# BUILDING STATES

COLUMBIA STUDIES IN
INTERNATIONAL AND GLOBAL HISTORY

COLUMBIA STUDIES IN
INTERNATIONAL AND GLOBAL HISTORY

*Cemil Aydin, Timothy Nunan, and Dominic Sachsenmaier, Series Editors*

This series presents some of the finest and most innovative work coming out of the current landscapes of international and global historical scholarship. Grounded in empirical research, these titles transcend the usual area boundaries and address how history can help us understand contemporary problems, including poverty, inequality, power, political violence, and accountability beyond the nation-state. The series covers processes of flows, exchanges, and entanglements—and moments of blockage, friction, and fracture—not only between "the West" and "the Rest" but also among parts of what has variously been dubbed the "Third World" or the "Global South." Scholarship in international and global history remains indispensable for a better sense of current complex regional and global economic transformations. Such approaches are vital in understanding the making of our present world.

For a complete list of books in this series, see page 379.

# BUILDING STATES

THE UNITED NATIONS, DEVELOPMENT,
AND DECOLONIZATION,
1945–1965

---

EVA-MARIA MUSCHIK

Columbia University Press
*New York*

Columbia University Press
*Publishers Since 1893*
New York   Chichester, West Sussex
cup.columbia.edu
Copyright © 2022 Columbia University Press
All rights reserved

Library of Congress Cataloging-in-Publication Data
Names: Muschik, Eva-Maria, author.
Title: Building states : the United Nations, development, and decolonization, 1945–1965 / Eva-Maria Muschik.
Description: New York : Columbia University Press, 2021. | Series: Columbia studies in international and global history | Includes bibliographical references and index.
Identifiers: LCCN 2021038649 (print) | LCCN 2021038650 (ebook) | ISBN 9780231200240 (hardback) | ISBN 9780231200257 (trade paperback) | ISBN 9780231553513 (ebook)
Subjects: LCSH: United Nations—History—20th century. | United Nations—Libya. | United Nations—Horn of Africa. | United Nations—Bolivia. | United Nations—Congo (Democratic Republic) | Nation-building—History—20th century. | Decolonization—History—20th century. | World politics—1945–1989.
Classification: LCC JZ4984.5 .M88 2021 (print) | LCC JZ4984.5 (ebook) | DDC 341.2309—dc23
LC record available at https://lccn.loc.gov/2021038649
LC ebook record available at https://lccn.loc.gov/2021038650

Cover image: 1961, Secretary-General Dag Hammarskjold of the United Nations before meeting with the UN Security Council on the situation in the Republic of Congo. Keystone Press / Alamy Stock Photo

Cover design: Lisa Hamm

A version of chapter 5 was published as "Managing the World: The United Nations, Decolonization, and the Strange Triumph of State Sovereignty in the 1950s and 1960s." *Journal of Global History* 13, no. 1 (2018): 121–44. Reprinted with permission.

TO MY MOTHER

# CONTENTS

Introduction: Managing the World   1

1. The UN and the Colonial World: International Trusteeship and Non-Self-Governing Territories   26

2. How to Build a State?: The UN in Libya   61

3. If Ten Years Suffice for Somaliland . . .   97

4. Moving Beyond Advice: Pioneering Administrative Assistance in Bolivia   125

5. Hammarskjöld, Decolonization, and the Proposal for an International Administrative Service   166

6. State-Building Meets Peacekeeping: The UN Civilian Operations in the Congo Crisis, 1960–1964   198

Epilogue   251

*Acknowledgments*   255

*Notes*   261

*Bibliography*   341

*Index*   363

#  BUILDING STATES

# INTRODUCTION

## Managing the World

*One day it may seem paradoxical to have urged territories towards national independence at a time when it is acknowledged that world peace and the chance of survival are solely dependent upon the good will with which so-called sovereign states consent to sacrifice a part of their sovereignty.*

— Jean de la Roche, United Nations Secretariat, September 1946

Writing in the wake of World War II, Jean de la Roche, a mid-level French civil servant with the United Nations (UN), argued that the two World Wars had sounded the death knell of both colonialism and nationalism. There was a palpable sense of a new beginning among those invested in international cooperation at the time, but also considerable uncertainty with regard to the future shape of the world order and the role that the UN might play in it. To de la Roche, it was clear that "the idea of the colonizer and colonized" had to be abolished and replaced by "cooperation and mutual assistance for the common good and the stability of the world." Yet, dividing the world into "watertight compartments" of nationalism offered no solution to the imperial question. Such a development would only breed ignorance and suspicion, as the two World Wars had made abundantly clear. Doubtful that true independence could even be achieved in the twentieth century in anything but name, de la Roche thought that *inter*dependence had to be recognized as a fact of international life. It would be a folly, he argued, "to form states on already outmoded lines," only to retrace one's steps later on. What was called for, then, was something entirely new: a reimagination of state sovereignty and international relations for the postcolonial world, a transformation in which the UN would play a central role.[1]

Multilateral cooperation is often presented as an attempt to overcome the limitations of the nation-state system. This book, by contrast, explores how the UN was involved in establishing said system and examines the organization's role in the transition from a world of empires to one of nominal nation-states in the 1950s and 1960s. When the UN was founded in 1945, it had fifty-one member states. European colonial powers were still, and in some cases again, in control of large parts of Asia, Africa, and the Pacific. Twenty years later, UN membership had jumped to 117, and a majority of the new members were former colonies.[2] This book explores the role of the UN Secretariat in New York, the bureaucracy of civil servants that carry out the day-to-day work of the organization, in contributing to this strange triumph of state sovereignty.[3]

The rapid proliferation of newly independent states after 1945 might be perceived as strange, first because, at the outset of postwar decolonization, there were a number of alternative political projects to empire, from nonhierarchical associations between "metropoles" and colonies to regional federal arrangements.[4] Second, during this era of decolonization, state sovereignty became an increasingly less meaningful barrier to outside intervention because the process of state proliferation went hand in hand with an expansion of the activities of international organizations, especially in "developing countries."[5] As Guy Fiti Sinclair notes, it would be overly simplistic to suggest that this development resulted in a loss of sovereignty by states. To the contrary: the expansion of the activities and powers of international organizations was intimately bound up with the creation of states, the construction of state power, and the very constitution of modern statehood in the postwar period.[6] The post-1945 triumph of state sovereignty, then, represents no extension of a European, Westphalian model of international relations to the rest of the world, but a new phenomenon of the postcolonial world, which brought into being a multitude of "developmental states" that depend on foreign personnel and funding in exercising their sovereignty.[7]

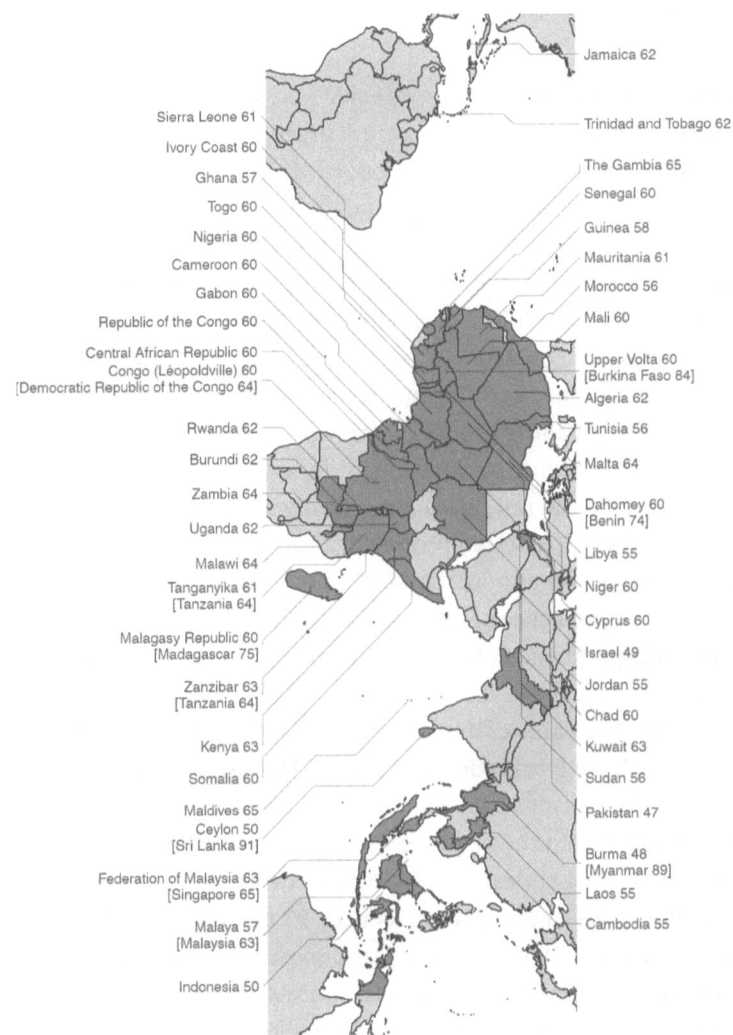

**FIG. 1** States Emerging from European Rule Admitted to the UN Between 1945 and 1965

Year of Admission:
1947: Pakistan
1948: Burma (Myanmar in 1989)
1949: Israel
1950: Indonesia
1955: Cambodia, Ceylon (Sri Lanka in 1991), Jordan, Laos, Libya
1956: Morocco, Sudan, Tunisia
1957: Ghana, Malaya (Malaysia in 1963)
1958: Guinea
1960: Cameroon, Central African Republic, Chad, Congo (Brazzaville), Congo (Leopoldville), Cyprus, Dahomey (Benin in 1974), Gabon, Ivory Coast, Malagasy Republic (Madagascar in 1975), Mali, Niger, Nigeria, Senegal, Somalia, Togo, Upper Volta (Burkina Faso in 1984)
1961: Mauritania, Sierra Leone, Tanganyika (Tanzania in 1964)
1962: Algeria, Burundi, Jamaica, Rwanda, Trinidad and Tobago, Uganda
1963: Kenya, Kuwait, Zanzibar (Tanzania in 1964)
1964: Malawi, Malta, Zambia
1965: The Gambia, Maldives, Singapore

Source: Data drawn from https://www.un.org/en/about-us/growth-in-un-membership. Image by author.

In 1945, when some 750 million people were living under colonial rule, the UN was founded as both a creature of empires and of nation-states.[8] European colonial powers initially hoped that the organization—like its predecessor, the League of Nations—might help to newly legitimize imperial rule at the international level.[9] And indeed, the UN Charter, the organization's foundational, constituent treaty, explicitly recognized and thus legitimized colonialism as a form of international trusteeship in the name of the advancement of the inhabitants of a given territory under foreign rule.[10] Yet, in the years to come, a growing number of "Third World" states gave new meaning to the Charter's principle of self-determination and turned the UN into an instrument for ending formal colonialism.[11] This development did not flow automatically from the letter of the Charter, but was a hotly contested process of confrontation and negotiation.[12] *Building States* looks at how the UN Secretariat tried to reconcile these two competing projects: the internationalization of empire and the Third World campaign to end colonialism. It examines how UN officials managed the tension between the organization's commitment to international trusteeship in the name of development as well as its simultaneous commitment to self-determination and respect for state sovereignty.

The provision of international "technical assistance"—the dispatch of experts to assist requesting governments with any number of issues—became key to this endeavor. This type of development assistance, this book argues, enabled the UN to reconcile its position as both "arbiter of the universal and defender of the particularism of the nation-state."[13] It provided the organization with a means to support the nation-state form and thus widen the base of UN clientele, while simultaneously giving it a privileged position to influence national policies. Moreover, technical assistance allowed the Secretariat to work with and build on colonial development initiatives, while leaving room for national governments to determine policies. In short, development assistance seemed to offer a way of accommodating competing political projects and thus peacefully managing and facilitating decolonization.

By shifting away from the high politics of the Security Council and the General Assembly to the nominally "technical" work of the organization, *Building States* challenges the narrative of the organization as a mere "talking shop" that was largely paralyzed during the Cold War by the superpower standoff.[14] As UN officials responded to the distinct pressures of decolonization in a Cold War context, they extended the activities of the organization from development assistance to peacekeeping, far beyond the scope and powers that its founding fathers had envisioned.

Focusing on Secretariat initiatives represents just one way of telling the history of the United Nations.[15] The UN system is confusingly vast, with multiple headquarters, intergovernmental bodies, subcommittees, regional commissions, affiliated organizations, and programs. The organization as such can be approached as an international public forum that states can use for propaganda purposes, negotiation, and norm-setting. It can also be seen as an international venue for informal networking among government representatives, activists, and communities of experts.[16] A focus on the Secretariat (and not just the secretaries-general), however, allows us to see more clearly the agency of the organization itself in global affairs—as well as the limits thereof.[17]

As with many other features of the UN, its international bureaucracy—which possesses diplomatic immunities and is supposed to be loyal only to the world organization—was an innovation pioneered by the League of Nations.[18] Like the League Secretariat, the UN bureaucracy was divided into functional units, corresponding roughly to the principal organs of the world organization (the General Assembly, the Security Council, the Economic and Social Council, and the Trusteeship Council).[19] In comparison to national or even municipal bureaucracies, in the early years, the UN Secretariat was a fairly small "club" of only a few thousand employees.[20] While the secretary-general was appointed by the General Assembly on the recommendation of the Security Council, the hiring of permanent UN staff fell to the Secretariat itself, which relied heavily on the professional networks and contacts of its earliest members.[21] Despite officially aspiring to broad geographic representation, the early Secretariat—much like the League bureaucracy before it—was dominated by Western civil servants.[22] In 1956, for example, nationals from the United States, the United Kingdom, and France filled about half of all high-level posts within the UN bureaucracy.[23] Though presented as an apolitical administration, the Secretariat did much more than simply execute directives from the organization's main intergovernmental organs. By shaping how member states framed their interests, by developing and lobbying for their own aid proposals, and by interpreting requests for assistance from member states, UN officials were not simply intergovernmental or bureaucratic conduits, but assumed a proactive role in international governance.²⁴ At the same time, UN employees were in no position to simply impose their ideas and initiatives on member states and aid recipients.

Until now, scholarship on the UN and development has largely focused on ideas rather than practice and privileged the goings-on at the headquarters over activities in the field.²⁵ A second deliberate choice in writing this book was therefore to focus primarily on the activities of the organization in select settings abroad—in the former Italian colonies of Libya and Somaliland, in Bolivia, and in the Congo—rather than on New York or Geneva. This approach follows from the conviction that UN thinking and practice did not result from isolated contemplation of abstract issues at the headquarters, but was shaped by the organization's engagement in member states and territories bound for UN membership.²⁶ This book's rather unusual geography is a result of the sites deemed interconnected and important for UN development assistance by the world organization's staff members at the time. To be clear, the book does *not* offer a history of those sites, but rather a history of the United Nations told mainly through its archival trail and the personal papers of key Western UN officials. As a result, non-Western voices are not as well represented in the following pages as one would like them to be. This approach—though necessarily limited—nevertheless illuminates biases and interests, decisions and unintended consequences, as well as the hidden diplomacy that shaped international assistance in the postwar decades. Hopefully, it will also encourage further studies that broaden the UN cast and probe how the world organization affected the societies it engaged in various ways and vice versa.²⁷

The book advances three basic, interrelated arguments. First, the UN should be taken seriously as more than an intergovernmental forum: namely, as an important actor in global history that was substantially shaped by its employees.²⁸ Second, although Western member states, especially the United States, enjoyed disproportionate influence on the day-to-day work of the organization, the Secretariat was no simple handmaiden of powerful Western nations, but pursued its own agenda. Third, in its attempt to manage decolonization, the UN Secretariat made important contributions to development thinking and practice: it helped shape an understanding of state-building as a universal technical challenge (rather than a unique political or historical process) that required the expertise of myriad specialists in order to succeed. And UN staff helped push international development assistance from an earlier emphasis on advisory services into a more operational direction that focused on getting the job done on behalf of aid recipients. Recovering this history helps us to better understand the role of the UN in the end of empire, the Cold War bloc competition, and the history of development.

## THE UN, EMPIRE, AND DECOLONIZATION

Formal empire had taken multiple hits both before and during World War II. While the large European land empires dissolved as a result of World War I, most overseas empires—save for the comparatively short-lived German one—survived the war and even extended their reach. At the same time, the "Great War" also catalyzed anticolonial resistance.[29] The severe ramifications of the Great Depression of the early 1930s led to additional pressure by causing strikes and riots in many colonies. During the Second World War, European imperial powers appeared vulnerable in the eyes of colonial soldiers, who fought on their behalf, and vis-à-vis subject populations, when their colonies in East Asia were seized by Japan. The Free French, the antifascist government-in-exile, was thrown back completely on colonial territory when continental France fell to Germany in 1940. The Allied anti-Nazi propaganda further discredited racist ideas of superiority as a legitimation for colonial rule, and important voices within the emerging superpowers, the United States and the Soviet Union, assumed anticolonial positions.[30]

By signing the Atlantic Charter in 1941, the British technically approved of a people's right to self-determination, while France explicitly recognized the contribution of the colonies to the war effort at the Brazzaville conference in 1944.[31] In their need to newly legitimize empire before international, domestic, and colonial audiences during and after the war, European imperial powers turned to the promise of welfare and development as well as a closer association between "metropole" and colonies. As a result of new commitments in this regard, imperial governance became increasingly costly for European powers, which were already struggling with the economic legacies of the war. Some "metropolitan" policymakers thus began to wonder whether they had more to gain from close-knit post-independence relationships with their former "charges" than from continuing to maintain formal sovereignty in the colonies; much as they had done with regard to colonies that had come under international oversight in the interwar period.[32]

Following World War I, League of Nations oversight of select colonial administrations, so-called mandates, had raised the stakes of imperial governance. As a result, some "metropolitan" policymakers began to view formal independence in combination with significant informal influence as a good alternative to continued colonial rule under international purview. The British and indeed the *international* granting of formal independence to the League mandate of Iraq in 1932 provided a model for postcolonial informal rule, as London maintained extensive military and economic rights in the new state. As Susan Pedersen has argued, Iraq's transition to sovereign statehood—to a degree—robbed formal independence of its terrors and helped make the end of empire imaginable in British eyes.[33] This is not to suggest that decolonization thereafter unfolded peacefully as the result of a sober cost-benefit analysis in the European capitals. Prolonged and brutal wars, such as the ones in Indonesia, Kenya, and Algeria, which ultimately led to these countries' independent statehood, illustrate the continued European unwillingness to give up empire. It took several developments—in the colonies, in the "metropoles," and at the international level—that together led to the acceleration of decolonization after 1945.[34] The UN was one among many factors in that story.[35]

As is often acknowledged, the world organization was not just remade by decolonization, but played an important role in the end of empire itself. Yet, this story is less straightforward than UN informational material, which depicts decolonization as *the* success story of the world organization, might suggest.[36] The UN was *not* originally intended as an instrument of decolonization. The planners who were instrumental in setting up the world organization contemplated a number of plans with regard to the colonial world, ranging from immediate independence for all colonies to an extension of League-style international supervision to all imperial holdings.[37] At first sight, the UN founding conference in San Francisco in 1945 offered no New Deal for the Black man, as frustrated contemporary observers put it.[38] The League of Nations regime of international supervision for a few select territories was reestablished under a new name: the UN trusteeship system—with the important difference that a special category of so-called *strategic* UN trust territories was created, which effectively allowed the United States to administer Pacific island territories without UN supervision.[39] Another important difference to the League was the inclusion of a "Declaration Regarding Non-Self-Governing Territories" in the UN Charter, which established general principles for colonial rule by UN member states. On the one hand, this declaration newly legitimized *all* colonial rule at the international level as "a sacred trust" in the name of protection and advancement of the territories in question.[40] On the other hand, it officially turned imperial rule in general into a matter of international concern, which anticolonial member states within the General Assembly soon seized upon.[41]

At the San Francisco conference, the ultimate goal of colonial trusteeship, framed as a choice between eventual self-government or political independence, was a hotly debated issue. In the Charter, independence was spelled out as a *possible* goal for UN trust territories, but not for other colonies. Yet, within the General Assembly, a growing coalition of Arab, Asian, and African states—often supported by the Soviet Union and its allies as well as some Latin American countries—increasingly championed political independence as *the* goal for colonial territories.[42] The fiercely contested 1949 General Assembly decision to grant independence to the former Italian colonies of Libya and Somaliland after a temporally limited period of colonial trusteeship had a signal effect: if such "poorly advanced" territories (in terms of economic resources, professional personnel, and infrastructure) could be established as independent states within a relatively short period, why did other, "more advanced" colonies have to continue to rely on colonial trusteeship for their development for an undeterminable time?

At the same time, UN representatives began to scrutinize imperial powers' developmental promises with regard to their colonies, not just in the Trusteeship Council but also in the General Assembly. Against resistance from the imperial powers, the first General Assembly—aided by Secretariat officials—set up a Committee on Information from Non-Self-Governing Territories, composed of imperial and nonimperial powers alike. The committee would henceforth review and discuss reports submitted by the colonial powers, relating to ostensibly *technical* matters in "dependent territories,"[43] as colonies were now called in UN parlance: that is, a colony's economic, social, and educational conditions. By drawing up the detailed questionnaire on the basis of which colonial powers drafted their annual reports for each territory, Secretariat officials had a hand in promoting an expansive view of national development. As Jessica L. Pearson has shown, the Committee became an important site for both pro- and anticolonial government representatives at the UN to discuss which territories would be considered colonies, as well as how and to what end colonial rule should be practiced. It created a significant opening that allowed the world to see "the inner lives of empires."[44]

Going beyond scrutiny of imperial rule and holding imperial powers accountable to their lofty promises of protection and development, representatives from the Middle East, Asia, and Africa—aided by the Soviet Union and its satellite states—mounted an active campaign within and outside the UN to end formal colonialism. This culminated in the 1960 UN General Assembly Declaration on Granting Independence to Colonial Peoples, which called for the immediate transfer of power "without any conditions or reservations" and thus, as Adom Getachew has argued, marked a watershed in the history of decolonization.[45] The Committee of 24, which was subsequently established in order to oversee the implementation of the 1960 Declaration, featured an overwhelming number of anticolonial powers and thus quickly became a year-round source of critique of the remnants of imperial rule.[46] While this campaign gave momentum to individual liberation struggles, as was the case in Algeria, there were naturally limits to what critiques in New York could achieve on the ground.[47] A case in point was recalcitrant South Africa, which continued to rule South West Africa (Namibia) until 1990, despite manifold UN protestations.[48] And, of course, there were limits to the kinds of claims to self-determination that were recognized as legitimate within the halls of the General Assembly; those excluded, for example, the ones that were made by ethnic minorities within established nation-states.[49] Nevertheless, the UN General Assembly was an important site for government representatives from the Global South to lobby for a more egalitarian, postimperial world order.[50]

Departing from a focus on these intergovernmental deliberations, *Building States* examines the hands-on-role that UN officials sought to play in processes of decolonization. In heeding the increasingly vociferous calls within the General Assembly for a break with formal colonialism, the Secretariat soon offered to assume "impartial" trusteeship in the postcolonial world itself, to fill the presumed void left by the departure of the colonial powers and to guide national development after empire. Governments in the Global South, many of whom were struggling with very real shortages in terms of professional personnel, relied on UN assistance to varying degrees. Though limited in scope, the UN project of international trusteeship clashed with the organization's pronounced goal of noninterference in the internal affairs of member states. It also put the world organization in direct competition with imperial powers' attempts to manage decolonization and maintain strong informal ties with their former colonies after independence.

Despite increasingly confrontational rhetoric in the General Assembly, Secretariat officials who managed to get a foothold in decolonization processes in "dependent territories," such as the former Italian colonies, prior to independence generally sought to build on the colonial experience and cooperate with often highly reluctant imperial administrators. Initially, colonial officials in Libya and Somaliland perceived the world organization as a nuisance or even a threat: a useless drain on resources and an incompetent challenge to imperial expertise and authority. Eventually, however, some imperial administrators came to regard UN officials as useful allies.[51] The Secretariat, in any case, hoped to build a supposedly neutral bridge from an imperial past and present to an international future and at the same time avoid a Cold War superpower confrontation over Third World development.

## A COLD WAR INSTRUMENT?

The United States is widely recognized as the main driving force behind the UN's establishment, though scholars continue to debate Washington's intentions and influence.[52] How exactly Western states tried to steer the day-to-day operations of the organization once it was set up has received less scholarly attention. Of course, the world organization was by no means the impartial body it presented itself to be. As noted above, in the first two postwar decades, the majority of UN funding and staff, particularly in key senior positions, came from Western nations.[53] Throughout the

1950s and 1960s, European colonial powers constituted the principal (though not exclusive), recruiting grounds for UN development experts.[54] As this book demonstrates, the United States—as the main financial sponsor and host country of the organization—enjoyed outsized informal access to and influence on many UN civil servants.

Prior to visiting aid recipient countries, UN officials would usually consult policymakers in Washington, D.C. as well as the relevant imperial "metropoles." "In the field," they mingled with Western diplomats and often relied on the U.S. embassies' communication services. It is thus no surprise that in Bolivia in the late 1940s and early 1950s, for example, the United States and the UN were often seen as synonymous. At the same time, reactionary forces in Washington attacked the UN as a seedbed of communism, embroiling the Secretariat in McCarthyist witch-hunts.[55] Eastern European and Third World countries, meanwhile, continuously pushed for a diversification of UN staff in terms of geographic representation, especially after the sudden expansion of UN membership in 1955, when sixteen new member states joined the world organization. By the early 1960s, the push to diversify the Secretariat was increasingly successful.[56]

But even the Western staff covered in this book, which dominated the work of the organization in the first two decades, were a fairly diverse, though generally left-leaning group that included former colonial officials such as de la Roche, African-American scholars such as Ralph Bunche, League bureaucrats such as the Dutch Adrian Pelt, and "exponents of Swedish socialism" such as economist John Lindberg. Given the diversity of experience and outlooks this brought to the table, UN officials did not always agree on how best to assist member states and promote development. More importantly, the Secretariat was no straightforward instrument of American or European politics. Rather, UN staff pursued their own agenda, reflecting a degree of disunity in the "Western camp" when it came to matters of development.[57] At times, specific UN developmental recommendations were thwarted by American or European resistance (e.g., with regard to the monetary arrangement for Libya); other times, UN thinking influenced Western policies (e.g., the U.S. decision to support a revolutionary regime in Bolivia). Often Western powers found more useful allies in employees of the International Monetary Fund (IMF), as the British did in Libya, and the United States in Bolivia.

An examination of U.S. and European influence on the Secretariat thus complicates schematic chronologies that suggest "years of Western domination" at the UN up until the early 1960s, followed by a Western turn away from the world organization (when it became too "unwieldy" as a result of decolonization) toward ideologically more reliable organizations such as the IMF and the World Bank.[58] To policymakers in the United States and the European "metropoles," it seems the UN was a rather unreliable instrument for imposing their agendas from the get-go.[59] As a result, Washington did not put much weight behind any of the UN initiatives covered in this book, with the important exception of the organization's intervention in the Congo Crisis, but here, too, the Secretariat pursued its own agenda.

Generally, the UN officials portrayed in this book were keen to work in close consultation with European colonial administrators and U.S. representatives and hoped to guide the development of UN member states in a social democratic, capitalist direction. While some thought that multilateral assistance offered a path to "win the Cold War by other means," most were more concerned with peacefully managing the end of empire.[60] The UN, in any case, was far from paralyzed during the Cold War. Indeed, in the two postwar decades covered here, it pioneered certain practices such as developmental state-building and peacekeeping, which ultimately outlasted the superpower conflict and was taken to new heights in the 1990s.[61]

## INTERNATIONAL TECHNICAL ASSISTANCE AND THE LIMITS OF UN AGENCY

While no simple tool of an all-powerful West, the idea of the UN as a neocolonial force in its own right is equally misleading. The organization's employees could only hope to affect national development by persuasion, not by coercion. In the early years of the UN (even before U.S. president Harry Truman's famous Point IV speech), the primary means to deliver on the promise of development was "technical assistance"—that is, the extension of knowledge and skills, usually by dispatching international experts to advise governments, but also by offering training or scholarships in various fields to select nationals of interested member states. International technical assistance was based on the uncontroversial ideas that lack of expert personnel and know-how was among the factors impeding development and that requesting governments should be in full control over the kind of foreign assistance rendered.[62] (The insistence by poorer countries at the UN that substantial *capital* assistance was also needed to promote development found less support among the richer member states.[63]) Upon request, technical assistance experts would conduct a visit to study a particular problem or the country's overall potential for development and then submit a report making certain policy-recommendations, which the recipient government was free to accept or reject.

The UN framework for improving the world's welfare and development was thus decidedly national, even though many of its officials were painfully aware of the limitations of such an approach.[64] UN economists Hans Singer and Raúl Prebisch, for example, demonstrated as early as 1950 that the terms of world trade were detrimental to many countries in the Global South, which depended on the export of primary commodities.[65] Drawing on this insight, Secretary-General Dag Hammarskjöld conceded in the mid-1950s that much more could be achieved if the goodwill that had led to the establishment of postwar international aid programs was applied to improving world trade relations for these countries.[66] Yet, it was only in the late 1960s and 1970s, when the balance of power within the General Assembly shifted more decisively toward Third World states, that arguments in favor of *global* policies to tackle inequalities among nations gained new momentum with the establishment of the UN Conference on Trade and Development and the call for a New International Economic Order.[67] The 1950s and early 1960s by contrast, were not just the prime time of the "high modernist" projects that have received much scholarly attention, but also of small-scale technical assistance projects.[68]

Though UN officials would often present it as such, postwar technical assistance was not a new phenomenon.[69] In the interwar period, the League of Nations' Committee on Technical Cooperation had sent several expert missions abroad, to India, Palestine, China, and Chile, with the goal of improving public health and fostering economic growth. The League-affiliated International Labor Organization (ILO) had also dispatched small teams of advisers to support various governments in the introduction of labor legislation and social security programs.[70] During World War II, this type of practical international assistance increased and—in addition to setting up the UN Organization itself—the Allies also established a number of so-called UN specialized agencies: independent UN-affiliated international organizations that would focus on specific economic and social problems and thus, it was hoped, help stave off unrest and war in the postwar period. In 1942, the Allies set up the UN Educational, Scientific and Cultural Organization (UNESCO), and the following year, the UN Food and Agriculture Organization (FAO). In 1944, the UN Monetary and Financial Conference in Bretton Woods, New Hampshire, established the IMF and the International Bank for Reconstruction and Development (IBRD), which later came to be known as the World Bank. Each UN agency would offer technical assistance in its respective field.[71]

Many states initially hoped that the IBRD would serve as the main economic development agency of the UN system, but were soon disappointed.[72] Accordingly, poorer countries turned directly to the UN, where voting power was not tied to economic might, to provide an overall framework for the many proliferating assistance services. In the Charter, UN member states had vaguely vowed "to employ international machinery" "to promote economic and social progress and development" around the world in order "to save succeeding generations from the scourge of war."[73] During the very first meeting of the General Assembly in London in 1946, representatives from Colombia and Lebanon took up the issue and placed the inequalities in economic development among member states on the organization's agenda, calling for a UN plan to remedy the situation.[74] Their initiative set the ball rolling and, supported by Latin American, Asian, and Arab countries, led to the December 1948 General Assembly decision to fund "technical assistance for economic development."[75]

Although the UN goal of promoting better living standards worldwide was ambitious, the means made available to this end were miniscule: the General Assembly initially appropriated no more than $288,000 from the organization's regular budget for development assistance. A month after the UN's decision, however, U.S. president Truman followed the world organization's lead and called for "a bold new program" of international technical assistance "for the improvement and growth of underdeveloped areas" in his famous Point IV inaugural speech. While Truman is often credited with ushering in the "great American mission" of global modernization in the postwar period, it is mostly forgotten that he called on all nations to work together through the UN and its specialized agencies for this purpose.[76]

Even though critics charged that the president's foray was neither bold nor new, his speech caused great excitement among UN officials, and the subsequent U.S. commitment of funds to development propelled the organization's fledgling assistance activities to another level. Following Truman's speech, Western UN member states allocated $20,000,000 to the UN on a voluntary basis for technical assistance purposes and the contributions continued to increase in the years to come. Denouncing technical assistance as an imperialist design to exploit the resources of poorer countries, the Soviet Union and its allies refused to donate money to the UN program until 1953. Even when they joined the effort after Stalin's death, the socialist contribution to the UN assistance budget remained minimal, hovering around 5 percent throughout the late 1950s and early 1960s, as opposed to the 87 percent shouldered by Western European and North American countries.[77]

The donated technical assistance funds were distributed among the specialized agencies and the UN Secretariat according to predetermined shares, but the Secretariat also assumed a coordinating function for the UN assistance program, called the Expanded Program for Technical Assistance (EPTA), in which the agencies participated.[78] Within the Secretariat, a new department—the Technical Assistance Administration (TAA)—was created for that purpose in 1950.[79] In aid recipient countries, the UN build up a system of so-called resident representatives to help governments plan for development and formulate requests for assistance. Though officially in charge of the UN system's program, the Secretariat was just one among a number of technical assistance providers—and not the best endowed one, at that—in a rapidly expanding and professionalizing field covered by the specialized agencies (which had their own technical assistance programs in addition to EPTA), philanthropic organizations such as the Rockefeller and Ford Foundations, and bilateral assistance programs offered by the United States and Western European countries, and eventually Eastern European states as well.[80] Within EPTA, the Secretariat initially assumed primary responsibility for assistance in the fields of economic and industrial development, transport and communications, public finance and fiscal questions, social development, and public administration.[81] As this book will show, it was in the latter field where UN officials soon saw the opportunity of offering a unique service to "developing countries."

## FROM PUBLIC ADMINISTRATION TO STATE-BUILDING

The Secretariat viewed technical assistance in government administration as a comparatively cheap, ostensibly apolitical type of aid with the biggest possible impact on a country's development. Like many of their contemporaries who were professionally concerned with development, UN officials in the postwar period thought of the state as the main provider of national welfare and the principal driving force behind a country's progress. But they went a step further in identifying proper government administration as the key to ensuring both national self-determination and development. UN representatives presented public administration as a universal technical skill, separate from politics and thus legitimate terrain for outside assistance. Yet, they also thought of such assistance as central enough for their intervention to have an important effect on national policies. The UN, so the argument went, would take care of governance while leaving actual government to national actors.

For the UN officials covered in this book, development was a complex process, involving political, economic, social, and educational progress. They did not promote any one-size-fits-all solutions, nor did they call for a radical redistribution of power and wealth. Rather, they advocated incremental, progressive change in all spheres of public life, which they believed could be stimulated and sped up by government intervention. The "modern state" was to ensure public welfare, education, and infrastructure while also continuously improving existing industries and kick-starting new ones to diversify the country's economy and increase its overall productivity. Especially in decolonizing countries, the perceived challenge was how to meet rising public expectations of prosperity and welfare, despite generally declining state revenues and lack of professional staff. For ambitious national policymakers in these countries the room to maneuver was very much constrained.[82] Hence, the UN insisted on the necessity of impartial foreign assistance in terms of both personnel and funding, for what they perceived to be an essentially national endeavor of development.

Following James Ferguson's landmark study of development as an "anti-politics machine," scholars have repeatedly shown how development work depoliticized contentious issues by presenting them as technical problems.[83] The UN officials in this book were often well aware of the politics behind any given request for assistance. Still, they interpreted their mandate to respect state sovereignty as a ban against becoming involved in contentious national issues such as labor conflicts, and instead chose to subsume them within the broader framework of national development. Many national governments embraced this framing for their own reasons. Ferguson's other finding, which has received less attention, suggests that the expansion of bureaucratic state power was a "side effect" of development efforts. This book suggests that UN officials quite consciously put heavy emphasis on strengthening administrative structures as a prime objective of development.

Although tackling the world's administrative problems threatened to be a rather dull undertaking, it steered the UN head-on into serious controversy. The notion of public administration as distinct from politics and thus the rightful terrain for international experts did not go unchallenged: many UN member states jealously guarded their sovereignty and independence and, in the case of former imperial powers, the ties to their former colonies. While London and Paris perceived UN assistance in this field as unwelcome competition, some "developing countries" expressed well-founded concern that the UN might simply reintroduce colonial administrators under international auspices. International civil servants, meanwhile, worried about the repercussions of UN overreach, cautioning that the specter of "world government" might jeopardize member states' support for the organization as a whole. Yet, many governments—for varying reasons—ultimately welcomed international administrative assistance as a means to bolster their national state-building projects.

In that sense, UN development assistance was neither a neocolonial imposition nor a triumph of international understanding.[84] Rather, it was the result of negotiation between international civil servants and sovereign states of vastly different bargaining power. UN assistance came to function as a voluntary state-building program in which the tension between foreign tutelage in the name of expertise and the self-determination of sovereign states was continuously renegotiated.[85] There was no literal "rule of experts," much as there was no world government.[86] The United Nations, as Daniel Speich Chassé has argued, established norms of government but did not rule. It functioned neither as a globalized nation-state nor as an empire ruled from New York. Instead global governance as practiced by UN experts drew legitimacy and gained adherence through the communication of scientific rationality.[87] Where the UN failed to convince recipient governments of the soundness or utility of its advice or operations, there was little the organization could do to determine national policymaking.

Ultimately, the UN never provided the large-scale administrative assistance it envisioned as necessary to overcome the imperial past and build a peaceful international future. The global "age of functionaries" that some of its officials had dreamed of, envisioning an international brotherhood (there were few female UN experts) of scientists, technicians, and educators working side by side in the administration of sovereign states to develop the world's resources and ensure global prosperity and security, never came to pass.[88] It should nevertheless be taken seriously as one vision of world order—a managerial, technocratic internationalism—that competed with many other visions at a time when the outcome of processes of decolonization seemed far from certain. A version of this dream lives on today in instances of so-called international territorial administration, where nonelected international officials perform public policy functions in post-conflict settings.[89]

The United Nations initiatives discussed in this book thus had significant repercussions. First, in their attempt to manage decolonization, UN officials helped to establish an understanding of state-building that is still relevant today: namely, as a technical challenge for international experts rather than a unique political or historical process.[90] Whereas prior to 1945, the road to statehood led through political negotiations, under UN auspices, it became a process increasingly reliant on international "technical" expertise in an ever-expanding range of fields, from constitution writing to public health.[91] Importantly, international state-building efforts did not conclude upon formal political independence but, to the contrary, were often pursued more vigorously in newly sovereign states and also became a central feature of many peacekeeping missions in the postcolonial world.

Second, UN officials helped push international development assistance more generally from an earlier emphasis on advisory services into an increasingly operational direction that focused on getting the job done on behalf of aid recipients.[92] A sense of frustration over the limits of advisory assistance among both the recipients of the UN's advice and the organization's technical experts set in motion a reformulation of international assistance almost as soon as it had been agreed upon by UN member states in the late 1940s. As a result, foreign personnel were soon integrated into national government bureaucracies to carry out a multiplicity of jobs rather than merely provide advice on specialized problems. Taken together, this story helps to explain how international actors came to occupy increasingly important public policy functions in many of today's "developing countries," culminating in international attempts to assume virtual trusteeship of "weak" or "failed" states in the name of expertise and impartiality.[93]

## STRUCTURE

The UN role with regard to empire had been one of the most contentious issues of the wartime planning that led to the creation of the world organization. This book's first chapter, "The UN and the Colonial World," revisits this history. It examines the codification of general principles of colonial rule applicable to *all* colonies in the UN Charter—the so-called Declaration Regarding Non-Self-Governing Territories—and the establishment of the UN trusteeship system in the 1940s. The trusteeship system functioned as an apparatus of international oversight for specific colonial administrations, and was intended to ensure the trust territories' advancement toward self-government. Initiatives from within the UN trusteeship division, then directed by African-American political scientist Ralph Bunche, to shape this advancement and influence the day-to-day politics in the trust territories largely failed in view of imperial powers' claims to sovereignty. This chapter argues that UN assistance *after* the nominal independence of former colonies was thus often more significant for the development of individual territories than formal UN trusteeship prior to independence.[94]

FIG. 2  UN Headquarters, New York City

As seen from Roosevelt Island in the East River in 1955. The skyscraper houses the Secretariat's offices. Council chambers and conference rooms are located in the low building at the river's edge, and the General Assembly in the domed building at center.

Source: UN Photo, UN7635336

Chapters 2 and 3—"How to Build a State: The UN in Libya" and "If ten years suffice for Somaliland . . ."—examine the crucial, largely unexplored role of the world organization in two former Italian colonies that became early testing grounds of UN state-building in the 1950s. When the wartime Allies failed to agree on the fate of these territories after the war, decision-making was left to the General Assembly, which stipulated in 1949 that both Libya and Somaliland were to become independent states within a fixed period of time under international supervision. The question of how they might achieve independent statehood was largely left open. Confronted with the problem of how to build a state, UN employees—journalist-turned-diplomat Adrian Pelt in Libya and former

FIG. 3  UN Department of Economic Affairs

Library of the Department on the thirtieth floor of the Secretariat building (1951).

Source: UN Photo, UN7768692

French colonial official Jean de la Roche in Somalia—called upon the nascent UN development assistance services. Initially, development missions were dispatched to conduct economy, health, education, and agriculture surveys in an attempt to understand how these states might endure after political independence. Eventually, development assistance came to provide an answer in itself when UN experts framed the new polities as sovereign states that depended on continued international assistance for the foreseeable future.

Chapter 4, "Moving beyond Advice: Pioneering Administrative Assistance in Bolivia," examines one of the earliest UN assistance missions dispatched to a member state in 1949. This mission proved crucial in shaping UN thinking about the unique contribution that the organization could offer to member states' development more generally and to newly

FIG. 4  UN Cafeteria

Temporary cafeteria on the fifth floor of the Secretariat building (1951).

Source: UN Photo, UN7757643

independent states in particular. The UN, represented by Canadian civil servant Hugh Keenleyside, suggested that Bolivian administrative instability and incapacity presented the main obstacles to successful national development. To solve this problem, the UN offered to integrate foreign "administrative assistants" into Bolivia's governmental bureaucracy. These international "experts," it was hoped, would not only reform the country's administration, but also carry out, rather than merely advise on development policies. Although highly controversial for its potential breach of Bolivian sovereignty (and thus time-consuming and difficult to negotiate), the scheme was by no means imposed on the country, but readily embraced by vastly different governments in La Paz, highlighting the negotiated nature of UN development assistance.

FIG. 5  UN Staff Lounge

A view of the staff lounge on the fifth floor of the Secretariat building (1960).

Source: UN Photo, UN7768101

Chapter 5, "Hammarskjöld, Decolonization, and the Proposal for an International Administrative Service," uncovers how Secretary-General Dag Hammarskjöld sought to build on the Bolivian experiment to respond to the ongoing dissolution of European overseas empires and shape the emerging world of postcolonial states. In 1956, the Swedish head of the UN proposed the creation of a new service that would offer "nations emerging from foreign rule" seasoned, high-level administrators from abroad to help manage their newly independent polities. While many new states enthusiastically embraced this idea, the opposition of an odd alliance of representatives of select Third World nations, imperial powers, and Eastern European countries ensured that Hammarskjöld's far-reaching vision was considerably weakened. The resulting UN program for the provision of operational and executive personnel (OPEX) nevertheless proved significant in pushing what member states and other aid agencies thought of as acceptable international development assistance away from advisory services into a more operational, paternalist direction.

The final chapter, "State-Building Meets Peacekeeping: UN Civilian Operations in the Congo Crisis, 1960–1964," examines the UN's intervention in the former Belgian colony, also known as *Opération des Nations Unies au Congo* (ONUC). Under Hammarskjöld's lead, UN officials sought to use the multifaceted emergency that followed the Congolese rush to independence and the unique superpower agreement sanctioning a UN military intervention to showcase the organization's capabilities in managing decolonization through development assistance and in particular, through OPEX-type services. In the Congo, the Secretariat set up the largest UN assistance program in the organization's history to that date. Operating parallel to the Congolese government, it covered every conceivable field of public administration, from transportation and communications to health, education, agriculture, finance, and the judiciary. ONUC thus expanded the scope of international peacekeeping beyond its original simple policing function, by including the maintenance of a state's public services in the name of stability and development—with lasting effects for similar endeavors today.

Initially mounted as a campaign to demonstrate the world organization's efficacy and importance, the intervention in the Congo proved a sobering experience for UN officials and member states, one that demonstrated the limits of UN state-building capacities and brought the organization close to political and financial collapse. As the epilogue notes, it was not until the end of the Cold War and the apparent proliferation of "state failure" that international administrative management as practiced by the UN in the Congo in the 1960s reemerged and was indeed taken to new heights, e.g., in Kosovo and East Timor. Recovering the story told in this book helps us better understand not only the genealogy of current-day international territorial administrations, but of the United Nations more generally as both a creature of empires and nation-states. What this book seeks to offer is a sober analysis of the history of the world organization in the two formative postwar decades that reveals both the UN's limitations and its impact on global history, as well as its flexibility to adapt to new circumstances and change over time.

# 1

## THE UN AND THE COLONIAL WORLD

International Trusteeship and Non-Self-Governing Territories

> [I]t was the usual business of "freedom now" against "freedom when ready," but from many remarks that were made I felt . . . that the members of Parliament from all these countries were well aware . . . that the UN Charter had given colonial powers and non-colonial powers alike a platform from which to argue either way. This is in itself a phenomenal achievement.
>
> — George Ivan Smith, Director of the UN Information Center in London, reporting to his colleagues in New York about a 1950 meeting of the Inter-Parliamentary Union, an international organization of national parliaments

One of the most contentious issues in the wartime planning effort to set up an international collective security organization was the future role of the United Nations with regard to the colonial world. To their imperial allies' dismay, the United States had until 1941 argued for political independence as the goal for Europe's colonies, and then briefly considered an Anglo-American partnership to police the postwar world.[1] National liberation—with the option of a "voluntary union of equal people in the socialist family"[2]—was the objective the Soviet Union would vociferously defend throughout the war years and beyond. Countries such as Egypt, India, and China, with their own experiences of various degrees of imperial subjugation, likewise favored independence as a goal for the colonies.

Starting in 1942, postwar planners in the U.S. administration began to toy with an alternative idea: establishing a system of international trusteeship for all "dependent territories," as colonies came to be called.[3] The UN predecessor organization, the League of Nations, had already overseen the colonial administration of select territories, so-called mandates, which the defeated powers of World War I had lost.[4] European imperial powers abhorred any talk of independence and strongly opposed an extension of international supervision. Yet, instead of withdrawing from international cooperation altogether, they hoped to turn the tables and codify the colonial project through such channels—much as they had done after World War I within the framework of the League of Nations—and thus newly legitimize colonial rule at the international level.[5]

This chapter examines the resulting political compromise formalized in the UN Charter[6]: the Declaration Regarding Non-Self-Governing Territories, a codification of general principles of colonial rule applicable to *all* colonies, and the UN trusteeship system, a framework of international oversight of colonial administration that would encompass eleven territories in Africa and the Pacific (with the exception of Italian Somaliland, all former League of Nations mandates).[7] While the wartime fight over the issue of independence for colonial territories has been well documented, its unintended outcome—the Declaration and the trusteeship system—has received less attention.[8] Fewer scholars still have been interested in exploring how exactly UN employees sought to build on the Charter in order to shape the postwar transformation of colonial rule that we now refer to as decolonization.

Despite or perhaps because of relatively sparse scholarship on the topic, there exists a stubborn willingness to believe that decolonization was the "rare success story of the UN in the Cold War"[9] and that the trusteeship system and towering figures such as Nobel laureate Ralph Bunche, the American director of the UN Secretariat's Division of Trusteeship, did much to help accelerate or at least "pave the way for [the] gradual, peaceful" unfolding of this process.[10] In his seminal study of the origins of UN trusteeship, Wm. Roger Louis even suggests that the "system had teeth and often bit."[11] Surprisingly, given the dearth of in-depth studies on how the trusteeship system actually worked in practice, scholars across the political spectrum have called for its resuscitation to deal with what they call "failed states."[12] The less the system is known, it seems, the more easily it can be presented as a constructive policy proposal.

There is a convincing argument to be made that the unrelenting advocacy of anticolonial activists and their allies helped establish a measure of UN oversight that put constant pressure on colonial powers.[13] Yet a comprehensive study of UN trusteeship in practice remains wanting.[14] In general, the number of unpublished dissertations seems to suggest that the trusteeship system is a topic where book projects go to die; presumably, this is because many studies examine in detail the machinery and procedures in New York (which make for a rather dry read), rather than the effect of the system on individual trust territories.[15] If the rare case studies of the evolution of individual trust territories under UN supervision are any indication, international oversight usually slowly raised, and then fairly quickly disappointed the expectations of the indigenous inhabitants.[16] The system's supervisory mechanisms, as will be discussed below, were limited, making it a questionable template for proposals seeking greater accountability in current efforts of "international territorial administration."[17] Accordingly, some historians have suggested that the system really functioned as a "safe space" for imperial powers.[18]

As for Ralph Bunche, celebratory statements regarding his contributions to the UN Charter directives concerning the colonial world, as well as his impact on UN policy toward colonies as an international civil servant, require qualification.[19] While Bunche was involved in drafting the final U.S. proposal for trusteeship at San Francisco, he was a fairly junior State Department official, and American postwar planning regarding the colonial world had largely taken shape by the time that he arrived on the scene.[20] On the other hand, Bunche worked with delegations from Australia and China to introduce his ideas about international oversight into the proceedings at San Francisco and the first General Assembly session in 1946. Still, Bunche was nominally junior to the department's head, assistant secretary-general Victor Hoo, whose ideas about the role of international public servants and the purpose of UN oversight of colonial rule were far more conservative. More importantly, Bunche's energies were soon consumed by his role mediating conflict in the Middle East, after the state of Israel succeeded the British mandate of Palestine.

More generally, this chapter seeks to move beyond the questions whether UN oversight was a success or failure of decolonization, and whether UN supervision accelerated the independence of individual trust territories, questions that either suggest a misleading binary or would require more detailed case studies.[21] Rather, it examines the specific principles and oversight mechanisms for colonial rule that the Charter brought into being (as well as the limits thereof), and examines the attempts by Secretariat officials (including, but also going beyond Ralph Bunche) to shape ensuing UN discussions, definitions, and practices with regard to the colonial world.

First, this chapter will review wartime planning with regard to the future world organization and the colonial world, a largely uncoordinated Anglo-American affair, and discuss how the resulting political compromise – the Declaration and the trusteeship system – differed from the League set up. Much as the League covenant, the Charter explicitly affirmed and internationally legitimatized the concept of colonial trusteeship. At the same time, the Charter reformulated the purpose of said trusteeship from being *protective* (guarding against abuse) to being *proactive* (promoting development). While League oversight of colonial rule was officially limited to the mandates system, the UN Charter moreover sought to regulate and provide a measure of oversight for colonial rule in general. According to the Charter, "self-government" (a vague "weasel word ... deliberately designed ... to offer the shadow but never the substance of independence to subject peoples," as Indian UN delegate Vijaya L. Pandit put it[22]) was the agreed-upon goal of all colonial trusteeship. The achievement thereof, however, was tied to an indefinite period of foreign tutelage of "dependent peoples" in political, economic, social, and cultural matters.

The Charter itself, finalized and signed at the San Francisco UN Conference on International Organization in the spring of 1945, thus did little to settle the heated debate about where "dependent territories" were headed and what role the UN might play in them. Its directives were vague enough to lend themselves to competing interpretations and continued discussions, giving imperial and anti-imperial powers alike ammunition to argue either for continued colonial trusteeship or for immediate independence. It was also far from clear how progress along political, economic, social, and educational lines (considered a precondition for self-government and called for by the Charter) would be defined and achieved, and what role the UN itself might play in that process.

As this chapter explores, some officials in the UN Secretariat sought to give direction to the ensuing discussions, and by extension to processes of decolonization. While they were largely convinced that the colonial age as they knew it was coming to an end, like many of their contemporaries, UN civil servants were unsure what political constellations might replace empire in the future. Instead of rushing to foregone conclusions and deciding the political fate of the colonies in 1945, they counseled caution and attempted to square the circle of combining the foreign tutelage of "dependent peoples" with the malleable concept of self-determination, much as the League founding fathers had tried to do in the interwar period.[23] Though unsure about the endpoint of the imperial transformation ahead, UN officials hoped that the world organization would play a significant role in that process, especially in trust territories.

As will be discussed below, the actual impact of UN officials on day-to-day rule in colonies and trust territories was severely limited, owing to both systemic as well as personal confines. Nevertheless, Secretariat agency with regard to the colonial world should not be dismissed: first, Secretariat officials helped establish a Generally Assembly oversight mechanism, the Committee on Information from Non-Self-Governing Territories, which unlike the Trusteeship Council dealt not just with select territories, but with colonial rule in general. Second, the Secretariat's Trusteeship Division helped draft questionnaires on the basis of which colonial powers submitted information on their trust territories and colonies to the UN. In drawing up questions about progress in "dependent territories," the Secretariat helped define an expansive understanding of (national) development as well as the necessary prerequisites for self-government, that would be echoed beyond the confines of the trusteeship system and the colonial world. The UN thus created certain international benchmarks for development as well as a public space to hold colonial powers accountable to their own lofty promises. Much as the mandates system had in a few select territories, UN oversight of colonial rule thus helped make imperial governance more burdensome and in that way—indirectly—contributed to the end of empire.[24]

Beyond this, the Secretariat also proposed to offer hands-on *technical* assistance in political state-building, and to showcase the world organization's practical abilities in that yet-to-be-established field in trust territories. This 1950 initiative, however, led nowhere. Perhaps Secretariat officials ultimately realized the inherent contradiction in their proposal; perhaps lacking leadership or commitment in the Secretariat Department of Trusteeship and Information from Non-Self-Governing Territories played a role. But most importantly, colonial powers insisted on their sovereignty in "dependent territories" and displayed no interest in further broadening the scope of UN "interference." Nevertheless, the ideas contained in the state-building proposal discussed below prefigured more ambitious development missions that the UN would pursue in member states in the years to come.

## WARTIME PLANNING

How did the colonial world become an issue of concern to the UN? In the eyes of many U.S. government officials who were the main driving force in setting up the world organization, European empire posed a threat to international security. Colonies had long been regarded as a source for inter-imperial strife over economic outlets and resources. During World War II, American officials started to believe that the suppression of nationalist movements, particularly in Asia, would sow the seeds of the next world war. The future of the European colonial empires thus provided a central concern of American postwar planning and, to their imperial allies' distress, the common theme of independence ran through the thoughts of high-level U.S. policy makers.[25] In response to American schemes, which they inferred from public statements as well as from largely informal policy discussions, the British worked hard to gain the international initiative on the colonial issue. They sought to preempt American plans, of which they had only a partial understanding and which were themselves continuously evolving, with constructive policy proposals of their own.

Mark Mazower has argued that the central role long accorded to the United States in setting up the UN owes itself to something of an "optical illusion," as American planners during the war were essentially revising the League system, which, to a large extent, had been shaped by Great Britain.[26] Stephen Wertheim, by contrast, has suggested that American planners based their designs for the UN on a thoroughgoing critique of the League.[27] Largely based on Roger Louis's study, my reading of the wartime debates leading up to the establishment of the trusteeship system and the Declaration Regarding Non-Self-Governing Territories suggests a more dynamic, if largely uncoordinated Anglo-American back-and-forth.[28] It also acknowledges the role played by other states, as well as anticolonial activists, in shaping the UN system. It was only shortly before all UN founding member states agreed on the Charter that the United States, the United Kingdom, France, China, and the Soviet Union convened to reach a prior agreement on the UN and the colonial world. Yet accord proved hard to come by, as both China's nationalist government and Moscow lobbied for including independence in the Charter as an explicit goal of colonial rule.[29] At the San Francisco conference, a public event, anticolonial activists and their state allies worked hard to shape the Charter and, by extension, the future of the world organization in such a way that it would allow them to challenge colonial sovereignty.[30]

I also argue that while officials in both the U.S. and British administrations initially focused their attention and energy on the big question of formulating an abstract, ultimate goal for the colonies (that is, independence or self-government), their wartime discussions resulted in a highly consequential reformulation of the purpose of colonial trusteeship from being *protective* (guarding against abuse) to being *proactive* (promoting development). Though the League of Nations' foundational treaty, too, had enshrined the concept of tutelage for the "well-being and development" of peoples "not yet able to stand by themselves," its emphasis, at least for mandates that were considered less advanced, was decidedly on protective measures, such as guaranteeing the freedoms of conscience and religion and the prohibition of abuses.[31]

In August 1941, U.S. president Franklin Roosevelt and British prime minister Winston Churchill signed the Atlantic Charter. Although intended above all as a declaration to cement Anglo-American partnership, this agreement famously served to focus international attention on the issue of national self-determination by proclaiming "the right of all peoples to choose the form of government under which they will live."[32] The formulation had appeared innocuous enough to its signatories at the time, but British colonial officials soon realized that it invited a host of unwelcome questions about its application to the empire—an opening that was quickly seized upon by anticolonial activists.[33] Consequently, colonial officials pushed for government clarification that the Atlantic Charter's proclamation pertained to the European context only.

The search for a constructive statement to accompany the dismissal of the Atlantic Charter's applicability to empire plunged British officials into a far-reaching controversy over the goals of imperial policy: while some argued that "the Empire, animated by a spirit of liberty, pursued the goal of self-governing institutions," others were convinced that even subscribing to the limited goal of self-government was a step too far, as some territories within the empire, such as Mauritius or Aden, were simply too small or too strategically important to ever become self-governing units—an argument with remarkable staying power in the postwar period.[34]

For many American observers, by contrast, the future of European empire appeared clear-cut. Writing in the wake of the British surrender of Singapore to Japan in February 1942, the influential journalist Walter Lippmann opined that Western nations had to drastically reorient their wartime policy, "purging themselves of the taint of an obsolete obviously unworkable white man's imperialism." He called on them to "identify their cause with the freedom and security of the peoples in the East" and assure them independence. U.S. Undersecretary of State Sumner Welles publicly proclaimed the age of imperialism dead, essentially repeating Lippmann's suggestion that the war was fought for the liberation of all peoples, regardless of race, creed, or color in sovereign equality.[35] In Parliament, British representatives expressed concern about American calls for an end of empire. To counter such declarations, they proposed formulating a supplement to the Atlantic Charter, a British "Colonial Charter" that would spell out the benefits "dependent peoples" would reap from an Allied victory.[36]

While British parliamentarians debated the pros and cons of a Colonial Charter, wondering how to give a new lease of life to empire, the U.S. State Department formulated its own policy commitment to "dependent peoples" to be made by all "United Nations," as the Allied nations began to call themselves, in order to motivate the "colonial subjects'" war effort.[37] Key to American planning was Roosevelt's conception of international trusteeship as a general interim phase that would, as he put it condescendingly, lead the "many minor children among the peoples of the world" toward independence. Ambitious American promises to bring all colonies under the same regime of international control, however, were soon scaled back. Fear of a "boomerang effect," i.e., international supervision of U.S. dependencies such as Guam, Hawaii, and Alaska, as well as concern for British "sensitivities" and political feasibility, likely played a role in this decision.[38] U.S. policy makers instead agreed to bring only "ex-enemy overseas territories" under direct international supervision, as the League had done after World War I.[39] In addition to updating the geographically limited interwar mandates system, American officials further wished to pledge all imperial powers to observe certain universal principles of colonial administration. More importantly, they proposed to have them subscribe to specific objectives of imperial rule, namely eventual national independence.[40]

In the summer and fall of 1942, the Colonial Office, in consultation with Dominion governments, set out to develop a counterstrategy in response what it believed to be the thrust of the State Department's planning.[41] British officials aspired to a joint Anglo-American declaration on colonial policy that would robustly reaffirm British authority, while simultaneously offering the people in the colonies a stake in the imperial project. They further hoped to appease the U.S. appetite for the internationalization of empire, while abolishing any schemes for international control or oversight favored by the Americans. In contrast to U.S. plans, the declaration envisioned by the British bound the "Trustee State" to actively develop the social, economic, and political institutions of colonial peoples until they were able to discharge the responsibilities of self-government. Thus, gradual progress, or, more precisely, tutelary development was offered in lieu of imminent liberation. The prospect of self-government—once highly controversial among British officials—was espoused as the lesser evil to the assumed American obsession with independence.[42]

To counter the second U.S. idée fixe, the internationalization of empire, the British proposed the establishment of international regional commissions. According to their proposal, the "Trustee State" would be responsible for the safety and administration of dependencies (albeit "within the wider framework of a postwar international security system"), relying on regional commissions yet to be created for advancing the welfare of "dependent peoples."[43] What the British had in mind were essentially international consultative bodies without executive or supervisory functions, something along the lines of the Anglo-American Caribbean Commission, a contemporary, now largely forgotten international organization that was founded during World War II.[44] Cooperation of this kind, the colonial secretary explained, would provide the necessary "element of internationalism" to please both Americans and the British Left without giving away "anything essential," i.e., control of individual colonies.[45] No specific mention was made of either mandates or newly "parentless" ex-enemy dependencies. The old League system of international oversight of colonial rule in specific territories (which the British themselves had done much to shape) would have died a silent death.

Upon receiving the British proposal for a joint declaration on the colonies, the U.S. State Department proceeded to formulate yet another American version based on the British draft as well as earlier U.S. plans.[46] The result was the "Declaration by the United Nations on National Independence" of 9 March 1943. As the title indicates, the American Declaration hinged on the word "independence." One distressed British Foreign Office official noted that this appeared no fewer than six times in a single opening sentence. The new American Declaration also introduced the idea of setting specific dates for independence, which, in British eyes, was a particularly hideous proposition.[47] According to this Declaration, it was the "duty and purpose" of the UN—that is, the wartime alliance—to help "dependent peoples" in general become "qualified for independent national status." Echoing the British Declaration, the American draft now declared colonial governments responsible for giving "protection, encouragement, moral support, and material aid" for the educational, political, economic, and social advancement of "dependent peoples."[48]

British officials were aghast at the American insistence on eventual independence of the colonies, but being on the receiving end of U.S. financial and military assistance, they tried to avoid the issue as best as they could. By June 1944, however, American postwar planners faced much more powerful opposition to their plans closer to home. As an early study of the topic put it, the Departments of War and the Navy had developed "strong feelings" about U.S. postwar control of bases in the Pacific for security purposes.[49] Accordingly, these departments pressed for uncompromised American sovereignty over the formerly Japanese-mandated islands, which the U.S. military had occupied during the war. The U.S.

military command insisted on pure and simple "acquisition" of these islands, not for American "colonization or exploitation," as former Governor-General of the Philippines turned U.S. Secretary of War Henry Stimson was quick to point out, but rather for the defense of the postwar global order. According to this logic, the islands would serve as U.S. strategic "outposts" rather than colonies, and therefore should not come under international purview as other "dependent territories" would.[50]

The State Department, however, was anxious that such action would make the United States vulnerable to charges of territorial aggrandizement, which Roosevelt had disavowed in the Atlantic Charter. Its representatives thus pushed for a consistent application of international trusteeship to *all* former mandates and newly "parentless" ex-enemy territories. As a result of this "Battle of Washington" and the prolonged failure to reach an agreement on official American policy, the United States excluded close consideration of the topic from the big power preliminary talks (attended by the U.S., the Soviet Union, the United Kingdom, and China) at Dumbarton Oaks in October 1944, where the future setup of the world organization was laid out and discussed.[51] It was only five days prior to the beginning of the official discussions about the issue of trusteeship at San Francisco that the great powers—now including the French as well—came together to reach a prior agreement. This proved elusive, however, because of Chinese and Soviet insistence on independence as the ultimate goal of colonial rule.[52] Consequently, there was still some scope for delegates at the San Francisco, which brought together all UN founding member states from April to June 1945, to flesh out the Charter directives with regard to the colonial world.[53]

By the time of the conference, official American plans for a UN role in colonial affairs were watered down considerably to accommodate U.S. military demands within the promised trusteeship system. The formerly Japanese-mandate islands were designated as "strategic" trust territories and placed under the purview of the Security Council rather than the Trusteeship Council, so that the United States could veto any interference or even discussion of matters relating to them.[54] The UN trusteeship system, with its special category of "strategic territories" reserved for American-occupied mandates, thus served to both obscure and legitimize the territorial expansion of U.S. military power. It thus neatly fit with broader American designs to graft UN universalism atop a U.S. power base as the true enforcer of world order.[55]

In waging the internal battle over trusteeship, the Americans had temporarily lost sight of their previous interest in a declaration of general principles for the administration of all "dependent territories."[56] As the war drew to a close, such a declaration likely appeared less necessary as a propaganda tool to rally colonial peoples' support for the war effort. More importantly, the U.S. military objected to an expansive statement for fear of unrest among local populations at U.S. "outposts" such as Guam, Wake Island, or Samoa, which were administered by the Navy.[57] The British arrived at San Francisco largely unaware of the "Battle of Washington." Anticipating a much more far-reaching American draft, they introduced their own comparatively tame declaration of general principles into the proceedings.[58]

The delegations at San Francisco all agreed—though some, like the French, rather grudgingly—on the advisability of having a broad general policy statement with regard to colonies in the UN Charter.[59] The resultant Declaration Regarding Non-Self-Governing-Territories (Chapter XI) was much more detailed than the corresponding phrasing of the League covenant had been.[60] While the latter had simply pledged signatories "to secure just treatment of the native inhabitants of territories under their control," the UN Charter declared the interests of the inhabitants of non-self-governing territories paramount and obliged colonial powers "to promote to the utmost ... [their] well-being." This meant ensuring "political, economic, social and educational advancement" as well as "just treatment" and "protection against abuses." Self-government was an explicitly declared goal, as were the promotion of "constructive measures of development" and, to that end, cooperation among colonial powers and, "where appropriate," with specialized international bodies. Going beyond a declaration of the purposes of colonial rule, the Charter, in response to anticolonial calls for a supervisory mechanism, also asked "administering authorities," as colonial powers were called in official UN parlance, "to transmit regularly ... information of a technical nature relating to economic, social and educational conditions in the territories for which they are responsible."[61] Even this seemingly small concession was subject to limitations related to colonial powers' security and constitutional considerations.[62] Nevertheless, it was one on which anticolonial governments in forthcoming General Assembly sessions would build to establish a UN oversight mechanism for colonial rule: the Committee on Information on Non-Self-Governing Territories.[63]

While pledging colonial governments to the active advancement of their "dependent territories" toward self-government (once staunchly opposed by the British) now appeared rather uncontroversial and was adopted without much discussion, it was the issue of whether or not to include independence as a goal for "dependent territories" that generated the most discord at San Francisco.[64] It is important to note that San Francisco differed from other wartime meetings that would shape the UN not only in terms of the scope of participating governments, but also by virtue of being open to the press as well as to civil society organizations and activists. The U.S. delegation invited more than forty organizations—among them the National Association for the Advancement of Colored Peoples (NAACP), represented by W. E. B. Du Bois—to attend the proceedings as official consultants in an effort to increase public support for the future world organization. Anticolonial activists and organizations were thus able to use multiple channels (ranging from public pronouncements to informal influence with consultants and sympathetic state delegations) to put pressure on government representatives to ensure colonial peoples' representation at the UN, extend international supervision, and eventually end colonial rule.[65] Among the most outspoken supporters of this cause was the head of the Filipino delegation, Carlos P. Romulo, who made valiant attempts to have independence written into charter, but he was ultimately "squared" by the U.S. delegation.[66]

The debate about whether to identify independence as an explicit goal of colonial rule was ultimately concluded with a trade-off: under Western pressure, anticolonial representatives agreed to back down from their insistence on including independence in the general declaration if it was explicitly included as a possible objective for UN trust territories.[67] The UK delegate, moreover, put on record that "self-government"—the pronounced goal for all colonies—did not *preclude* independence. The trust territories, so the more hopeful attendees thought, might become a shining example and measuring stick for other "dependent territories."[68] Yet, even for them, the goal was formulated as the progressive development towards self-government *or* independence as may be appropriate to the particular circumstances of each territory and its peoples and the freely expressed wishes of the peoples concerned, and as may be provided by the terms of each trusteeship agreement.[69]

Given these caveats, the hard-won compromise did little to settle the debate about where colonies were headed in the postwar world order.

San Francisco, moreover, established only general principles of colonial rule as well as the outlines of the international trusteeship system. "Administering authorities"—one or more states or, theoretically, the UN itself—would rule the trust territories. The Trusteeship Council, one of four principal intergovernmental bodies of the UN, would supervise the administration of these territories by reviewing annual reports and petitions as well as dispatching periodic visiting missions. The latter provisions, which promised the inhabitants of trust territories an unprecedented degree of access to the UN, were no small achievements for anticolonial activists and their state allies.[70] Yet at the Yalta summit in February 1945, the United States, the Soviet Union, and the United Kingdom had agreed that for specific territories to effectively come under UN oversight, individual and detailed trust agreements would have to be reached by unspecified "states directly concerned."[71] Making the trusteeship system a reality and shaping the ultimate contours of international trusteeship was thus up to the colonial powers. Shaping UN oversight of colonies in general, in turn, would require the initiative and activism of anticolonial states at the inaugural session of the General Assembly in 1946.

## A SECRETARIAT VIEW ON TRUSTEESHIP

Anticipating continued discussion regarding the final objectives of trusteeship, the future of the colonies and, by extension, the world at large, some in the UN Secretariat sought to give shape to that debate or, rather, to bring to an end discussions about independence and self-government, which they perceived as "somewhat theoretical and unlikely to lead to agreement."[72] In September 1946, former French colonial official turned UN Secretariat member Jean de la Roche wrote a memo on "the objectives of international trusteeship" for that purpose.[73] There is no evidence to suggest that the document carried any weight in "metropolitan" policy debates (as de la Roche had hoped it would), nor even that other Secretariat officials weighed in on the matter. Nevertheless, it constitutes an interesting testament to the thinking of a UN official at the time, conveying a general sense of a new beginning, but also considerable uncertainty with regard to the future shape of the colonial world and the role the UN might play in its transformation.

De la Roche was born in 1904. He studied law in Paris, spent three years in the Navy, and, while working for a French furnace firm in the late 1920s, traveled widely in North Africa, Latin America, and the Caribbean. In 1931, he entered the colonial service in the French West Indies (Martinique and Guadeloupe), where he likely met Félix Éboué, a Black colonial administrator and reformer. Between 1939 and 1942, de la Roche served under Éboué in Chad, before transferring again to New York to head the French Colonial Information Service there. During this time, he also served as a Free French delegate to multiple wartime meetings related to international organization, among them the 1944 International Labor Organization conference at Philadelphia, the meeting at Hot Springs in 1945 that led to the establishment of the Food and Agriculture Organization, and the conference in San Francisco that same year that decided the final shape of the UN Charter.[74]

In 1945, de la Roche co-published a book called *La Federation Française: Contacts et Civilisations d'Outre-mer*, which advocated for the reconstitution of the French Empire as a federation, "uniting Metropolis with Colonies and allowing each of them to move at ease in the context of their particular worries."[75] The book portrayed French imperialism, despite its shortcomings, as an essentially humanist, protective force, but heralded the end of "the colonial cycle" and the coming of truly novel times of association and assimilation. Taking its cue from proponents of colonial reform such as Éboué, the book called for the improvement of labor rights, health provisions, state schooling, and civil protections across all of "Greater France." De la Roche's career and intellectual pursuits prior to entering the UN Secretariat's Division of Trusteeship in 1946 thus testify to the linkages and continuities between imperialism and international governance, but also suggest that a particular kind of reform-oriented colonial officials were drawn to serving the world organization.[76]

Writing for the UN in 1946, de la Roche thought it was clear that "the idea of the coloniser and the colonised" had to be abolished and replaced by "cooperation and mutual assistance for the common good and for the stability of the world." He continued, "The so-called colonial world has in fact entered upon an era of profound change," yet "none of the nations responsible for the administration of dependent territories," with the important exception of territories of strategic interest, he argued, "is at present in a position to define its aims in these territories clearly." De la Roche saw two extremes: on the one side were "colonials" hoping "to give a new lease of life to obsolete methods (colonial pacts, economic privileges, compulsory labor, political subordination etc.)." On the other were "men of good will trying to liquidate the 'colonial age.'" Between the two poles were a "considerable number of ideological theories, practical considerations, immediate needs, economic interest and compromises between ideals and material necessities." To de la Roche, it was unclear what might become of empire in the postwar period.[77]

De la Roche discerned two possible, desirable options: autonomy from, or equality of rights with the "Mother Country." The "evidence," he stated, counter to the argument presented in his own 1945 book, was not yet "conclusive or convincing" as to which direction would best serve the needs of "dependent peoples."[78] In assimilationist policies, which he linked to closer association, de la Roche saw the dangers of standardization and the loss of local traditions and customs. On the other hand, he was doubtful that true independence could be achieved in the twentieth century in all but name, and that *inter*dependence had to be recognized as a fact of international life. Politically independent territories, he thought, ran the risk of being mere "playthings of foreign governments or economic systems, and of advanced [local] cliques and 'chefs de race.'" Dividing the world into "watertight compartments," he argued, only bred international ignorance and suspicion, as the two world wars had made abundantly clear. The challenge for the UN was thus to help steer a middle ground between global standardization and a compartmentalized world.[79]

The world wars, de la Roche thought, had sounded the death knell of both colonialism and nationalism. Like his French contemporaries, he looked to some form of federalism, or the formation of "geographical groups based on ethnical and economic considerations," as he put it, as a desirable alternative to both colonial "business as usual" and international "balkanization."[80] De la Roche believed that one day it would seem paradoxical that dependencies were urged toward national independence at a time when world peace depended "upon the good will with which so-called sovereign states consent to sacrifice a part of their sovereignty." It was contradictory to ask highly developed states to limit their national sovereignty in the name of the common good of the UN while "exalting the principle" or even "bringing it prematurely to birth in the case of communities in the formative stage." The main difficulty, de la Roche thought, was forging some kind of political belonging within the state without falling prey to the "obsolete virus of nationalism." His hope was that the "exploitation of natural wealth, the training of professional and administrative staff, the education of the masses" might prove to be "sufficiently absorbing tasks." In other words, developmental state-making might take the place of literal nation-building.[81]

"Neither those in power," de la Roche argued, nor the inhabitants of "dependent territories," "were at present qualified or in a position to decide" on an ultimate political goal for the colonies. After all, trusteeship had been applied because the inhabitants of colonies were deemed "not sufficiently mature." The UN, not being "directly concerned in the consequence of a choice," he thought, could be more objective. Yet it was not for the UN to make "a premature choice between political systems," but rather to bring the masses of "dependent peoples" to a point where they themselves could make a "deliberate choice" about which type of government they preferred—"with the full knowledge of facts and in complete physical and moral freedom." De la Roche did not determine at what point "dependent peoples" would qualify for self-determination, or who would decide that question, nor was he concerned with the nuts and bolts of promoting development. He merely envisioned the UN as "profit[ing] from the long and varied experience of colonising nations" in this regard. According to de la Roche, it would be up to the "administering authorities," under UN supervision, to master the "delicate task ... [of ensuring] the rapid but impartial awakening of consciousness of the masses." Ultimately, his memo reads as an effort to move beyond both colonialism and nationalism, but also reflects an understanding that the UN—as a creature of both empires and nation-states—could not quite do without either.[82]

## THE CONFINES OF THE TRUSTEESHIP SYSTEM

Counter to de la Roche's hopes, colonial powers did not appear to use any UN Secretariat guidelines in drawing up trusteeship agreements and establishing the legal basis for their administration of individual trust territories under UN supervision. In fact, much as they had done after World War I, they dragged their feet on concluding these agreements at all. The League mandates of Palestine (ruled by the British) and South West Africa (Namibia today, at the time governed by South Africa) were never formally placed under UN trusteeship.[83] It took some polite prodding by UN Secretary-General Trygve Lie for the first trust agreements for former League mandates to be submitted to the General Assembly for approval in December 1946.[84]

Even so, these agreements were drafted by the "administering authorities" themselves (that is, the United Kingdom, France, Belgium, New Zealand, Australia, and the United States), who decided which states to consider and thus consult as "directly concerned." There was little leverage for other UN member states, let alone the UN Secretariat, to influence the terms of the trust.[85] When the General Assembly discussed the first trust agreements, anticolonial member states suggested over 200 amendments. Yet, the future "administering authorities" accepted virtually none of the suggested changes, threatening to withdraw their voluntary submissions to the system altogether.[86] The General Assembly ultimately approved of the agreements on the assumption that it was better to bring the trusteeship system into operation on the terms the colonial powers desired than to have no international oversight at all. Nearly all Arab-Asian states, as well as some Latin American members, however, abstained from voting.[87]

To Secretariat officials and journalists with high hopes regarding the benefit of international supervision of colonial administration, this arrangement soon proved a "pyrrhic victory" or worse, a "squalid farce."[88] Authority over day-to-day policy lay firmly in the hands of the colonial powers. It was not so much that the Trusteeship Council, the intergovernmental UN supervisory body, had no teeth, as one contemporary observer deplored, but rather that, because of its composition, it did not even want to take a bite.[89] UN member states had agreed at San Francisco that the Council would be composed of an equal number of representatives from states "administering" trust territories (Australia, Belgium, France,

New Zealand, the United Kingdom and, eventually, the United States and Italy) and those that did not, and that it would include the permanent members of the Security Council. There were thus no anti-colonial majorities in the Council as there would be within the General Assembly.[90]

In 1947, the Trusteeship Council took up its work. It met twice a year at the UN headquarters to review annual reports written by "administering powers" as well as any petitions relating to the trust territories. The reports were written in response to a detailed questionnaire, which the Secretariat helped shape. The questionnaire that was officially approved by the Trusteeship Council in 1952 was composed of eleven parts, numerous subsections, and 190 questions altogether. Most of these, by far, concerned the economic (47), social (70), and educational advancements (36) in each trust territory, while fourteen questions were related to its political advancement. These questions covered everything from "colonial subjects'" participation in government and the civil service to suffrage, the legal system, public finance, economic activities, human rights, living standards, public health, housing, penal organization, schools, and higher education. Taken together, they suggested a uniquely expansive definition of (national) development.[91]

For Council members sympathetic to the plight of colonial peoples, however, the comprehensive information thus compiled proved difficult to handle.[91] What was more, colonial powers hoped to use the statistical information thus compiled to defend imperial rule and shame anti-colonial delegates on the Council by comparing developmental achievements in trust territories with those of their countries of origin.[92] While the colonial powers on the Council "showed profound respect for the principle of dog does not eat dog,"[93] as one observer put it, and indeed the British, French and Belgians coordinated their policy at the Council beforehand, two to three Council members usually expressed cautious criticism of the "administering powers." Initially the representatives of "non-administering" member states focused on the expansion of social and educational facilities; later on, the political advancement of the inhabitants of the territories became a prominent concern.[94]

The only consistent radical challenge to the colonial powers' position came from the Soviet representative, who—after an initial boycott of the proceedings, because the USSR had not been consulted on the trust agreements—used the Council as a "knob for attacks" on the West.[95] For example, the Soviets mocked the claim of the British representative to the Trusteeship Council, Hilton Poynton, who had portrayed the British Empire, although separated by seas and oceans, as a "single international organism," much like the Soviet Union. The argument was later picked up by Poynton's successor, Sir Alan Burns, and presented as the so-called "salt water fallacy." Burns complained that the "expansion by a country over land, and the incorporation of large areas of territory inhabited by other races and peoples [was] apparently perfectly praiseworthy," but that the "extension of one's jurisdiction over sea," by contrast, was "stigmatized in certain quarters as 'Colonial imperialism,' [and] 'oppression of subject races.'"[96]

In an open letter to Poynton published in the *Literary Gazette* of the USSR, Kirghiz writer Kassymaly Bayalinov drew on his own experience to ridicule the Soviet-British comparison.[97] The Soviet state, Bayalinov wrote, had cured him of illiteracy and ignorance; it had established Kirghizia (Kyrgyzstan) as a Soviet Republic and turned Kirghiz into a written language, introducing translations of foreign classics, as well as honoring Kirghiz literature and poetry. He continued:

> It would be very kind of you, Mr. Poynton, to let me know in what town of your mandatory and colonial possessions the plays of Shakespeare, Ostrovsky, Gogol and Griboyedov are performed. I should also like you to send me some information regarding the national bards of the peoples in your possessions . . . which books have been translated into English and what libraries in English towns are adorned with the portraits of Sikhs, Copts and Bechuanas. . . . Have many of them been elected to Parliament? Whose books are read in Birmingham and Liverpool?[98]

But even if the Soviet representative put the "administering authorities" on the defensive, his comments on the Council did not reach a broad audience and, so the colonial powers thought, could easily be dismissed as propaganda.[99] They initially considered the other "non-administering" powers "a more difficult problem" than the Soviet attacks. Here, a "conciliatory approach" seemed necessary, which they feared might have "undesirable effects upon certain sections of the populations in the trust territories." To support their case, the colonial powers worked for U.S. support. They presented a united front, working closely with U.S.

delegates at the UN and "educating American public opinion" "on the achievements of the Colonial powers in technical fields."[100] This strategy must have worked well enough so that, according to Evan Luard, the Council's examination of annual progress reports quickly became a lengthy routine.[101] As was the case with the mandates system, however, UN oversight certainly made imperial governance in trust territories more burdensome.[102]

While the examination of annual reports was a feature inherited from the League of Nations mandates system, formalized petitioning was a novel aspect of the trusteeship system that offered colonial peoples unprecedented access to the new world organization. The UN Secretariat shaped that access by preselecting, organizing, and summarizing the content of petitions. In theory, anyone could send petitions relating to trust territories to the Secretariat, hand them over to UN visiting missions dispatched to trust territories, or present them in person to the Trusteeship Council. While substantial practical hurdles in terms of travel restrictions as well as costs had to be overcome in order for a petitioner to appear in person before the Council in New York, the potential rewards were also higher, offering a chance to network with foreign allies and raising one's profile at home. Submitting written petitions was less costly and grew increasingly popular as more inhabitants learned about the special status of UN trust territories—to the extent that the Secretariat became unable to handle the volume.[103] Yet many petitioners from trust territories, who had initially been hopeful about the UN's weighing in on their behalf with regard to specific grievances, were by and large disappointed by the late, tepid, and generic responses they received from the Trusteeship Council.[104]

In addition to formalizing the petitioning process, the UN Charter also provided for periodic visiting missions of Secretariat officials and government representatives to trust territories as an oversight mechanism. Yet these, too, did not necessarily function as safeguards of the local population's interest. While the Trusteeship Department staffed and assisted visiting missions to trust territories and prepared their final reports, these missions were largely at the mercy of the receiving "administering authority" and, furthermore, specifically instructed by the UN headquarters to not investigate petitions on the spot, should colonial officials object to this. A Secretariat directive noted that visiting missions were supposed

FIG. 6  UN Visiting Mission to Trust Territories in the Pacific

Sir John MacPherson, UK Chairman of the UN Visiting Mission, is greeted by an unnamed "Kukukuku warrior chief" upon arrival at Menyamya Airport in Papua New Guinea (1956). Notice the different image the UN sought to project in the photographs from the organization's Congo intervention four years later (see chapter 6), where Black UN experts are foregrounded and at least some Congolese are named in the captions.

Source: UN Photo, UN7686256

to "forge ties rather than inspect." Their purpose was not to report abuses or mistakes on part of the colonial administration, but instead, as one internal UN memo put it, to promote the advancement of the territory.[105]

According to Luard, the first visiting mission, dispatched to Western Samoa in the summer of 1947 at the request of the "administering authority," New Zealand, to judge calls for immediate self-government, set the tone for subsequent missions. The mission report was generally favorable to New Zealand and encouraged other "administering authorities" to be less cautious about official UN visits.[106] To be sure, some activist Secretariat members would not follow the official restrictive guidelines. Ulrich Lohrmann suggests that the 1954 UN visiting mission to Tanganyika, for example, proved a catalyst for the nationalist movement. Yet, he also recounts that the maverick Secretariat officials in question were quickly reined in and, on subsequent visiting missions, replaced with UN representatives more agreeable to the colonial authorities.[107] More insistent pressures on "administering authorities" eventually came from the General Assembly, which discussed a summary report from the Trusteeship Council's every year. Increasingly impatient with the lack of progress in the trust territories, the Assembly's Fourth Committee on Trust and Non-Self-Governing Territories eventually began to take over some of the functions of the Trusteeship Council, reviewing oral statements and even dispatching visiting missions on its own.[108]

## PERSONAL CONFINES

By and large, there was only limited room for UN Secretariat officials to directly influence policy in the trust territories. Nor, it seems, did the top officials in the UN Secretariat's Department of Trusteeship and Information from Non-Self-Governing Territories show much initiative. The assistant secretary-general in charge of the Department, Chinese career diplomat Victor Hoo, had enjoyed a thoroughly elitist upbringing. Hoo was the son of a largely absent high-level diplomat and a mother who passed away when he was young. He grew up among family friends in a Russian aristocratic household in pre-revolutionary St. Petersburg, which counted more servants than family members. Hoo studied diplomacy and law at the Sciences Po and spent his summers at Oxford and Cambridge before taking up first diplomatic assignments with the Chinese delegation to the Paris Peace Conference and the League of Nations in the interwar period.[109]

According to a biography by his daughter, Hoo was a bon vivant through and through, who was far more interested in maximizing the amenities of diplomatic life than in any progressive cause that his work at the UN might serve. Generally, Hoo believed that the Secretariat should be told what to do, rather than "carry the burden of political responsibilities."[110] His diary entries concerning a visit to trust territories in East Africa in 1951 show him preoccupied mainly with the (mediocre) quality of the caviar he was served, his colleague's amorous adventures and naughty jokes, and sensationalist accounts of local customs. In Rwanda, he was impressed by conditions maintained by Belgium:

> In Astrida we saw the best kept hospital for natives that I have ever seen... The beds had coloured bed covers that lent a happy note to the atmosphere. There were pillows for everyone with clean pillow cases and an anesthetic machine in the delivery room.[111]

Upon taking up his post in the Trusteeship Department, Hoo expected cosmopolitan diplomacy interspersed with the occasional adventure here and there (he imagined encounters with lions and cannibals), not international accolades or uplift. In a 1946 broadcast, he conceded quite frankly that he did not expect UN supervision to bring about immediate and radical changes for the people in the trust territories.[112]

Hoo's nominal second-in-command, Ralph Bunche, the director of the Department's Trusteeship division, was a more likely candidate to push for a progressive Secretariat role in the trust territories.[113] By all accounts, Bunche, who was born in Detroit in 1904, was hard-working, highly intelligent, and, perhaps more importantly, deeply concerned about "the great moral issue" of one people ruling over another, which he found irreconcilable with the democratic principles invoked by the victorious Allies.[114] Bunche also boasted an unusually longstanding and intimate knowledge of, as well as a personal investment, in the issue of international trusteeship. During his graduate studies—he was the first African-American recipient of a PhD in political science, in 1934—Bunche had traveled to West Africa to compare French policy in the League of Nations mandate Togoland and the neighboring colony of Dahomey. As a postdoctoral student, Bunche mingled with African students in London (some of whom would play important roles in the independence struggles of the postwar

FIG. 7  Victor Hoo, Trygve Lie, and Ralph Bunche

Victor Hoo, assistant secretary-general in charge of the Department of Trusteeship and Information from Non-Self-Governing Territories; UN Secretary-General Trygve Lie; and Ralph Bunche, director of the Trusteeship Division, at the first session of the Trusteeship Council (1947).

Source: UN Photo, UN7728119

period) and visited South Africa, Kenya, and Uganda, as well as the Belgian Congo.[115] During World War II, he joined the State Department, where he became an important contact for emerging African leaders and also, as discussed above, helped shape the American planning effort for the postwar order.

Both his early Marxist convictions as well as his personal observations in Africa led Bunche to conclude that imperialism equaled brutal exploitation. In a 1936 booklet, he wrote that "powerful industrial nations had raped Africa under the false pretense of shouldering 'the white man's burden' . . . to expose them to the benefits of an advanced European culture."[116] His doctoral dissertation offered a meticulous survey and critique of colonialism in practice and he expressed hope that the imperial age was coming to an end.[117] But his appraisal of how one might get there, or what the new age might look like, remained somewhat vague; as it did for other Black internationalists at the time.[118] For a time, Bunche placed his bet on colonial "tutelage" and "apprenticeship." In his 1934 dissertation, he wrote:

> Though the time when the ... African will be able, in the words of the League Covenant, "to stand alone in the strenuous conditions of the modern world," is probably many generations removed from the present day, he should be serving an apprenticeship in the art of self-rule under the tutelage of his immediate rulers. ... It must be made possible for him now to acquire the experience and develop the leadership essential to sound government everywhere.[119]

Again, it was unclear what form this tutelage might take.

Bunche was on firmer ground when it came to the role he envisioned for international organizations in this uncertain process of guided, gradual decolonization. He thought that mandate principles "had operated generally to liberalize and humanize the policies of colonial powers," yet he saw the accomplishments of the League in this field as only the beginning of "great work" ahead.[120] In general, he found little difference in the treatment and status of people under the Togo mandate and that of their neighbors in the colony of Dahomey.[121] To Bunche, international cooperation was important not for ensuring a concrete improvement of colonial administration through oversight, but in establishing certain principles for colonial rule.

In that sense, Bunche had also been an enthusiastic supporter of the International Labor Organization's Recommendation on Minimum Standards of Social Policy in Dependent Areas, also known as the "Charter for the Colonies," proclaimed in Philadelphia in 1944. Largely drafted by Wilfried Benson, who would later join Bunche as a colleague in the UN Trusteeship Department, the Recommendation (which was ratified by ILO member governments) had called for a subordination of all colonial policies to social objectives—active promotion of economic and social development on part of colonial governments—as well as increased participation of the colonies' inhabitants in decision-making. The desirability of an internationalization of social policy was also hinted at. Daniel

Maul suggests that the Philadelphia session had an enormous effect on social and political movements in the colonies, as the Recommendation invited a range of new claims from their inhabitants. In Maul's assessment, it was a "huge stride forward for reform-oriented forces and a source of inspiration for all those committed to the emancipation of colonial peoples."[122] Bunche saw the UN Charter as building on, but going beyond Philadelphia's narrower social focus.[123]

As noted above, some scholars credit Bunche with a "central role in the evolving process of decolonization," suggesting that his input on U.S. and UN colonial policies "helped pave the way for gradual peaceful" emancipation from imperial rule.[124] Yet, as his former colleague Lawrence Finkelstein pointed out, Bunche was a fairly junior State Department official, and American postwar planning regarding the colonial world had largely taken shape by the time that he arrived on the scene.[125] Nevertheless, he was involved in drafting the final American trusteeship proposal "at the eleventh hour" aboard the train to San Francisco.[126] Apparently dissatisfied with the official U.S. version, Bunche introduced his own ideas for the trusteeship system into the official proceedings via the Australian delegation.[127] He later described the discussions about trusteeship as the "toughest fight of the Conference," telling his wife that the Charter section on trusteeship was not as good as he would like it to be, "but better than any of us expected it could get." A good part of the final phrasing, he continued, was drafted exclusively by him. "It's a thrill even for your blasé old hubby to see his own writing in [the Charter]—writing over which he struggled for long, long hours in a desperate effort to break with what often seemed to be impossible impasses."[128] Together with other delegates such as Romulo of the Philippines and Wellington Koo of China, Bunche supported the introduction of official accountability mechanisms both for trust territories (in the form of petitions and visiting missions) and with regard to other colonies (in the form of information to be submitted to the secretary-general).[129]

Later in the Trusteeship Department, according to Finkelstein, there was by and large "little opportunity for direct and open participation [on the part of UN officials] in the making of international policy affecting the colonies."[130] Bunche did the best he could with the means available to him. For example, he worked closely with the Chinese delegation to the UN, led by Koo, in order to convince the 1946 first General Assembly session in London to set up the ad hoc Special Committee on Information Transmitted under Article 73e of the Charter which, much like the Trusteeship Council, was composed of an equal number of colonial and noncolonial powers that would review and discuss reports submitted by the imperial powers on their colonies on a regular basis.[131] As noted above, the Charter required UN members responsible for the administration of "non-self-governing territories" (that is, colonial powers) to regularly transmit to the secretary-general "information of a *technical* nature relating to economic, social and educational conditions in the territories."[132]

Initially, the major European colonial powers were reluctant to submit said information to the UN at all, pointing out that the Charter requirement was subject to "security and constitutional considerations." French officials tried to suggest that the newly proclaimed "French Union" was, in fact, no longer a form of empire.[133] When such arguments failed to gain purchase at the General Assembly, colonial powers pushed back against the public discussion of the reports that they eventually submitted, by pointing out that the Charter did not specify what the secretary-general would do with the information he received. Ultimately ditching their defensive position to assume, in the words of a British official, "a position of moral leadership based on our record of colonial achievement," the colonial powers agreed to a UN publication based on their reports.[134] This reflected an early change of British strategy, from stonewalling the UN to appreciating the importance of the world organization as a potential tool for deflecting anticolonial pressure by playing "as constructive and as co-operative a part as possible in the work of the Special Committee."[135]

From that point on, the quantity rather than the scarcity of the information on colonies submitted to the Committee became a problem (mirroring a similar trend at the Trusteeship Council). Handling this information required a "drastic" preselection process by the Secretariat.[136] Cooperative imperial powers—Belgium left the Committee in the early 1950s—submitted reports on their colonies in response to a detailed questionnaire, which was based on a Secretariat draft and similar to the one concerning trust territories. The main difference was that the questionnaire for "non-self-governing territories," unlike the one on trust territories, did not feature any questions with regard to the territory's "political advancement."[137]

Secretariat officials sincerely hoped that since the ad hoc Committee was officially set up to discuss only *technical* matters relating to economic, social, and educational conditions in the territories, it might constructively channel political issues toward the advancement of colonial territories, while the "rhetorical fireworks" concerning colonialism would be reserved for the General Assembly.[138] As more and more data were gathered, the Committee's recommendations indeed became increasingly specific. Ultimately, the Committee became an important site for government representatives at the UN—both procolonial and anticolonial—to discuss which territories to consider colonies in the first place, as well as how colonial rule should be practiced and to what end.[139] As Jessica L. Pearson has argued, it created a significant opening that allowed the world to see into the inner lives of empires.[140]

While Bunche tried hard to make the UN the most effective possible advocate of the rights and interests of the people in "dependent territories," as early as 1947 his energies were no longer focused on colonies per se, but on peacekeeping in the Middle East.[141] Because Palestine was a former League of Nations mandate, the Trusteeship Department became involved in the work of the UN to decide the territory's future. In mid-May 1947, the General Assembly set up a Special Committee on Palestine and Secretary-General Trygve Lie appointed Victor Hoo as his representative there. According to Brian Urquhart, an early Secretariat member turned UN chronicler, Lie appointed Bunche as Hoo's special assistant to give some "heavyweight assistance" to Hoo's "vain, pleasure-loving lightweight."[142] On 6 January 1948, Bunche became principal secretary of the UN Palestine Commission, to which—per General Assembly resolution—the British were to cede authority for a two-month transitional period before two separate states would be established. As Urquhart put it, the fact that Arab countries had denounced this program and the British had said that they would not give effect to it made the work of the Commission "somewhat academic."[143] In May, the General Assembly and the Security Council dispatched Count Folke Bernadotte of Sweden as a UN mediator to Palestine, accompanied by Bunche as a chief representative of the secretary-general. When Bernadotte was assassinated in Jerusalem in September 1948, Bunche was appointed acting mediator. In 1950, he was awarded the Nobel Peace Prize for his work, which resulted in armistice agreements between the new state of Israel and four of its Arab neighbors: Egypt, Jordan, Lebanon, and Syria.[144] Given this important work, there was little time for Bunche to focus on the question of trust territories and other colonies.

Within the Trusteeship Department, the lack (or part-time nature) of Bunche's leadership resulted in a considerable slump in morale among his staff. Asked by Bunche to comment on the weaknesses of the Department and how they might be overcome, Taylor Shore, his friend and colleague, wrote:

> With the exception of your hardy immediate staff and one or two others on a personal basis very few ever get into your office, which is constantly besieged by visitors from outside. Most of your officers see you in the corridor as you dash from one meeting to another. They do not feel free to come to you.[145]

It is therefore of little surprise that a 1950 proposal drafted in the Trusteeship Department, which argued for the UN Secretariat to take a more proactive role in delivering on the promise of development in the trust territories, came to nothing. The proposal nevertheless provides an important testament to ideas prevalent among UN officials at the time, who increasingly sought to approach the politics of state-building as a technical challenge.

## TECHNICAL ASSISTANCE IN POLITICAL ADVANCEMENT

As noted in the introduction, in the 1940s and 1950s "technical assistance"— the transfer of knowledge and skills conveyed by advisory experts to requesting governments—functioned as the UN's primary means for delivering on the promise of global development. Much of the UN's own work, during and in the first years after the war, focused on the problems of rehabilitation and reconstruction of those parts of the world, mainly in Europe, that had seen large-scale destruction as a result of the war. The very first official UN body to come into existence in 1943, the UN Relief and Rehabilitation Administration (UNRRA), had been dedicated to this cause. When UNRRA was ripped apart by a growing East–West divide and formally terminated in 1946, the General Assembly resolved that the UN Secretariat should continue "the important advisory functions in the field of social welfare" that had been furnished to member countries.[146] A sum of $436,000 was allocated from the regular UN budget to finance technical assistance in this field.

Yet many UN member states were discontented with the UN's focus and spending on the industrialized world. Brazil, for example, claimed that it had given 1 percent of its national income to UNRRA and argued that it was time for the world organization to now turn to the special problems of "underdeveloped" countries.[147] During the first General Assembly sessions, several representatives raised the issue of glaring inequalities in economic development among UN member states, warning that these presented a threat to world peace. Carlos Lleras Restrepo, a former finance minister of Colombia, who had previously represented his country at the Bretton Woods negotiations, fleshed out his view of the linkages among economic interdependence, global growth with equity, and international peace and stability.[148] Charles Malik of Lebanon, supported by the Chinese delegation, called for the creation of a UN Advisory Board that would provide experts and guidance to underdeveloped countries in various fields of economic and social development.

Malik's initiative resulted in the Economic and Social Council's very broadly phrased resolution on "Expert Assistance to Member Governments" of March 1947. The resolution asked the UN Secretariat to assist member states in obtaining information on expert personnel, research facilities, and resources available through the United Nations and the specialized agencies (autonomous international organizations affiliated with the UN, such as the FAO, the ILO, and the WHO) and organizing the dispatch of teams of experts, who would study specific problems and recommend solutions.[149] Haiti was one of the first member states to request UN assistance under this resolution. In the last months of 1948, the UN Secretariat dispatched a team of eleven experts in various fields covering agriculture, industry, finance, education, and health to the island to study the country's overall potential for economic development.[150] Given its comprehensive nature, Secretary-General Lie thought that the UN mission to Haiti "deserved attention as a new departure in UN activities."[151]

But the Secretariat was initially slow to embrace this new enterprise and, indeed, recognize it as such. Comparatively little money was budgeted for expert assistance to member governments—the secretary-general expected to spend about $14,800 in 1947—and government requests were handled on an ad hoc basis by different Secretariat sections. The conditions and nature of UN support varied so greatly from country to country, so the argument went, that assistance could not be centralized or standardized. UN officials believed that the experience of different countries should not be generalized and that each government request for assistance should therefore be handled as a special case.[152] Yet a number of countries, including Burma, Chile, Egypt, and Peru continued to push for the UN to offer and allocate funds for specialized assistance to underdeveloped countries. Despite already existing technical assistance activities of the UN specialized agencies, the delegates of these countries argued that there was still a broad area of development in which assistance was lacking and best provided by the world organization.

As a result of this campaign, the General Assembly appropriated the modest sum of $288,000 for "Technical Assistance for Economic Development" to "under-developed areas" in December 1948.[153] A month later, U.S. president Harry Truman followed the UN's (or rather, the poorer countries') lead and called for "a bold new program" of technical assistance "for the improvement and growth of underdeveloped areas" in his famous Point IV speech.[154] The subsequent U.S. commitment of funds substantially expanded the world organization's existing assistance activities. Following Truman's speech, Western UN member states allocated $20,000,000 to the UN and its specialized agencies for technical assistance purposes and the Secretariat assumed a coordinating role for the UN Expanded Program for Technical Assistance, or EPTA.[155]

Reporting back from a trip to Europe shortly after Truman's speech, a UN Secretariat member noted that within all the UN specialized agencies, "very considerable and perhaps exaggerated interest [was] being shown in the possibilities of technical assistance." To a greater extent than at the UN headquarters, he continued, "it seems to be felt that the Non-Self-Governing Territories are areas in which technical assistance may be most effectively offered."[156] By 1950, the excitement generated by Truman's speech also reached the shores of the Trusteeship Department. Two memoranda explored the potential role of technical assistance in the trusteeship system and the significance of the system for UN assistance more generally.[157]

The memos noted that technical assistance was one of the most important aspects of the work of the UN, that trust territories were among "the most under-developed areas of the world," and that economic and social advancement was one of the basic objectives of the trusteeship system. Yet attention to the development of these territories, in the eyes of the Trusteeship Department, had so far been insufficient. For reasons of prestige, the memos suggested, the UN should prioritize these places in its technical assistance program. In the trust territories, the UN could showcase its assistance capabilities and the territories' development could serve as a shining example to other colonies. The author imagined the Trusteeship Council to have more leverage vis-à-vis the "administering authorities" than the Economic and Social Council (one of the six principal UN organs) had regarding sovereign UN member states, and that it was thus easier to push for direct involvement of the UN in the trust territories.

The memo stated that work in the trust territories would allow the UN to venture into entirely new fields of development beyond the economic and social realm and thus to pioneer new forms of assistance. The political advancement of the inhabitants and their progressive development toward self-government or independence was one of the most important aims of the trusteeship system. "It seems to be certain that . . . some kind of technical assistance [in this realm] is possible and desirable," the memo insisted. Indeed, the authors imagined a "wide field of technical assistance towards self-government" opening up to the UN for tilling, a quite literal project of institutionalized technical state-building.[158]

As far as the trust territories were concerned, such dreams on the part of the Secretariat went largely unfulfilled. Requests for assistance from the UN had to be formulated by the "administering authorities" (the colonial powers), which were by and large ardently opposed to seeing the world organization involved in the politics of their dependencies.[159] As one UN official put it: "I am doubtful whether any metropolitan government would—for the small advantages involved—be prepared to accept the precedent of direct United Nations help."[160] While the principle of international assistance to trust and "non-self-governing territories" was firmly established, observed another, it could hardly escape notice that demands on the UN program of technical assistance would likely be minimal, so that important UN contributions to the development of colonies were unlikely in the near future.¹⁶¹ In other words, while the United Nations helped to frame colonies as dependent upon international assistance for further advancement toward self-government and did much to promote an increasingly expansive vision of development, for the most part, UN representatives themselves would play no important roles in that process.

―

As Evan Luard pointed out in his seminal study of the UN during the age of decolonization, the world organization's significance lay less in its impact on day-to-day rule in the colonies than in its emphasis on political, educational, social, and educational advancement as the purpose of colonial trusteeship.¹⁶² Its significance also lay in fleshing out quite concretely in questionnaires what exactly advancement or development might mean in a broad number of fields. While the Trusteeship Council itself provided a relative "safe space" for colonial powers, the establishment of ostensibly universal goals of colonial rule in combination with novel oversight mechanisms nevertheless created a space for holding colonial powers accountable for their lofty promises and providing a benchmark against which to measure progress.

The Secretariat's efforts to more directly influence policy in trust territories (as well as colonies) ultimately failed, partly due to lack of personal investment on the part of Trusteeship Department officials, but above all in view of "administering powers'" claims to sovereignty and noninterference. As noted above, more insistent pressures on "administering authorities" and colonial powers emerged from several General Assembly committees: notably, the Committee on Information from Non-Self-Governing-Territories, the Fourth Committee, and, after 1960, the Committee of 24.¹⁶³ Yet, as Luard writes, the UN could persuade but not compel, demand but not impose, condemn but not coerce. The power of decision-making ultimately lay with individual UN member states.¹⁶⁴

The former Italian colonies, the subject of the next two chapters, proved an exception to this rule. When the Allies could not agree on these territories' fate, the decision was ultimately passed on to the General Assembly, where government representatives decided to establish both Libya and Somaliland as sovereign states within a fixed time period. They also asked UN personnel to assist in the process. Libya and Somaliland thus became important early testing grounds for more immediate UN trusteeship and the organization's capabilities in literal state-building. It was here that UN officials began to approach state-building as a technical challenge and an operational activity, the domain of bureaucrats and experts, rather than as a unique political or historical process. Otherwise, as subsequent chapters will show more clearly, political independence oftentimes became the de facto starting point rather than the end of UN trusteeship for the purpose of advancement.

# 2

## HOW TO BUILD A STATE?

The UN in Libya

*Are freedom and independence the right only of wealthy people; are they the only people who deserve independence?*

—Mustafa Bey Mizran, head of the National Congress party of Tripolitania, Libya

In 1949, Libya and Somaliland became laboratories for a new method of state creation that one observer referred to as the "deadline method":[1] when the victorious Allies could not agree on the fate of the Italian colonies after World War II, decision-making was left to the General Assembly, which stipulated that both Libya and Somaliland were to become sovereign states within a fixed time limit. While UN member states thus decided the supposed fate of the colonies, the question of how to prepare the territories for independent statehood within the given timeframe was delegated to the "administering authorities," as colonial powers were called in UN parlance. They were assisted in this task by both UN government representatives and Secretariat staff on the ground.

The General Assembly framed state-building in these nations above all as a political project that called for the creation and transformation of key political institutions: a legislative assembly, a constitution, a government.

UN officials in Tripoli and Mogadishu, however, soon called attention to nominally *technical* aspects of statecraft that urgently needed attention and investment so that the incipient sovereign states would survive beyond independence: that is, public administration, finance and economic development, education, and health. Confronted with the problem of crafting a sovereign polity, UN bureaucrats called upon the nascent UN development services. Initially, UN development missions were dispatched to conduct surveys covering broad categories such as economics, health, education, and agriculture with the aim of understanding how these soon-to-be-independent states might endure. Eventually, development assistance came to provide an answer in itself, as UN experts framed the new polities as sovereign states that were dependent on continued international assistance for many years to come.

Because of this dependence on financial and personnel assistance, some observers at the time deemed the new states—the United Libyan Kingdom (1951) and the Somali Republic (1960)—failed at birth, or sovereign in name only. Others viewed their tenuous status after achieving formal sovereignty as a necessary transitory period on the road to postcolonial modernization, which could be overcome with substantial foreign assistance and lead to full independence at a later stage. Still others questioned what independence could even mean in an increasingly interconnected world. What emerged from these discussions was a new understanding of sovereignty and the state in the postwar period, of how it would be financed and staffed.[2]

For the UN officials who were closely involved in the Libyan and Somali transformations on the ground, these "experiments of international decolonization" were a mostly depressing experience: the "administering authorities" and, later, the national governments disregarded democratic procedures; international material support for the new states was lacking; and both countries entered clientelist relationships with wealthy sponsor states. However, other officials who were further removed from these experiences soon began to regard the work of the world organization in Libya and Somaliland—which in turn was influenced by other UN missions at the time—as a model of what it could do for "developing countries" more generally: offer comprehensive developmental surveys, draw up plans for national development, and assist where possible with the administration of governmental affairs.

Though some historians have examined the UN debate leading up to the decision to grant independence to Libya and Somaliland, little attention has been paid to the UN involvement that followed in the transformation of these territories.[3] Most scholars have focused on Anglo-American interests in the run-up to the decision to grant independence and, to a lesser extent, its aftermath.[4] More recently, historians have explored the Somali trusteeship period through the analysis of Italian archival records.[5] To date, no scholarship on either nation seems to have drawn on UN archival materials, though some work references its officially published records.[6] This chapter and the next, by contrast, are based on a review of the archival papers of the UN Secretariat in New York, where the records of the UN missions in Tripoli and Mogadishu are kept.[7]

Analysis of these documents reveals the UN as a mostly supportive actor of the colonial powers' lead in the Libyan and Somali state-building projects. When there were substantial differences of opinion between UN representatives and colonial authorities (for example, with regard to the internationalization of post-independence financial assistance) the colonial powers usually had the last word. For the most part, Britain, France, and Italy found quite reliable, useful allies in the UN staff. The latter were only too willing to approach political issues as technical problems calling for expert investigations rather than political discussions. The UN experience in Libya and Somaliland thus helped to establish an understanding and practice of state-building as more of a technical challenge for international experts than a political problem to be solved by government representatives. UN staff, moreover, lobbied tirelessly for international assistance so that the incipient states could properly function beyond independence, thus helping to legitimize a form of sovereign statehood heavily dependent on foreign assistance in terms of both financial support and personnel.

## DECIDING THE FATE OF THE ITALIAN COLONIES

The 1947 Paris Peace Treaty, which the Allies negotiated with Italy, divested the former Axis power of all her colonies. The major powers disagreed on what to do with Italy's African territories: Libya, Somaliland, and Eritrea.

While the United States, Great Britain, the Soviet Union, and France discussed bringing them under UN trusteeship in some form, they had differing ideas on how they should be administered and whether there should be a time limit to trusteeship. Rather than finding a solution through the recently established United Nations, the four powers first tried to reach an agreement through the extension of the wartime practice of great-power summitry by convening the Council of Foreign Ministers.[8] Proposals there ran the gamut from schemes of collective trusteeship to a three- or four-power division of the territories to a restoration of Italian authority, with or without fixed dates of independence, with each power shifting positions from one meeting to the next. The main question in these discussions was not so much how and to what end the territories would be administered, but rather by whom.[9]

As a "collection of deserts," the Italian overseas empire primarily held strategic importance for the great powers because it lay astride significant sea routes: Libya extended 1,200 miles along the Mediterranean opposite Greece and Italy; Eritrea's 600-mile shore commanded the Red Sea approaches to the Suez Canal; and Italian Somaliland, with a 1,000 mile coastline, faced the Indian Ocean.[10] The Soviet Union was interested in gaining a foothold in the Mediterranean—or at least in neutralizing the British presence in Libya, which already served the UK as a sea, air, and military base. Western powers adamantly opposed a Soviet advance in the region. The French were, moreover, resolutely opposed to the American fixation with timetables, fearing similar demands in their neighboring territories. Both sides had an interest in finding a solution that would reflect favorably upon them in the eyes of the electorate in Italy, where a Communist victory in the national elections seemed possible in 1948.[11]

Unable to reach an agreement, the former Allies decided to dispatch a four-power commission of investigation to visit the former colonies and survey the conditions on the ground.[12] In late 1947, the commission set out on a seven-months' sojourn first to Eritrea, then Italian Somaliland, and finally the three territories that would eventually comprise independent Libya. Although the visit was stage-managed by the occupying colonial powers, the differences among the government representatives, according to one historian, led to a fairly thorough survey and a revealing portrait of nationalist sentiment in North Africa.[13] There were serious clashes between Italian-sponsored and anti-Italian factions in Eritrea and especially in Somalia. After several deaths occurred in Mogadishu upon the arrival of the investigative commission, the British authorities took a series of precautions against similar incidents happening in Libya. The final report of the commission brought the Allies no closer to agreement, except on the points that the inhabitants seemed unprepared for self-government, that the territories were economically poor and not self-supporting, and that a majority of the people did not seem to wish for a return of Italian rule.

In late 1948, when the Council of Ministers failed to reach an agreement regarding the colonies a year after the peace treaty, the issue was brought—by default—before a largely unprepared UN General Assembly.[14] Here, the challenge shifted to finding a solution that would satisfy both a staunchly pro-Italian Latin American voting bloc (which advocated for a restitution of the colonies to its former imperial master) and the anticolonial Arab and Asian states (which vehemently opposed Italian rule), in order to achieve the necessary two-thirds voting majority for a decisive resolution. The Western Allies, meanwhile, had come to an agreement on the disposition of the colonies with the so-called Bevin-Sforza compromise, signed in May 1949. This plan envisioned the carve-up of Libya among the British, the French, and eventually the Italians, plus Italian trusteeship for Somalia and the ceding of most of Eritrea to Ethiopia.[15] Not least because of considerable protests in the territories in question, the plan met with opposition from African and Asian representatives at the UN and was narrowly rejected by the General Assembly.[16] All in all, it took two General Assembly sessions, extended hearings with Italian officials as well as some "colonial subjects," innumerable proposals, and prolonged heated debates, greeted with protests, "disturbances," and repression in the colonies, for the delegates to finally reach a compromise solution in November 1949.[17]

The November 1949 General Assembly resolution on the "Disposal of the former Italian colonies" stipulated that Libya (that is, the territories Tripolitania, Cyrenaica, and Fezzan) was to "be constituted an independent and sovereign State" as soon as possible and no later than 1 January 1952.[18] To aid the people in the formulation of a constitution and the establishment of an independent government, the General Assembly appointed a UN commissioner, choosing the former Dutch journalist turned international civil servant Adrian Pelt, who had been nominated by Secretary-General Trygve Lie.[19] To assist and advise Pelt, the Assembly

FIG. 8 Residents of the Former Italian Colonies Present Their Case at the United Nations in New York

Representatives of the Somali Youth League, Ali Bin-Nour and Abdullah Issa (left), are seen with UN representatives of Eritrea (1949).

Source: UN Photo, UN7779931

called for the constitution of a ten-man Council for Libya in Tripoli, composed of foreign government representatives (from the U.S., the UK, France, Italy, Egypt, and Pakistan) as well as one politician from each of the three Libyan provinces and one representing the country's minorities.[20] Somaliland, by contrast, was to become an official UN trust territory under Italian administration, assisted by a UN Advisory Council in Mogadishu, to be composed of government representatives from Colombia, the Philippines, and Egypt and assisted by UN Secretariat staff on the ground. The territory was to be prepared for independence within ten years. Eritrea, it was later decided, would become an autonomous territory in a federation with Ethiopia.[21]

Ironically, Libya's two-stage advisory system of a UN commissioner *and* a UN Advisory Council (which was first proposed by the Soviet Union) gave more of a role to the world organization in the soon-to-be-independent colony than in the official UN trust territory of Somaliland, which, save for the Secretariat staff supporting the Advisory Council in Mogadishu, had no independent UN representative in residence. It is important to note that both of these UN advisory councils essentially functioned as political bodies composed of government representatives rather than UN bureaucrats or experts. As the following chapters will show, such international "political filters" would play less of a role in subsequent UN experiments in decolonization and statebuilding, which were increasingly approached as technical challenges for international experts rather than political problems.

## LIBYA: FROM COLONY TO INDEPENDENT STATE

The vast bulk of Libya's 1,750,000 square kilometers lies within the Sahara on the shore of the Mediterranean. In 1950, it was bordered by Egypt to the east (then a British protectorate), the colonial federations of French Equatorial Africa and French West Africa to the south, as well as well as Algeria, which the French considered an integral part of their country, and the southern tip of Tunisia, a French protectorate, to the west. Cut off from one another through desert, the three territories that comprise Libya today—Tripolitania in the northwest, Cyrenaica in the east, and Fezzan in the southwest—developed by and large separately, despite the common spread of Islam and Arabic in the region during the Middle Ages. Home to many different, mostly Muslim ethnicities, in the early 1950s, the three territories were home to a very unevenly distributed population of a little over one million. Tripolitania counted about 750,000 inhabitants, Cyrenaica about 300,000 and Fezzan about 50,000. An early UN report estimated that the Muslim population—broadly divided into Berbers and Arabs—comprised about 1,050,000 people, while there were about 47,000 Italian settlers left in Tripolitania (Cyrenaica's having been evacuated in 1942).[22] Most inhabitants lived in the coastal regions of Tripolitania and Cyrenaica. Agriculture and animal husbandry provided the main source of livelihood, though poor soil, desert winds, limited access to water, and occasional locusts, according to UN reports, made for a rather hostile natural environment.[23]

After an attack on Ottoman rule in the region in 1911, Italy established her first colonial presence in the three territories. Tripolitania, Cyrenaica, and Fezzan were conjoined as Italian Libya in 1934, following prolonged, brutal fighting interspersed with periods of relative peace.[24] Resistance to Italian rule encouraged some pan-Libyan cooperation and nationalism in Cyrenaica and Tripolitania.[25] Fascist Italy placed heavy emphasis on settler colonization and agricultural development, accompanied by investments in utilities and public works. By 1940, 225,000 hectares of Libyan land were being cultivated by some 110,000 Italian settlers. The territory possessed a basic modern infrastructure, including a coastal highway that connected Tunisia with Egypt, which necessitated continuous, considerable expenditures from Rome. Libyans, however, had been systematically excluded from Italian investments in the territory—or worse, displaced and prevented from farming productively. Beyond the agricultural sector, local handicrafts faced unequal competition from Italian imports, which often survived only through state subsidies. Under Italian rule, Libyans were largely barred from political organization, administrative positions, and educational facilities. In the coastal cities of Tripolitania and Cyrenaica, many were forced to become low-wage menial laborers.[26]

World War II and the slow expulsion of German and Italian troops from North Africa by Allied forces caused large-scale destruction in Libya: damaged or destroyed infrastructure, abandoned farms, and the extensive spread of land mines.[27] At the same time, the Axis powers' retreat fostered hope for autonomy among Libyans, who attempted to wring concessions from the Allies in return for supporting their war effort.[28] In 1943, the British established separate military governments in Cyrenaica and Tripolitania. In the latter territory, the U.S. also established an Air Force base that would become one of the largest American military facilities abroad. The Free French, the government in exile led by Charles de Gaulle, established a military administration in Fezzan. In contrast to the period under Italian rule, Libyan political activities flourished under the Allied military administrations. While the great powers could not agree how to dispose of the former Italian colonies, opinions with regard to Libya's political future increasingly consolidated within the three territories. Many Tripolitanians demanded a unified, independent Libya. Cyrenaicans insisted on the future rule of the Sanusi Order, which had long dominated the territory's political life, over either a unified Libya or an autonomous province. In Fezzan, almost half the population expressed its support for continued French rule.[29]

Though decision-making was ultimately delegated to the General Assembly in 1948, as mentioned above, the Western Allies sought to get ahead of the matter through the Bevin-Sforza plan, announced in May 1949. With regard to Libya, the plan, named after the British and Italian foreign ministers, proposed ten-year trusteeships for France in Fezzan, Great Britain in Cyrenaica, and Italy in Tripolitania. When the announcement was greeted with violent demonstrations in the two latter territories, supported by vocal Arab and Soviet protests at the UN, the plan was narrowly defeated in the General Assembly. The Western Allies then decided that an independent, though disjointed Libya might also accommodate their interests well—perhaps even more so than an official UN trusteeship could.[30] Accordingly, Britain, again in an effort to obviate UN decision-making, unilaterally decided to grant self-government to Cyrenaica even before the General Assembly reached an official agreement with regard to the territories. France followed this lead in February 1950 and set up a transitional government in Fezzan.[31]

By that time, the UN delegates in New York had finally reached an official decision: the November 1949 General Assembly resolution 289 stipulated that Tripolitania, Cyrenaica, and Fezzan were to become a unified, independent state in no less than two years: that is, by January 1952. Until then, the British in Tripolitania and Cyrenaica and the French in Fezzan were to act as UN "administering authorities." Adrian Pelt would be dispatched to assist the people of Libya in the formulation of an independent government, advised by the ten-man Council for Libya. UN delegates had acknowledged both in the General Assembly discussions as well as in the final resolution that economic and social problems might play a role in state formation. They placed explicit primary emphasis, however, on the political act of forming a government and drafting a constitution.[32]

Apart from overviews of Libyan history, there is little historical scholarship that deals with the formative transition period that followed the General Assembly decision and none, it seems, that takes UN archival sources into account.[33] With support from the Carnegie Endowment for International Peace, Pelt himself wrote a 1,000-page account of his experience as commissioner, which was originally published in 1970.[34] Wm. Roger Louis examined the Libyan state creation from a British perspective, suggesting that independent Libya was not so much a triumph of the much-invoked principle of self-determination as essentially a British creation that depended on U.S. support and UN collaboration.[35] Though the UN records indeed reveal a close, supportive relationship between the commissioner and the British authorities, they also testify to a number of disagreements, most importantly, on the issue of Libya's post-independence monetary organization and financial aid to the country. The records also reveal a growing tension between the commissioner and the UN Council for Libya, where the representatives of Egypt, Pakistan, and Tripolitania pushed for a much more confrontational UN approach toward the "administering powers." Pelt rejected the Council's directives, and the commissioner himself was sidelined by the British and French when it came to matters of importance to their administrations. The UN involvement in Libya nevertheless helped Secretariat officials rethink the practice of state-building as going beyond the drafting of a constitution and forming a government. It also prompted them to rethink how a newly sovereign polity in the postwar world might operate.

## SETTING UP THE UN PRESENCE IN TRIPOLI

According to Pelt, UN Secretary-General Trygve Lie had suggested his name for nomination as UN commissioner in Libya because of his expansive "experience of international life."[36] Pelt began his career as a journalist and joined the League of Nations Secretariat's Information Section in 1920. As a League staff member, he served on several international missions, visiting British India, the Dutch East Indies, Manchuria, and Austria. During the war, he led the Netherlands government in exile's information service in London and represented the country at the UN founding conference in San Francisco in 1945. He joined the UN Secretariat a year later as head of the Department of Conference and General Services, where he was in charge of the transfer of relevant League of Nations files to the UN. After his return from Libya, Pelt served as director of the European Office of the United Nations in Geneva from 1952 to 1957.

Pelt himself had serious misgivings about his own suitability for the assignment in Tripoli (a recurring motif among UN officials sent abroad): his knowledge of Libya's history and geography was superficial, he possessed no constitutional expertise, was not familiar with Arabic or "the Islamic world," and had not, until his appointment, even paid close attention to the question of the former Italian colonies.[37] Despite feeling ill-prepared for his assignment, Pelt was adept at assembling a fairly large team of Secretariat employees to support his work in Tripoli.[38] He thought that his mission could only work effectively if it enjoyed the trust of the UN member governments invested in Libyan affairs, that is, those represented on the Council for Libya. The best way to secure this trust, Pelt thought, was by appointing some of their own or other "sympathetic" nationals to his staff. Pelt thus set out to appoint an Englishmen, a Frenchman, "an Arab" (apparently regardless of nationality), and a U.S. citizen to mediate between London and Paris, a Latin American to placate the Italians, and someone "of Mediterranean origin" in the hopes of appeasing the Jewish, Greek, and Maltese minorities in Libya. Citing Eric Drummond's report on the lessons learned from the experience of the League of Nations, Pelt suggested that the ideal civil servants were neither men without a country nor extreme nationalists, but those who felt their country's interest was best served by international cooperation.[39]

Aside from paying attention to national representation, Pelt, by his own account, also favored an inclusive working environment with frequent staff meetings, few secrets, and a free exchange of opinions.[40] Thomas Power, a U.S. historian-turned-diplomat dispatched from the permanent American mission to the UN in New York, became Pelt's second-in-command as principal secretary of the UN mission in Tripoli.[41] In addition to a deputy principal secretary, four political officers, and administrative and clerical staff (secretaries, interpreters, guards), Pelt also insisted on the immediate appointment of an expert on Sharia and constitutional law, a post filled by an Egyptian, Omar Loufti, "a mild-mannered lawyer with a penchant for quoting political philosophy" who would later represent his country at the UN in New York.[42] The subsequent dispatch of social and economic experts, Pelt thought, would have to await an appraisal of needs on the spot.[43]

Before setting out on an initial two-part reconnaissance mission in January 1950, Pelt consulted with the governments that would be represented on the Council for Libya and solicited proposals from them for the appointment of Libyan Council members. At that point, it was unclear where, how often, and in what format the Council would meet (that is, open or closed to the public). From January 19 to February 7, and again from March 17 to March 28, Pelt traveled widely throughout Libya. By his own account, he and some his staff consulted several hundred individuals: political and religious leaders, representatives of minority groups, and private individuals. Pelt's trips were as much about soliciting Libyan views on the country's future as they were introducing the General Assembly resolution to the Libyan public and explain the functions of the UN commissioner and the Council. (No adequate Arab translation was available in Libya.) Above all, he sought to address two major misunderstandings: to explain that the UN would not *govern* Libya and that the commissioner and the Council would not *impose* a constitution on the country, but merely act in an advisory capacity. In private, though, Pelt admitted his intention to steer something of "a middle course between imposing solutions and giving advice," in order to educate Libyans to formulate their own plans.[44]

After his initial sojourn in the territory, Pelt appointed the Libyan representatives to the Council for Libya in consultation with the British and French administrations. In Fezzan, representative Hajj Ahmed al-Senussi Sofu was chosen based on a large-scale consultation of public opinion. The French reluctantly approved, after initially insisting that no Fezzanese was qualified to serve on the Council. In Cyrenaica, the leader of the Sanusi Order, Sayyid Idris, presented Pelt with a list of eight candidates, from which Pelt chose Ali Assad al-Jerbi, the minister of public works and communications in the Cyrenaican government. Choosing a representative for Tripolitania proved more difficult. Ultimately, Pelt settled on Mustafa Bey Mizran of the National Congress Party. Although Mizran was accused of being a British stooge—and his appointment was indeed supported by the British administration in the territory—Pelt notes that he turned out to be anything but a mouthpiece, but rather a critical voice challenging the colonial administrations.

According to Pelt, it was hardest to settle on a representative for the minorities in Libya. The General Assembly had not spelled out which groups would be recognized as minorities, but the Latin American governments, which had insisted on the addition of a minority representative in the first place, had had Italian interests in mind. Ultimately, Pelt was able to convince the Jewish, Greek, and Maltese minorities in the territory to accept the Italian representative Giacomo Marchino. The Berber people, though too a minority living along the Tunisian frontier, were apparently not consulted.⁴⁵

Ultimately, the governments represented on the Council agreed for the UN advisory body to convene in Tripoli. The British and the French had initially opposed this, fearing that critics on the Council might instigate "local agitation." In his book, Pelt noted that he had been "of two minds" about the matter: on the one hand, he saw an advantage in having the Council meet in Tripoli, which would allow him easy access to its representatives and not require costly travel arrangement for the Libyan members. On the other, the commissioner feared having to share his scarce staff resources with the Council if it were to operate in Libya. To appease British and French concerns, Council members later decided—despite

FIG. 9   UN Commissioner Adrian Pelt Leaves for Libya

Adrian Pelt (center) with Thomas Power (right), principal secretary to the UN Libya mission, and David Vaughan (left) of the UN Department of Conference and General Services (1950).

Source: UN Photo, UN7710630

Egyptian, Pakistani, and Tripolitanian opposition—to hold their bimonthly meetings in Tripoli in private, so as not to "stir up public opinion."[46]

Pelt and the UN mission were off to a somewhat rocky start with the "administering powers." Before he started his assignment in Tripoli, an unnamed "high UK official" in New York had ominously warned Pelt's wife over dinner that her husband would likely "break his neck" during the upcoming Libyan mission. Moreover, on instructions from London, the British chief administrator in Tripoli canceled a welcoming reception for Pelt at the very last minute to put the UN representative in his place. This left the commissioner, though greeted at the airport by other foreign officials as well as Libyan political and religious leaders, quite literally out in the cold. Sitting and chatting that same evening beside a blazing fire at the British residency, however, the incident was soon cleared up. According to Pelt, British civilian and military personnel blamed the UN for making their lives and work in Libya more difficult, and for ultimately depriving them of their jobs. They also accused the UN staff and their somewhat higher salaries for causing rent hikes in crowded Tripoli. Despite these initial resentments and continuing differences of opinion, by his own account, Pelt quickly established an "exceedingly pleasant and cordial" rapport with the British and French authorities.[47]

As will be further discussed below, Pelt's relationship with the Council, by contrast, very soon deteriorated: Pelt blamed the Pakistani-Egyptian desire to control both him and the colonial powers for the tensions that developed. The commissioner insisted on his independence vis-à-vis the Council and pointed out that the "administering powers" only had to answer to the General Assembly; both the Council and his own position, he emphasized, were merely of an *advisory* nature.[48]

## FORMING A GOVERNMENT

Pelt's most immediate task in order to fulfill the General Assembly resolution was the creation of an all-Libyan governmental organ, which could then decide the form of the future state, draft a constitution, and form a government. The UN commissioner was greatly concerned about the separatist tendencies supported by the colonial powers' policies of granting autonomy, if not outright independence, to the provinces under their control.[49] In order to best protect British military interests in Cyrenaica and allow the Americans in Tripolitania and the French in Fezzan to follow suit, London wished to establish independent Libya as a loose federation. A federal arrangement also seemed like good compromise to many Libyan political groups, who insisted on regional autonomies.[50] As mentioned above, both the British and the French administrations initially sought to create a series of *faits accomplis* by quickly granting far-reaching autonomy to the provinces they administered. Ultimately, however, Pelt convinced the British and the French to slow down the process of federalization, in exchange for his promise to assist with the negotiation of long-term agreements regarding military-base rights in independent Libya.[51]

The General Assembly resolution had called for the establishment of a *unified* independent state, an all-Libyan constitution and government. To achieve this goal, Pelt submitted a plan to the Council for Libya in May 1950, based on his prior consultations with foreign officials and Libyans: elected bodies in the three territories would dispatch delegates to form a preparatory committee, which would then decide a procedure for electing a National Assembly and draft a constitution. Months-long discussions followed, which concluded with an agreement to form a preparatory committee, but with *appointed* rather than *elected* members, which, in turn, would *appoint* a National Assembly (with equal rather than proportional territorial representation).[52] Libyan representatives of the three provinces further agreed to the creation of a loosely federated state, to be headed by the Cyrenaican Sanusi leader Idris.[53] The flip side of the loose federation arrangement was a heavily bloated government bureaucracy: in addition to two capitals, Tripoli and Benghazi, newly independent Libya would have one federal as well as three provincial administrations with government payrolls eventually amounting to 12 percent of the total GNP.[54]

When it came to the appointment of the representatives to the National Assembly in October 1950, Tripolitanian nationalists felt sidelined in the process. With Egyptian, Pakistani, and Arab League support, they called for widespread protests of the procedure as undemocratic.[55] Demonstrators took to the streets in Tripoli and Pelt received thousands of petitions. Arab delegates attacked the arrangement at the General Assembly, and Cairo launched a sustained press campaign.[56] The protests continued well into 1951, to the extent that a scheduled visit by Trygve Lie to Tripoli in March was canceled out of security concerns.[57] At the same time, the British authorities in Tripolitania ordered a crackdown on the opposition, as a result of which approximately 850 people were exiled, put under house arrest, or imprisoned.[58]

## TECHNICAL STATE-BUILDING

Though Pelt was unhappy with the undemocratic process of forming a government and deciding the future shape of the state, he was even more concerned about the lacking administrative and economic basis for Libya's impending sovereignty.[59] "My main preoccupations are not of a purely political nature," he wrote to Lie in August 1950.[60] The commissioner drew a distinction between political and constitutional independence on the one hand and administrative and economic independence on the other. It was one thing, he argued, to draw up a constitution and organize a provisional government as requested by the General Assembly, messy as the process could be. But the question of the basis on which the future Libyan state would operate, he suggested, had been given little thought—both in terms of personnel and finances.[61] For two years, Pelt would lobby for international attention to this issue. He initiated UN developmental surveys to find out on what basis the future Libyan state could function and ultimately presented international assistance itself as a temporary solution to that problem.

The UN commissioner pushed for attention to nominally technical matters from early in his tenure. When the Council for Libya first met in April, Pelt asked for advice regarding the scope of his work: should he limit it to consulting on the formation of the political institutions that the General Assembly resolution had called for, or should he also pay attention to the establishment of administrative services of the future Libyan state and its economic and social development? Pelt later noted that he received all the support from the Council that he could have hoped for, although members were "also sensitive to the possibility that he might tackle economic and social questions without adequately consulting [the Council]."[62] When the matter was discussed at the General Assembly in the summer and fall of 1950, Pelt's broader understanding of his mandate was again generally confirmed, though a variety of fears and suspicions came to the fore. The Pakistani and Egyptian delegates, for example, favored avoiding any reference to public administration, fearing that the colonial powers would manipulate any UN efforts in that regard to perpetuate their power. To Pelt's great satisfaction, their objections were ultimately overruled: the final General Assembly resolution recognized the need for continued technical assistance to Libya "even after the attainment of its independence, for the development of its economy, for its social progress and for the improvement of its public administration."[63]

But even before receiving this intergovernmental endorsement, the UN commissioner reached out to the UN headquarters and specialized agencies to seek support for his mission in the form of technical assistance. Pelt asked for an immediate expansion of his staff, to include expert advisors on such issues as agriculture, currency, banking, administrative and budgetary organization, and problems of land tenure.[64] He also requested expert missions to draw up preliminary surveys of the country's needs: a general one concerned with economic development from the UN headquarters and two more in the fields of education and health from UNESCO and the WHO respectively.[65] Significantly, the first UN reconnaissance or preparatory mission to plan more comprehensive technical assistance for the country-in-the-making was initiated by the commissioner himself and sponsored from the regular UN budget, as opposed to being requested and funded in part by member states (in the case of Libya, the "administering powers"), as was customary for UN assistance.

The UN commissioner had earlier advised the British and the French to request a technical assistance expert who could make an initial survey of the country's needs and coordinate technical assistance matters later on. Initially, Pelt encountered "hesitancy bordering on unwillingness to cooperate" on the part of both powers. It was only in June, when Secretary-General Lie had already agreed to green-light a first technical assistance reconnaissance mission to Libya *without* an official request from the British or French, that both powers agreed to request a comprehensive UN survey mission. As late as August 1950, however, Pelt complained about increasing difficulties with the "administering powers" with regard to technical assistance. Both France and the UK were reluctant to efficiently cooperate and were "almost obstructing" the UN technical assistance effort, Pelt reported, without going into further details. He warned that if the situation did not improve, it would be necessary to bring it to the attention of the General Assembly.[66]

## THE GOODRICH RECONNAISSANCE MISSION

Representatives at the UN headquarters agreed with Pelt that the world organization had a major stake in the success of the Libyan transformation. Andrew Cordier, the American executive assistant to the secretary-general in New York, warned that a failure would be serious for the UN, which had a direct responsibility for the nascent country. While he deemed Libya's constitutional development "satisfactory," Cordier, much like Pelt, insisted on the urgent need for "training in administration and self-government" and making the Libyan economy "viable." To UN personnel, these issues were closely connected. "The problem of economic viability and financial solvency is grave," an early UN memo noted. "Could Libyan resources go further if properly managed and honestly administered?"[67]

To find an answer to this question, David Owen of the Secretariat's Department of Economic Affairs suggested the dispatch of a UN technical assistance reconnaissance mission to help Pelt and the government(s) concerned think through their needs and prepare the ground for a more comprehensive developmental survey, which could then form the basis for a UN development "action plan."[68] He suggested Carter Goodrich, who half a year earlier had led a very similar mission to Bolivia (discussed in chapter 4). Goodrich, a professor of economic history at Columbia University and former U.S. representative to the International Labor Organization (ILO), readily accepted the task and embarked on a three-week reconnaissance mission in July of 1950. Goodrich described himself as part of the New Deal generation and dedicated much of his academic career to studying government involvement in economic development. Through the ILO, he had lobbied for the extension of a New Deal to "dependent territories" and the internationalization of colonialism, with a view to awarding them full independence as soon as possible.[69] Goodrich was accompanied on his mission by African-American UN economist William Dean, who subsequently led a very similar reconnaissance mission to Somaliland (see chapter 3), and Belgian civil servant W. A. Kooy of the Social Activities Division of the UN Secretariat in Geneva.

Before setting out for Libya, Goodrich had been advised by the UN headquarters to consult with as many government representatives and officials of UN specialized agencies as possible.[70] After consultations in Washington, Paris, London, Geneva, and Rome with government representatives and FAO, UNESCO, WHO, IBRD, and IMF officials, the UN reconnaissance mission arrived in Tripoli on 9 July 1950. Goodrich and colleagues then traveled widely by UN aircraft. Commissioner Pelt was convinced that the success of technical assistance depended in large part "on the enthusiastic collaboration of those who were to profit by it," and thus arranged for the UN mission to meet numerous "leading Libyans," including the representatives on the Council for Libya.[71]

Unfortunately, there is scarcely any testimony in the reviewed archival papers as to what Libyans thought of the UN effort or how their input shaped how UN representatives perceived the country's needs.[72] Pelt later wrote about a broad skepticism among many Libyans with regard to technical assistance: they had seen Italian experts come and go in large numbers, followed by British and French experts, without deriving much practical benefit from these visits. Pelt thought that this attitude was not altogether fair, though understandable enough in a people who had long been exploited, only to come later into a "caretaker regime" under UN supervision.[73] Many Libyans argued that it was preferable to receive *financial* rather than *technical* assistance, but UN experts insisted that an economic appraisal had to precede any requests for financial aid.[74] Beyond this, Pelt suggested, the meetings with Goodrich and his team had the important effect of making Libyans "accept the fact that their country was really in the red," which many had previously assumed to be a pretext used by the colonial powers to delay independence. Presumably, the meetings thus allowed UN representatives to drive home their point about an overwhelming need for outside assistance to support the Libyan state-building project.[75]

To better assist Libyans in this project, the Goodrich mission recommended immediately expanding the permanent UN presence in the country. Twenty or more specialists in the fields of public finance, agriculture, social welfare, and statistics, they said, should assist the commissioner to advise the Libyan government on these matters. A deputy principal secretary should coordinate all technical assistance efforts in the territory and, when possible, initiate an expansion of assistance. Goodrich noted that UN staff extensions in the fields of currency, banking and exchange, public administration, and land tenure had already been authorized and deferred recommendations in the fields of education and health to UNESCO and the WHO, which had already sent their own technical assistance missions to Libya.[76]

One of the most important aims of any assistance effort, Goodrich thought, was to help the new government build up the state's administrative, social, and economic services. Pelt later noted Libyan suspicions with regard to existing public administration training schemes: was the training of young Libyans not merely a pretext to keep British and French administrators in power? "Would they not take advantage of the selection of trainees to push their friends and protégées and thus avoid accepting Libyans from critically minded nationalist parties?"[77] Without explicitly addressing such fears, Goodrich pointed to the difficulty, if not impossibility, of embarking upon administrative assistance while the future Libyan state and government were only beginning to take shape. Once a provisional government was formed, Goodrich envisioned bringing in a team of UN experts covering the various branches of public administration to help set up a government bureaucracy.[78]

Goodrich's emphasis on investing in bureaucracy reflected a growing consensus among UN officials that an effective public administration was a sine qua non for true sovereignty, or at least for successful national development. In a September 1950 letter to Pelt, FAO Director-General Herbert Broadly wrote that he agreed wholeheartedly with the UN commissioner's assessment that the most difficult challenge in Libya was the creation of a functioning state bureaucracy. This was indeed the problem faced by many "underdeveloped" countries, Broadly thought. "It is very well for us to send technicians to offer advice, but unless some machinery is created for translating advice into actions," he warned, "all our efforts will be futile." He believed that all experiments in the field of international organization had thus far suffered from a lack of authority. In the script for a radio broadcast that he shared with Pelt, Broadley laid out his technocratic dream of a new "age of *functionaires*"—an international brotherhood of scientists, technicians, engineers, and educators—working side by side in the administration of sovereign states to develop the world's resources and thus bring about global prosperity and security. What the UN was currently recommending for Bolivia—the injection of international administrators into the state's bureaucracy—Broadly thought might pave the way to this dream of a "New Rome."[79]

The introduction of UN personnel into sovereign state bureaucracies was still wishful thinking on the part of international officials when Goodrich—or rather his deputy, Dean—was finishing the UN reconnaissance mission's report on Libya. While the United Kingdom was invited to comment on early drafts (and asked, for example, that the proposed survey consider the territories as *separate* but *related* entities), Swedish sociologist Alva Myrdal, who would later win the Nobel Peace Price and was then working in the Secretariat's Social Affairs Department, also shared her views on the matter. Myrdal warned that social problems should not be lost sight of, in Libya in particular but also in UN development efforts more generally. While Dean thought that Myrdal was combating a straw man, Goodrich insisted that, given the "primitive" state of the Libyan economy, any social program in the country necessarily needed to be modest.[80]

The final report called for immediate practical assistance in various fields, but also insisted on the need for a general economic appraisal. Goodrich hoped that an economist "of recognized distinction, who has an understanding of the problems of an under-developed and agricultural economy" would be found for the job.[81] Libya's per capita income was so low, the report noted, that although government services were minimal (especially in the social and educational fields), they had depended on substantial "metropolitan" subsidies for a number of decades. An appraisal was necessary to determine which government services would even be sustainable in independent Libya; as a basis to ask for loans or other types of financial assistance; and to indicate how to increase the productivity of the Libyan economy and thus serve as a guide to the new government. Goodrich's report emphasized that such a study would not have to start "de novo," but could build on and extend existing knowledge of the country produced by the previous and current "administrations"—if they were willing to share it.[82]

## THE LINDBERG APPRAISAL AND THE DISPUTE OVER LIBYA'S MONETARY ARRANGEMENTS

As mentioned above, British and French authorities in Libya were initially reluctant to accept or even request a UN developmental survey.[83] They thought that their own staff could do a much better job more cheaply, but they also resented the UN emphasis on approaching Libya as a whole, rather than as three separate territories.[84] Yet when the Council for Libya (the UN advisory body in Tripoli composed of both foreign government representatives and Libyans) ventured to get involved in the matter and sought to establish priorities of assistance based on public inquiries, the colonial powers shifted position and insisted on leaving the matter to international experts instead. According to Pelt, British and French officials "smelled a rat" in the Council's proposal to invite Libyans to express their opinions on technical assistance matters, fearing that public discussion might result in criticism of their rule.[85] Because the UN moreover agreed to waive most of the local costs of the projected UN survey mission, both colonial powers—first the British, then the French, too—eventually signed the formal request for a comprehensive UN developmental appraisal.[86]

Other government representatives in Libya had mixed feelings about UN technical assistance—though for entirely different reasons. Selim Bey, the Egyptian delegate to the Council for Libya, for example, noted that he generally supported international assistance, since many social and economic issues in Libya required urgent expert attention. However, he disapproved that such assistance would be based on the recommendations of UN staff and, ultimately, on Pelt's personal directives and desires. The survey envisioned by Goodrich, he argued, was ultimately far too elaborate and must have been "drawn up mainly for propaganda purposes... to create the impression abroad that something useful was being done in Libya."[87] What the country needed, Bey argued, was not "flying visits by experts, who merely produced reports," but a few specialists, preferably from the Middle East, who would stay in the country and work with the current "administering powers" and eventually the government of the new state. Bey thus presented a vision of hands-on international assistance quite similar to the one featured in many UN proposals at the time, with the important difference of stressing anticolonial or regional solidarity.

Above all, however, the Egyptian delegate insisted that *financial* rather than *technical* assistance was essential to help "penniless" Libya at this point.[88]

According to Pelt, most members of the Council commended the Egyptian remarks and it set up two subcommittees in the hope of exercising control over or at least supervising the UN technical assistance effort. Pelt suggested that neither subcommittee ultimately "did much harm nor much good": the Council members lacked the necessary knowledge of and experience in economic affairs to effectively question or supervise foreign technical experts.[89] He concluded that what really motivated the critiques on the Council was fear, borne out by events, that the Council representatives would lose their influence on Libya's development. They were afraid that the UN's and the "administering powers'" push to view the country's problems as technical rather than political would relegate them to the remit of international experts rather than politicians.[90] As mentioned above, Pelt rejected the idea that he functioned as an executive agent of the Council and insisted that the advice his office provided to the Libyan people was impartial.[91] The developmental survey mission as envisioned by Goodrich, endorsed by Pelt, and eventually approved by the French and the British went forward despite the Council's misgivings.[92]

From January to June 1951, Swedish economist John Lindberg set out to draw up a "balance sheet" or "inventory" of the Libyan economy with the help of the UN technical assistance team in Tripoli. Lindberg, who was born in 1901, had studied economics at the University of Stockholm and worked for the Swedish Royal Commission for Unemployment before joining the ILO's statistical office in 1930. In 1936, he switched to the League of Nations' economics section, where he was in charge of studies on world production. Along with other League staff, during World War II, Lindberg transferred to Princeton's Institute for Advanced Studies. He then took up the position of visiting professor at Swarthmore College in 1948/1949.[93] Before heading the UN technical assistance mission to Libya, Lindberg was part of the technical assistance mission to Bolivia. There, the American ambassador had accused Lindberg of being "an eminent exponent of Swedish socialism" and of wreaking havoc in the country by recommending questionable policies. Accordingly, Goodrich expressed reservations about Lindberg's appointment as chief UN economist in Libya, but Lindberg was dispatched to Libya nevertheless.[94]

According to Pelt, Lindberg's mission report on Libya in September 1951 constituted the first all-encompassing study of the territory.[95] More importantly, perhaps, it was the first comprehensive survey to be published in Arabic and the first tangible result of the UN technical assistance effort in the country that was shared with what UN officials perceived as an increasingly impatient public.[96] Lindberg encountered considerable trouble in drafting his report.[97] This was due in part to delays on the part of the individual experts working for him and in part to disagreements with the deputy principal secretary of the UN mission in Tripoli about who was in charge of the survey. The main issue, however, was Lindberg's caution with regard to the monetary system that the British envisioned for Libya.[98] From the very beginning of his assignment, the Swedish economist advised against committing the future sovereign state prematurely to joining the Sterling area (nations whose currencies' values were tied to that of the British pound sterling) as London wished, in order to bolster the postwar British economic recovery. Lindberg feared that such a move might hamper Libya's independence and economic development.[99] This position—though shared by Pelt—ultimately not only put Lindberg at odds with the International Monetary Fund advisors to the UN mission in Tripoli, but also cost him his job.[100]

To the dismay of the British, who would have preferred to leave the settlement of Libya's future monetary arrangements to the British Treasury and the Bank of England, Pelt had asked for IMF expert support to advise him on the issue in early 1950.[101] In September of that year, after Pelt pressed Secretary-General Lie for months to reach an arrangement with the IMF, two staff members were finally seconded to Tripoli: G. A. Blowers, an American who had previously worked on currency matters in Liberia and Ethiopia, and A. N. McLeod, a Canadian who had participated in a technical assistance mission to Haiti.[102] Alongside Tom Power, the principal secretary of the UN mission in Tripoli, both IMF experts consulted British officials and reached out to Paris, Rome, and Cairo to collect data and exchange views on Libya's monetary future before their arrival in Tripoli. They then toured the country-in-the-making and spoke with Libyan political and business leaders.[103] By the end of October 1950, Blowers and McLeod had submitted their preliminary recommendations to Pelt and the secretary-general.

The two IMF experts recommended that the future Libyan currency unit be equal in value to four shillings sterling. The "administration" of the monetary system, they wrote, should rest with a Currency Board domiciled in Libya and composed of both Libyan nationals and foreign experts. The currency should be tied to an exchange standard, they advised, but the eligibility of foreign currencies for reserve purposes and the currency of redemption should be at the full discretion of the Board. A 100 percent reserve in foreign exchanges was to be maintained at all times. A Stabilization and Development Bank should be established and furnished with capital by "all nations with an interest in the Libyan economy."[104] At the insistence of the British and French authorities, Pelt bypassed the Council for Libya and instead invited the UK, France, the U.S., Italy, and Egypt to dispatch representatives to a "Meeting of Experts on Libyan Financial, Monetary and Development Problems," held in London in March 1951, to discuss the IMF experts' proposal. Pelt later wrote that London and Paris insisted on such removed discussions "at the technical level" to avoid presenting the Egyptian, Pakistani, and Tripolitanian members of the Council with an opportunity for "political polemics."[105]

According to Pelt, UN staff kept the Council informed of the progress of the technical assistance programs and the discussions on currency, foreign aid possibilities, and related matters. But when their reports were shared with the Council in the summer and fall of 1951, Pelt found that the critics of technical assistance "appeared to be totally uninterested" in the findings and recommendations and seemingly failed to report to their governments on the matter. He also admitted, however, that he had neglected to seek the Council's formal advice on important issues or did so only pro forma. What was more, he opined, "those prone to criticize might well have thought twice before exposing themselves to the embarrassment of a devastating barrage from the Commissioner's side, which not only could turn the documentation to the best advantage, but also draw on the professional knowledge of a highly expert team." In other words, while Pelt showed understanding toward the disadvantages delegates from poorer countries faced in terms of technical preparation and staff, he was generally happy to leverage UN expertise to sideline the Council's critics from having a say in Libya's future development.[106]

Pelt himself asked Lindberg for his opinion on the recommendations of the IMF experts. The UN chief economist subjected the proposal to "grave criticism," mainly because it did not explicitly discuss alternatives to Libya's joining the Sterling bloc, but also because he thought that its policy statements about fiscal belt-tightening were contrary to prevailing economic thinking at the time. Lindberg advised "utmost caution" to avoid any premature commitments by Libyan politicians in the direction of the Sterling area.[107] Pelt subsequently asked Lindberg to pay special attention to monetary problems in his own survey report, despite the IMF experts' work on the issue on behalf of the UN.[108]

On the eve of the intergovernmental Meeting of Experts in London in late February 1951, British authorities shared their own proposal for Libya's monetary future with the UN commissioner and his staff.[109] In a nutshell, the British proposal promised that London would support the Libyan budget and take care of the country's balance of payments deficits if a "sound currency" backed by a 100 percent sterling reserve would be established and adequate budget controls guaranteed through the installation of a senior British financial comptroller. Note issues would be made by a currency authority, which would operate "simply and virtually automatically."[110] States other than the United Kingdom could invest in the country by contributing to a development and stabilization fund (rather than the IMF's suggested central bank). Only the UK, however, would directly support the Libyan budget.[111]

Pelt was unhappy with the proposal. For his opening remarks at the meeting he summarized the arguments against joining the Sterling bloc as follows:

> 1. Decisions on Libyan foreign trade and other financial matters might be taken on the basis of their effect on the Sterling area as a whole, rather than on what was in the best interest of Libya itself. 2. Membership in the Sterling area hampers a country, which wishes to develop its own economic resources. 3. Membership in the Sterling area discriminates against trade with other (non-Sterling) countries, and also against financial transactions with them.[112]

Pelt argued for *international* support of the Libyan budget or at least international rather than British budget control. (Libyan budget control, it appears, was not even up for debate.) He also urged that the country be allowed to retain some dollar earnings, which it would likely incur from the American military presence in Tripolitania. Earlier, Pelt had advocated tying foreign financial subsidies to Libya explicitly to the grant of a military-base right, but both the UK and the U.S. were adamant about not setting an expensive precedent for analogous arrangements elsewhere.[113] All in all, Pelt thought that the monetary arrangement proposed by Britain would establish London's de facto dominance over Libya's economy and likely prove unacceptable to the General Assembly. British officials reportedly responded to this concern with an unimpressed "so what?"[114]

By the time of the third "Meeting of Experts," which took place in Geneva in late May and early June of 1951, the other governments consulted had come around to supporting the British position.[115] More importantly, the finance minister of the provisional Libyan government, Mansur Bey Qadara, announced that Libya would join the Sterling area and that his government had agreed to a 100 percent sterling reserve. Pelt later wrote that their failure to discuss the decision with him beforehand "was so unexpected a breach of confidence that normally prevailed between [us] that the event took on a quite exceptional character."[116] Pelt criticized the Libyan decision as premature, leaving no time to devise alternatives. More importantly, he thought the arrangement ran counter to the General Assembly's decision to establish a truly independent state. Feeling *"plus royaliste que le Roi,"* the UN commissioner ultimately gave in.[117] It appears that Pelt did not have much of a choice, given that British authorities were prepared to "run him down" had he not played along.[118]

Shortly after the Meeting of Experts concluded to British satisfaction, in July 1951, an early draft of Lindberg's report was circulated among members of the Council for Libya and submitted for comments to British, French, and American officials as well as the staff of the UN Department of Economic Affairs. Representatives of the Tripolitanian National Congress party complained about the lack of time to study the report properly. To do so, they needed impartial expert advice, but British authorities, they charged, made it impossible for them to obtain or retain reliable men on the spot.[119] London, in turn, swiftly demanded to delete anything from the UN report that could be construed as criticism of the recently agreed-upon monetary arrangement, threatening to withdraw budget support to Libya.[120] In response, New York "drastically revised" the report accordingly and "released" John Lindberg from his position as chief technical assistance economist.[121]

UN representatives thought that the final revised document strikingly illustrated the weakness of the Libyan economy, so that the problem of development appeared even more difficult than many Libyans had anticipated.[122] "Lindberg's report" noted a hefty balance of payments deficit, as well as a budget deficit of almost $5 million, about 30 percent of total expenditures, and concluded that foreign subsidies were a sine qua non for the "viability" of the Libyan State.[123] It also stressed the need for a long-term development plan. Given Libya's largely illiterate and unskilled population, no domestic savings to speak of, and destitution in terms of raw materials and energy sources, the UN argued—much as Italian Fascist officials had previously—that its "natural line for economic development" was in agriculture and animal husbandry. Although the country was predominantly agricultural, the report noted, Libya was not self-sufficient in terms of food production.[124] Industry would likely remain of small importance for the foreseeable future. The report concluded that the United Nations had a special responsibility to afford Libya the help necessary for economic independence. At best, the road to a "viable" economy and adequate standards of living would be long and hazardous, entailing considerable economic obligations for the world organization for many years to come.[125]

## THE HIGGINS DEVELOPMENT PLAN

According to Pelt, the final version of Lindberg's somber appraisal ultimately reflected "a distinct warming toward UN technical assistance" on the part of the "administering authorities." British and French officials had realized that UN experts, "far from being ogres, were in fact, quite inadvertently, reliable allies, in that they advised the Libyans not to embark on projects, which were impracticable or would require greatly increased subsidies." Pelt noted that Libyans, meanwhile, continued to voice their disappointment that the UN supplied no means of providing loans and grants or budget subsidies to their country.[126] The British and the French, however, readily agreed to request a third, still larger UN technical assistance mission to Libya with the goal of formulating a comprehensive development plan for the territory.[127]

From July 1951 to January 1952, a team of twenty-seven UN experts led by North American economist Benjamin Higgins—whose penchant for colorful shirts paired with very brief shorts and sandals reportedly irritated Libyan notables—prepared a six-year plan for the economic and social development of Libya.[128] Higgins was born in 1912 in Ontario, Canada, and studied economics at the University of Western Ontario and the London School of Economics, as well as public administration at Harvard. He received a PhD from the University of Wisconsin in 1941 and became a U.S. citizen the same year. Higgins taught at American, Canadian, and Australian universities and served as an advisor on various technical assistance missions in Indonesia, Lebanon, the Philippines, Greece, and Brazil. In Libya, he was eager to collaborate closely with the UN specialized agencies to work out a comprehensive development plan, hoping to set a precedent that might be followed elsewhere.[129]

As early as September 1950, UN officials had noted "local confusion" with regard to technical assistance owing to the rapid succession of expert visits.[130] "In this day and age," one UN report noted, "investigators, advisers, fact-finders, technical engineers and the like are found on every plane."[131] In July 1951, Higgins noted that "local officials" (presumably Libyans as well as British and French) would prefer material assistance—subsidized imports, reparation for war damages, and financial aid—or concrete development projects rather than the provision of more experts.[132] Study trips that allowed Libyans to travel abroad, visiting Egypt and Tunisia, for example, to learn about agriculture and taxation, were also viewed favorably.[133] To make matters worse, UN experts were essentially "birds of passage" on short assignments. Though most meant well, worked hard, and did good work, one UN report noted, they added to the "wear and tear" on officials in the British and French administrations, who often felt unfairly judged and ill-compensated for their cooperation with the world organization's staff. As one such official complained:

> You come here on a fantastic salary to write us up. I introduce you to everybody, show you around, answer your questions, and attend to your comforts.... You take my photo, which goes into an album with cactuses and canals. After a few weeks you retire to an alpine hotel to write down what I told you, leaving me to catch up with work.[134]

In addition to the UN teams' comparatively high salaries, European officials particularly resented the effect of their large groups on local prices.[135]

To ease the work of Higgins's team, the UN mission in Tripoli issued some behavioral guidelines that give clues about the comportment of previous UN experts. Experts were instructed to ask for interviews with colonial officials well in advance of their arrival and prepare their questions ahead of time, based on all publicly available materials. UN representatives were not to bother these officials with requests for tours, souvenirs, or entertainment, nor to ask for snapshots with servants. As far as Libyans were concerned, the guidelines patronizingly called for the UN experts' patience, suggesting that the local population was not accustomed to planning for the future. The memo advised UN officials to be polite, accept invitations for drinks and food, and generally ignore the women. In another memo, experts were instructed to abandon the word "native" because of its "colonialistic" implications. Libyan requests for consultations without the presence of colonial officials were to be "handled with great care," which testified, again, to the generally cautious approach of a UN unwilling to antagonize Western powers.[136]

Like Lindberg before him, Higgins noted that his team and the UN mission in Tripoli had differing ideas about the competencies of the other. However, his work caused much less of a stir than his predecessor's.[137] Higgins's report was submitted as a recommendation to the Libyan government and officially accepted by it shortly after the country gained independence in December 1951. Late that year, the provisional Libyan government had established six working parties, whose (unspecified) members discussed the report's findings with the UN team. "Many of those who attended the meetings," Pelt noted, "were later to hold important political and administrative appointments in the government of Libya, and their participation in the preparation of what came to be known as the 'Higgins Report' undoubtedly contributed substantially to its acceptance and to much of its implementation."[138]

Following Lindberg's lead, Higgins's plan was deliberately rural. He noted, "To anyone who thinks of 'economic development' as the process, which took place in the Western world during the last two centuries," the plan devised for Libya "may seem strange."[139] Though development was then often used synonymously with industrialization and urbanization, the future that the UN envisioned for Libya, much as Italy had before it, was decidedly agricultural. With its emphasis on the countryside, Higgins's plan also anticipated the recommendations of prominent American modernization theorists later in the decade.[140] The UN's primary goal for Libya lay in low-cost improvement of agriculture. On the one hand, Higgins recommended experimental work to determine the most fruitful lines of improvement; on the other, he envisioned labor-intensive "action" projects such as forestation, range improvement, the sinking of livestock-watering wells, and the building of check dams and other irrigation works. It was essential, Higgins wrote, that early results would be dramatic enough to demonstrate to the Libyan people that progress was possible, "to jerk the country out of the lethargy that," according to Higgins, "had engulfed it in the past."[141] Much like U.S. modernization efforts later, he recommended prioritizing UN development projects according to their perceived ability to symbolize the arrival of modernity.[142]

The main goal of the plan, Higgins explained confidently and condescendingly, was "teaching the Libyans to do better what they [were] already doing" in order "to raise productivity per capita to the level where want disappears." Education thus played a central role. The UN experts unanimously agreed that a solid basic educational foundation was essential for any developmental effort. Top priority was given to "an attack" on illiteracy and investments in teacher training and school facilities. More broadly, Higgins distinguished between worthwhile "social development" efforts and luxury "social welfare" measures. The former referred to programs and projects (for example, in education, public health, or housing) that were designed to raise the level of productivity by improving the conditions in which people lived and worked. Care for the aged or blind, by contrast, would fall into the "luxury" social welfare category. While the UN team reluctantly concluded that Libya could not afford social welfare programs at that point, Higgins thought that much "useful . . . work could be done by women on a volunteer basis," particularly by expatriate wives.[143] Strapped for money, the UN—like nationalist governments later on— recommended substitutes for "developmental labor" in women's uncompensated care work.[144]

Though the UN plan contained no proposals for new industries, new transport facilities, or, as Higgins put it, gigantic investment projects of any kind, the restoration and repair of the Italian-built harbor facilities, water supplies, power plants, roads, and other infrastructure figured prominently in the projected development expenditures. Higgins's emphasis on repair and maintenance was in part a response to Libyan requests for compensation and reconstruction of war damages, which, Pelt conceded, were "not only an economic problem but also a moral responsibility."[145] In his book, the UN commissioner did not elaborate whose "moral responsibility" it was to help Libya recover from the "ravages of war and occupation," though to be fair, Pelt repeatedly raised the issue at the General Assembly—where member states failed to agree on a solution. Pelt ultimately concluded that his only chance to make the Assembly recognize the existence of a war damage problem in Libya was by dropping all reference to compensation and linking the issue instead with that of development.[146] Accordingly, Higgins's plan framed reconstruction as a problem of Libyan economic development rather than the moral responsibility of those who had inflicted the damage on Libya. UN talk of reconstruction, it appears, was reserved for Europe, while Libya had to aspire to development.[147]

Other UN authors framed the challenge in Libya, much like their colleagues writing about the Congo a decade later, as a very peculiar problem of development: namely one of *maintenance*. In this view, Libyans had inherited a "ready-made modern state" from the colonial powers, which one report unconvincingly likened to a "mansion" in need of expensive upkeep. In a similar vein, Pelt noted that the UN found itself in the paradoxical position of compelling Libya to reduce its weak administrative and social services, even though in the long run, international assistance promised to bring about improvements in the administration of the country and its standard of living.[148] Overall, the Higgins plan required a budget of £2 million for the first year and somewhat larger amounts for the following five years—a small sum, he noted, in comparison to the needs of the country and the money that the Italian colonial regime had previously spent on development there. While Higgins hoped that the Libyan government would be able to shoulder about half of these costs, he also counted on assistance from the UN and the recently established, bilateral Libyan-American Technical Assistance Service. And indeed, Pelt later received assurances from the State Department that there would be full and close cooperation between the U.S. and the UN in Libya.[149]

Aside from financial resources, Higgins thought that the success of the plan would require "a great deal of skilled administration and much further planning." Given the dismal educational situation in Libya, he concluded that administrative personnel would have to come from abroad. Yet even if it were politically and administratively feasible to integrate foreigners into the Libyan civil service, he thought, the country would be in no position to pay for their salaries. The "logical source" for experts, Higgins concluded, was the United Nations and its specialized agencies. He wrote that it would be "psychologically preferable" that foreign civil servants not be nominated by any single government. Their high salaries could be paid according to a formula recently worked out for UN administrative assistants in Bolivia, who were remunerated by both the specialized agencies and the UN under the Expanded Program for Technical Assistance (EPTA).[150]

When Higgins's report was published, the administrative assistant scheme that integrated UN experts into the Bolivian civil service had only just been negotiated between the world organization and La Paz in late 1951. According to the principal secretary of the UN mission in Tripoli, it roused considerable interest in Libya.[151] Going beyond the more limited proposal for UN assistance that was ultimately provided in La Paz, Higgins suggested that a UN resident representative in Tripoli coordinate the work of all foreign experts in independent Libya, while a UN deputy should serve as chief economist, helping to continuously revise and adjust the development plan. In addition, a large team of international experts, headed by senior UN officials from the specialized agencies in the fields of agriculture, health, and education, should "form an integrated whole" to help the new state operate properly—a vision strikingly similar to the UN program that Secretary-General Dag Hammarskjöld would launch in the Congo in 1960 to help manage that country's crash transformation from colony to independent nation-state.[152] The Libyan government was in its infancy, Higgins concluded. For some years to come, it would need a good deal of outside help in the general training of civil servants and especially with administrative posts requiring scientific and technical training or expertise.

## LIBYA AT INDEPENDENCE

The technical assistance program that was eventually established in independent Libya was the largest per capita UN program of the early 1950s, and in Pelt's estimation, constituted one of the most intensive and most successful ones ever mounted.[153] Some UN experts were indeed appointed to administrative positions in Tripoli, leading one UN leaflet to boast that the world organization helped govern the new nation not only by assisting ministers with policy advice, but also by "running an important segment of the government." The evidence: one UN expert subsequently ran the government's statistical bureau; others worked out new tax legislation and revised the social security system; another served as advisor to the National Bank.[154] UN personnel also helped to draft the statutes for the country's development institutions, the Libyan Public Development and Stabilization Agency (LPDSA) and the Libyan Finance Corporation (LFC) and a UN representative would later serve on their respective boards.[155] Yet, UN officials never assumed the central coordinating role for Libya's development that Higgins had recommended.

An international fund to channel financial assistance to Libya was eventually established by the General Assembly, but no UN member states ever contributed to it. Turkey, Egypt, and Pakistan made "modest contributions" to the LPDSA for varying numbers of years. However, until revenues from oil began to flow into Libya's coffers after 1959, the bulk of the administrative and development budget deficits were met by payments from the United Kingdom and the United States, while the much smaller French subvention barely served to redress the financial imbalance of Fezzan.[156] As the main long-term sponsor of the budget of independent Libya, London generally had the last word with regard to developmental decisions. Projects begun under the British administration rather than the novel ones envisioned by the UN development plan were thus the majority of those sponsored by the LPDSA.[157]

The majority of foreign personnel within the Libyan administrations both before and after independence were former British and, in Fezzan, French officials.[158] A UN memo noted that these foreign civil-service employees enjoyed substantial authority.[159] At the Secretariat's prodding, UNESCO helped to establish a training center for Libyan civil servants, but this was led by a British principal, staffed with British-nominated teachers, and built on British curricula and syllabi. The French apparently ignored the training center altogether, preferring instead to send qualified Fezzanese to France or Algeria for training.[160] Most importantly, London continued to insist on its monopoly to advise or even control the Libyan government with regard to financial and budgetary matters in return for financial assistance. In October 1951, the former British chief administrator in Tripoli wrote to Adrian Pelt that his government was unable to accept that the preparation of a development program should come within the competence of the UN resident representative; nor could the British agree that the UN representative should have even advisory functions vis-à-vis the Libyan government. "I wish to make this point quite clear," the letter concluded.[161]

Reporting to Secretary-General Lie on his two-year mission in the country in May 1952, Pelt noted that a principal flaw in Libyan independence was its financial dependence on other governments. He argued, however, that the assistance came from different sources, and that, although the British were dominant, these influences tended to balance themselves out, allowing the Libyans some room to maneuver. (Tripoli ultimately received substantial financial support from the UK, the U.S., and France. In the run-up to independence, the British promised to spend £1.5 million a year for a twenty-five-year period. Washington offered to pay $1 million a year for twenty years.[162]) Without discussing the bloated bureaucracy mentioned above, Pelt worried that the new polity, which the UN had helped to set up, was weakest from the point of administration. The country, he thought, did not have a sufficiently large number of Libyan civil servants and foreign employees held most of the top posts in the Libyan government.[163] As noted above, Pelt's concern with public administration was very much in tune with the work of other UN technical assistance missions, regardless of whether they were visiting trust territories, newly independent states, or longer-established underdeveloped countries. In the golden years of state-led development, UN officials saw government bureaucracies as the main impediment or engine of national progress and self-determination—and paradoxically, also as the most fruitful point for outside intervention.

Pelt's discussion with the secretary-general turned to the question of the "applicability of the Libyan pattern to other parts of Africa."[164] When driving through neighboring Tunisia (then a French protectorate), the UN commissioner noticed that "the new Libyan license plates had certainly drawn the attention from nationalist crowds."[165] Yet he also warned vaguely of "a danger for the UN to undertake too much" on the African continent and elsewhere.¹⁶⁶ Along with many observers at the time, Pelt was unsure of how UN experiments in state-building would turn out; he wondered whether they would contribute to world peace or, rather, cause further disruption.¹⁶⁷ In many ways, the Libyan experience had been more sobering than exhilarating to the UN officials involved, demonstrating that it was one thing to declare the founding of an independent state in New York and quite another to build one.

While Pelt thought of the Libyan transformation as a unique international experiment in handling decolonization peacefully, his colleagues at the UN headquarters soon came to regard it as a model. Paul Hoffman, a U.S. automobile millionaire who led the implementation of the Marshall Plan and headed the Ford Foundation before joining the United Nations as director of the Special Fund, presented UN assistance to Libya as "a kind of microcosm of what the UN tries to do for a traditional society" more generally.¹⁶⁸ And indeed, the UN experience in Libya set an important precedent in presenting state-building increasingly as a technical challenge and an operational field for international experts rather than a political process. Pelt himself suggested in 1970 that while a UN "decolonization operation" akin to the one in Libya had not been repeated elsewhere, in recent similar processes, development agencies had tended to play an increasingly important role, whereas "political filters" such as the Council for Libya were no longer considered a useful device for state-building.¹⁶⁹ UN officials involved in the parallel, though longer-lasting Somali state-building project took away a very similar lesson about the futility of "political filters" and the necessity of continued international assistance to the newly independent state for many years to come.

# 3

## IF TEN YEARS SUFFICE
## FOR SOMALILAND . . .

*The problem here is interesting. I suppose that economically things are pretty tough and it appears that a very small percentage of the people are literate. However the human material seems so good that even in ten years the thing can be done. . . . [I]f we put our backs into it we could have the country ready for self-government in a relatively short time. This could be a bright spot in [the] UN's history.*

— UN Secretariat official reporting from Mogadishu to the New York headquarters in 1950

In a contemporary review of the Somali state-building process, one observer noted that, although initially not intended as an experiment in the feasibility of international state creation, conditions in the territory were so unfavorable that if the UN approach proved effective there, it would be expected to meet with success anywhere else. A decade later, a former UN official similarly suggested that the 1949 General Assembly decision to grant independence to "backward" Somaliland within ten years had "a profound influence" on expectations in other colonies. If ten years was considered sufficient time to turn pauper Somaliland into a state, why should other, much more "advanced" colonies have to wait longer? The UN trusteeship system as such, he argued, played only a secondary role in transforming expectations about colonial rule.[1]

After the UN member states decided to turn Somaliland into a UN trust territory under Italian administration for a ten-year period, a special committee of the Trusteeship Council (composed of representatives from France, Iraq, the Philippines, the Dominican Republic, the United Kingdom, and the United States) was given the task of drafting a trusteeship agreement, according to which Italy would administer the territory. Italy was invited to participate in the drafting process without a vote, as were Egypt and Colombia, the latter two because they would dispatch representatives to a UN Advisory Council to be set up in Mogadishu. Ethiopia received a similar invitation because of its "special interest in East Africa," as did India, because the country's representatives had previously drafted a set of constitutional principles to be included in the trusteeship agreement for Somaliland.

The final agreement registered a compromise between two drafts, one proposed by Italy and one by the Philippine delegation. According to a former colleague of his, the "Philippine" draft was actually written by American Secretariat member Tom Power (who would later serve as Adrian Pelt's deputy in Libya; see previous chapter). Power was then still working for the U.S. State Department and, by his own admission, possessed little knowledge about the Italian colonies.[2] During the draft negotiation, according to one Secretariat observer, representatives of the Philippines and Iraq strove determinedly to make the trust agreement for Somaliland a model expression of trusteeship. The agreement promised detailed guarantees for the population and sharp curbs on the "administering authority's" freedom of action, imposing, for example, stringent restrictions on Italy's power to claim land and natural resources.[3]

The final document thus differed from other UN trusteeship agreements on several points: trusteeship in Somaliland was limited to a ten-year period; it contained a declaration of constitutional principles meant to guarantee the rights of the inhabitants of Somaliland; it called for the establishment of institutions designed to facilitate the transfer to full self-government; it explicitly declared sovereignty to be vested in the people of the trust territory; and its provisions relating to, for example, education and land alienation were spelled out in greater detail. Finally, the agreement stipulated that a UN Advisory Council, situated in Mogadishu and composed of one representative each from Colombia, Egypt, and the Philippines, was to assist the Italian administration of the territory, the *Amministrazione Fiduciaria Italiana della Somalia* (AFIS). The intergovernmental UN Advisory Council, so the more optimistic observers hoped, would act as a "watch dog" for the UN in Somaliland by reporting to New York.[4] On the ground, the Advisory Council was supported by a handful of UN Secretariat officials, who were seconded from New York to the Somali capital.[5]

Despite their initial high hopes, UN representatives in Mogadishu were largely sidelined during the trusteeship period. The Advisory Council was highly dysfunctional. Personal animosities and political differences among government representatives as well as Secretariat officials played a role, as did lack of specialized knowledge and diplomatic tact. Some council members simply resented being sent to Mogadishu—in the eyes of one UN official "a godforsaken place with a lousy per diem."[6] The Italian administration regarded the Advisory Council at best as a joke and, given the anti-Italian stance of the Philippine and Egyptian delegates, at worst as a threat, and thus by and large ignored it.[7] Successful mediation efforts between Somalis and Italians by individual UN representatives seem to have been the exception rather than the rule. In addition to its strained relationship with the Advisory Council and the Italian administration, the UN mission in Mogadishu was also troubled by staff shortages, lack of language skills, unfamiliarity with legislative matters, and a mostly distant, often patronizing attitude toward Somalis.

Nevertheless, the UN played a significant role in the territory. From early on, Secretariat officials in Mogadishu, much as in Libya, lobbied for the notion that "a viable economy" was a necessity for true independence and indeed the survival of the state. Pointing to the experience in Libya, the New York headquarters also pushed for increasing training in public administration, and technocratic assistance more generally, as a necessary part of any state-building project in Somaliland.[8] UN reports tied Somali sovereignty to the need for foreign assistance and international cooperation. In view of lacking *material* support from the "international community" (that is, from UN member governments), these initiatives helped push Somalia toward a clientelist relationship with sponsor countries, namely the United States and Italy. To the distress of UN officials on the ground, both Washington and Rome were happy to turn a blind eye, or indeed actively support antidemocratic developments in the territory, as long as "radical" politicians were barred from government. Much as in

Libya, the UN's involvement in state-building in Somalia proved a rather sobering experience to those closely involved.

## ITALIAN TRUSTEESHIP OF SOMALILAND

Situated on the Horn of Africa, where the Gulf of Aden meets the Indian Ocean, the UN Trust Territory of Somaliland under Italian Administration, formerly known as Italian Somaliland or *Somalia Italiana*, bordered British Somaliland in the northwest, Ethiopia in the west, and Kenya in the southwest. Italy's colonial presence dated to the late 1880s, when European colonial powers carved up the Horn of Africa, inhabited mostly by Somalis, who shared a common language, culture, and religion. In the 1950s, the trust territory, which spanned approximately 500,000 square kilometers, had a population of about one million, of whom 70 to 80 percent were nomadic or seminomadic pastoralists. At the time, it had no known mineral resources—and, according to UN reports, due to the arid climate, livestock raising and agriculture provided only a bare livelihood for many Somalis. Fascist Italy's efforts to turn deserts into fertile fields had mainly concentrated on Libya, though there had been some investments in infrastructure and settler agriculture in Somaliland as well.[9]

While Italians had largely barred Somalis from receiving formal education and forming political associations, the British Military Administration, which occupied the territory from 1941 to 1950, provided some openings in this regard. Somali party politics flourished under the British military occupation. Many Somalis were hopeful that, under British patronage, a unification of all Somali-speaking regions might be feasible, which would have included neighboring British and French Somaliland, as well as parts of Ethiopia and Kenya.[10] The prolonged period of uncertainty after the signing of the Peace Treaty, which divested Italy of its colonies in 1945, and especially the great power investigative commission dispatched in 1947 to survey local opinion, further encouraged Somali political organization.[11]

At the same time, Italians mobilized a pro-Italian Somali umbrella organization, the *Conferenza per la Somalia*, which clashed violently with the anti-Italian opposition centered on the main nationalist party, the

Somali Youth League (SYL) in 1948.[12] It was against this background of fierce opposition to Italian rule that Rome deployed a large number of troops to Somaliland in the somewhat hasty transfer of power from the British in early 1950. The official beginning of the UN trusteeship period thus resembled the advent of a foreign military occupation rather than the arrival of an internationally sanctioned civilian administration. Though the British Military Authority had forbidden demonstrations protesting the Italian return, a dockworker strike, which forced the Italians to unload their own cargo, demonstrated Somali resistance to the transfer of power.[13]

Save for the head of the new administration, Giovanni Fornari, and his second-in-command Pier Pasquale Spinelli, Rome staffed AFIS above all with fascist-era colonial officials—an issue Somalis repeatedly raised at the UN to no avail.[14] To counter opposition to Italian rule, AFIS initially severely restricted Somali party activities and incarcerated many people suspected of opposition to the new administration, to the point that the number of prisoners in Mogadishu rose threefold within the first two months of trusteeship.[15] Somalis, particularly the SYL, sought to counter these measures by petitioning the United Nations (which offered no remedy) and organizing frequent and widespread protests in the territory. The conflict between Somalis and AFIS reached a climax in August 1952, when two representatives of the administration were stoned to death during a demonstration against the authorities in the port city of Kismayo and Italian officials temporarily closed down the SYL headquarters.[16] After the incident, Fadel Bey, the Egyptian delegate to the UN Advisory Council in Mogadishu, held many talks to facilitate reconciliation between the opposing groups, and the relationship eventually became less confrontational.[17]

By the mid-1950s, after the SYL achieved its first decisive electoral victory, the party was closely cooperating with AFIS, and indeed asking the Italian administration to remain in the territory until the end of the trusteeship period and support the Somali state beyond independence. Scholars have listed several reasons for this about-turn of the party, which would rule Somalia until Siad Barre's military coup in 1969; among them were AFIS' carrot-and-stick policies (repression coupled with select educational opportunities), changes in leadership of both AFIS and the SYL, and the disappointed hope for British support of Pan-Somali unity after London ceded Somali-speaking territories to Ethiopia in 1954.[18] The growing realization that international assistance was necessary for the continued survival of a sovereign Somali state—a notion the UN tirelessly promoted in the trust territory—likely played a role as well.

## THE UN IN SOMALILAND

The first UN Secretariat officials set foot in Mogadishu in May 1950, a month after the Italian arrival, to support the work of the UN Advisory Council. Impressed by Somali intelligence and initiative, some UN representatives—as the opening quote indicates—were initially optimistic about the prospects of state-building in the territory and presented it as a potential "bright spot" in the history of the United Nations. Though "economically things are pretty tough,... the human material seems so good, that even in ten years the thing can be done," predicted one UN staff member in a bout of "24 hour expertising," for which he apologized.[19] Others were decidedly less confident. In a private meeting with secretary-general Trygve Lie in late November 1950, Egon Ranshofen-Wertheimer, the first principal secretary of the UN mission in Somaliland, suggested that the situation was complicated.

Ranshofen-Wertheimer was born in 1894 in what was then the Austro-Hungarian empire and grew up to study law and history in Vienna, Munich, and Heidelberg. From 1924 to 1930, he worked as a foreign correspondent for the social democratic newspaper *Vorwärts* in London, before joining the League of Nations in Geneva. In 1940, he immigrated to the United States, where he worked at the American University in Washington, DC as a consultant to the State Department, and as a journalist. In early 1946, he joined a mission to arrange the transfer of funds and functions from the League to the UN and was offered a position in the UN Secretariat upon his return to the United States. In January 1949, he served as principal secretary of the UN mission charged with overseeing the peaceful withdrawal of American troops in Korea and negotiating the unification of the North and South. Ranshofen-Wertheimer's background testifies to the relative diversity of UN officials as well as to their general lack of specialized preparation for assignments abroad.[20]

It is unclear on what basis Ranshofen-Wertheimer formed his opinions about Somaliland, but he suggested to Secretary-General Lie in 1950 that the population was "at the lowest level of development of any African people" since most were nomads without an interest in agriculture. Even if they could be convinced to change their ways, he reported, 80 percent of the territory was wasteland unsuitable for agriculture or animal husbandry. Few Somalis had enjoyed formal education, and none, he thought, had any training or experience with democratic institutions. "Without a tremendous effort ... to educate and train people, supplemented by a large-scale technical assistance program aimed toward converting the population from a nomadic to a settled experience," Ranshofen-Wertheimer concluded, it would be difficult to realize true independence for Somaliland within the space of ten years.[21]

As noted above, the UN remained largely on the sidelines of the actual state-building effort in Somaliland. The UN Advisory Council in Mogadishu was supposed to act as a guardian of the world organization and assist AFIS with the administration of the territory. Yet the fierce personal and political differences already noted, coupled with AFIS' disinterest in actually consulting the Council on policy matters, severely hampered its effectiveness. Five months into the UN's presence in Somaliland, A. J. Lucas, the principal secretary from France, who replaced Ranshofen-Wertheimer as head of the UN mission in June, resigned because of "violent attacks" by the Philippine delegate to the Council, Victorio Carpio. Carpio accused Lucas and the Colombian representative to the Council of not supporting the Somali cause and tweaking UN reports to the Trusteeship Council in New York accordingly.[22] (Lucas, who also had health issues, was replaced by the Canadian Germanist Taylor Shore for a year, before fellow Frenchman Jean de la Roche, whose internationalist vision for a new, postcolonial age was discussed in chapter 1, took over.[23]) AFIS and the pro-Italian Somali parties, in turn, accused the Philippine delegate of exceeding the terms of reference of his appointment by "meddling" with political parties and thus inviting "widespread bloodshed."[24] After Rome declared Carpio a persona non grata, he was recalled to Manila in early 1952.[25] Secretariat officials, who had considered Carpio "stupid," gullible, "cunning," "treacherous," "greedy" and cheap, if also "hard-working" and generally well-intentioned toward the Somali cause, were full of praise for his successor, Vicente Pastrana, describing him as conscientious and willing to compromise.[26]

After Carpio's departure, relations between Council members improved somewhat, though long-serving Colombian representative Edmondo de Holte Castello, according to Secretariat officials, often behaved in a "childish and unpredictable" way.[27] While principal secretary Lucas apparently got along well with Castello, his successor Shore considered the Colombian delegate a "smart cookie," but also a "bastard" who didn't have "an honest bone in his body." Shore saw in Castello an even "greater evil" than in Philippine delegate Carpio.[28] Shore reported that in addition to suffering from alcoholism, Castello was vain, vicious, megalomaniac, and "extremely pro-Italian."[29] In one instance, Castello refused to sign the annual report to the Trusteeship Council—even if all it said was "Mogadishu is very hot"—to spite the other delegates.[30] Later on, he refused to sign the report because he did not understand the technical details of the section on the economy.[31]

Successive Egyptian delegates to the Council were for the most part less confrontational. Indeed, principal secretary Shore praised delegate Fadel Bey as "intelligent and easy to get along with." Though he reported that Bey was "monkeying around" with things beyond his terms of reference, Shore thought that overall he was doing much practical good, e.g., by smoothing hostilities between Arab and Somali communities in Mogadishu.[32] Shore described Bey as wildly popular with Somalis—a "mob" of "hundreds and hundreds" came to greet him at the airport after a home leave—and wielding "*tremendous* influence."[33] Soon, and with a tint of jealousy ("a refrig and a radio is [sic] being imported from Aden"), Shore began to worry about Cairo's investment in the region, which he saw as bent on "impress[ing] the gullible with Egyptian importance." In addition to the seemingly lavish spending on Bey's representational comforts in Mogadishu, Shore was alarmed by the promise of twenty Egyptian fellowships for Somali students to study in Cairo, as well as Egypt's intention to send two Koranic and a number of secondary-school teachers. Maybe no other power wanted to influence Somaliland, he mused ("naturally, I'm thinking of Great Britain and especially the U.S.A"), before suggesting the U.S. take "a load of young Somalis" for study in America as a "counterbalance" to Egyptian efforts.[34] De la Roche, too, worried that Egyptian delegates were ultimately less invested in making the Council work and assisting AFIS in the administration of the territory than in using their UN-sponsored position in Mogadishu to campaign for Egyptian interests in the region: that is, the widespread use of Arabic in Somaliland and, more generally, subsuming the Pan-Somali project into Pan-Arabism, led by Cairo.[35]

While representing Cairo's interests in Somaliland was surely important to Egyptian Council delegates, the initiatives pursued by the Philippine and Egyptian representatives suggest a markedly different understanding of the Council's role. Both generally sought to bolster the "watch-dog" function of the Council, arguing, for example, for Somali representatives and reports to be sent to the General Assembly, where colonial powers were a minority, rather than to the Trusteeship Council, where they were not outnumbered. UN staff, by contrast, saw the Advisory Council in Mogadishu as a body that was supposed to constructively support the Italian administration.[36]

Regardless of these different conceptions about the Council and the role of the UN, when it came to the day-to-day decision-making in Somaliland, the Advisory Council remained on the sidelines. The Italian administration simply had no interest in involving the Council in policy decisions. If AFIS sent it ordinances for advice at all, they were usually dispatched in a last-minute face-saving measure. Often Council members and Secretariat officials would only learn of important political decisions made by the administration from reading the local newspaper, the *Corriere della Somalia*. The news of post-independence Italian foreign aid, for example, was only announced to the Advisory Council a few hours after it had been published in the *Corriere*.[37]

By 1953, Colombian delegate Castello wished to reveal the "futility" of the Advisory Council to the Trusteeship Council, so that delegates in New York would put an end to the charade. He suggested that the Advisory Council be replaced with some kind of technical UN body staffed with legal, economic, and educational experts, which might be in a better position to constructively assist AFIS in the administration of Somaliland. In a confidential assessment of the work of the Advisory Council, principal secretary Jean de la Roche supported Castello's proposal. As discussed in the previous chapter, colonial officials in Libya, in cooperation with the UN, had taken exactly this route of depoliticizing state-building by circumventing political discussions with regard to the country's future monetary arrangements and leaving the matter to technical experts instead. In Mogadishu, the UN preference for technocratic advice rather than politicized discussions was not simply rooted in a Machiavellian desire to assume control of the Somali state-building process. Rather, it should also be understood as a response to the very real dysfunction of the Council. "Somalia is supposed to be taken care of, but it is not," de la Roche noted in 1953, worrying about the prestige of the UN that he thought was at stake.[38] Yet, because the Secretariat was afraid of pushback from the Philippines and Egypt in the General Assembly, it took no initiative to abolish or transform the Council and AFIS simply continued to ignore it.[39]

The Council's relationship with the first Somali administration, it appears, was not much better. A year after the first Somali government was elected in 1956, SYL prime minister Abdullahi Issa Mohamud assured the UN that his government wished the Council to continue its operations until the end of the trusteeship period. Apparently, up until then, the Somali government had not been familiar with the Council's offers of assistance—perhaps a testament to its marginal role.[40] Subsequently, according to Secretariat officials, members of the Advisory Council would frequently advise Somali government officials on important problems. Their comments on the country's labor code, for example, reportedly made a great impression on the Somali government. The latter also sought support from Council members with regard to the unresolved border issue with Ethiopia, before it was discussed at the General Assembly.[41]

By the end of 1958, however, the relationship deteriorated rapidly when the Council protested the introduction of a new voting law designed to obstruct opposition parties.[42] In October, the Somali Constitutional Independent Party (HDMS) had done very well in the municipal elections, while the ruling SYL did not achieve its desired result. UN officials had been impressed by the "dignified and peaceful atmosphere" of these elections and especially by the high turnout of women, who voted for the first time. The UN received no complaints regarding the conduct of these elections.[43] However, in the wake of their disappointing results, the SYL ratified a new electoral law that prevented opposition parties from fairly competing in the upcoming national elections.[44] Amid rising tensions and violent clashes between the Somali government and opposition parties, the Advisory Council tried to mediate, to no avail.[45]

Much like Council delegates, Secretariat officials were largely removed from Italian and later Somali decision-making. Though successive principal secretaries described the relationship with the Italian authorities as "quite cordial," they blamed AFIS's "somewhat fuzzy and unsystematic" manner of operating for the lack of cooperation with the UN.[46] Meanwhile, their relationship with Somali politicians and the population at large was hampered by language issues as well as a patronizing, if not racist attitude on the part of UN officials. Somali pleas for an Arab-speaking principal secretary of the UN mission in Mogadishu were never answered or apparently even considered a possibility. For long stretches during the trusteeship period, no "responsible" UN staff member in Mogadishu was a speaker of Arabic, leaving the mission, by its own description, "mutilated."[47] Early on, Lebanese political officer Goro Deeb, who served as the UN mission's "contact man" with the Somalis, accused acting principal secretary Taylor Shore of "racial bias."[48] Shore, who had described Somalis in personal letters as "no fools" but occasionally a "pretty demanding, unreasonable and cocky bunch," rejected the accusation, which ended in a public brawl at an Italian party and an apology from Deeb the next morning.[49]

The UN remove from Somali concerns was also reflected and supported by the choice of its headquarters-cum-housing-facility in Mogadishu, a compound called "the Lido" outside of the city center. Living conditions, according to one staff member, were "fairly primitive, but tolerable enough," save for only "rudimentary" medical services.[50] UN staff members, however, lamented the problem of "staff living and working too close together for comfort," and Shore partly blamed his dramatic falling-out with Deeb, which involved whiskey-throwing and a knock-out blow, on this issue. Yet they saw no other solution to this accommodation, pointing to "greedy landlords" who believed the UN to possess its own "dollar-printing shop," as well as the ubiquity of robberies. (Ignoring such concerns, the Egyptian delegate to the Advisory Council moved out of the compound to a house in town in early 1952.[51])

Despite the language barrier and the UN's physical distancing, many Somalis continued to visit "the Lido" throughout the trusteeship period. While most inquired about job opportunities, others asked the UN to intervene with the Italian and, later, Somali authorities on their behalf, often in the form of petitions. Officially, the Advisory Council in Mogadishu was not allowed to receive, much less investigate such petitions on the spot. Only the Trusteeship Council in New York was allowed to receive and examine petitions from trust territories. Understandably, the procedure was confusing and annoying to Somalis, who expected the supposed UN "watch dog" in Mogadishu to intercede on their behalf with the authorities.[52] Though successive Philippine and Egyptian delegates to the Advisory Council continued to protest this, a Secretariat paper concurred that the Council "should be kept as much as possible far from the field of local passions and struggles."[53] It was the exception rather than the rule if individual Council delegates were able to successfully mediate between Somalis and AFIS (as was the case after the Kismayo incident described above) and, after the introduction of self-government following national elections in 1956, among the population of the territory, AFIS, and the Somali government.

De la Roche noted that Advisory Council members were freer to act as intermediaries between AFIS and, later, the Somali government and the people, if *no* formal petitions were involved. One example was the case of Abgal political leaders, who, after not being able to obtain an interview with the Italian administration to protest the digging of a well on their land, visited the UN compound in 1953. More precisely, they sought out Algerian UN officer Abdelamek Lakhdari, whose expertise lay in both mining engineering and Arabic philology and literature. Lakhdari notified the Egyptian delegate to the Advisory Council, Mahmoud Moharram Hamdy, who in turn was able to arrange a meeting with Italian administrator Enrico Martino, which ultimately resulted in a halt to the digging. De la Roche noted that Lakhdari acted with great diplomacy in this awkward situation: while he was not able to give the impression that the Advisory Council was allowed to investigate Somali petitions, he did not dryly refuse people who came to the compound to get the UN's attention.[54] In another instance in 1958, a crowd of 200 merchants gathered before the UN compound to protest the introduction of a new market tax by the Somali government. After Philippine delegate Mauro Baradi informally approached Prime Minister Abdullahi Issa about the issue, the government lowered the tax.[55] Such episodes of successful mediation or lobbying on the part of UN representatives, however, seem to have been the exception rather than the rule. By and large it was left to AFIS, and later the Somali government, to determine the shape of the actual state-building process.

## THE ROAD TO SELF-GOVERNMENT

With regard to the transfer to self-government, the trusteeship agreement drafted by UN delegates had laid out some guidelines for AFIS: namely, that a national consultative organ, a Territorial Council, as well as local consultative organs, were to be set up immediately. The former, constituted in late 1950, provided Somalis with the first opportunity under colonial rule to gather in a central organ of government and confront national issues in an advisory capacity. The thirty-five appointees chosen by AFIS dealt with substantive matters of governance, ranging from the regulation of the cotton industry to the organization of the school system, and gained experience in dealing with the "intricacies of a modern parliamentary system."[56] In *appointing* representatives, however, AFIS by and large neglected the political developments in the region since the 1940s and favored "traditional" community leaders over party representatives.[57]

It was only in 1956, following General Assembly pressure for increased Somali participation in government and territory-wide elections, that the Territorial Council was replaced by a new seventy-seat *elected* Legislative Assembly, which, under the lead of the nationalist SYL, assumed responsibility for the territory's domestic affairs.[58] Still, the electoral procedures adopted by AFIS, a mix of direct male voting in urban areas and representative voting in rural areas without a reliable census of the population, invited severe electoral tampering. The procedures, moreover, formalized the institution of the *shir*, an essentially spontaneous meeting of men belonging to the same clan or subclan, as representative of a community, to the exclusion of women and minorities.[59]

At the local level, the trusteeship agreement had called for the constitution of District and Municipal Councils as consultative and eventually representative organs of government. It was hoped that such local councils would serve as instruments of civic education for the larger population by drawing Somalis into official decision-making processes and eventually granting them financial, executive, and legislative powers over local matters. Some scholars at the time suggested that the Municipal Councils were indeed successfully transformed into elected, largely autonomous bodies of local governance.[60] The District Councils, by contrast, were characterized by a highly autocratic structure built around a community leader. The majority nomad population, moreover, failed to identify with Italian-created districts. AFIS projects, from roads to schools, seemed remote from their own daily needs: the search for and competition over pasturage and water. Equally important, although the UN Advisory Council and the two UN visiting missions that toured the country in 1951 and 1954 continuously urged greater autonomy for the District Councils, Somali representatives at the national level opposed an increase in power of these local bodies, arguing that such a move would strengthen the forces of "tribalism" rather than democracy. The District Councils thus remained above all consultative bodies, leaving authority firmly with the central government, which, following the introduction of self-government in 1956, set out to create a highly centralized one-party state on AFIS's and the UN Advisory Council's watch.[61]

## UN PLANS FOR ECONOMIC INDEPENDENCE: THE DEAN MISSION

When it came to educational and economic initiatives for turning Somaliland into an independent state, UN delegates at the General Assembly had not provided AFIS with any guidelines. From the outset, Italian authorities (at least those higher up) were eager to share that "tremendous effort" with the UN—contrary to other colonial powers, as shown in the previous chapter. On November 20, 1950, AFIS submitted a request for technical assistance for the development of Somaliland to the world organization.[62] One likely cause was that Rome, in the early 1950s, was still trying to get into the UN's good graces. Even though it was the designated UN "administering authority" in Somaliland at the time, Italy was not yet a member of the world organization; it was only admitted in 1955.[63] More importantly, perhaps, despite Marshall Plan aid, Italian resources were limited and Rome's priority was the national recovery from war damages and the development of "metropolitan" territories that were considered economically and otherwise backward.[64] As a result, AFIS faced continuous budget cuts, starting with a drop from 8,000 to 6,000 million lire for 1951.[65]

In their technical assistance request to the UN, the Italians asked for no less than a general survey of the economic and social needs of the territory, with particular attention to the development of agriculture and of fundamental education; for a program to improve conditions; an outline of further necessary UN assistance; and an overall cost assessment of such a development effort.[66] AFIS officials thought that three people should be able to do the job in three months: one chief economist, one expert in social development, and one general agricultural and zootechnical economist.[67]

As chief economist and head of the mission, the UN Secretariat in New York saw William H. Dean as a great fit. At the time, Dean, a Harvard graduate and one of the first African Americans to receive a doctorate in economics, served as chief of the Africa Unit in the UN Secretariat's Department of Economic Affairs. Much like his colleague Ralph Bunche (see chapter 1), Dean had initially worked in academia and, despite graduating at the top of his class, encountered difficulties likely related to racism when it came to securing permanent employment in higher education. Again like Bunche, Dean entered government service during the war (serving with a federal agency established to prevent inflation in Haiti and the Virgin Islands), and left segregated Washington, D.C. to join the UN Secretariat in New York in 1946.[68] As a junior secretary, Dean took part in the first comprehensive UN technical assistance mission, in which twelve experts of the UN and the specialized agencies had taken stock of Haiti's potential for development in 1948.[69] As noted above, Dean had also participated in the reconnaissance mission to Libya in 1950 (discussed in the previous chapter) and came highly recommended by his senior colleague Carter Goodrich. Goodrich prized Dean as an "admirable colleague" who was both "knowledgeable" and "sensitive to the political implications of the problems" they had encountered in Libya, which he thought Dean had handled "with considerable tact and discretion."[70]

Drawing on this prior experience, Dean thought that the Italian request for UN assistance in Somaliland was rather delusional, in that it expected far too much of too few people in too limited a time.[71] He agreed to serve as chief economist to the mission to Somaliland only if the assignment was clearly defined as a manageable one. He suggested undertaking a mission of a more exploratory nature, one that would briefly review the economic and social problems, which could subsequently be dealt with in more detail by individual experts. His mission could make a partial and preliminary evaluation of existing development projects and Italian plans for the territory, and broadly indicate the direction of economic and social advance, without, however, working out a detailed development plan as well as a cost analysis, as Italian authorities had suggested.[72] When the goals for the mission were scaled back accordingly, Dean felt obliged to accept, "though with many reservations."[73]

In the end, Dean's mission included six experts, who visited Somaliland from late August to late November in 1951.[74] The UN team first gathered in Rome on August 23 to organize and collect material on Somaliland and to meet with Italian officials from the Foreign Office and the soon-to-be-disbanded Ministry of Italian Africa. Dean's hopes to embark on a "constructive task in a spirit of scientific humility" were soon disappointed. Although he found most conversations satisfactory, Italian officials appeared reluctant to offer economic information, which Dean considered essential for his mission, such as the balance of payments or the record of investments.[75] The UN mission left Rome for Somaliland on August 25, conducting "very fruitful" conversations on matters of agriculture and livestock with officials from neighboring French as well as British Somaliland during the journey.[76]

In Mogadishu, the UN team tried to establish a working relationship with the technical services of the Italian administration before embarking on field trips to survey the territory. As in Rome, Dean found that the conversations with Italian officials in Somaliland "proceeded with great difficulty."[77] He attributed this to the lack of statistical data, the absence of a fellow economist at AFIS, the manifold pressing duties of the Italians he met, and the "lassitude of the tropics."[78] In private, he told a colleague that he thought of the Italians as "hopelessly disengaged & archaic."[79] Principal secretary Taylor Shore had a slightly different take on Dean's difficulties: he thought that Dean, "in his anxiety to get cracking," tried "whipping the Italians along like a bunch of schoolboys and this they naturally resented."[80] As AFIS was largely staffed with fascist-era colonial officials, racism surely played a role in Dean's difficulties as well. Generally, his trouble with bureaucrats "on the ground" also testifies to a divide in the Italian willingness to work with the UN among top officials and their mid- to lower-level staff on site.

In the absence of facts on Somaliland, Dean ultimately offered little more than his general impressions of the economy as a whole in conclusion of his work. He thought that chief administrator Fornari's request for the UN to draw up a development program for Somaliland with a spending limit of 6 billion lire was an "impossible task."[81] The central problem as he saw it was the question of how to facilitate the economic and social advancement of the indigenous population despite chronic deficiencies in government revenue.[82] Ever since the beginning of Italian colonial administration, the territory had been plagued by budget deficits, which Rome had covered through grants. In 1950, AFIS had raised about $3 million in territorial revenue (a measly 13 percent through direct taxation and 73 percent through import and export duties), while close to $17 million had been provided by Rome. Although the deficit was later reduced (largely due to a reduction in military spending from about $10 million in 1950 to about $3 million in 1958), still only 50 percent of the overall $14 million 1958 budget was supported by internal revenue. [83] In other words, the costs of government, even at the bare-bones level that was not yet committed to significant social spending, appeared staggering in comparison to governmental income. Fornari hoped the UN mission would provide a hint where help would come from in the future.[84]

Dean was at a loss to provide one. He never wrote a final report on the work of his UN mission to Somaliland. Shortly after his return to New York, on January 8, 1951, Dean ended his own life. *Jet* magazine quoted Ralph Bunche, then director of the Secretariat's Trusteeship Division, as suggesting that Dean had been "physically exhausted" by overwork on his Somaliland mission.[85] His colleagues, as well as an unnamed "specialist closely associated" with Dean, finished the report, which was published in early 1952.[86] Conflating the costs of the Italian administration of the colony with "the economy," its introductory remarks noted that the latter had not been "viable, even at a low level, since the advent of European administration."[87] The UN technical assistance mission did not pretend to foresee any rapid improvement in the "fundamentally deficitary character of the economy." Nevertheless, the report indicated some possibilities for progress. Much like the UN recommendations for Libya, the Secretariat's report for Somaliland emphasized the development of agriculture, and the "direct needs of its inhabitants," recommending sound investment in education, health, and social welfare as an "absolutely essential prerequisite for economic development."[88]

## AFIS'S "FARMED-OUT" DEVELOPMENT EFFORTS

AFIS chief administrator Fornari pressed Rome for additional funds to invest in Somali social and economic development. He even threatened to resign over impending budget cuts, complaining that AFIS would not be able to cover even routine administrative expenses, much less develop the territory as the trusteeship agreement required. Although Rome ignored his pleas, Fornari carried on, downsizing military expenditures and pushing the rapid "Somalization" of the state bureaucracy as both a cost-saving measure and a necessary step toward national independence.[89] By 1956, Somalis had replaced Italians in all senior administrative positions, though Italian "counselors" continued to assist Somali ministers.[90] Rome, meanwhile, continued to cut the budget subsidy to Mogadishu (by 1955, it was reduced to 5,500 million lire) and gave no assurances for continued Italian budget contributions until 1960, much less for financial support to the Somali state after independence.[91]

Amid this uncertainty, AFIS outsourced developmental activities to the UN specialized agencies, particularly in the fields of education and health. Most significant, perhaps, in this regard was the UN Educational and Scientific Organization's (UNESCO) Five Year Program for Educational Development, drafted in 1952.[92] While in 1948, there were an estimated 1,222 students in Somali schools, by the 1957–1958 scholastic year this figure had increased to more than 30,000 students, most enrolled in primary schools. However, only slightly more than 1,000 students at that time received some kind of secondary education, of whom only 25 percent actually graduated. Because these students were the main source of clerical employees for government and commerce and the only source for teacher training and higher education, one contemporary observer noted that—despite UNESCO's achievements—the bottleneck in secondary education would likely retard the country's overall development in the future.[93]

UNESCO's attempts to turn nomads into Somali citizens via educational projects likewise showed mixed results. A project at Dinsor that offered teaching in handicrafts, health measures, and new techniques in farming and animal husbandry to "semi-nomads" was considered a success by contemporary observers. A similar project at Afmedu, by contrast, which unsuccessfully sought to provide "more elementary, fundamental education" to members of the same group of nomads was soon abandoned.

Secretariat officials in Mogadishu thought of the Afmedu project as poorly conceived, because it lacked Somali participation. More importantly, they thought of the assigned expert, a Dr. Zöhrer, who was a meteorologist by training, as woefully ill suited for the job, given his view of Somali nomads as "culturally backward" and generally "lacking in mental perceptive facilities."[94]

The World Health Organization and the UN Children's Emergency Fund (UNICEF) assisted AFIS in an extensive campaign to fight malaria, tuberculosis, and other diseases in Somali schools.[95] In 1956, AFIS requested emergency aid from UNICEF to combat famine in the region of Midjertain. The "emergency" situation in the region continued for at least another two years. In February 1959, a UN memo noted that life in Midjertain was hard. The mortality rate of children, the report speculated, was probably high, though "naturally," there were no statistics. One district commissioner had lost twelve of his seventeen children between the age of one and three and he believed this to be a normal proportion. The report's author, however, pointed out that the commissioner's living standards were certainly higher than those of a shepherd living in the same region. Without going into any details, UN officials blamed the Somali government for mishandling UNICEF food supplies meant to lessen the suffering. Elsewhere, they reported that the government was restricting access to water to enforce party membership.[96] A similar scenario with regard to UNICEF food supplies seems possible.[97]

Although the UN specialized agencies were altogether more active in Somaliland than in any other trust territory, the UN Secretariat in Mogadishu did not provide any sense of direction for the territory's overall development activities. In fact, in many cases experts dispatched by the UN agencies were completely unaware of the special role that the UN played in the territory and the presence of a UN Advisory Council and Secretariat staff in Mogadishu. At first, the New York headquarters did little to remedy this situation. It was only in late 1956 that the Secretariat Division of Trusteeship asked to be informed of impending expert visits to Somaliland and for experts to be briefed on the special role and presence of the UN in the territory.[98]

As more and more agencies and countries—above all, the United States—became interested in extending technical assistance to Somaliland in the late 1950s, UN officials in Mogadishu continuously stressed the need for better coordination of international assistance on the ground.[99] U.S. assistance to Somalia dated to an Italian-American agreement in late 1954, which established a joint technical assistance fund. In August 1956, the UN Secretariat in Mogadishu noted that a large number of American experts were arriving in connection with Point IV aid. Relations between the UN officials and American representatives were at first quite cordial, with a hope of coordinating or even "dovetailing" the two technical assistance programs. By July 1958, cooperation was proceeding so well that the principal secretary of the UN mission in Mogadishu was concerned about not becoming too involved with the American operation, "since this might be misunderstood in certain circles."[100]

## COORDINATING AND PLANNING DEVELOPMENT UNDER UN PRESSURE

While the UN provided no sense of overall direction or coordination of development efforts in Somaliland, AFIS was slow to introduce a comprehensive plan of its own. It was not that no initiatives existed, Jean de la Roche, then principal secretary of the UN mission in Mogadishu, reported in December 1953. But there was no definition of a general policy, no coordination between scattered plans and efforts.[101] When the Secretariat asked the administration for a simple overview of outside aid being provided to Somaliland, AFIS was unable to comply with the request. "The budget of the Territory can hardly be called a budget," de la Roche noted.[102] No one knew the proportion of expenses devoted to education or social services—or perhaps, no Italian was willing to share the data. To inform the UN Advisory Council of the financial situation of the territory, the Secretariat had to make up its own budget estimate.[103]

The fact that a development plan did not emerge until 1954 provided a source of constant concern to government representatives at various UN intergovernmental organs, in particular the Trusteeship Council and the General Assembly's Fourth Committee for Non-Self-Governing and Trust Territories.[104] By late 1953, de la Roche reported that the necessity for economic development had also become *"a l'ordre du jour"* among educated Somalis and the population in general, as well as within administrative circles. There was no real economic crisis, but rather a psychological "malaise," he diagnosed. Merchants reportedly displayed no confidence in the future of the territory, smuggling their capital abroad. Somali party leaders were thus becoming extremely concerned about creating a moral climate of confidence to prevent funds from leaving the country and also to attract new capital.[105]

On several occasions, the Trusteeship Council heard various delegations from Somaliland express the idea that support from international agencies was necessary to remedy this situation. The importance of material help from the UN and other nations was also a leitmotif of virtually all conversations between UN representatives in Mogadishu and Somalis. The latter—much like their Libyan contemporaries—were tired of seeing so many experts "roaming about," de la Roche reported, of hearing so many speeches while no material help was forthcoming. Political independence after 1960, many Somalis concluded, would not mean much if people were starving.[106] It was in this context that representatives of the Somali Youth League leadership, once fiercely hostile to Italian rule, asked Italy to stay in Somaliland until the end of the trusteeship period and to provide post-independence assistance to the country. One of the SYL's first official acts of government after winning the national democratic elections in a landslide victory in 1954 was to pass a motion that guaranteed the protection of foreign investments in Somalia after independence.[107]

In 1954, the Italian administration finally presented a seven-year development plan, first to the Somali Territorial Council (the national consultative organ) and then to the UN Trusteeship Council in New York.[108] The plan was ostensibly based on a report by Italian lawyer and politician Giovanni Malagodi that AFIS had commissioned in 1953.[109] Malagodi's report, in turn, relied on a number of individual studies by AFIS personnel, the United States International Cooperation Agency (ICA, later renamed the U.S. Agency for International Development, or USAID), and various UN agencies. Much like the UN plan for Libya, the "Italian" development plan for Somaliland placed heavy emphasis on "improving" indigenous agriculture and animal husbandry, chiefly through the digging of wells and water catch basins, but also through the clearing of land, the construction of storage facilities, the provision of modern machinery, and the establishment of rural credit facilities. The remainder of the projected expenditures, about 20 percent of a total of $10 million, was to be spent on the upkeep of roads and ports.[110]

AFIS officials' fears that the UN might find the plan, and the economic situation in the territory more generally, severely lacking were well founded. The 1954 UN visiting mission, which had been briefed on the economic situation in the territory by South African UN staff member Edith Walton, severely criticized the "so-called plan."[111] The final report of the mission noted that Malagodi's plan was essentially "a catalogue of very useful public works" that lacked an overall assessment of the economic position of Somaliland and a year-by-year breakdown of developmental objectives to be achieved. Crucially, there was no detailed information as to how these public works would be financed. To the UN mission, it seemed "essential that a complete Development Plan should be prepared immediately with the assistance of highly qualified experts in each field." Only with a proper appraisal of the economic situation and an outlook for 1960 and beyond would it be possible to seek substantial foreign assistance for the soon-to-be sovereign state.[112]

Other outsiders, too, found the Italian plan unconvincing. American economist Mark Karp, for example, examined the transformation of Somaliland into an independent state as a case study of "economic problems caused by anticolonialism in Africa" for his PhD thesis, which was published in 1960.[113] In Karp's analysis, economic development was not the primary objective of Malagodi's plan. The listed projects were, above all, designed to strengthen the subsistence sector and provide security for the indigenous population, even though this would bring only slow economic progress and no substantial changes to the structure of the economy. This choice, he suggested, was motivated by "non-economic" reasons: water projects, for example, were designed to induce a sedentary way of life, which, it was thought, would make the task of providing Somalis with a modern education easier. Without education, so ran the thinking, there could be no participation in the democratic process. Karp also argued that the Italian plan displayed "limited" development ambitions because of the looming independence date and the necessity to focus on projects that could be realized before 1960.

Karp was critical of the seemingly pervasive belief in planning as a tool that allowed politicians to overcome economic realities. At the same time, he warned against the belief that more could be accomplished by going to the other extreme, laissez-faire. Inspired by the work of the turn-of-the-century Austrian economist Eugen Böhm von Bawerk, Karp simply wished to insist that the attainment of economic objectives did not depend entirely on either human will or objective economic forces. The economic policies that he himself recommended for Somaliland were further investments in agriculture, technical research, and experimentation, in hopes of making the country more productive. He advocated a trial-and-error process, which would necessarily entail failures and setbacks. Because he considered the Somali economy too weak to withstand violent shocks, he, too, argued that success depended on a large measure of international assistance, material as well as technical. Without such support, Karp opined, the decision to grant independence to the country in 1960 would be "tantamount to international dereliction."[114]

## INTERNATIONAL ASSISTANCE TO SOMALILAND

At the 1954 session of the UN Trusteeship Council, AFIS asked the world organization for foreign capital assistance to finance development in the territory.[115] In response, the council referred the matter to the General Assembly, which in turn passed the baton to the International Bank for Reconstruction and Development (IBRD), inviting it to send yet another mission of experts to study the situation and the possibilities of economic development in the trust territory.[116] It took the bank two years to produce a report on the matter, which was of rather limited help: it pointed out that, as Somalia approached independence, incentive for foreign capital to make new investments or expand old ones would decrease. At the time, the Bank itself only gave financially viable loans, so it excluded its own potential assistance, pointing out that, for Somalia, aid would have to come in the form of grants.[117]

In 1957, the IBRD report and its discussion in the Trusteeship Council was picked up in the U.S. press, including an opinion piece in the *Milwaukee Journal* titled "Attempt to Create a Nation Where There is No Nation."[118] When the article was subsequently reprinted in the *Corriere della Somalia*, there was considerable concern among Somalis that it reflected the official position of the U.S. government. According to UN officials, many Somalis had hoped for American support for their state-building project, in view of Washington's pronounced world-wide goal of fighting communism and spreading democracy. Given the sorry state of the Somali economy and the bank's prediction that it would depend on outside assistance for at least some twenty years, the *Milwaukee Journal* article argued that the UN decision to grant the territory sovereignty had been a mistake. Somaliland, the author concluded, was the perfect example of the "extreme ridicules" toward which the "irrational worship of the cult of nationalism" was dragging the modern world.[119]

A few days later, the *Corriere* printed a rebuttal of both the assumption that the *Milwaukee Journal* reflected the official position of Washington and of the arguments advanced in the opinion piece.[120] In a great democratic country like the United States, freedom of speech and press had a long tradition, the article explained, and every newspaper was free to publish any opinions it desired. Everyone knew, the author continued, that with regard to foreign aid, no other country rivaled the United States and that Washington, representing the largest among anticolonial countries, supported the political aspirations of former colonial peoples. The unnamed *Corriere* author argued that the *Milwaukee Journal* article was based on two mistakes. The first was to believe that a country could not achieve full *political* independence without economic self-sufficiency. Because most sovereign countries, including Italy, had been far from self-sufficient at independence, the assumption revealed gross historical ignorance. Historically, the *Corriere* insisted, material difficulties were overcome in time by "the moral unity of the people and the will and capacity of the ruling class."[121]

Without denying the importance of economic facts, the author noted a tendency to dismiss Somalis as inferior on this basis, now that that the assumption of a hierarchy based on race was no longer "fashionable." The article continued, "To the consolation of the obstinately reactionary and colonialist mentality has remained the so-called 'economic factor' that should indefinitely condemn us Somalis to not having what . . . we absolutely want." It was this tone of bad faith in the discourse about the "poverty" of Somaliland that the author found the most irritating. But was it true that the country was indeed poor? Absolutely not, in the pessimistic, irredeemable sense suggested by many; including those arguing for Somaliland to be annexed by other countries.[122] The possibility of economic development, albeit limited, very much existed, the *Corriere* insisted. While the situation did not allow for excessive optimism, it certainly did not justify the excessive pessimism of the IBRD report, either. To the contrary: with appropriate investments and "suitable measures," the author foresaw "vast possibilities of development in this country," and—much like the UN report—emphasized especially the agricultural and livestock sectors.

In early 1958, the United States, Italy, and, to a much lesser extent, Great Britain decided to promise substantial post-independence financial aid to Somalia to assure its continued functioning and promote the country's development. The promise was conditional, however, on the victory of "moderate," in other words, pro-Western SYL politicians in the national election later that year.[123] Italy promised expenditures of $2 million (which would mostly circle back to "metropolitan" coffers through salaries for Italian experts and fellowships enabling Somalis to study in Italy); the United States pledged $2.7 million and Britain $300,000.[124] At the time, rather than confronting a potential communist threat, U.S. interest in Somaliland was focused, above all, on containing the considerable anti-American Egyptian influence in the region.[125]

UN officials in Mogadishu were concerned that the strategy to make financial support conditional on electoral outcomes might backfire and play into the hands of Somali "extremists," who would accuse any government backed by Western bilateral aid of continuing imperialism. "I wish the history of Irak [sic] should teach us a little bit," UN principal secretary J. J. Cebe-Habersky noted in November 1958, expressing his hope that the General Assembly would recommend to channel financial assistance to Somalia into a multilateral fund under UN guidance—a proposal also supported by the Somali government, but that never came to pass.[126]

## SOMALI INDEPENDENCE

By early 1959 Italy had become increasingly anxious to disband its responsibilities in the Horn of Africa and petitioned the UN to advance the end of trusteeship for Somaliland by half a year.[127] Despite misgivings among some delegates, given the discouraging information relating to widespread poverty and illiteracy, continued tribal and boundary disputes, serious political repression of opposition parties, and limited and poorly developed resources, the General Assembly complied with the Italian request.[128] On July 1, 1960, the independent Somali Republic was born, presenting to social scientists of the day a "distressing picture."[129] Economist Mark Karp concluded: "As an experiment in the feasibility of meeting nationalist aspirations in dependent areas by setting time limits for independence, trusteeship in Somalia must . . . be adjudged a failure."[130]

Others rejected the assumption of a failed experiment of decolonization, a state failed at birth. In response to Karp's book, American political scientist Alphonso Castagno, who had studied the Italian colonies both in Italy and during an eighteen-month research trip to the Horn,[131] wrote: "No one seriously anticipated that at the end of ten years of trusteeship Somalia would have a balanced budget, a favorable balance of payments and an effective economy." Castagno rejected the conclusion "that economic laws, being 'logical laws,' set limits to what politics can achieve and that transgression of these limits can impose adverse consequences." More specifically, he rejected the argument that by granting political independence to Somaliland, the UN had in fact *hindered* the development of the territory. He, too, rejected the conclusion that—given the ostensible failure of the Somali experiment—in the future, political decision makers needed to more seriously consider the role of economic forces before making "drastic political changes." Pointing to W. W. Rostow's "competently argued" theory on the stages of economic growth, Castagno insisted that the building of an effective, independent nation-state was a decisive aspect of a precondition period before the Somali "takeoff" into modernity could begin.[132]

Other reviewers simply took Karp's book as a plea for a fuller study and understanding of the whole problem of development and for a wider recognition that there were limits to what could be achieved by political action in the field of economic development. Anthropologist I. M. Lewis, who has been referred to as the "doyen of Somali studies" and whose work was read by UN officials at the time, noted that until that point, in the "scramble for self-government" in Africa, economic considerations, which ultimately affected political autonomy, had simply not been adequately emphasized.[133] In a foreword to Castagno's own treatise on Somalia, published by the Carnegie Endowment for International Peace in 1956, editor Anne Winslow presented a somber outlook: "Sovereignty . . . will be but another step in a long, hard road, with few economic resources to hold out a promise of future prosperity."[134] The United Nations, which had taken a series of unprecedented steps in Somaliland during the period of official trusteeship, she predicted, might find itself with even graver responsibilities in the years ahead. In other words, although independence marked the official end of international trusteeship of the Somali state, in important ways it was also seen as a starting point. Ultimately, the end of the UN relationship framed Somalia as a nominally independent state, which would be dependent on continued international development assistance for many years to come.

The debate about whether the Somali state could ever be "viable" continued beyond the trusteeship period and emerged in a new form in the 1990s, when the country came to be associated with ethnic warfare as well as abstract notions of "state failure" and "state collapse." Apparently ignorant of the earlier iteration of the debate, many observers in the 1990s suggested that in 1960, the Somali Republic had looked like one of the "brightest stars" among newly independent African countries, "one of the true nations on the African continent" given its relatively homogenous culture and society.[135] While scholarly attention since has focused above all on theorizing "state collapse" and determined the role of the clan system as a cause of Somalia's troubles in the 1990s, little attention has been paid to colonial legacies, the process of decolonization, and the construction of the postcolonial state in the 1950s—or the cautionary voices at the time of independence.[136] This is not to suggest that the Somali Republic was doomed to fail from the start, but rather to call attention to the serious challenges to the state's functioning since its incipience, the haphazard way in which it was created, and the outsize responsibility that UN member states had for that process, while lacking the necessary commitment to see to its success.

---

Though in many ways unique, the UN-mandated international state-building exercises in Libya and Somaliland shared many similarities beyond the imposition of a deadline for independence. In both cases, UN officials increasingly framed state-building as a technical challenge for international experts rather than as a political process—a notion that provided a useful argument for the colonial powers that had no interest in inviting a public discussion of developmental matters. This effected a distinct warming on the part of the administrators (especially the British and the French) toward the UN, which they had initially approached with great apprehension, if not outright hostility. Italian authorities, at least those higher up in the political and administrative hierarchy, were less hesitant with regard to UN technical assistance, though they, too, rejected close cooperation with the world organization in managing the day-to-day affairs of Somaliland. While Secretariat officials had hoped that UN experts would play a pivotal role in the decolonization of the former Italian colonies, helping to build their new government bureaucracies and directing national development, in both Libya and Somaliland they never assumed such a central, coordinating role.

Yet the UN emphasis on planning for development and investment in government personnel to use existing resources most effectively proved useful for deflecting attention from insufficient international material support for the states-in-the-making. Moreover, the UN recommendation for hands-on international *technical* assistance in governmental matters in both Libya and Somaliland—which was connected to UN assistance in Bolivia at the time—anticipated both Dag Hammarskjöld's proposal for the provision of more expansive, standardized UN governmental assistance for newly independent countries more generally, as well as his fateful blueprint for managing the Congo's transition from colony to nation-state in 1960. Taken together, these efforts contributed to a new understanding of political sovereignty, according to which nation-states could farm out essential state services to international experts and depend on foreign financial assistance to pay for the state's day-to-day operations.[137]

# 4

## MOVING BEYOND ADVICE

Pioneering Administrative Assistance in Bolivia

*It was the first duty of the UN mission to find a satisfactory explanation [for the] contrast between the potential wealth of Bolivia and the failure of its people to translate that wealth into . . . a prosperous national economy. It is the belief of the Members of the Mission . . . that the explanation of the paradox is to be found in the governmental and administrative instability that has consistently marked the history of that nation.*

—Keenleyside Report, 1951

In 1953, the newly elected UN secretary-general, Dag Hammarskjold, wrote that the "exceptional character of the Bolivian programme," which the UN had recently embarked upon, "must draw the attention of everyone" even marginally interested in technical assistance.[1] As one UN memorandum on the topic explained, the "Bolivian program [was] initiated as an attempt to develop methods of technical assistance that would penetrate more deeply than most into the economic problems of the nation and into the administration of development programs."[2] As discussed in the previous chapters, UN officials in both Libya and Somaliland had indeed paid careful attention to the organization's activities in the Andes. More importantly, the UN engagement in Bolivia heavily influenced how the headquarters would come to think about the unique contribution that it could offer newly independent states to help them manage the decolonization process. When the conservative government of Enrique Hertzog had first approached the world organization for help five years earlier, it was not at all evident that UN assistance to the country would play such an exceptional role.

In the summer of 1949, Hertzog's government sought assistance in mediating a conflict among workers, mining companies, and the government in the national tin industry. A miners' strike at Catavi, one of the country's major tin mines, had previously escalated into violence: journalists and company personnel were beaten, property was destroyed, the labor minister was taken hostage and two American engineers killed. In response, the government arranged for the detention and exile of 200 labor and opposition leaders.[3] In August, La Paz reached out to the UN for help, asking for a team of experts that would appraise Bolivia's tin production, advise on proper taxation of the mining industry, and determine fair wages for the workers.[4]

Although impressed by the urgency of the issue, UN officials professed to have no "magic solutions for conflicts between labor and capital."[5] Instead, they offered to send a comprehensive survey mission to Bolivia that would examine a multitude of fields, including mining, and assess the country's overall potential for economic progress. The violent conflict in the tin industry would thus be subsumed into a larger developmental framework. Workers' demands for a redistribution of profits would be transformed into a question of national economic growth to be achieved through expert-led international development efforts. Hertzog, who at the time was struggling to stay in power amid dire economic circumstances and a barely contained civil war against leftist forces, readily embraced this UN proposition.

Once the broad development survey was underway, the world organization offered to go one step further, beyond the provision of written advice on how to cure Bolivia's socioeconomic ills. The UN not only recommended policies, but also volunteered to dispatch international personnel to implement them on behalf of La Paz. UN officials argued that the key to developmental success in Bolivia lay in governmental stability—the country had seen some 60 presidents in 125 years of independence—as well as careful governmental planning for development. To ensure the former and facilitate the latter, the world organization offered to assume trusteeship of Bolivia's governmental affairs. Foreign experts, so-called administrative assistants, were to serve as civil servants in key positions within the Bolivian administration. These assistants were meant to both reorganize the bureaucracy and see to the sound implementation of development plans. The overarching goal was incremental progressive change through the promotion of stability and long-term continuity in policies in what was perceived as a highly unstable, yet paradoxically stagnant governmental environment. The postwar state was thus promoted as the central agent of national well-being, while governance or administration was presented as science or a technical skill. Failure to achieve development called for outside intervention in governmental affairs.

The proposed UN scheme was highly contested. Critical voices within Bolivia and neighboring countries, as well as within the world organization itself, denounced it as an infringement of Bolivian sovereignty by an organization that, by its own statute, was not to meddle in the internal affairs of its member states. Several high-ranking international civil servants at the UN headquarters in New York raised objections, arguing that the plan would give ammunition to those who accused the organization of aspiring to world governance.[6] However, successive Bolivian governments—through radically different in political outlook—welcomed the dispatch of technocrats under UN auspices. Beyond the shared belief in UN expertise, Bolivian hopes that UN assistance might pave the way for financial support surely played a role. Given the governmental support for the administrative assistance proposal, this episode illustrates that although certain UN representatives lobbied intensely for this heavily interventionist program, even disregarding any Bolivian input, one can hardly speak of a neocolonial imposition on poorer countries on the part of international organizations.[7] Rather, assistance must be seen as the result of a negotiating process, involving in this case not just UN and Bolivian representatives, but also U.S. officials. Without a request from La Paz, let alone Bolivian governmental approval of the proposed scheme, there would have been no UN intervention. The world organization did not possess much leverage to enforce its vision for the country, save for the lure of expertise and impartiality, as well as its proximity to Washington.

Informally, a UN presence in their country seemed to promise Bolivians special access to American officials. Despite official announcements regarding the independence of the international mission dispatched from

New York, UN representatives arrived in La Paz via Washington, DC and mingled extensively with U.S. embassy personnel on the ground in Bolivia. Still, the UN hardly served as the covert handmaid to the "Colossus of the North." Rather, its officials developed their own prescriptions for the country's ills and lobbied U.S. representatives on behalf of UN plans. While most Americans cautiously welcomed UN initiatives, some—most importantly, the U.S. ambassador to Bolivia—were quite hostile to the world organization's efforts in Bolivia. Ultimately, Washington decided to neither oppose nor push for Bolivian acceptance of the proposed UN administering assistant scheme. American embassy officials in La Paz, however, came to accept the basic propositions of the UN position: namely, that international administrative assistance provided a potential key to developmental success. Embassy officials told the U.S. State Department that the attitude of any future Bolivian government toward the UN proposal was more important than its political orientation—a consequential suggestion.

A month after the first UN administrative assistants arrived in La Paz in March 1952, Bolivia was swept up in a revolution led by the popular left-wing *Movimiento Nacionalista Revolucionario* (MNR). To many observers in the United States, the MNR's platform came dangerously close to communism, as the party promised to nationalize the partially U.S.-controlled tin industry and to redistribute agricultural land, which until then had been owned by a tiny elite. Yet, in stark contrast to U.S. policy elsewhere in the hemisphere, Washington chose to tolerate and indeed supported the revolutionary experiment in Bolivia. The MNR's reliance on UN assistance likely played a role in this decision. Prior to taking power, the revolutionary government had publicly denounced the agreement with the UN for the provision of administrative assistance as an infringement of the country's sovereignty. Yet the MNR was deeply committed to the idea of economic development and, in principle as well as in practice, welcomed international assistance to help achieve this goal. In fact, the new regime was slow to revise the existing agreement with the world organization and de facto expanded the UN presence in the country.

In practice, UN assistance to Bolivia hardly proved as far-reaching as supporters of the scheme had hoped and critics had feared. The 1953 UN-authored monetary stabilization program was a case in point. While UN officials worked out the substantive proposal, it was the MNR government of Víctor Paz Estenssoro that decided Bolivia's policy. The principal author of the stabilization measures, Hungarian-born UN financial expert Arthur Karasz, later complained about his lack of decision-making power. The notion of a "rule of experts," of development advisors gaining unprecedented powers in the postwar period, as promoted by much of the scholarly literature on development, thus needs to be qualified.[8]

In analyzing the MNR's early reliance on international assistance, this chapter contributes to a better of understanding of the Bolivian revolutionary period. It uncovers an important antecedent to the technocratic turn of the regime, which is usually associated with International Monetary Fund–led economic reforms of the late 1950s and early 1960s.[9] By highlighting the informal contacts between UN and American officials, the chapter also sheds light on the very close working relationship between the world organization and the U.S. government—without ignoring their respective independence from one another. More importantly for the purposes of this book, the chapter recovers an overlooked episode in UN history that later served as model for the world organization's response to European decolonization and the nation-building efforts of newly independent states. In Bolivia, the UN came to pioneer a form of international assistance that went beyond the provision of written advice, and inserted foreign experts into the management of the governmental affairs of one of its sovereign member states.

## FORMULATING A BOLIVIAN REQUEST FOR ASSISTANCE

Bolivia's conservative government had first approached the world organization about the possibility of receiving assistance as early as January 1948. Yet, none of La Paz's requests conformed to the language of UN resolutions on technical assistance. The government wavered between asking for specialized assistance with individual problems and, later on, a comprehensive, developmental country survey of the type first conducted in Haiti in 1947.[10] On the recipient end, there was little coordination among the Department of Social Affairs and the Department of Economic Affairs, the two UN departments dealing with requests for technical assistance. More importantly, UN officials disagreed about how to best provide assistance to La Paz. They ultimately settled on an exploratory approach that built on the dispatch of UN officers to Bolivia to inquire about the needs of the government and help formulate a request for UN assistance. In the future, UN officials concluded, the Secretariat would need to take a much more proactive role in shaping governments' petitions to the world organization.

Beginning in January 1948, the permanent Bolivian delegate to the UN, Eduardo Anze Matienzo, had been in touch with the Department of Social Affairs about the possibility of the UN's furnishing social experts as advisors to the government in La Paz in the fields of juvenile delinquency, penal administration, and general welfare administration. All Bolivian requests, however, had referred to General Assembly resolution 58, which dealt with the continuation of social welfare services previously furnished by the UN Relief and Rehabilitation Administration (UNRRA) to countries devastated by World War II. Because Bolivia did not fall into this category, the UN Department of Social Affairs "willingly admitt[ed] that no forceful action was undertaken by it," save for the dispatch of several letters intended to elicit a reformulation of Bolivia's needs.[11]

In February 1949, having learned of the previous year's comprehensive UN survey mission to Haiti, which had taken stock of and advised on the country's potential development, delegate Matienzo approached the UN Department of Economic Affairs about the possibility of furnishing similar assistance to Bolivia. Yet again, the Secretariat asked La Paz for "a more definite and clear-cut request" and sent Mexican economist Gustavo Martínez Cabañas, then executive secretary of the UN Economic Commission for Latin American and the Caribbean, to Bolivia to sound out the government.[12] Upon his arrival at the end of March, Martínez Cabañas discussed the possibility of technical assistance with several Bolivian officials, yet found the government unprepared to give any specific definition of the kind of mission desired. In July, Secretary-General Trygve Lie received a letter from President Hertzog asking for UN assistance, "without specifying of what nature."[13]

In August, shortly after the escalated strike at Catavi, delegate Matienzo informed the Economic Affairs Department that the Bolivian government had changed its mind about the need for a comprehensive mission and now desired the advice of three UN experts with regard to the tin industry: a geologist, who would appraise the country's tin production and its possible expansion, a public finance expert to suggest proper taxation rates with regard to the tin companies, and a social welfare expert, who would determine fair wages and benefits for the workers. Given the confused picture of Bolivian requests, the UN instructed yet another Secretariat official, Venezuelan economist Manuel Pérez-Guerrero, who was then traveling in South America, to visit La Paz to determine what kind of assistance the government desired. However, his trip to the Bolivian capital in the first days of September coincided with violent uprisings against the conservative order led by the MNR. Pérez-Guerrero thus quickly left town without further clarifying the government's wishes. In late September, delegate Matienzo addressed another letter to the secretary-general, which switched the Bolivian technical assistance request squarely back to one for a comprehensive survey mission.[14]

In view of this confusion, Alva Myrdal, the Swedish sociologist and later Nobel laureate, who was then head of the UN Department of Social Affairs, deduced two important insights in October 1949.[15] First, better coordination was called for between the UN departments in handling government requests for technical assistance. Second, Bolivia had not been able to understand "the intricacies of the UN machinery" and the differences between the various resolutions on technical assistance. Government officials in La Paz had not been able to follow UN terms of reference, Myrdal wrote, because "they [had] not seen the needs of their country in the lights of our texts and in the categories we use." Instead of continuously asking them to specify and reformulate their petitions, she thought, the Secretariat should have simply framed a request for them. In future technical assistance work, Myrdal concluded, it should be up to the United Nations to advise the government, help formulate a country's needs, and teach member states how to think in UN categories.[16]

At the same time, UN officials themselves were divided over how best to assist La Paz. Myrdal, for example, thought that the country's problem was not so much one of finding new means to promote economic development, but rather of correcting the social effects of "misguided development." The sociologist suggested dispatching "a high-level personality" to La Paz who was familiar with the UN machinery, to gradually build up a UN representation in the country, which could help mitigate the labor conflict in the tin industry and the devastating effects of development gone awry.[17] Myrdal's colleagues disagreed. David Weintraub of the Department of Economic Affairs, a New Dealer who had previously worked for the State Department and then UNRRA, thought it unwise to define the problem as social rather than economic. He argued that assistance in both social and economic fields was necessary and that the two were necessarily intertwined in the broad concept of development. Weintraub and others also counseled not to "waste" high-profile officials at this point, but rather to send a "very good officer" to La Paz to find out, once and for all, what it was that the Bolivian government itself desired and how the UN might best be of assistance within its terms of reference.[18]

The UN mandate in Bolivia, an earlier memo advised, should ideally be broad. Although the Bolivians insisted that the UN focus on problems related to the tin industry, other aspects of the country's economic and social life should be addressed as well. In this way, the more contentious issues would be subsumed into a larger developmental framework.[19] To help formulate the country's needs in acceptable UN language, the Secretariat decided to send Carter Goodrich, a professor of economic history at Columbia University and former chairman of the governing board of the International Labor Organization (ILO), on an exploratory visit.[20] (As discussed in chapter 2, Goodrich would lead a very similar UN reconnaissance mission to Libya half a year later.)

Goodrich's first stop en route to La Paz took him to Washington, DC, where he consulted with officials of the U.S. Department of State, the Export-Import Bank, and the UN Food and Agriculture Organization (FAO) about Bolivia and existing international assistance efforts there. The U.S. government had started to sponsor technical assistance in Latin America in 1940 as part of a broader campaign directed by Nelson Rockefeller's Office of Inter-American Affairs (OIAA). This was intended to combat fascist influence in the region and pave the way for American commercial interests by winning the hearts and minds of the populace. U.S. technical assistance was rendered through so-called *servicios:* executive agencies attached to national government ministries, but led by U.S. directors. *Servicios* were originally supposed to provide services in fields not covered by regular government departments or by private enterprise. They were designed to attack public health problems and increase the production of vital wartime resources: they covered, for example, teacher training and health education programs; the construction of warehouses, laboratories, and health centers; and farm extension and credit services.[21]

The Export-Import Bank, the official export credit agency of the American government, had no representation in Bolivia at that time. In their conversation with Goodrich, representatives of the bank nevertheless ambitiously suggested kick-starting the country's development with large-scale population transfers of indigenous peoples from the Altiplano (the mountainous regions) "to seize the economic opportunities of lowland agriculture." The FAO had recently completed a survey of agriculture in the Altiplano and, in contrast to the bank, advocated improving agricultural conditions in areas where indigenous peoples were living. Their representatives had identified an urgent need for assistance in the areas of agricultural administration, rural credit, and the building of extension services, but wished to send no further experts to the country until the Bolivian government committed more funds to its Ministry of Agriculture.[22]

## BOLIVIA IN AND PRIOR TO 1949

Equipped with this information, Goodrich arrived in La Paz on 11 November 1949. There, he encountered one of the most unstable, indebted, unequal, and impoverished countries in the Americas. Just a few weeks before his arrival, President Hertzog had resigned amid the civil war to make way for his vice president, Mamerto Urriolagoitia, who would step up the repression of the leftist opposition. Bolivia contained a treasure trove of mineral wealth and abundant, potentially fertile soil.[23] Yet, a tiny elite—the three excessively wealthy tin magnates and, to a slightly lesser degree, the landed aristocracy, who were for the most part descendants of the Spanish *conquistadores*—had dominated the country for decades. The indigenous workforce in the countryside was, according to one historian, "almost indistinguishable from serfs," and the Bolivian tin mines, in the estimation of one U.S. official at the time, made "Russia's Siberian labor camps look like Labor Day picnics."[24] The "tin barons" resided overseas, where they incorporated and invested all of their profits. Although the landed elite lived in Bolivia ("in ease and idleness"), they displayed little inclination to invest in the country's economy and relied on imports from abroad for their daily necessities.[25]

As Glen Dorn summarized, racially charged inequity and ruthless exploitation fueled leftist opposition to the established order and left the nation on the perpetual brink of social and political unrest.[26] In December 1943, Major Gualberto Villaroel had seized control of the government in a bloodless coup with support from the popular MNR. The revolutionary party stood for social welfare measures, a redistribution of land and mining profits, and a diversification of the national economy, as well as the incorporation of the illiterate, disenfranchised indigenous majority into the Bolivian democracy. Villaroel's government thus presented a first attempt (if an ultimately unsuccessful one) to challenge the old order. He was hanged by a mob in 1946, which ushered in the reign of successive conservative governments—the so-called *sexenio*—dedicated to upholding the old order and suppressing leftist opposition.[27]

In view of the resistance of local elites and the incapacity of the rest of the population to pay significant taxes, the Bolivian state kept afloat financially mainly through customs revenues from the mining industry and foreign loans. Mineral products, of which tin was by far the most important, accounted for around 95 percent of total Bolivian exports. The "barons" controlled 80 percent of the industry. While Britain had purchased nearly 99 percent of Bolivian tin before World War II, the U.S. established a purchasing monopoly for the metal during the war, setting the price in an annual contract with La Paz. Yet the Bolivian government was not only dependent on revenues from U.S. tin purchases, but also—increasingly—on American loans to cover deficit spending to finance public works, an expanding bureaucracy, and its payments on previous loans. Between 1908 and 1931, its foreign debt soared from zero to over $60 million. By 1928, virtually all of La Paz's public debt rested in North American hands.[28]

To obtain further American loans, Bolivia had since the 1920s hosted a number of North American financial advisors ("money doctors") and had "surrendered exceptional sovereignty" to foreign financial houses and inspectors during that period: La Paz officially adopted economic regulations and practices desired by its creditors, and furthermore allowed North Americans to oversee Bolivian adherence to those rules—at least in theory. In practice, the nation often paid only lip service to foreign codes and proctors.[29] In 1931, Bolivia defaulted on its debt and turned away from U.S. models and mentors for a decade.[30]

During World War II, U.S. investment in Bolivia intensified as Washington sought to secure Latin American allegiance in the war effort as well as vital wartime resources. In 1941, the State Department offered to plan long-term assistance in the fields of communication, transportation, agriculture, mining, and currency stabilization, with an eye to increasing Bolivia's material contribution to the Allied war effort. At the end of the year, a group of U.S. government officials led by foreign-service officer Merwin Bohan spent several months in Bolivia to assess the country's needs in these fields. Around the same time, La Paz received armaments from the United States under the newly enacted Lend-Lease program. A few months later, the Export-Import Bank granted the country several loans to finance some of Bohan's recommendations, most importantly the construction of highways. The Office of Inter-American Affairs, moreover, launched public health programs in areas where rubber and quinine were produced.[31]

Yet Bolivia's most crucial source of income during the war was tin, which was used for the production of cans and armaments. After the major British tin producing areas in Asia fell under Japanese control in 1941 and 1942, Bolivia became the only secure source of ore for the Allies. When striking miners threatened to disrupt the supply in late 1942 and thirty-five were killed in a clash with government forces at Catavi, U.S. government officials—in consultation with ILO representatives—offered to dispatch an expert mission to Bolivia to mediate. (Two years before, the ILO had dispatched a British officer, David Blelloch, to advise La Paz on reforming the country's labor code. He would also join the postwar UN mission to the country.) The American initiative resulted in a joint U.S.-Bolivian investigative mission in early 1943, which was informally supported by ILO staff and led by U.S. federal judge Calvert Magruder, who had previously advised the Roosevelt administration on labor relations.[32]

Magruder thought that the crux of Bolivia's problems was the low U.S.-set tin price. Although U.S. secretary of state Cordell Hull had instructed the mission not to discuss the issue in its report, Magruder privately raised it with Hull upon his return to the United States. The judge inquired why the United States would send a mission to Bolivia in the first place when it was not willing to help out with a higher tin price. Everybody knew that the conditions in the Bolivian mines were deplorable, he wrote in a letter to Hull, but where could the money to ameliorate the situation come from if not from the U.S.? Other mission members, however, recommended a very different U.S. approach. According to Robert J. Watt from the American Federation of Labor, Bolivia's economy was almost unsalvageable. His recommendation was that the United States take the country over for a quarter of a century and run it "autocratically in the interests of revamping economic conditions completely."[33] Ultimately, few reforms were carried out as a result of the Magruder mission, but it forms part of the long history of foreign assistance and ambitious schemes of intervention in the country on which the postwar UN mission built.

## THE GOODRICH RECONNAISSANCE MISSION

In the capital city, Goodrich received a warm welcome from President Urriolagoitia, who had taken office in the preceding month. Yet, in his first meeting with cabinet members, Julio Alvarado, Bolivian undersecretary of foreign relations, whom Goodrich described as a "Spanish racialist" who was "rather difficult to deal with," argued that the UN headquarters had misunderstood Bolivia's request for assistance. La Paz had asked for two UN missions, Alvarado insisted: an urgent one relating to the mining industry, and a more comprehensive mission of the nature that Goodrich was advocating. Alvarado noted the overriding need for an authoritative opinion "on the critical and dangerous issue of wages in the mines" that would be respected by everyone with stakes in the conflict—workers, tin companies, and "extremist parties." At that time, he suggested, no one in Bolivia was in a position to deliver a judgment that would be accepted by all sides.[34] Goodrich, "impressed by the urgency of the mining problem," though afraid of not being able to offer "magic solutions," pointed out that his instructions did not cover the possibility of an urgent mining mission. He would consult with UN headquarters, if this was what the government wanted, but went on to speak of the benefits of a broad approach.[35] President Urriolagoitia, while also noting the urgency of the mining problem, soon approved of the UN-recommended broader mission.[36]

The result of Goodrich's discussions with the Bolivian authorities was a list of fields in which the UN would be asked to send experts to further investigate the country's situation and potential. "The subjects themselves," Goodrich later wrote, were "conventional enough": electric power, labor, transportation, irrigation, taxation, tropical crops, treasury, living standards, social welfare, education, mining, soils, and forestry.[37] What was new was that previously discrete interventions now appeared as component parts of a comprehensive development effort. The list of experts who had been dispatched to Haiti served as an illustration of the fields that might be included in a survey of Bolivia's potential for social and economic progress.[38] The Haiti list, however, was not presented as a one-size-fits-all solution to a seemingly generic problem of national development. Nor were the conclusions of the Haiti mission presented as a general panacea for the "developing world."[39] Rather, Goodrich's preparatory visit to La Paz ensured that the mission was tailored to the specific requests of the Bolivian authorities. He later noted, "In some cases, the reasons for the selection [of certain fields] were directly related to the dissensions and disorders at the mines."[40] The expert on administration and social legislation, for example, was to look into a revision of the labor code and the experts on public finance and mining were to determine how much taxation the tin companies could be expected to bear, while the expert on living standards was supposed to help settle the controversy over the miners' wages.[41]

While the conservative Bolivian government had sought UN assistance primarily to mediate the conflict in the mining industry, it received a broad survey mission that would advise on the country's potential for development. This was not, however, a one-way imposition of UN services on a shiftless member state, but the result of a negotiating process. Although Bolivian authorities placed overriding importance on finding a solution to the mining conflict, they were inclined to accept the broad survey mission the UN offered, as it promised, in their words, a "highly authoritative" judgment on contentious issues.[42] What was more, it provided an opportunity to change the national conversation from one centered on the conflict among government, capital, and labor to one concerning the nation's overall development. It could potentially also lead to further foreign investment. Concluding his assignment with a visit to the UN headquarters in New York, Goodrich compared his visit to Bolivia to the UN job ahead: while it was easy to win consent for the study of contentious issues, he thought that coming up with palatable recommendations and, more importantly, winning consent for their implementation would be difficult. To succeed, he suggested, the UN would need to convey a sense of unity of the mission's task. "You are not going on fourteen tasks," he told the outgoing officials, "but on one."⁴³

## THE KEENLEYSIDE MISSION

The man chosen to direct this difficult job was Canadian Hugh L. Keenleyside, a former professor of history whose research had focused on the social and economic development of the United States. Born in 1898, Keenleyside was described as a "brisk and good-looking man with an attractive plainness of delivery." He had grown frustrated with academia in the late 1920s and, after a brief stint in publishing and some time serving as a diplomat in Japan and Mexico, had become a high-ranking civil servant in Canada.⁴⁴ A journalist at the time opined that the honor of being appointed head of the UN mission "wasn't entirely personal"⁴⁵ but, to a large extent, based on Keenleyside's nationality:

> [The UN] thought it better not to have an American in charge—might rouse Latin-American prejudice against the Colossus of the North. On the other hand, industrialists now engaged in Bolivia are mostly American and the U.S. Government will put up most of the money for whatever is done; therefore they needed someone whom Americans would trust and who could speak the U.S. language. Where to find a man with these particular qualifications? There seemed to be only one answer—Canada.⁴⁶

That Keenleyside confessed to having only "an indifferent knowledge" of the history of Bolivia and even less of an idea of its current social and economic circumstances apparently mattered very little—as was customary for the UN.⁴⁷ Given the centrality of the mining issue, Keenleyside's former position as Canadian deputy minister of mines from 1947 to 1949 may have contributed to his qualifications for the job in the eyes of the UN Secretariat.

With the assistance of the UN specialized agencies, the Secretariat recruited an additional fourteen expert advisors to serve on the roughly four-month survey mission to Bolivia. They were drawn equally from

FIG. 10  Hugh L. Keenleyside

Head of the UN mission to Bolivia in 1950. After returning from the mission, Keenleyside became director of the Secretariat's newly created Technical Assistance Administration (1954).

Source: UN Photo, UN7485374

national government services, the staff of international organizations, and academia. Five experts came from the United States, six from different western and northern European countries, and one each from Canada, South Africa, and Mexico.[48] Before traveling to Latin America, most members of the mission met at the UN headquarters in New York for a week crowded with briefings, medical examinations, contract signings, individual study sessions, and conferences with journalists. The North American press took an active interest in what many—ignoring the UN's previous involvement in Haiti—described as "the first comprehensive mission to study the whole social economy of a member state."[49] The heightened U.S. public interest was likely a result of President Harry Truman's recent Point IV commitment to technical assistance, in which he had explicitly asked "all nations to work together though the United Nations and its specialized agencies."[50]

The Bolivia mission left New York on 21 April 1950 for Arequipa in Peru, where the UN officials remained for two nights to acclimatize to the altitude and to "pull themselves together," as Keenleyside put it.[51] He used the time to establish some guidelines: working hours would conform to those of the Bolivian public service (9:00 to 1:00 and 3:00 to 6:00), Saturdays were reserved for group discussions, and Sundays were off. Keenleyside warned the UN experts not to associate too closely with any national embassies in order to maintain the international character of their mission—a directive he personally chose to ignore.[52] As his travel diary shows, Keenleyside met almost daily with officials from either the U.S. or the British embassy in La Paz in the following weeks. (The latter represented Canadian interests in Bolivia, "such as they were."[53]) Through them, he arranged for his group to participate in the U.S. embassy consumer cooperative, and, more importantly, to have access to any files that would be of interest to the mission.[54] Keenleyside also mingled quite extensively with Bolivian and foreign business representatives based in La Paz. Most notably, he repeatedly met Carlos Víctor Aramayo, one of the country's three tin magnates. In contrast to the other two, Aramayo was actively involved in Bolivia's national life, as he controlled an important section of the press. Keenleyside thought positively of Aramayo as a "very cultured English-type gentleman" whose "angle on things in Bolivia... supplemented and confirmed what [he himself] had already read and been told."[55]

Aside from his contacts with embassy officials and business representatives at lunches, receptions, dinners, and bridge parties, Keenleyside also had official meetings with "various ministers" of the Bolivian cabinet, who, although "bubbl[ing] with good will," struck him largely as "pleasant, but unimpressive" and thus went unnamed in both his diary and memoirs.[56] "We heard again the same story of the need for UN assistance," Keenleyside noted after one such meeting. "It would be tiresome and platitudinous if it didn't deal with such important subjects affecting the lives and happiness of so many people."[57] None of the Bolivian officials, including the president, it appears, provided any particular impetus to Keenleyside's thinking about Bolivia's problems. At his first meeting with the president in late April, he and Urriolagoitia exchanged pleasantries and discussed "England, economics, golf, Canada, [and] various other things."[58]

Based on trips to the countryside and mining areas, Keenleyside became aware of the stark inequalities in Bolivia and the fact that "merciless poverty was endemic" to the country.[59] He believed that the big mining companies "had raped the country of its wealth for generations" and he thought no better of the landed elite.[60] In a mid-May diary entry, Keenleyside contemplated the violent overthrow of the old order:[61]

> Incidentally, a good revolution in the country with a few landlords killed and haciendas burned might be a useful step in Bolivian progress. It is difficult to see how any change in the peonage system can be effected without something dramatic of this sort.

Yet, Keenleyside also considered Bolivian workers and peasants to be ignorant "poor devils" who had no alternative government to offer, and were in any case too disorganized to cooperate in support of any cause.[62] He feared that revolution might lead to chaos, which would either enable a right-wing Peronist intervention as in neighboring Argentina or allow the left wing "to set the whole of Latin America on fire." The latter, he believed, would help Moscow and embarrass or even endanger the U.S. and its allies.[63]

Instead of advocating for revolution, he thus proposed a technocratic fix.[64] "The United Nations," Keenleyside thought, "should provide Bolivia with competent foreign administrative personnel to strengthen the public service."[65] In his view, Bolivia's problems stemmed in large part from governmental instability due to frequent changes in ruling personnel, which impeded any coherent line of policy. His opinion was that foreign administrative assistants could stay put as part of the national civil service irrespective of government turnover and, if sufficiently authorized, could carry out the sound development advice that UN specialists were to give in their respective fields of expertise.

It is unclear how exactly Keenleyside arrived at the administrative assistance proposal. He later claimed that it was based on an idea by British UN labor expert David Blelloch, who had previously visited Bolivia on the abovementioned ILO advisory missions.[66] Blelloch was born in New Southgate (London) in 1896 and read Latin and Greek at Oxford University, where he also served as vice president of the university's socialist

FIG. 11  Unnamed Laborer with Baby at Tin Mine near Oruro, Bolivia (1950)

Source: UN Photo, UN7447446

student society. Before joining the UN mission to Bolivia, Blelloch served as chief of the Non-Metropolitan Territories Division at ILO headquarters, which had just moved back to Geneva. As a permanent ILO staff member, Blelloch had already advised Bolivia on drawing up a labor code in 1940. He had furthermore assisted the 1943 U.S.–Bolivian investigative mission led by Judge Magruder as an external advisor, after which he complained to colleagues about the ineffectiveness of bringing about change through recommending legal standards.[67]

Whatever Blelloch's influence on Keenleyside, it is not surprising that the latter, as a civil servant himself, would emphasize public administration. It was indeed quite common for technical assistance experts to view their particular field of expertise as key to a country's overall development. Public health experts argued that a healthy population was a precondition for development; rural specialists insisted on prioritizing the modernization of agriculture based on the overwhelming share of that sector in national economies, and so on. On the other hand, the proposal likely was not just a result of the personal predilections of the specific UN staff in Bolivia, but part of a larger international emphasis on public administration as key to national development in the postwar period.

Following a Brazilian initiative in the General Assembly, UN member states had in 1948 officially recognized the importance of public administration as key for socioeconomic progress.[68] The Brazilian delegate had noted at the time that in recent years, the functions of government had extended more and more into social and economic fields and the complexity of administrative duties had consequently increased considerably. Without proper administration, neither the formulation of a development plan nor its execution was likely to be successful. Although critics—such as the Soviet representative to the UN—charged that administration was an aspect of government and necessarily unique to a country's political organization, UN member states ultimately agreed that the organization should provide their countries with assistance in public administration through expert advice, training courses, scholarships, conferences, and publications.[69] (See also chapter 5.)

One UN memo on public administration, dated November 1949, had found its way into Goodrich's briefing materials before he set out on his exploratory visit to La Paz. It argued that UN technical assistance should "primarily—or at least concomitantly—[be] directed to the improvement of public management in the under-developed countries." Echoing the Brazilian position, the memo noted that the growth "in number and complexity of the functions of the State [was] one of the most striking phenomena of our time . . . especially . . . in the social and economic fields." It said that the responsibilities placed on public administration had seen a manifold increase in recent years and could only be fulfilled efficiently if public administrators embraced the principles and norms of scientific management. Yet, waste, "corruption, awkward and obsolete methods, nepotism, inefficiency, even disorder . . . [plagued] many public offices, especially in the under-developed countries." Any UN plans for social and economic improvement therefore ran the risk of total failure. "All systematic efforts toward economic development," the memo proclaimed, precipitating Keenleyside's proposal, "must . . . be preceded by efforts toward the improvement of government personnel and machinery in order for them more effectively to discharge their basic function in developmental activities." Goodrich seems to have concurred with the memo's advice: a scribbled "Yes" punctuates the margin next to the suggestion to focus technical assistance on public administration.[70] Keenleyside would have likely received similar briefing materials before embarking to Bolivia.

The dispatch of foreign administrators by international organizations was not an entirely new phenomenon. The League of Nations, for example, had granted stabilization loans to Hungary and Austria in the interwar period on the condition that they install a foreign trustee who would control their finances.[71] The League had also recommended the appointment of high-level administrative assistance to Liberia.[72] Keenleyside, however, was proposing a far more comprehensive takeover of administrative functions than the League had ever realized. Aware of the controversial nature of his proposal, which would reach far into the internal affairs of a sovereign UN member state, the Canadian cautiously tested the reaction to his ideas among La Paz businessmen, diplomats, UN experts, and Bolivian politicians before approaching President Urriolagoitia himself. Keenleyside received a rather unexpected response, in that Bolivians were in his view quickly taken by his proposal, while several UN representatives raised concerns. U.S. diplomats appeared cautiously in favor of his plan.

By Keenleyside's own account, tin magnate Aramayo and other business leaders provided an "unexpectedly favorable response."[73] British and American diplomats, though largely sympathetic to his recommendations, were skeptical that Bolivians would accept them. Still, the U.S. embassy in La Paz recommended holding off the expansion or extension of American bilateral aid to Bolivia until the UN had completed its mission to the country.[74] According to Keenleyside, La Paz's social democratic and liberal opposition leaders "swallowed the foreign control idea without gagging," while Bolivian cabinet members "took it all and asked for more!"[75] (In a later edit of the typescript of his travel diary, Keenleyside exchanged the term "foreign control" that he had repeatedly used throughout the text with "administrative assistants.") He reported that the only real resistance to his proposal came from *within* the UN team of experts: Richard Goode, a professor of economics at the University of Chicago and the UN's taxation specialist, turned out to be a fairly stubborn champion of the principle of self-reliance. Keenleyside complained:

In our discussion, [Goode] went so far as to say that he would not support my plan for foreign administrators *even if the Bolivians asked for it*. It would be bad for them, therefore they should not be allowed to have it.⁷⁶

The Bolivian president was more favorably attuned to a technocratic fix of his country's problems. According to Keenleyside, Urriolagoitia agreed at once to receive administrative assistants and asked for a draft proposal.⁷⁷

The president's apparent ease in accepting Keenleyside's proposal can be explained by the rather desperate situation in which he found himself at the beginning of June 1950. While Urriolagoitia had emerged victorious from the civil war with revolutionary militias in 1949, this had motivated the U.S., which had effectively controlled the world price of tin through an independent government agency, the Reconstruction Finance Corporation, to decontrol the metal for the first time since World War II. When tin's price fell thereafter, Bolivian production declined and La Paz's revenues, which were dependent on the industry, dwindled. Bolivian tin producers chose to lay off workers, thus further fueling public discontent. In February 1950, the U.S. embassy in La Paz predicted "a complete economic collapse" if the price of tin continued to fall. Embassy officials expected Urriolagoitia's government to be ousted by the military within six months.⁷⁸

In a desperate move in April, the president had alienated the tin barons and the newspapers they controlled with a decree that had, unsuccessfully, attempted to force them to turn over their foreign exchange earnings to the government.⁷⁹ The following month, Urriolagoitia demanded the resignations of his ministers of government and labor, who had gone behind his back to meet workers' demands for a pay raise in the face of runaway inflation. According to historian Glen Dorn, Urriolagoitia was unable to find competent loyal civilians to fill the vacant positions and appointed "reactionary, possibly incompetent" military officers instead, which led to intensified labor strife.⁸⁰ Given these pressures, Keenleyside's proposal to put UN technocrats in charge of key administrative positions likely struck the president as a welcome relief, or at least as a last straw to hold onto. Moreover, he hoped that UN administrative assistance might persuade international aid agencies and lending institutions to invest in the country and, according to Keenleyside, even suggested that the proposed five-year term for foreign officials be renewed if Bolivians were "unable" to take over when that time was up.[81]

Exhilarated by the enthusiasm of the Bolivian president, Keenleyside went out of his way—traveling to New York, Washington, D.C., and Geneva at a time when long-distance travel from Bolivia to Europe required no fewer than six layovers—to convince a skeptical UN Secretariat of his ambitious plan. If necessary, he announced, he would go to UN Secretary-General Lie himself.[82] Ultimately, Keenleyside talked to several midlevel UN officials at the New York headquarters, then still located in Lake Success, Long Island, and confided in his diary that "initial reactions were most favourable as to the *desirability* of our plan but not so favourable as to its *practicality*."[83] Final decision-making was relegated to the directors-general of the ILO, WHO, and other UN specialized agencies on the Technical Assistance Board in Geneva. According to Keenleyside, they thought that Latin American countries had already been "advised to death" and thus welcomed his proposal as "extraordinary and epoch-making," with the potential to change the whole course of the technical assistance.[84]

In early July, Keenleyside returned triumphant to Bolivia. The president, he wrote, "was thoroughly delighted" and as anxious as the head of the UN mission to proceed with the implementation of the proposal.[85] The La Paz newspaper *La Razón* soon carried the first official public indication of the recommendations of the UN mission, as well as the Bolivian government's disposition to accept the UN prescriptions.[86] "I do not expect any more trouble from now on," Keenleyside concluded, "except as the result of *pressure of time*."[87] His optimism, however, proved premature.

## OBJECTIONS FROM WITHOUT AND WITHIN

On the day that Keenleyside left La Paz, President Urriolagoitia passed another decree intended to ensure greater state control over the mining industry's foreign-exchange earnings, apparently hopeful that the United States and the United Nations would support his government in this regard.[88] However, the American ambassador to La Paz, former Broadway lyricist and inventor Irving Florman, was adamantly opposed to these measures. The ambassador was moreover convinced that the UN mission was to blame for what he thought of as an ill-advised decision by the president. More specifically, Florman suspected that economist John Lindberg, the Swedish Princeton professor who had joined the UN mission as an expert on living standards, had designed the decree. (For Lindberg's later controversial role in Libya, see chapter 2).

The U.S. ambassador thought of Lindberg as "well intended," but ultimately and problematically also as "an eminent exponent of Swedish socialism."[89] He told the State Department, "The United Nations reforms are attempting to dissolve an era of good feelings and create a benign [sic] atmosphere harmful to the U.S.A." The UN mission to Bolivia, he thought, had "dealt more in personalities than in issues." Florman did not think highly of the "opinions of the eminent [UN] scientists ... from eleven countries with thirty-seven degrees." "It [was] a fallacy to assume," wrote the musical-lyricist-turned-diplomat, "that when a man developed competence in one field, he possessed expert knowledge and wisdom in all fields of human activity."[90] The UN mission's views of Bolivia, he concluded, were "without foundation."[91]

Keenleyside, for his part, had not been highly impressed by Florman on their first encounter. He recognized the ambassador as a "neophyte in diplomacy," who was "certainly a bit gauche and awkward." Nevertheless, he thought that Florman's "heart [seemed] to be in the right place." In one encounter, according to Keenleyside, Florman "talked pretty emphatically and in good heart, but not too intelligently, about some of the economic problems of Bolivia. . . . But at least" Keenleyside continued, "he is not the usual American businessman-turned-Ambassador who would be inclined to 'damn the niggers' or alternatively 'the reds' for demanding decent conditions of labour."[92]

Florman believed that if Urriolagoitia's decree went into effect, the Bolivian tin industry would be destroyed, the U.S. government deprived of the steady supply of a strategic mineral, and the Bolivian president, whom the ambassador lionized, overthrown.[93] He therefore pressured Urriolagoitia (who wrongly assumed that Florman was acting on Truman's direct orders) to meet the tin barons' demands for a "supplement" to the new decree. Urriolagoitia agreed to this, which resulted in even greater earnings for the mining elite. Florman also told Bolivian officials that they "did not need to worry about the recommendations of the UN mission because the United States would take care of Bolivia."⁹⁴ The ambassador's ill-conceived intervention and bombastic, arrogant style ultimately alienated his own embassy staff and U.S. State Department officials, as well as the Bolivian government. Yet it took the State Department another eight months to remove him, reflecting the generally low priority assigned to Bolivia in Washington.⁹⁵

Assistant Secretary of State Edward Miller expressed surprise at Florman's outburst against the UN and disavowed it.⁹⁶ Secretary of State Dean Acheson personally cabled Florman that the government was aware of the work of the UN mission and hopeful that the final recommendations now being coordinated at Lake Success would provide the basis for sound Bolivian economic and fiscal reforms, which would lead the country to stability and prosperity.⁹⁷ A U.S. interdepartmental meeting on "Economic Assistance to Bolivia" had earlier found that the idea of UN administrators "with real authority" working in various ministries worth trying and "probably the only way to force Bolivians to take measures to put the country on a sound economic and political basis." The "carrot" of "future prosperity and well-being," it was agreed, was likely not enough to incentivize Latin American countries to "straighten out their internal affairs . . . especially in the case of Bolivia." Although U.S. policy had previously insisted on self-help, the government now thought that "throughout Latin America, [the U.S.] probably [had] to help countries help themselves."⁹⁸

Keenleyside himself sought out a meeting with State Department officials on 1 September 1950, to reassure them that the UN mission had nothing to do with Urriolagoitia's August 11 decree.⁹⁹ He also assuaged American concerns about a possible UN recommendation to nationalize the tin industry, admitting that his remarks to the press upon his return to Lake Success in mid-August might have given the wrong impression. The UN was convinced, Keenleyside explained, that Bolivia needed both private and public foreign capital for its development, which in turn required a "favorable atmosphere" to investments, and therefore assurances of "reasonable treatment and continuity in policies," i.e., no nationalization. Finally, Keenleyside seized the opportunity to vent his own concerns, namely that he was "troubled by the Bolivian tendency to look to the United States 'to bail it out' of its difficulties." He believed that UN assistance could solve the country's ills, but feared it would be "necessary to force Bolivian compliance with the details of the program." He hoped that the U.S. would make it clear to Bolivia that it could not back out of "the onerous reforms needed."[100] To Keenleyside's great satisfaction, Edward Miller replied that, provided the UN program was in harmony with U.S. objectives and policies, the State Department would tell Bolivia that the United States would discontinue "handouts" to La Paz if its government decided the recommended reforms were too unpalatable.[101] Keenleyside thus successfully dodged ambassador Florman's blow against the UN mission and even tentatively secured U.S. support to force Bolivian compliance with his recommendations.

A few weeks later, however, the UN headquarters threw up another roadblock: senior international civil servants now opposed Keenleyside's proposal. In late November 1950, both Henri Laugier, the head of the Department of Social Affairs, and Byron Price, the Secretariat's head of Administrative and Financial Services, "expressed serious disagreement with and concern at key proposals" of Keenleyside's draft report.[102] The fact that these high-level UN officials raised major objections to the proposals months after Keenleyside's tour of the UN headquarters in New York again testifies to the lack of communication among the various Secretariat departments and speaks to the irony that the world organization professed to be in a position to streamline Bolivian governance but was struggling with administrative issues of its own.

After apologizing for the delay in commenting on the paper due to his difficulties with English, Laugier, a French scholar and civil servant, objected to Keenleyside's report on two grounds: first, he thought it was impermissible, or at the very least undesirable for the UN to criticize the government of one of its members, "its administration, its integrity and its politics."[103] A public exposé of a member state's weakness, Laugier believed, would cause great political backlash against the world organization, both from within Bolivia and from other member states. Second, he thought that the adoption of the proposed administrative assistants scheme would lead to disaster for UN technical assistance activities and for the United Nations as a whole."[104] The proposal would likely be exploited by UN member states that opposed any interference of the organization in national politics.[105] Until Stalin's death in 1953, for example, the Soviet Union had rejected technical assistance under UN auspices as a cover for imperialist exploitation.[106] The colonial powers, on the other hand, were critical of UN meddling in what they considered their sovereign affairs and warned against its aspiring to "international government."[107] Laugier concluded that the report of the Keenleyside mission to Bolivia should not be made public and that UN experts dispatched to the country in the future should merely act as "[c]onsultants who [would] enjoy within the Governments concerned the authority that they can win by their personal qualities." He thought that the ultimate decision with regard to Keenleyside's report should lie with an intergovernmental UN body, namely the Technical Assistance Committee of the UN Economic and Social Council, where representatives of member states rather than international civil servants convened.[108]

Price, an American former journalist who had been director of the U.S. Office of Censorship during World War II, likewise objected to the idea of administrative assistants. If UN officials were to become full-time appointees of national governments, he suggested, this would violate article 200 of the UN Charter, which stipulated that UN staff members were not allowed to receive instructions from any government. Furthermore, Price envisioned that such a scheme would bring the UN Technical Assistance Fund to bankruptcy, as "pauper governments" would come to rely on the UN payroll in great numbers. "Unless technical assistance will help only those who help themselves," he concluded, there was no hope for the program's future.[109]

Ultimately, the Secretariat referred the matter to the head of the organization, Secretary-General Tryvge Lie, who, according to Keenleyside, did not have "any deeply felt and consistent interest in or knowledge of the principles and practices of international aid."[110] Lie agreed with Laugier that the severe criticism of Keenleyside's report should be toned down. He nevertheless decided that the document could be passed on to the Bolivians as a confidential paper.[111]

## THE KEENLEYSIDE REPORT

The Report of the United Nations Mission of Technical Assistance to Bolivia, also known as the Keenleyside Report, was submitted to the government in La Paz at the end of 1950.[112] It promised to offer a general review of Bolivia's present strengths and weaknesses, its specific economic and social problems. It also offered some proposals that were intended to serve as the basis for a comprehensive development program.¹¹³ The international mission focused almost entirely on Bolivia's *national* capacities to effect change—and UN capacities to provide assistance in that effort—as if the country strove for progress in an isolated vacuum rather than within an interconnected global economy. Most importantly, variations in the world tin price resulted in frequent dislocations of the Bolivian economy. Glenn Dorn states, "To Bolivians of every political stripe, the annual tin contract with the United States," which had maintained a purchasing monopoly on the metal since World War II, "eclipsed all other international issues and most domestic ones."¹¹⁴ Keenleyside's report, however, did not address international trade relations. Aside from stressing the general need for outside investment, the world organization approached the achievement of global prosperity as essentially a national task that each member state would have to tackle individually, if with UN assistance.

After a very general description of Bolivia's economic and agricultural life, as well as its natural resources and people, the report turned to what it called the "Bolivian Paradox": the contrast between the country's potential wealth and the failure to translate its generous resources into a prosperous national economy. The problem diagnosed by the UN was governmental instability and administrative incompetence. The report conceded that this instability might be the result as well as the cause of economic "under-development," suggesting that "governmental weakness and economic debility [formed] ... two segments of a single vicious circle," a notion that prominent UN development economists such as Hans Singer and Gunnar Myrdal would later repeat in their writings.¹¹⁵ On the other hand, Keenleyside promised that progress could be spectacularly rapid under favorable governmental auspices. Indeed, anticipating the dramatic promises that U.S. modernization theorists would make a decade later, UN mission members believed it possible "to telescope into a single generation or less the economic and social advance that [would] otherwise involve a slow progression over many decades."¹¹⁶

The key, the report maintained, lay in overcoming the problem of "constantly fluctuating official policy and erratic administration." The long-term provision of a number of experienced and competent administrative officials could be a solution to this problem. On the one hand, these international officials would carry out the "hard but practical measures" recommended by the UN mission's experts in their various fields of expertise and outlined in much of the rest of the report.¹¹⁷ On the other hand, they would set out to reorganize Bolivia's governmental administration as such, to make it more efficient. In jumping from bountiful resources to the problem of administration, the UN report was able to evade addressing a number of dicey questions relating to the country's stark inequalities, such as proper wages in the mining industry or the fair distribution of land in the agricultural sector.

The discussion of the mining industry, once considered by the mission members "the most important and at the same time an exceedingly difficult aspect of their task," was buried midway through the 130-page document.[118] Until Bolivia was able to diversify its economy, the report stated, mining had to be regarded as the country's economic mainstay.[119] Instead of addressing international trade relations or wages, however, the experts focused on means to increase national productivity to keep revenues flowing. The UN mission proposed various modernization measures relating to equipment, transportation, and training as a remedy. Their report identified workers' "low efficiency" as a drag on profits and productivity. Coca chewing and "high absenteeism" on the part of the workers due to fiestas and strikes were part of the problem, but so was "the outrageous practice" of seven-day weeks and the absence of training facilities for workers, as well as the lack of a statutory code of safety regulations in an industry with an exceedingly high number of accidents, injuries, and fatalities. The report pronounced that tin companies were no longer accruing the tremendous profits they once had, suggesting it might be time for the government to reconsider its approach to the industry as a "milk cow." However, it also criticized companies for being slow "in realizing and accepting their social responsibilities" with regard to labor. The report thus placed the blame for conflict in equal measure on workers, companies, and the government. [120]

The UN mission did not dare offer any "highly authoritative" recommendation on the issue of fair wages, as the Bolivian government had initially hoped. The report merely stated that "[in] general, the miners employed in the larger mines [were] now better off than most workers in Bolivia," while "[conditions] in some of the smaller mines [were] exceedingly bad. In all mines," however, "the work [was] difficult and dangerous."[121] UN experts expressed their hope for a better understanding between the industry on the one hand and the government, labor, and the public on the other, timidly suggesting that "such an understanding [would] certainly be facilitated if the mine operators [demonstrated] more clearly than in the past their interest in assisting the general development of the country."[122] This was, of course, no revolutionary call to arms: "Even if nationalization of the mining industry were theoretically desirable," the report maintained, "it would be wholly impracticable in Bolivia under present conditions." The development of the industry would have to be carried out by private enterprise.[123]

Similarly, although the report found that the "antiquated and confused system of land tenure" in Bolivia "blocked the development of progressive agriculture," the UN shied away from advocating wholesale land reform.[124] Arguing that there was no easy solution, its experts merely recommended abolishing price subsidies on imported foodstuffs so as to encourage domestic agricultural production, and investing in infrastructure, rural credit facilities, and education. (Mass transplantation of the indigenous population from the Altiplano to more fertile regions—as the Export-Import Bank had suggested to Goodrich prior to very first UN exploratory mission—was seen as unlikely to be successful.[125]) The report ended on a final recommendation to negotiate "a firm agreement or treaty" between the Bolivian government and the UN, under which the former would commit itself to implement such parts of the mission's report "as are within its power," and the UN would agree to provide any required assistance.[126]

## NEGOTIATING AN AGREEMENT

After the document was submitted to the Bolivian government, Keenleyside personally carried a copy of it to the District of Columbia to again express his hope that the U.S. would not "undermine" the UN's work by offering to solve Bolivia's problems if La Paz did not accept his recommendations. Somewhat surprisingly, the State Department now raised serious concerns about the desirability of the "UN establishing economic trusteeships . . . in Latin American countries" and, in an internal memo, recommended to "oppose such plans wherever possible." "U.S. special interests" in the region would be at risk if the economic development of these countries was entrusted to "a heterogeneous [UN] group beyond the control of [the American] Government." In the case of Bolivia, however, things had already gone too far for any changes to be made and Washington decided to neither push for nor oppose a Bolivian agreement with the UN. Though doubtful about the acceptability of the UN recommendations, State Department officials assured Keenleyside that the U.S. had no intentions of offering to solve La Paz's problems bilaterally.[127] Similarly, at Keenleyside's request, the UN specialized agencies "reluctantly agreed not to accept requests for assistance" from Bolivia for the time being.[128]

The government in La Paz, meanwhile, faced wholly different pressures. When the revolutionary MNR and its leader, Víctor Paz Estenssoro, emerged victorious from elections on May 6, 1951, Urriolagoitia resigned from the presidency and called on the armed forces to take over the country under the leadership of General Hugo Ballivián. Expecting a fierce backlash by MNR supporters, the junta declared a state of siege, outlawed strikes, imposed censorship on newspapers, banned public gatherings, established a curfew, and detained a number of politicians, journalists, and union leaders.[129] It was not until late July of 1951 that the new military government considered Keenleyside's report, accepted it "in principle," and asked for a UN representative to be sent to La Paz to negotiate a technical assistance agreement.[130] The American embassy credited Alfonso Crespo Rodas, a Bolivian ILO employee, for having pressed consideration of the UN report by the new Bolivian government at a "propitious" time. After having been in power for some months, the junta's record in facing basic economic problems, the embassy noted, was marked with indecision, writing, "Entry into an agreement with the UN ... could be pointed to as an achievement at a time when the junta may feel the need to point to some action being taken in meeting the country's problems." Accordingly, it "grasped the straw offered by the UN with both hands."[131]

At the beginning of August, the La Paz newspaper *El Diario* published a Spanish translation of the Keenleyside Report, without any comment, editorial or otherwise. The government-friendly *La Razón*, in turn, initiated a series of columns on the topic by Crespo Rodas, the Bolivian ILO official. In late August, the junta appointed a special civilian commission to study the UN report.[132] One member confidentially informed the American embassy that the civilian group found Keenleyside's recommendations to be a "package of such proportions" that it would be impossible to implement them entirely. The commission thought that UN assistance efforts should be concentrated in three critical ministries: Finance; Mining, Petroleum and Power; and Labor and Social Welfare. They further insisted that the overall coordinator of the UN effort should be a Bolivian national rather than a foreigner.[133]

To negotiate an agreement, the UN again relied on Carter Goodrich, the Columbia professor of economic history who had led the first UN exploratory mission to the country. Goodrich arrived in La Paz in the middle of September 1951, after first having paid another visit to Washington, DC for "informal conferences" with officials of the International Bank for Reconstruction and Development (IBRD), the International Monetary Fund (IMF), and the U.S. government. The State Department thereupon instructed the U.S. embassy in La Paz "to give Goodrich and his party all aid consistent with the objective of eventual close coordination between U.S. and UN programs in Bolivia." All sides agreed, however, that it was best for the Americans not "to put on a show" for the UN representatives. "[To] do so," an American embassy official noted, "might intensify the impression in simple Juan Quispe's mind that the U.S. and the UN were synonymous."[134]

The UN Secretariat had anticipated a certain debate with regard to the status and power of the administrative assistants. Yet, according to Goodrich, the Bolivian negotiating committee was "anxious that technical assistance should lead promptly to economic aid" and was thus "fully prepared to accept" the Keenleyside Report's general prescriptions.[135] UN officials, in turn, readily agreed to downsize the originally more comprehensive list of administrative assistants, accepting, for example, administrative assistance to the Interior Ministry as too "highly political" a subject.[136] The only minor point of debate resulted from La Paz's insistence that a Bolivian coordinator, rather than a UN representative, needed to direct the administrative assistants' work. The committee considered this "essential for the purpose of convincing public opinion both in Bolivia and other Latin American countries that the Agreement involved no essential sacrifice of Bolivian sovereignty."[137] Goodrich sympathized with the Bolivian plight and cabled to the UN headquarters that the political protection such an arrangement offered far outweighed the administrative difficulties it would present. In any case, a special representative of the secretary-general would really coordinate the overall UN effort in La

Paz, while the Bolivian "coordinator" would serve as more of a liaison between the UN mission and the government.[138]

The final agreement, reached by the end of September, provided for the appointment of eleven UN technical experts and ten senior administrators, who would stay for an initial period of two years in the Ministries of Finance, Agriculture, Mines, Petroleum and Economic Affairs, Labor and Social Welfare, and Public Works and Transport, as well as in the Budget Bureau, the office of the Controller-General, the Central Bank, and the Social Security Administration. One additional UN administrative assistant would see to the general reorganization of public administration in the country in cooperation with the Bolivian coordinator. The UN administrative assistants were to have direct access to their respective ministers; they would help determine personnel policy, train Bolivian counterparts on the job, advise on organizational changes and policy, and have a word in budgeting. Yet they enjoyed no veto power over their Bolivian superiors and the government could dismiss them at any point.[139] A U.S. embassy dispatch reported that "the local reaction to the Agreement [had] been uniformly favorable."[140] All the La Paz daily newspapers had published editorials complimenting the government on the agreement. Members of the civilian negotiating committee, the U.S. embassy reported, had moreover prudently reached out to Hernán Siles Zuazo, a leader of the revolutionary MNR, in the hopes that "if and when" his party came to power, it would not abrogate the agreement with the UN.[141]

U.S. officials themselves were divided about the UN agreement, largely reflecting their own "Bolivian Dilemma." On the one hand, Americans decried "the corrupt inefficiencies" of Bolivia's successive conservative governments, as well as "the rigid self-interested inflexibility of the tin barons," resulting in continued Bolivian poverty.[142] On the other hand, they were fearful of a left-wing revolution. Some considered that the UN endeavor might be doomed from the start, for, in order to streamline the Bolivian bureaucracy, UN officials would have to dismiss "some 2,000 dead-wood employees" and thus step on too many toes.[143] Not only would this fuel opposition to the current regime in La Paz, but a large share of the resentment against outside interference in Bolivia's sovereign affairs would likely be directed toward the United States. After all, "on the part of the man on the street, there [was] still confusion between the U.S. and the UN."[144] Even Bolivian newspapers and government officials occasionally conflated the two acronyms.[145] The anti-American press in Argentina and Brazil further pushed this angle, attacking the UN operations in Bolivia as a cover for *Yanqui* imperialism, which was rapidly transforming the "unhappy Bolivian nation" into an "exploited colony."[146]

American officials accepted the UN assumption that Bolivia's basic problem was a vicious circle of government instability and underdevelopment. Indeed, one comprehensive analysis of Bolivian affairs, written by an American embassy official on the eve of the MNR's takeover in April 1952, effectively reproduced Keenleyside's argument—without crediting the UN report. The embassy's analysis, moreover, explicitly lauded the UN for attempting an integrated, simultaneous attack on a variety of Bolivia's problems rather than offering another piecemeal approach to progress. It noted that, crucially, the UN mission appreciated "that the focal point of the various bonds constricting Bolivian development [was] *political*" and "approached the *political* segment of the closed circle as closely as it could, by inventing a form of 'administrative assistance.'" Success of this experiment, however, depended on UN officials having de facto high-level influence. "No improvement," the embassy analysis noted, "[could] be expected from the mere presence of experts, however well qualified."[147] Bolivians themselves needed to realize that "a complete revamping of the national economy" was necessary. If successful, UN officials would likely encourage supplementary use of American assistance and thus effect a "drifting" policy on the part of the Bolivians toward the U.S..[148] The attitude of the next Bolivian administration toward UN technical assistance, the analysis concluded, should therefore be of greater significance for U.S. policy than its "political complexion."[149]

## IMPLEMENTING THE KEENLEYSIDE REPORT AMID A REVOLUTION

At the request of the Bolivian authorities, Carter Goodrich was chosen to oversee the implementation of the Keenleyside plan in Bolivia, in spite of earlier deliberations that the secretary-general's special representative in La Paz should *not* come from a "great power." The Bolivians themselves had asked for the ban on certain nationalities to be dropped, as they expected U.S. citizens to have more of an influence on the American government's "purse strings."[150] The U.S. State Department, by contrast, continued to worry about a conflation of the U.S. and the world organization and expressed concern about the preponderance of Americans in the UN program. In consultation with the Bolivian government, the UN Secretariat recruited administrative assistants and technical experts by reaching out to select governments (the archival evidence reviewed does not reveal which) as well as the UN specialized agencies. Before setting out for La Paz, the UN team went to Washington, DC for another round of consultations with officials from the IBRD, the IMF, and the State Department.[151]

The first UN mission members arrived in Bolivia in March and, according to Goodrich, were warmly received by their counterparts in the respective ministries. Yet, official meetings aside, the UN team encountered a less welcoming attitude. As they strolled through the city on their first Sunday afternoon, Goodrich and colleagues soon discovered that the walls in La Paz were covered with such slogans as "*Fuera el yanqui* Goodrich!" or "*Abajo el plan* Keenleyside!" ("Out with the Yankee Goodrich!" "Down with the Keenleyside plan!").[152] To some extent, such views were likely rooted in anti-U.S. sentiment, which ran high in Bolivia at the time, as the "man on the street" tended to conflate the world organization with the "Colossus of the North." More importantly though, the slogans mirrored the position of the widely popular MNR, which had publicly denounced the agreement with the UN as an infringement of Bolivian sovereignty.

Shortly before the MNR took power, however, Goodrich received the "entirely unexpected opportunity" to meet in secret with Hernán Siles Zuazo, who was preparing the party's insurrection from within the country.[153] Siles repeated that the MNR considered the UN program an attack on Bolivian sovereignty. He rejected the agreement with the world organization as illegal because it had been reached with an unrepresentative government. In principle, Siles believed in the UN's good intentions and held out the prospect of a revision of the program once the MNR came to power. After all, the revolutionary party considered itself far more committed to Bolivian development than any of the conservative governments had ever been and intended to make serious use of international assistance for that purpose. When the party indeed emerged victorious after three days of fighting in mid-April 1952 and Paz Estenssoro assumed the presidency, he quickly accepted Goodrich's offer for UN emergency assistance with medical supplies and the reconstruction of housing.[154]

While the new government in Bolivia was thus willing to rely on UN assistance, the MNR placed no priority on revising the military government's assistance agreement with the UN, despite having previously denounced it as illegal and scandalous. Paz Estenssoro did not impose a temporary embargo on the UN's work, either. His government quietly decided that those UN experts and administrative assistants already under contract should come to Bolivia as soon as possible; he even signed the agreed-upon outstanding contracts for UN personnel "in accordance with a policy of scrupulous regard for the obligations of the preceding government."[155] In other words, despite public attacks on Keenleyside's plan, once in power, the MNR not only continued, but in fact expanded the UN program in the country, albeit with new Bolivian counterpart personnel.

According to Goodrich, the "nature and tone of the new contacts differed from case to case."[156] While the Italian administrative assistant for social security, for example, was promptly sent off as head of a government mission to study social conditions in the mining camps, the Bolivian controller-general of finances "refused for six months to use the services of the able and correct Frenchman assigned to his office" by the world organization.[157] The U.S. embassy reported in late August 1952 that UN personnel were "for the most part treated with indifference" by the Bolivian administration and estimated that the UN accomplishments were "virtually nil."[158] Goodrich, by contrast, suggested that the new Bolivian government made "increasingly effective use" of UN assistance.[159] For example, international experts were involved in preparing an emergency budget, investigating social conditions in the mining areas, and drawing up a plan in cooperation with ministry officials for experimental farming stations.

When he began to notice a decrease in anti-UN graffiti on La Paz's walls, Goodrich started to push for an official revision of the technical assistance agreement.[160] The head of the UN mission in Bolivia suggested that the two central tenets of the MNR platform—nationalization of the mining business and land reform—presented new opportunities for UN technical assistance. A revised agreement could allow the world organization to venture into new realms of assistance and provide Bolivia with the opportunity to take advantage of the expanding UN financial resources. More importantly, Goodrich considered a new agreement vital for public relations reasons, and ultimately for the success of the UN program as a whole. The effectiveness and the influence of the UN experts, both within the administration and with the general public, he argued, had thus far been limited by the uncertainty surrounding the status of the agreement. This had been exacerbated by public attacks on the program in workers' demonstrations, in certain Communist publications, and also by prominent MNR politicians.

The ambiguous attitude of widely popular left-wing labor leader Juan Lechín was a case in point. Lechín marshaled the MNR's main support among workers and thus, according to Dorn, "held the fate of the regime in his hands." As opposed to Siles and Foreign Minister Wálter Guevara Arze, who favored a more gradualist approach, Lechín called for the immediate, radical restructuring of the country. In an interview with Latin Americanist Robert Alexander, Goodrich noted Lechín's "peculiar" attitude toward the UN mission: when he talked to UN representatives, Lechín had not only told them he wanted the UN to stay, but had also asked for five additional UN mining experts. According to Goodrich, Lechín had "struck up a particular friendship" with Canadian mining expert John Carman (whom Alexander described as Goodrich's chief assistant). In cabinet meetings, by contrast, Lechín reportedly demanded that all foreigners be thrown out of the country and many of his supporters agreed. Lechín's position, Goodrich thought, depended "a good deal on political pressures brought to bear upon him."[161]

After much delay, the UN reached a first informal agreement with the new regime in October 1952, resulting merely in a name change for the administrative assistants, who became "*asesores técnicos*" or "technical assistants."[162] It was not until May 1953, a year after taking power, that the MNR reached an official agreement with the UN. The new accord no longer listed the elaborate functions of the former administrative assistants, but retained their status as members of the Bolivian civil service. By and large, Goodrich concluded, "the revised agreement reflected the arrangements that had already been worked out in practice."[163] UN experts worked under the supervision of Bolivian ministers, and their assignments were more often concerned with the execution of policies than with administrative reorganization.[164]

## MONETARY STABILIZATION IN 1953

The 1953 program of monetary stabilization was illustrative of the functioning of UN assistance in Bolivia and the organization's reach and limits in the country. While the government in La Paz made difficult policy choices, the substantive preparation of the reform was almost entirely the work of UN personnel in the Central Bank and the ministry of finance. UN experts were only influential where they succeeded in convincing their Bolivian superiors of the soundness or utility of their advice. Yet, although the world organization possessed no direct leverage to force the Bolivian administration to accept its advice, the UN experts' work nevertheless proved important for securing American support for the revolutionary experiment in Bolivia.

At the end of 1952, the country continued to face dire economic conditions. The falling tin price following the U.S. trade liberalization of the metal during President Urriolagoitia's government had crippled the Bolivian economy. The long-term purchasing contract that Washington ultimately concluded with the new MNR government once Dwight D. Eisenhower assumed the presidency in 1953 left La Paz with a fraction of the revenue that previous Bolivian administrations had struggled to work with. At the same time, one of the first acts of the revolutionary government had been to retroactively increase wages of the working population by about 50 percent. Meanwhile productivity was decreasing. The resulting increase in domestic costs put Bolivia on the verge of a momentous inflation. While Paz Estenssoro was at first hesitant to take unpopular deflationary measures, in the beginning of 1953, he approached the Hungarian-born UN administrative assistant to the Central Bank, Arthur Karasz, to prepare a plan for a new, stable monetary system.[165]

In May, Karasz proposed a number of steps to reorganize the Bolivian economy. At the heart of his plan lay a devaluation of the currency, which the government introduced not as an isolated measure, but as part of an integrated net of legislation covering the entire field of monetary, fiscal, economic, and social policy. "The main purpose of the reform," Karasz explained, "was to stop the increase of consumption by creating monetary contraction."[166] To achieve this, the government simplified the exchange rate system, levied special taxes on nonessential and mineral exports, imposed credit restrictions, allowed prices to flow (save for rent and basic food items), and instituted a one-time flat-rate salary increase, followed by a wage freeze. These measures, according to Karasz, did not result in a definitive stabilization of the boliviano, but had the important short-run effect of checking the inflation for a time and allowing "business [to return] to normal."[167] The U.S. embassy likewise reported in June 1953 that the stabilization program "[appeared] to be thus far highly successful in meeting its first objective of pulling Bolivia out of an inflationary tailspin."[168]

The UN mission to Bolivia used the breathing space thus created to lobby the newly elected Eisenhower administration to support the country with financial aid. The president sent his younger brother Milton as a special envoy to La Paz, where Goodrich presented him with a memorandum on what the UN mission had achieved so far and what its financial experts expected the country's foreign investment or capital needs to be. The U.S. subsequently decided to grant $9,000,000 in emergency aid to Bolivia—"a country," as Karasz pointed out, "which had just nationalized an at least partially United States controlled industry!"[169] The "politically explosive" economic stabilization package was one condition for the U.S. to grant aid to Bolivia.[170]

From 1954 to 1956, bilateral U.S. aid to Bolivia amounted to an exceptional $60 million in the form of surplus goods, machinery, and technical advice—a clear break from America's otherwise austere policy in the hemisphere in the 1950s.[171] The *Wall Street Journal* at the time wondered why Bolivia was not treated like Guatemala or British Guiana, territories to which Washington dispatched troops to ensure that they stayed clear of communism.[172] Historian Kevin Young notes that the U.S. recognized the moderate nature of the MNR leaders in power, who promised to use foreign capital to exploit Bolivia's natural resources and gave foreign companies guarantees against expropriation and discriminatory taxes. At the same time, Washington acknowledged the country's socioeconomic problems.[173] Given the explicit recommendation of the U.S. embassy in

La Paz that the Bolivian government's attitude toward UN technical assistance should be of greater significance for U.S. policy than its "political complexion," the MNR's cooperation with the world organization likely contributed to Washington's surprising support of the regime.[174]

As Goodrich was preparing to leave the country in the summer of 1953, he took stock of the UN experiment in Bolivia. He recapitulated that the Keenleyside Report was based on the premise that the country had the natural resources that permitted extensive development but needed an efficient, stable administration to achieve this goal. Good governance, as it might be called today, was considered a prerequisite for securing foreign capital, which, in turn, was thought to be essential for national development. Aid in administration, the Keenleyside Report had concluded, was not the cure for all ills, but the point at which foreign assistance might most properly and most effectively be applied—without infringing national sovereignty.

In practice, UN officials had not necessarily confined themselves to administrative reform, but instead became involved in formulating and implementing policy. This was a far cry from the detached provision of learned advice of regular technical assistance experts, who came to a country for a number of weeks, surveyed a particular problem, wrote a report, and moved on. Yet the UN presence within the Bolivian administration constituted no actual "rule of experts," as some supporters of the scheme had hoped and critics had feared. UN officials worked under the instructions of Bolivian superiors. Only where they were able to convince La Paz of the usefulness of their advice did they become intimately involved in the governance of the country, as the example of the monetary stabilization program illustrates.

If UN assistance under the new scheme proved less controversial than expected, neither was it quite as beneficial as promised. Although President Paz Estenssoro allegedly told Goodrich that UN experts were producing results ("estan rindiendo"), the world organization's representatives themselves grew increasingly frustrated with the Bolivian development effort as time went on. Karasz, for example, confided in Goodrich in November 1954: "—*entre nous soit dit*—I continue *not* to be pleased. There is and has been a revolution, but there is *no development*."[175] Goodrich's successor as UN program coordinator in Bolivia, Mario Harrington, agreed: "Although I haven't seen any mention anywhere about the results of foreign aid in Bolivia, despite the modest UN contribution and the massive U.S. aid, one cannot claim that the experiment has been a success."[176]

A falling world tin price and the reduced productivity in the Bolivian mines after the MNR's ascendance diminished state revenues at a time that governmental social welfare spending was increasing. The resulting inflationary pressures deepened the country's economic crisis. The fact that the bulk of U.S. aid came in the form of food assistance did little to help diversify the economy.[177] Paz Estenssoro's regime responded to this challenge with an authoritarian turn. At the end of 1954, Karasz reported: "I am getting more and more concerned by the absolute lack of critique: a Bolivian is not allowed to say anything wrong about the present situation, otherwise he is an enemy of the people."[178]

As time went on, the Bolivian president increasingly came to rely on U.S. advisors. According to a U.S. embassy dispatch, Paz Estenssoro "jumped gleefully" at a 1955 proposal of the American ambassador to send a team of North American economists under the auspices of the IMF to help check Bolivia's newly soaring inflation.[179] By contrast, in the account of George Jackson Eder, the U.S. economist who headed the resulting stabilization mission in 1957, the IMF was only "invited" due to "duress and with repeated hints of the curtailment of U.S. aid."[180] According to Eder, the UN mission's "socialistic inclination" and "unfriendly political orientation" toward U.S.-favored free-market policies, as well as the "close rapport" between Karasz and President Paz Estenssoro were "responsible for Bolivia's long hesitation in inviting a U.S. [friendly] financial and stabilization team to help Bolivia put its house in order."[181]

Once Eder was established in the country as head of the newly created National Stabilization Council, he set out to undo all the "socialistic" policies that the revolutionary government had initiated in the previous five years with the assistance of the UN team. The supreme role of the state in socioeconomic management and redistribution gave way to the idea of the primacy of a free-market economy and closer integration into the capitalist world economy. The "Fifty-Step-Plan" that Eder drafted was loosely based on U.S. Treasury and State Department guidelines and centered on the stabilization of exchange rates, the reduction of government borrowing and spending, compensation to former mine owners, and the resumption of payment on Bolivia's foreign debt. The IMF plan also called for large-scale privatization of industries and utilities and a "restoration of labor discipline" through a wage freeze, the elimination of "burdensome labor legislation," and dismantling the country's "exaggerated social security structure."[182] This rollback had dire consequences for the country, resulting in national economic decline and rising income inequality.[183] U.S. policies with regard to tin and zinc were further disastrous blows to Bolivian revenues and brought about continued devaluation and layoffs.[184]

As North Americans watched the Bolivian revolutionary experiment flounder in the late 1950s, those still committed to foreign aid turned to the idea of "[increasing] U.S. control and direct involvement in daily operations of the Bolivian government."[185] Looking back on the UN "Experiment in Development" in Bolivia in 1959, Karasz wrote that "the original Keenleyside formula [of "foreign control" was] probably the only good approach. Perhaps it should be tried again with new people and in another country."[186] Indeed, Karasz was hopeful "that the [Bolivian] experiment [would] not only be repeated but even considerably enlarged," as the 1958 assembly of the UN Economic and Social Council had just accepted, "on a limited and experimental basis," Secretary-General Dag Hammarskjold's proposal for an International Administrative Service.[187] Under this scheme, Karasz hoped, foreign experts would soon be absorbed into the regular government service of various "developing countries" and at last be able to take control of global development.

# 5

# HAMMARSKJÖLD, DECOLONIZATION, AND THE PROPOSAL FOR AN INTERNATIONAL ADMINISTRATIVE SERVICE

*The long run may be very long and the need is urgent.*

— Dag Hammarskjöld, explaining the need for an International Administrative Service to serve newly independent countries in 1959

In a 1956 speech, UN Secretary-General Dag Hammarskjöld shared his thoughts about two of the major revolutionary developments of the time: the attempt to realize the principle of self-determination and the quest to improve the economic and social conditions of life for the vast majority of humanity. Realizing those twin aspirations, he declared, was one of the greatest challenges facing the postwar world, and efforts to tackle the issues on an international scale had fallen far short of expectations.[1] This chapter examines Hammarskjöld's 1950s initiative to establish a special kind of UN assistance—an International Administrative Service—that was meant to serve the particular needs of newly sovereign states emerging from colonial rule and enable them to achieve both self-determination and development. In making the proposal, Hammarskjöld built on the experience of UN administrative assistance in Bolivia discussed in the previous chapter. This chapter examines how the UN Secretariat tried to shape the process of decolonization on a global scale and how the dissolution of the European empires, in turn, affected the practice of international development assistance and contributed to a new understanding of state sovereignty in the postwar period.

In the 1950s, a rising number of states won independence from imperial rule at much greater speed than many observers at the time had anticipated. The new governments were caught between the commitment to nationalize state bureaucracies, which were mostly still dominated by former colonial administrators, and the urge to use state capacities to deliver on the manifold promises of development that had been made in the run-up to independence.[2] To assist them to meet this challenge, the secretary-general proposed creating a UN career service composed of seasoned high-level administrators who would temporarily help run the new states' bureaucracies. The feeble new polities, Hammarskjöld argued, needed a bit of "elbow room" to escape dependence—past and future, formal or informal—and establish their sovereignty on secure foundations.[3] In his view, only the dispatch of disinterested experienced administrators under international auspices, who could make the best use of both outside assistance and existing resources within a country, could guarantee such independence and ensure full sovereignty. "Fundamentally," he argued, "man is the key to our problems, not money."[4] In the long run, he was confident that national training programs would meet the personnel needs of the new states, but "the long run may be very long, and the need is urgent."[5] The UN could serve as a kind of stopgap organization, a bridge from imperial pasts to an international future.

Hammarskjöld's proposal was based on two assumptions: first, that economic development relied fundamentally on capable national governance; and second, that government administration was a skill or science that was separate from politics, and thus allowed for outside intervention without national sovereignty being compromised. Administrators merely carried out decisions, while elected officials made political choices. Hammarskjöld's initiative thus offered to simplify the complex political process of government as a technocratic question of management. The secretary-general presented UN administrative assistance as essentially unbiased and representative of a universal consensus reached by countries across political divides. A closer look at how his proposal was negotiated and reshaped by UN member states, however, reveals that communist countries' reservations were by and large ignored and that

Hammarskjöld and his staff hoped that ostensibly value-neutral UN administrative assistance would lead to capitalist development.

The International Administrative Service (IAS) never came into being quite as Hammarskjöld had envisioned it, and the UN did not play the premier role in individual decolonization processes that its representatives had vied for. While many newly independent countries such as Sudan enthusiastically supported the secretary-general's initiative, a rather odd alliance of countries acting with different motives—including "Third World" nations, imperial powers, and the Eastern European countries— ensured that Hammarskjöld's original vision was considerably reshaped.[6] The UN proposal was nevertheless consequential: it enforced the idea of the independent state as responsible for national well-being and development, as a "normal" member of the international community and as the logical outcome of European decolonization.[7] More importantly, the UN initiative tied state sovereignty to administrative capacity and suggested that the lack thereof called for outside intervention.

The eventual outcome of Hammarskjöld's proposal—the UN program for the provision of operational and executive personnel, or OPEX—assigned specialists in fields such as meteorology or broadcasting to executive posts in "developing countries."[8] It was soon copied by other aid agencies and ultimately absorbed into the regular UN assistance services with the creation of the UN Development Program (UNDP) in 1965. This evolution pushed international development assistance more generally from advisory services into an increasingly interventionist, operational role. Recovering this history helps account for the strange triumph of independent statehood as a result of decolonization—its global proliferation at a time when state sovereignty came to be a less meaningful barrier to outside intervention.[9]

Mark Mazower and Susan Pedersen have shown how colonial powers sought to protect the interests of empire by means of international organization.[10] The story of Hammarskjöld's International Administrative Service, by contrast, shows how UN officials actively supported the dismantling of formal empires and put the organization in direct competition with the attempts of colonial powers to manage decolonization and thereby maintain strong informal ties with their colonies. It also sheds light on how the officially apolitical international civil servants in New York City conceived of the role of the world organization in the Cold War battle for the development of the Third World. By providing new nations with a bit of "elbow room," UN officials hoped, these countries would naturally become more like "the West."

Under Hammarskjöld's supervision, UN civil servants offered administrative assistance as a state-building tool to newly independent governments. They did not seek to impose this assistance on member states, nor would they have been able to do so. The original UN proposal was substantially reframed through government negotiations, and OPEX, the actual operational service that emerged, was negligible in its impact. Yet the Secretariat initiative for an International Administrative Service had the important effect of prompting UN member states to redefine how government would be practiced in the postcolonial world.[11]

## HAMMARSKJÖLD, UN DEVELOPMENT ASSISTANCE, AND PUBLIC ADMINISTRATION

When recommending Swedish public servant Dag Hammarskjöld to be the new secretary-general in 1952, the Security Council had hoped for a "careful and colorless official" who would concentrate mainly on the administrative problems of the United Nations.[12] Yet, this son of a rather unpopular Swedish prime minister soon assumed the role of the "world's troubleshooter" and that of an outspoken advocate for the economic development of poorer countries.[13] Although Hammarskjöld had dabbled in philosophy and French literature as a student, he pursued a PhD in economics.[14] He studied briefly with John Maynard Keynes and was associated with the Stockholm School, a group of economists known for "proposing Keynesian policies before Keynes." In 1933, he completed a "sophisticated" dissertation on the propagation of business cycles.[15] Anne Orford argues that Hammarskjöld's economic thinking was closely aligned with Germany's "ordoliberal school," which favored administrative neutrality over state planning and expert rule over democratic interest-based politics.[16] Others described him as having "a certain inclination to patriarchism" and "an ability to let the state's guardianship go quite far."[17]

At the same time, the secretary-general had a deep sense of the inequality of nations, both in terms of opportunity and actual position. Yet,

FIG. 12  Secretary-General Dag Hammarskjöld in New York (1959)

Source: UN Photo, UN7758470

Hammarskjöld was generally hopeful that the establishment of international organizations signified a profound revolution in international thinking: the existence of a world community, for which all nations shared a common responsibility, was now generally accepted. This responsibility, he thought, entailed the duty to reduce the disparity in levels of living standards *between* nations, much as the need for greater economic and social equality *within* nations had earlier been widely accepted. He was determined that the UN, as the most democratic and broadly based international organization of the postwar landscape, should play a major role in the economic development of the less prosperous regions of the world. Echoing the basic assumptions of the UN Charter, which linked world security to global welfare, Hammarskjöld saw economic development as crucial to the foundation of a more stable global political order.[18]

His approach to attaining the goal of an international balance through the UN was a pragmatic one. Hammarskjöld noted that much more could be achieved if the goodwill that had led to the establishment of postwar international aid programs were applied to improving trade relations for "developing countries" (by, for example, stabilizing world commodity prices).[19] Yet, the secretary-general did not put his weight behind any UN initiative in that direction. According to John and Richard Toye, he even actively suppressed informal Secretariat discussion groups with government representatives that discussed such "controversial ideas," because of American complaints.[20] Instead, he hoped to work with, improve, and expand the existing UN services to promote economic development.[21] Hammarskjöld was keenly aware that the resources of the UN were "pathetically small" in relation to the vast and complex problems of world poverty. Nevertheless, he had "high hopes of the potentialities" of UN assistance and was determined that it should grow into an important vehicle for economic development.[22]

As noted in previous chapters, when Hammarskjöld took office, technical assistance, the transfer of knowledge and skills conveyed by advisory experts to requesting governments, functioned as the UN's primary means for delivering on the promise of global development. Initially UN member states' requests for development assistance from the organization were based on a December 1948 General Assembly resolution, which resulted from the initiative of Asian, Arab, and Latin American UN member states.[23] Such assistance was meant to help countries help themselves. The sovereignty of recipient governments had been the primary concern in negotiating the resolution. To prevent outside interference in domestic affairs, recipient governments were to be in full control of the kind of assistance provided.[24] Requests were addressed to the UN Secretariat, the New York bureaucracy composed of international civil servants that carried out the day-to-day work of the world organization. The Secretariat's Departments of Economic and Social Affairs then arranged the short-term dispatch of teams of experts or of individual specialists to conduct surveys and provide advice to the recipient governments. For the recruitment of experts, the Secretariat relied on personal networks and the UN specialized agencies.

To finance such "technical assistance for economic development," the General Assembly had initially allocated the modest sum of $288,000 from the regular UN budget, which was financed through fixed annual membership contributions. After U.S. president Harry Truman's Point IV call for a bold new development program under UN auspices, voluntary member state contributions to support technical assistance activities—$20,000,000 in total—were pooled in a separate fund.[25] While the U.S. commitment to technical assistance resulted in a quantum leap in terms of funding, it did not alter the nature of UN technical assistance activities. Assistance was meant to come in the form of advice or training—a transfer of knowledge—that could be taken or rejected by recipient governments. However, both governments and experts grew increasingly disenchanted with the limitations of advisory assistance. In practice, many UN development experts engaged in work that went beyond purely advisory tasks, calling this type of development work "operational" or "executive" assistance. A prospector looking for mineral wealth, for example, was not in the strict sense of the word offering his advice.

A 1957 study of technical assistance conducted by a former U.S. aid official stated that most "underdeveloped countries" felt that they had been "surveyed to death." Many of them saw successive assistance missions arrive, make a survey, publish a report, and depart to be unheard of again. As we seen in the previous chapters, this was a complaint frequently voiced in Libya, Somaliland, and Bolivia. It had become "a popular pastime" in government corridors of "developing countries," the study suggested, to make fun of these useless piles of paper.[26] Expert reports tended to be both lengthy and general, creating a daunting read that recipient governments by and large neglected. Yet length and scope, the study suggested, were not the sole reasons that such reports had so little effect: translating a broad survey's information into actual policy required a high degree of administrative competence. Unfortunately, the report argued, government personnel of the right caliber were scarce in "developing countries." Hammarskjöld's initiative for an International Administrative Service effectively catered to such concerns.

As noted in the previous chapter, the idea of linking public administration with development, and even the proposal to invest international experts with administrative power in national civil services, was not entirely new. In return for reconstruction loans, the League of Nations had dispatched resident "commissioners" to Austria, Bulgaria, Danzig, Estonia, Greece, Hungary, and the Saar Territory to influence governments' budgetary, fiscal, and administrative policies. It had also recommended similar arrangements for Ethiopia and Liberia.[27] In the early 1930s, the League was moreover heavily involved in reorganizing China's public health services and economic reconstruction efforts.[28] In 1948, Brazil initiated a discussion of the matter at the UN General Assembly, arguing that "spreading knowledge of *the art of science* of administration, [seemed] logically to be the first step in any effort for development."[29] In the preceding years, noted the Brazilian delegate, the function of government had extended more and more into social and economic fields, increasing considerably the complexity of government duties. Without proper administration, however, neither the formulation nor the execution of development plans could be successful. Anticipating Hammarskjöld's later statements, the Brazilian representative argued that the "promotion of economic and social progress depended on the human factor even more than on material resources."[30] Yet, whereas Hammarskjöld proposed the dispatch of foreign administrators to "developing countries" under UN auspices, Brazil asked for the establishment of a training and research center for international administration.

Brazil's proposal, inspired by recommendations made by the UN Economic Commission for Latin America, was supported by a number of Latin American countries, as well as India, Pakistan, and Haiti. Yet it met with strong criticism in the General Assembly. Administration was an aspect of politics, Brazil's opponents asserted, rather than a scientific system or a technical skill. There was no general method of public administration; each state had to develop its own approach. UN interference in administration—even if only through training—would constitute a direct intervention in the national affairs of its member states and thus a breach of their sovereignty. The communist countries were particularly vociferous defenders of the principle of noninterference in domestic politics. Other countries, such as Canada, insisted that the UN was essentially a coordinating rather than an operative agency: its mission was not "to distribute celestial manna in the guise of large funds or technical assistance," as the Belgian representative put it, but to solve problems between states by means of agreement. Still others, like the Republic of China (Taiwan), questioned the UN's competence, cautioning that "enthusiasm should not get the better of common sense": the UN had neither the resources nor the experience, nor even a philosophy of public administration. Poland likewise expressed doubt about UN capacities, arguing—in a surprising public bow to the West—that the organization could not hope to match established European and U.S. public administration research and training facilities. The Venezuelan delegate countered that following a single national school of public administration was undesirable and that the merit of an international center was to achieve a synthesis of different approaches. Haiti agreed, stating that the UN could not become an "international family" unless differences between its members were significantly reduced. Brazil finally expressed the hope that the organization would not "degenerate into a mere debating society."[31]

As a result of the pushback, the Brazilian proposal for a training center was rejected. Nevertheless, by a rather close vote, UN member governments decided that international technical assistance activities in the realm of administration (that is, seminars, scholarships, and the dispatch of advisory experts to requesting governments) would be permitted.[32] While not an outright success, this initiative in 1948 effectively resulted in the international recognition of public administration as a kind of technical knowledge. At the same time, it established the competence of the UN to render assistance in this field, for which the Secretariat assumed primary responsibility. International acceptance of public administration as a technical skill thus coincided with its recognition as an independent science and a discipline in Europe and North America in the immediate postwar period.[33]

Under the chairmanship of Hubertus van Mook, who had served as acting governor-general of the Dutch East Indies until 1948 (shortly before Indonesia gained independence from the Netherlands), the Secretariat convened a committee of experts to establish some guidelines, which would be published by the UN as "Standards and Techniques of Public Administration with Special Reference to Technical Assistance for Under-Developed Countries" in 1951. That same year, a Public Administration Division under van Mook's leadership was established within the Secretariat. Simply by virtue of continuities in personnel, there was thus a direct link between the late European colonial project and early UN efforts to render administrative assistance to "developing countries."[34] The new Secretariat division was to provide advice to governments regarding administrative reform and training centers, collect and exchange information on public administration, and analyze the problems of "developing countries" in the field. In the following years, the UN helped to set up several national and regional training centers and institutes of public administration, e.g., those in Brazil, Turkey, Egypt, and Costa Rica.[35]

UN publications on public administration promoted the idea that poorly structured institutions constituted a prime obstacle to economic progress. The process of modernization in "developing countries," UN writers argued, required thoroughgoing administrative reform: a transition from semifeudal or traditional arrangements to rational and efficient forms of government organization. Public administration was to be organized as a career service with selection and promotion choices being made on the basis of merit, reasonable assurance of tenure, an orderly classification of positions, a transparent salary plan, and a system of retirement. For further efficiency, governmental functions would have to be reassigned. Moving beyond the idea of rational organization, UN publications also promoted the idea that successful public administration depended on skilled personnel: namely, on experienced senior administrators who understood human psychology and would be able to foster morale among their employees.[36]

Although UN publications treated public administration as a universal science or skill, UN thinking and practice in the field, one scholar observed, was deeply steeped in the Anglo-American tradition of the discipline.[37] UN assistance in public administration was, moreover, based on the theory that politics and administration constituted separate realms. Some authors conceded that this vision "did not fit into the actual realities of life."[38] (By contrast, few Secretariat members noted the irony of the UN, with its infamously Byzantine organizational structure, claiming expertise in administrative matters.) A 1951 UN report stated that a permanent improvement in public administration could only be realized if based upon certain values and standards, such as political democracy, government stability, the rule of law, respect for fundamental human rights, and enlightened public opinion. The UN Charter, of course, precluded the organization from directly intervening in national affairs to promote these "fundamentals" of public administration. The Secretariat thus emphasized the promotion of techniques of public administration while "preaching goals and values at the same time and hoping that form [would] rise to function."[39]

The UN experiment with administrative assistance in Bolivia in the early 1950s had gone beyond the "preaching of goals and values." It provided the most immediate inspiration for Hammarskjöld's International Administrative Service proposal. As discussed in the previous chapter, a few months after taking office, Hammarskjöld opined on the "exceptional character" of the Bolivian program, suggesting that the UN experiment there ought to draw the attention of everyone even marginally interested in technical assistance.[40] Not content with merely replicating the Bolivian example (which had inspired a similar experiment in Indonesia in the early 1950s), the secretary-general advocated for the establishment of a new career service of international administrators available for immediate, temporary dispatch to UN member states.[41] The provision of this particular type of administrative assistance, he thought, needed to be readily available to interested governments without bureaucratic or legal hurdles.

## HAMMARSKJÖLD'S PROPOSAL FOR AN INTERNATIONAL ADMINISTRATIVE SERVICE

Hammarskjöld's reformulation of the Bolivian experiment into the idea for a general International Administrative Service had an immediate political cause: in making his proposal, the secretary-general was responding to, and hoping to shape, postwar decolonization. His proactive approach toward the dissolution of the European empires dovetailed with his increasing emphasis on preventive instead of merely reactive UN policies more generally. While Hammarskjöld had spent his first two years in office "quietly and unobtrusively learning the job," by the mid-1950s he was pursuing a more active role for the UN.[42] Part of his new approach of "meeting trouble halfway," as the *Economist* put it in 1960, were extensive tours to Asia and Africa to meet the leaders of newly sovereign states and "get a first hand idea of their problems."[43] It was around the time of his first such trip to twelve countries in the Near East and Asia at the beginning of 1956 that Hammarskjöld conceived of the idea for the International Administrative Service.[44] The secretary-general's trip to Asia came on the heels of the April 1955 Bandung conference, in which leading politicians of the postcolonial world had sought to assert their independence in matters of foreign policy. Government representatives at Bandung had also insisted that the Cold War was distracting rich countries from the much more pressing problem of economic disparities between nations.[45] It was shortly after the Bandung meeting, in July 1955, that Hammarskjöld argued for shifting UN attention away from the economic concerns of industrial countries and toward "the problem of underdevelopment."[46]

The first draft of the UN proposal for an International Administrative Service, which Hammarskjöld revealed to law students at McGill University in Montréal in May 1956, was written by David Owen, head of the Secretariat's Department of Economic Affairs and "midwife" of the UN's technical assistance services. Owen was born in 1904 in the Welsh town of Pontypool. He studied economics at the University of Leeds and worked briefly as a lecturer and on a range of publicly funded studies on topics such as living conditions, social services, and unemployment. In late 1941, Owen joined Sir Stafford Cripps on his unsuccessful mission to the British Raj, which was meant to secure Indian support for the Allied war effort. After a brief stint at the Ministry of Aircraft Production, Owen was transferred to the reconstruction department of the Foreign Office. In that capacity, he attended important conferences on postwar international organization (Philadelphia, Dumbarton Oaks, San Francisco), and served as deputy to Gladwyn Jebb, the British executive secretary of the UN Preparatory Commission. As deputy to Trygve Lie, Owen helped set up the UN Secretariat and afterward directed the Department of Economic Affairs.[47]

Owen's draft proposal for the IAS echoed the concerns voiced at Bandung. It bemoaned the failure of international organizations to come to terms "with the newly awakened, dynamic forces of nationalism" around the world and alluded vaguely to the Cold War as the reason for this neglect.[48] As many as twenty new states had been created during the previous fifteen years, his draft noted, "and there [was] every prospect that they [would] soon be joined by others the end of whose dependent status [was] now in sight."[49] In 1955 alone, sixteen new member states joined the UN, including five former colonies and four Eastern European countries.[50] Three African countries joined the organization in 1956, further swelling the ranks of the champions of anticolonialism.[51] Regardless of alternative political projects at the time (such as visions of "Eurafrica" or regional federations), from the UN's perspective, decolonization would result in a multitude of newly independent, sovereign nation-states.[52]

Thinking beyond the formal recognition of national independence, the UN proposal for an International Administrative Service stressed the need to establish sovereignty on secure foundations.[53] Repeating arguments that had already been made with regard to Libya and Somaliland (see chapters 2 and 3), the IAS proposal suggested that it was far too easily assumed that formal recognition of political independence equaled sovereignty. Yet, Owen's draft suggested that "the economic and social organization of all the newcomers [had not] kept pace with the evolution of their political status."[54] Most crucially, the administrative arrangements of the new polities fell far short of the requirements of an independent modern state. This posed a grave problem because the capacity of a country to absorb large-scale economic assistance and to make best use of domestic resources was "determined by the character of its administrative arrangements and by the caliber of its public servants."[55] In the final speech at McGill, Hammarskjöld added that every single UN or World Bank development survey made some reference "to the handicap imposed by poorly developed public administration and the shortage of competent officials."[56]

Noting this weakness, Owen's draft emphasized, constituted no disparagement of any of the new nations: "No one could fail to be impressed by the magnitude of the tasks with which the new leaders were grappling, or by the truly heroic character of their effort."[57] Most had had very little time to replace the colonial arrangements with their own organizations.[58] And even where former colonial powers had built up efficient administrative structures and sizeable cadres of national bureaucrats, they could "not meet the needs of peoples, whose awakening [had] stirred deeper feelings of hope and endeavor than were felt under the most enlightened colonial regime."[59] In other words, according to the UN, what was needed to meet the "revolution of rising expectations" in the newly liberated world were skilled foreign government administrators.[60]

The problem, the secretary-general argued at a press conference in Montréal, was essentially "a question of social structure." There were usually highly qualified men governing the newly independent states who were held back by serious personnel shortages further down the administrative line. Countries in Africa and Asia, Hammarskjöld suggested, were often led by a small intellectual elite who had received some form of "Western training." But there was no solid middle class, from which Western societies tended to recruit the bulk of administrators. Hammarskjöld was confident that a middle class would emerge "the moment we get the proper kind of economic and social development." He concluded, "It will grow naturally, as it has grown in the West."[61] Despite the secretary-general's insistence elsewhere that each country had to "find its own way, its own balance, its own form," the quotation reveals Hammarskjöld's ideas about the normal, desirable course of development or modernization: namely, that newly sovereign countries—if supported by the UN—would "naturally" become more like "the West."[62]

Other high-level Secretariat officials would more explicitly present UN assistance as a means to "win the Cold War." In an undated memorandum, Paul Hoffman, the former American Marshall Plan administrator who joined the Secretariat in 1959 and later became the first director of the UNDP, for example, argued that Western assistance should be taken out of the Cold War, that is, given through multilateral rather than bilateral channels, "not because it will not play a significant part in winning that war, but for tactical reasons."[63] Hammarskjöld's initiative for an International Administrative Service can similarly be read as an attempt to steer decolonization in a direction in harmony with undefined Western ideas of "proper" development through purportedly apolitical administration.

After Hammarksjöld first publicly announced his proposal at McGill University, a journalist pressed the secretary-general for his personal opinion on whether he thought any particular system was better suited than others to bring about development, presenting him with the eclectic choices of "free enterprise, Communism, Socialism, [and] Social Credit." In response, Hammarskjöld expressed his personal hope of getting "developing countries" into a system where economic life was self-sustaining, without any policy measures. "In that sense," he openly told the press, "you may find [my ideas] rather liberal in ... ideology, and [they] certainly [are] in [their] intentions." On the other hand, the secretary-general thought that even "the most staunch liberals" had to recognize that private initiative sometimes fell short of the need. The economic development of poorer countries, he argued, was a risky business rather than a safe, income-yielding enterprise. "Political common sense and responsibility" therefore had to come into play in most countries to supplement and, more importantly, prepare the ground for private initiatives.[64] While Hammarskjöld thus declared free-market capitalism the ultimate destination, he insisted that in "developing countries," international assistance in support of public initiatives would have to pave the way and create favorable conditions for such an economic system to establish itself.

In the long run, Hammarskjöld was convinced that national training programs would meet the personnel needs of the newly independent states.[65] But before this could happen, UN assistance might be the make-or-break factor in setting countries on the right path to development. In responding to decolonization, he emphasized again and again that time was of the essence: "What we need is . . . to be able to grant the assistance . . . with the necessary speed, at the right moment, when there is a kind of sur[plus]-value on all that we can do."[66] The period immediately after constitutional independence was characterized by a general uncertainty: many colonial administrators would leave the country, investors would hold back, and "metropolitan" funds would no longer be available. "The UN," Hammarskjöld offered, "should be there as a kind of stopgap organization, it [could] come in with the assistance needed during those days when assistance [was] a necessity, but when on the other hand, the government [needed] leisure to look around, to orient itself, to find its lines." The world organization, in other words, should provide the new polities "with a little bit of elbow room."[67]

Other outside assistance, especially from former colonial powers, the secretary-general thought, "[needed] the wider setting provided by the UN." He argued inconsistently that help "could then be given not as an act of patronage, but as from a senior to a junior brother, both having equal rights, self-respect and *potentially* equal status."[68] The bridge from the colonial past to the postcolonial future would best be provided by the UN, which, Hammarskjöld argued, was free of the suspicions associated with Western initiatives. Its assistance would thus come "without in any way getting that unpleasant overtone of dependence on any one country."[69] In the same vein, the secretary-general warned strongly against pushing his proposal in any paternal way: an idea such as the IAS was something that had "to be asked for, properly understood, and sponsored by the countries in need—not by the countries which wish to render services."[70] He was simply enlarging the general discussion of economic development, "bringing sharply into focus the existence of a major problem."[71] "This is the sort of case," Hammarskjöld told the press, "where I do feel that the international community has a responsibility which it could fill."[72] In the end, he said, it was up to the UN member governments to decide how best to tackle the problem.

The image of the United Nations as a bridge between imperial powers and their former territories was a favorite trope of the secretary-general. Alluding to the bridging function, Hammarskjöld allegedly once compared French relations with Africa to a good martini, telling author-statesman André Malraux that "France might be the gin, but the UN was definitely the angostura."[73] Yet, his proposal for an International Administrative Service in fact put the organization into direct competition with the "metropolitan" powers seeking to influence the newly independent bureaucracies of their former colonies. To encourage French colonial administrators to stay put beyond independence, for example, the French government allowed them to (re)join the "metropolitan" civil service once their employment abroad was discontinued. Alternatively, they could join one of two newly created corps for service abroad established within the Ministry of Overseas Departments and Territories: the *corps des conseilleurs des affaires d'outre-mer* for midlevel specialists and the *corps des administrateurs des affaires d'outre-mer* for more senior administrators.[74]

Only two weeks prior to Hammarskjöld's McGill speech, the British government had announced its determination to establish a similar "central pool of officers with exceptional administrative and professional qualifications" to be employed by London for secondment to overseas governments.[75] The proposal was only a partial victory for the British Colonial Office, which had hoped to establish a career service with a Commonwealth-wide remit to secure continuous employment abroad for all former British colonial civil servants.[76] The pool of administrative officers, however, fell short of providing the necessary long-term security that might have encouraged civil servants to remain in place in the territories transitioning toward self-government.[77] Indeed, the proposal did little to impede a "flood of expatriate retirements" as British colonies turned into newly independent states.[78]

Nigeria, the largest territory in the British colonial empire in the mid-1950s, presented a particularly pressing case. "Localization" of the administrative services, that is, incorporating Africans, had never been a priority of the colonial government in Lagos.[79] It was the prospect of a government breakdown "of mammoth proportions" in Nigeria, once the territory's self-government was in sight, that led an anxious Colonial Office to press the British Cabinet to create the above-mentioned career service for overseas administrative officers in 1956.[80] The British scheme, however, failed to attract enough colonial administrators in the country: only 400 out of 2,000 eligible officers chose to join. Faced with an impending staffing crisis, representatives of the emerging Nigerian state set out on a recruiting mission to the United States, Canada, and Europe in 1957, in search of some 600 employees. According to Heinz Wieschoff, acting director of the UN Secretariat's Division of Trusteeship, who consulted with the mission from Lagos, the Nigerians had expressed disappointment that the UN did not yet possess the means and facilities to meet their needs. The present UN technical assistance services could only serve a very different and, in their view, supplementary purpose.[81]

"The special circumstances of the African evolution," Wieschoff thought, "[made] the problem underlined by the secretary-general especially acute."[82] Numerous territories where training in public administration had long been neglected were almost simultaneously finding themselves confronted with the same pressing need for experienced staff. Popular expectations of immediate benefits from self-government placed increased pressures on administrations to provide better and more extensive government services. African governments were looking overseas to fill the gaps in their expanding bureaucracies. Yet, the new polities encountered "formidable difficulties": the market for administrative staff was highly competitive, especially in view of a rising number of countries assuming some form of self-government at the same time, and many newly independent states were not able to provide the "stability and security to match that of older countries." The new states' commitment to "Africanization," that is, educating and ultimately employing African staff, further diminished the little they could offer to overseas personnel. Wieschoff suggested, these countries could " [w]ithin reason, compete in matters of salary and housing but they [could not] offer the same *attractions of a permanent career*" to seasoned administrators as other countries could.[83] The new states' fundamental requirements, he thought, were best addressed by the secretary-general's proposal for an International Administrative Service.

## INTERGOVERNMENTAL DECISION-MAKING AND SECRETARIAT LOBBYING

Dag Hammarskjöld officially introduced the idea of the new service into the UN intergovernmental discussions through his annual report to the General Assembly in 1956. He was confident of a speedy approval, given a favorable press and his prior consultation with "key people on both sides"—presumably government representatives of potentially interested countries as well as donor nations.[84] Instead, for four years the study and discussion of Hammarskjöld's proposal bounced back and forth between various UN intergovernmental bodies: after some discussion the General Assembly referred the matter for further discussion to the Economic and Social Council (ECOSOC), one of the principal organs of the UN, which in turn referred the proposal for further examination to one of its subsidiary bodies, the Technical Assistance Committee (TAC). The TAC then made a recommendation to ECOSOC (e.g., "further study"), which then recommended a course of action (say, asking the UN Secretariat to produce a report on the topic) for referendum to the General Assembly. Meanwhile, the heads of the Food and Agriculture Organization, the World Health Organization, UNESCO, the International Labor Organization, and other specialized agencies of the UN also chimed in on the topic at the annual meeting of the Administrative Committee on Coordination (ACC).[85]

While decision-making was in the hands of UN member governments, the Secretariat worked behind the scenes, lobbying potential recipients and donor nations and tweaking reports and discussion papers on the subject. Hugh Keenleyside (who became director of the Secretariat's Technical Assistance Administration after returning from the mission to Bolivia discussed in the previous chapter) noted after the first round of inconclusive governmental debates, "This time, nothing that is possible to arrange should be left to chance."[86] Nevertheless, it took two years until UN member states could agree to start the service on an experimental basis, another for the program to get started, and yet another for it to become a permanent feature of UN assistance. The generally cumbersome operation of UN decision-making does not suffice to explain this lengthy process. Rather, the topic proved highly contentious, for in discussing

Hammarskjöld's proposal, government representatives set out to negotiate the meaning of state sovereignty and self-determination for an inherently unequal postcolonial world, and the role that international actors were to play in it.

Perhaps surprisingly, there was no neat East/West or what one might today call global North/South divide in the discussions.[87] Certain factions strongly supported the proposal from the start. Western countries without colonies presumably saw a welcome opportunity to gain influence overseas by sending their nationals abroad.[88] Ireland, for example, was "extremely interested" in the proposal, suggesting that, having never sought or possessed colonies, the Irish would make for particularly good international administrators.[89] Austria strongly welcomed the secretary-general's idea, and the Canadians even expressed an interest in "adopting" the proposal and making it a "high point" of their presidency of ECO-SOC in 1958.[90] Delegates from various potential recipient countries also welcomed the secretary-general's initiative. The Pakistani representative to the UN praised Hammarskjöld's idea as "excellent." Until national administrators "had become familiar with techniques appropriate to economic and social development," he suggested, international civil servants would be welcome.[91] The Sudanese delegate pointed out that it might be hard "for those coming from countries with long-established and efficient civil services, to appreciate the difficulties by which other countries were beset in solving the extremely complex problems of modern administration."[92]

Three groups of countries—communist, imperial, and "developing"—were staunchly opposed to the UN initiative. Communist representatives insisted again and again (much as they had done in the discussions about international support for public administration launched by Brazil in the late 1940s) that administration was inherently political and thus not the business of UN officials. "Host countries," warned the Czechoslovak delegate, faced the risk of a "birth of neo-colonialism, interference in their domestic affairs, and the impairment of their sovereignty."[93] Less loudly, socialist representatives expressed discontent with the fact that UN experts were overwhelmingly drawn from "a restricted group of countries" from the capitalist world.[94] As seen from east of the Iron Curtain, UN assistance to newly independent states was hardly as neutral as Hammarskjöld presented it to be.[95]

Representatives of European colonial powers also took issue with the vision of a proactive UN. In the words of the British delegate: "It was no function of the United Nations to act as a kind of international government." The world organization "was to provide a forum for international discussion of common problems and a channel through which help and advice could be sought." Hammarskjöld's proposed service, he suggested, might "lead to a degree of central control of under-developed countries' policies—a direction in which his delegation would not like to see the United Nations move."[96] Privately, British officials complained about "signs of 'Empire building' among members of the [UN] Secretariat who were toying with the alluring prospect of finding big important jobs for themselves and their friends administering colonial territories, when the present colonial powers withdraw."[97]

When it became apparent that arguments about the dangers of foreign control had only limited purchase with "developing countries"—particularly if coming from the representative of a major colonial power, as one UN official noted—this group tried a different strategy.[98] The Dutch delegate raised the following question: if administrative assistance of the type envisioned in Hammarskjöld's proposal had already been furnished to Bolivia, why was it necessary to speak of a new approach or call for the establishment of a novel career service? France took the same line, wondering why there was a need for separate funds; the British then argued that the UN should be allowed to make operational and executive appointments, but only under the existing terms of its technical assistance program. While the colonial powers did not want to find themselves isolated by taking a clear position in opposition to administrative assistance, one UN official concluded, they certainly tried to hamstring Hammarskjöld's more ambitious proposal and seemingly coordinated their positions for that purpose.[99]

To counter the British proposal, the Secretariat marshaled several unofficial "arguments for the corridors" and official "arguments for the conference room."[100] Within the first category belonged the statement that there was limited room for additional assistance to be provided under the existing UN machinery because 75 to 80 percent of technical assistance projects were running on a continuing basis. Only the allocation of additional funds, the Secretariat argued, would thus ensure a fair trial of Hammarskjöld's proposed approach. Moreover, in view of the pending independence of a multitude of former colonies, the secretary-general had stressed time and again that it was essential to fill existing gaps quickly and not lose time over drawn-out bureaucratic procedures that had delayed the deployment of administrative assistance under the existing program in the past—e.g., in Bolivia.[101]

In the conference room, UN representatives insisted that the difference in function of regular and administrative experts resulted in a number of managerial and legal differences that were better handled separately. For example, the Secretariat thought it was essential that governments pay for administrative assistants (whereas they did not usually pay for advisory experts) to make sure that they could hire a national officer once the UN official returned home. Ultimately, they argued, although the limited experience with executive assistance under the established technical assistance program had demonstrated the value of this type of aid, it had also demonstrated that the existing framework of technical assistance was not easily adapted to meet this need.[102]

To the delegations of India and Egypt, Hammarskjöld's proposal indeed smacked of UN overreach, as the British delegate had suggested. They thought it reflected badly on "developing countries" as a group, implying that they were incapable of governing themselves. Both countries, however, were eventually "persuaded to see the light," as head of the Secretariat's Technical Assistance Administration Hugh Keenleyside put it.[103] With Egypt, according to Keenleyside, Hammarskjöld used his personal "exceptional influence."[104] India was perhaps swayed indirectly, following the lead of FAO Director-General B. R. Sen's change of heart. Sen, a decorated former Indian civil servant and diplomat, had initially rejected the proposal for its "neo-colonial implications."[105] Extensive correspondence with Hammarskjöld, however, mitigated his initial hostility to the secretary-general's ideas.

Even though Sen was in principle supportive of the proposal, he still expressed some reservations. The most important service the UN family could render, he thought, was the training of nationals. The FAO director-general realized, however, that this could be "a somewhat long process in some countries," which thus needed additional stopgap assistance. Yet Sen strongly questioned that administrators could be readily transferred from department to department and country to country:

Administration today is a highly technical responsibility varying considerably with the department involved. Some fifty years ago [it] was a matter of the preservation of law and order and a trained administrator was competent to serve in a number of very different departments or ministries. Today [he] must have at his disposal wide technical knowledge and experience if he is to be able to render the services which governments need.

Rather than establishing a career service or a cadre of administrators, Sen argued (much like the British and French) that administrative assistance should be provided through the already established UN technical assistance program. Hammarskjöld was quick to assure Sen that his own conception of an international "cadre" or "reserve" of administrators was "figurative rather than literal." Individuals would not be employed continuously, but made available on an ad hoc basis. Only later, the secretary-general wrote, might one consider a more permanent setup.[106]

Mexico and Argentina proved more steadfast in their opposition than Egypt and India, emphasizing slightly different reasons: they were less concerned with the image of "developing countries" as a group than with perceptions of and attitudes toward the world organization. They asserted that if UN experts were involved in national governance, they would most certainly become subject to criticism, which in turn would reflect badly on the UN technical assistance program and the United Nations as a whole. The Mexican delegate could not help feeling that nothing the international administrative experts were expected to do could not be done equally well by providing advisors under the existing UN assistance program. Execution, authority, and responsibility, he concluded, should be left "where they should always be, namely, in the hands of elected national officials."[107]

The heads of the specialized agencies likewise voiced their strong opposition to Hammarskjöld's initiative. Jealously guarding their fields of expertise, the agencies were anxious to mark "their territory." The establishment of a centralized International Administrative Service, they feared, might prejudice the relationships they had already established with "developing countries" and thus impair their own work.[108] They further insisted on the primary importance and desirability of international and national administration training centers to educate national staff, instead of spending money on foreign administrators. Although the agencies had no decision-making power, their representatives sat in on intergovernmental meetings related to technical assistance, took part in the discussions, and—as proven providers of assistance—likely wielded a certain influence on aid-receiving countries.

Some countries sought to steer a middle course, or in the case of the U.S., as Caroline Pruden put it in a different context, to "balance awkwardly on the median strip in the middle of the road."[109] Americans, at least initially, showed no particular interest in this program as a desirable way of handling decolonization.[110] In informal conversations with UN staff, U.S. representatives appeared uninformed rather than hostile toward Hammarskjöld's "favorite child," as he himself called it.[111] Although avowedly "grateful and sympathetic" to the proposal, the American representative to the UN thought it doubtful that the proposed scheme was desirable to "developing countries." (Without elaborating further, he suggested that "experience in Latin America" had shown this.[112]) Ultimately, U.S. policymakers sought to square the circle by siding with their imperial allies (most importantly Great Britain) without antagonizing representatives of those countries they were simultaneously courting in the Cold War battle for the "hearts and minds" of the Third World.[113] In the classic international organization move to avoid any decision-making, the U.S. representative thus confined himself to suggesting "further study" of Hammarskjöld's proposal.

Others took a more constructive approach. The Indonesian delegate, for example, revived the 1948 Brazilian proposal for an international public administration research and training center. Though insisting that "fresh approaches" to "developing countries'" problems were needed, he rejected Hammarskjöld's vision of their simply following in the footsteps of "the West." In the absence of such an institute, he warned, the proposed career service would run the risk of being "manned by persons with outdated or invalid assumptions and preconceptions regarding underdeveloped countries" and turning into "a mere employment agency for former colonial administrators."[114] The Indonesian concerns were never adequately addressed. A subsequent Secretariat draft of Hammarskjöld's proposal simply referred back to the 1948 Brazilian initiative, pointing out that the training center establishment "had been found to be impractical." The reasoning, then, was that training was essentially a national matter: that "whilst certain general principles may be common to all administrations, the more specific requirements of particular Governments are conditioned by such factors as the political and economic structure . . . of the country concerned."[115] That such thinking ran counter to the very idea of a versatile corps of international administrators who could be employed in any "developing country," which lay at the heart of Hammarskjöld's proposal, was not addressed, let alone acknowledged by the Secretariat. The same was true for Indonesia's insistence that not only "nationals of under-developed countries" needed training in public administration, but also international administrative officers, to prepare for their work in "developing countries" so that the proposed program would not simply perpetuate colonial administration under international auspices. Curiously, the Indonesian delegation actively supported Hammarskjöld's proposal in subsequent discussions— perhaps so as not to jeopardize the large UN assistance program in the country, which, in the late 1950s, was a domestically hotly contested issue.[116]

While the Indonesian motion proved unsuccessful, other countries' recommendations carried the day. "As administrative duties frequently acquired political aspects," the Burmese delegate suggested that "it would be preferable to limit the role of the internationally-recruited specialists to purely technical matters and to speak of an 'international technical (or specialist) service.'"[117] Ceylon agreed, suggesting that the principal demand was for experts to perform executive and operational duties. Hammarskjöld was quick to reassure them that UN experts becoming involved in political issues "would be directly contrary to the whole idea of the service." The UN experts appointed would "be basically technicians. Policy [would] be the exclusive responsibility of the Government."[118]

Between intergovernmental meetings, UN officials worked hard to see some version of Hammarskjöld's proposal come to life. When the General Assembly asked the Secretariat to report on member states' views on the proposal after the first round of discussions, the international civil servants in New York interpreted their mandate to invite comments rather selectively: crucially, they did not solicit the opinions of any socialist countries. (The exception was Yugoslavia, which had contributed to and taken advantage of the UN assistance program from its inception.) As previously mentioned, the Soviet bloc had only reluctantly joined the UN assistance programs after 1953, having initially attacked such activities as imperialist and designed to exploit the resources of poorer countries. Even then, the socialist contribution to the UN assistance budget remained minimal, hovering around 5 percent throughout the late 1950s and early 1960s—as opposed to the 87 percent shouldered by Western European and North American countries.[119] UN officials clearly felt safe in circumventing the countries likely to play only a negligible role in any additional UN assistance scheme. This again demonstrates the hollowness of the organization's claim to neutrality and universal representation, and Hammarskjöld's suggestion that UN assistance was free of the suspicions surrounding Western initiatives.[120]

Before contacting potential donor countries, the Secretariat first approached potential aid recipients about their attitude toward an International Administrative Service. After gathering sufficient proof of interest, UN officials then approached potential donor nations through letters and visits by high-level UN officials to Western capitals. Initial responses collected in the UN archives appear at least mixed. Vietnam's first reaction, for example, was "absolutely unfavorable."[121] The local UN representative reported that, having recently acquired independence, the government did not wish to have foreigners on its staff. However, Vietnam's neighbor Cambodia, having likewise only recently gained independence, was very much in favor of the secretary-general's idea and in fact preferred the proposed assistance to the advisory type.[122] Ethiopia, the resident UN representative reported, was "curiously ambivalent."[123] Although the government in Addis Ababa had employed foreigners for a long time, and showed a continued interest in doing so, "there was evidently a reaction setting in to this practice."[124] The UN official speculated that this possibly owed to the fact that lending agencies such as the World Bank and the Export-Import Bank had made such "assistance" a requirement for getting loans. The Iranian government, for its part, expressed considerable interest in Hammarskjöld's proposal, precisely because it saw the proposed UN service as an opportunity to escape the World Bank's interference.[125]

Regardless of such nuances, the secretary-general was able to present the overall feedback as overwhelmingly positive because the great majority of countries—and even the heads of the specialized agencies—agreed to the proposal "in principle." Through a selective reading of responses from an already curated group of member states, UN officials were thus able to suggest that there was "overwhelming support" for Hammarskjöld's proposal. This, it appears, ultimately swayed the naysaying governments, or at least pushed them to go along grudgingly and refrain from outright opposition.

Yet the result of the extended intergovernmental deliberations, the UN program for the provision of operational and executive personnel (OPEX), which the UN Secretariat launched on an experimental basis in 1959, was no clear-cut victory for Hammarskjöld and his employees. The endless reports, discussions, and resolutions on the topic substantially changed the nature of the secretary-general's original proposal. Where Hammarskjöld had envisioned a service that would offer seasoned administrators the prospect of permanent careers, governments insisted on the "self-liquidating" and necessarily temporary nature of any international administrative assistance. Although the secretary-general had toyed with the idea of establishing a new agency, member states decided to make use of existing UN resources, namely the regular budget of the organization and the staff of the Secretariat in New York. Where Hammarskjöld had originally thought of dispatching versatile general administrators to relatively senior positions, recipient governments displayed greater interest in technicians in specialized fields such as meteorology or telecommunications to occupy the midlevel ranks of their administrations. OPEX was, in the eyes of one observer at the time, a "poor little thing for a big idea."[126]

The mere acceptance of OPEX, however, marked a significant shift in UN member states' attitudes toward national sovereignty and outside interference. "Not more than ten years ago, "public administration was considered too sensitive a topic for outside experts," a study of the topic noted in 1960.[127] Now, a majority of governments came to accept the theory that politics and administration were separate realms, and whereas the former did not lend itself to outside intervention, assistance with the latter constituted no infringement of state sovereignty. UN officials, for their part, continued to hope that form would give rise to function: that purportedly apolitical administration would serve to steer decolonization in a direction in harmony with vaguely defined "Western" ideas of proper development.

## THE UN PROGRAM FOR THE PROVISION OF OPERATIONAL AND EXECUTIVE PERSONNEL (OPEX)

Run with a skeleton staff by UN Secretariat officials and the miniscule amount of $250,000 from the regular UN budget, OPEX had a slow start in 1959.[128] That first year, only ten UN officials were dispatched under the program. Among them were a director of broadcasting, who was sent to Jamaica, a general manager at the Nepal Bank to Katmandu, an air traffic controller to Tunisia, a director for the National Centre for Administrative Studies to Laos, and an administrative director at the Finance Ministry to Panama.[129] Increasing demands for OPEX-type assistance convinced a majority of governments to end the initial "experimental period" the following year and put the scheme on a continuing basis in 1960.[130] Early skeptics such as Afghanistan came to speak at length about the value of OPEX and their own interest in such assistance. The Eastern European countries remained unimpressed, but abstained from voting rather than opposing the program. For the colonial powers, the realization that its negligible scale constituted no real threat to their ties with former colonies likely played the most important role in dispelling their doubts about OPEX.

The same year that OPEX was placed on a continuing basis, sixteen new African member states were admitted to the UN, yet only nineteen appointments were made through the program.[131] This hardly constituted the world-scale response to decolonization that Hammarskjöld had originally envisioned. Without a substantial increase in allocated funds, UN officials warned, there would be no resources to take care of burgeoning African needs.[132] The African share in OPEX at that time was high, but largely concentrated in countries such as Sudan, Libya, and Ethiopia that had a longer experience of independence. Newly independent African countries—the originally intended beneficiaries—were only just becoming aware of the possibilities of such assistance, but the UN, unfortunately, had little to offer them.[133]

Limited funds, however, were not the only obstacle to an expansion of the program. Since the inception of OPEX, recruitment of personnel under the new scheme proved difficult. Because OPEX officers served individual member states rather than the world organization, they were not entitled to standard UN benefits and diplomatic privileges, such as prolonged annual leave, medical coverage, and customs exemption. The Secretariat in New York spent much time trying to "iron out difficulties" to ensure that the conditions of service between OPEX officers and regular UN employees were equal—with only limited success.[134] Although $850,000 was allocated to the OPEX program in 1961, only $350,000 was used because of serious recruitment difficulties.[135] Even while member states' demands for administrative assistance steadily increased, the UN Secretariat thus found it difficult to convince governments of the need to further expand OPEX allocations.

At the same time, the Congo Crisis that followed the hasty retreat of the Belgian colonial power in 1960 dramatized the breakdown of public services as a result of decolonization (see chapter 6).[136] The UN Secretariat tried to harness the threat of a multiplication of "potential Congo situations" to persuade "the Governments, which [had] a principal interest in avoiding disaster (e.g., UK) ... to make supplementary [voluntary] contributions" to the UN, earmarked for administrative assistance.[137] Voluntary contributions were usually funneled through the UN Expanded Program for Technical Assistance (EPTA), reserved for regular advisory services. OPEX, by contrast, was funded through the regular UN budget, which was composed of membership contributions. This arrangement underlined the separate, experimental status of the OPEX program, but also reflected UN officials' initial hope that the service would eventually grow into an autonomous UN agency. When this prospect seemed more and more unlikely, Secretariat officials began to lobby for permission to use EPTA funds for OPEX purposes. They presented the idea by way of the Libyan delegation to the General Assembly, which approved it in December 1963. Since the Secretariat had not only prepared the Libyan delegate's speech on the topic, but also written the draft of the resolution, it claimed "a pretty large hand in getting this matter through."[138] Using regular UN technical assistance funds for OPEX appointments constituted a first step in blurring the line between advisory and operational assistance.

Another step in that direction can also be traced to the Congo Crisis, as a result of which the specialized agencies threw their initial misgivings about nonadvisory assistance overboard and set out to develop their own OPEX-type services. The UN's military and civilian response to the crisis, launched in the summer of 1960, encompassed the largest deployment of UN technical assistance to date. While UNESCO was called upon to recruit teachers and keep the bare minimum of educational services going after Belgian educators hastily left the country, the World Health Organization stepped in to staff Congolese hospitals. Subsequently, both UNESCO and WHO began discussing the provision of teachers and doctors as necessary operational assistance to newly independent states more generally.[139] The task at hand, as they came to see it, was not so much to build up or develop new services, but to prevent the collapse of existing ones.[140]

OPEX also had repercussions beyond the realm of the UN system. In 1964, the Organization for Economic Co-operation and Development (OECD) organized a conference to discuss technical assistance to East Africa, including the provision of operational personnel. According to one UN official, delegates "[drew] heavily upon UN forms of agreement and contract for defining the terms and conditions of service for both advisory . . . and operational personnel."[141]

Hammarskjöld and his employees were initially unhappy about the proliferation of OPEX-like schemes outside the immediate purview of the UN Secretariat.[142] They feared that a loss of Secretariat control and alternating conditions of service would lead to a general blurring of lines between advisory and operational experts. They were anxious because "bars [would] be dropped so that technical assistance advisors [could] freely serve in an OPEX-like capacity" without the necessary safeguards that protected OPEX officers from national jurisdictions.[143] Furthermore, important aspects of the original OPEX program, such as on-the-job training of national counterparts or the fact that countries had to pay for foreign specialists themselves so that they would budget accordingly and eventually fill the post with national staff, would be lost as a result of this blurring of lines. Yet UN officials conceded that a great need for operational personnel in newly independent states existed, a need that could never be satisfied with the meager resources of the OPEX program (even if supported by EPTA funds).[144] The more operational posts were on offer, they concluded, the better the needs of newly sovereign states could be met.[145] Some even thought that, if the specialized agencies established their own programs, this would allow the Secretariat to reserve their own funds for operational personnel for high-level executive posts.[146]

Staffing high-level administrative posts, as well as "a massive appeal" for the UN to respond to the needs of newly independent states, remained wishful thinking on the part of the Secretariat.[147] A 1967 in-house evaluation of UN operational assistance noted that "bilateral assistance of the OPEX type far [exceeded] OPEX assistance provided under the programs of the United Nations family."[148] In French-speaking Africa, only one or two countries received OPEX assistance from the "UN family," and that on a modest scale. The English-speaking countries were the predominant users of OPEX assistance furnished by the UN and the specialized agencies, but they, too, depended far more on bilateral assistance. Governments of virtually all African countries that had gained independence since World War II, as well as some countries in Asia and the Far East, made extensive use of OPEX-type services. Yet in practice these governments preferred bilateral over UN assistance because it allowed them to arrange appointments more quickly and with greater flexibility in terms of extensions.[149]

Another study, conducted for the Ford Foundation, noted that, in 1962–63, about half of the British government's technical assistance expenditure of no less than £25 million was spent on British personnel in public service posts employed by overseas governments. In East Africa, 90 percent of British technical assistance in these years was of that sort.[150] The study noted that large numbers of experts dispatched to "developing countries" were employed as engineers, policemen, tax collectors, doctors, veterinary or agricultural officers, and the like, continuing jobs they had previously held under the colonial regimes. The study concluded, "Many of them do not 'advise' or 'train counterparts'; they 'do the job.' In actual practice, technical assistance programs are not exclusively concerned with technical matters, nor only with teaching and advising."[151] The UN program did not fare better with regard to training. The 1967 in-house evaluation noted that more than half of the 165 OPEX officers in service at the time of writing did not even have "counterpart personnel," whom they were supposed to train on the job to eventually take over. Nevertheless, the report suggested soberly that "experts appear[ed] to function satisfactorily." Without noting the irony, the evaluation stated that the international officers—who had originally been summoned to help the newly sovereign states build proper administrations—functioned best where "reasonably modern" administrative structures already existed.

Despite these failures, the increasing reliance of governments on the OPEX program nevertheless affirmed the value of this type of assistance in the eyes of the United Nations. By 1964, the once-controversial operational services were considered a regular feature of UN assistance, as the head of the Secretariat's OPEX division pointed out: "It seems significant that the [1964 UN report on technical assistance] makes no mention of OPEX as such." If the report was any indication, he continued, the original idea behind OPEX, namely that the provision of operational, executive, and administrative personnel should be considered a *supplementary* form of technical assistance in public administration, appeared to have been completely abandoned. OPEX assistance now seemed to be treated as one technique of technical assistance more generally.[152] When the various technical assistance programs of the UN were converted into the UNDP in 1965, the organization found "ample justification for making the OPEX form of assistance," originally intended to serve as a temporary, post-independence bridge for newly independent states, "an integral part of the assistance normally provided by the [program]."[153] Semantically, "aid" turned into "cooperation" in the 1960s; in practice, development took a paternalist turn.[154]

Although Hammarskjöld presented the UN as the twentieth-century bridge between European "metropoles" and their overseas territories, his suggested response to decolonization at the level of international organization instead put the UN in direct competition with the services offered by imperial powers designed to maintain ties with their former colonies. Ultimately, however, the UN was unable to compete with the (former) colonial powers in the realm of public administration. While Hammarskjöld's proposal did not result in the large-scale response to decolonization that he had hoped for, his action was nevertheless far from inconsequential. The secretary-general's initiative ultimately helped bring about a substantial shift of international attitudes toward international development assistance: from the insistence on advisory services and the idea of helping countries help themselves to a more paternalist approach that focused on "getting the work done" on behalf of aid recipients. A mix of frustration on the part of experts and civil servants about advice not being taken, as well as the feeling in "developing countries'" governments of being "surveyed to death," contributed to this change in attitude during the first fifteen years of UN assistance services.

In practice, the line between advisory and operational development activities had never been as clear-cut as technical assistance theory purported it to be, but the Secretariat had hoped to achieve a separation between the two—and an official recognition of the difference—through the establishment of OPEX. Instead, the eventual dissolution of OPEX within the existing UN technical program and the proliferation of OPEX-type services within the wider UN system and beyond blurred the lines between the different types of assistance and officially sanctioned a more interventionist approach to international development as common practice. Ultimately, the UN was not important because of the immediate, practical impact of these and other development programs. Rather, the organization was influential in setting certain norms: UN initiatives and debates shaped what was soon recognized as the "natural" course of decolonization, the needs of a newly independent or "developing" state, and the range of acceptable practices to meet these needs.

Scholars have argued that postwar internationalism sprang from a conviction that the nation-state system was becoming increasingly obsolete.[155] This chapter, by contrast, suggests that the establishment of UN development aid not only acknowledged the primacy of that system, but also supported the proliferation of state sovereignty on a global scale.[156] If, as recent scholarship has stressed, this outcome was far from preordained at the outset of decolonization, the questions of why this explosion of state sovereignty happened in the 1950s and 1960s and what kind of sovereignties emerged become all the more pressing.[157] The UN played a considerable role in that process. Under Dag Hammarskjöld's lead, civil servants in New York shackled the realization of self-determination and the improvement of living standards to state sovereignty. They presented the independent state as the natural outcome of decolonization and people's aspirations, and as the prime agent for development. State sovereignty, however, was tied to administrative capacity, and a lack thereof necessitated outside intervention. The story of the UN proposal for an International Administrative Service thus helps to account for the renegotiation of the meaning of state sovereignty as a result of decolonization and the active role that international actors would come to play in the governance of the "developing world" in the second half of the twentieth century.

# 6

## STATE-BUILDING MEETS PEACEKEEPING

The UN Civilian Operations in the Congo Crisis, 1960–1964

*You try to save a drowning man without prior authorization and even if he resists you; you do not let him go even when he tries to strangle you.*

Dag Hammarskjöld explaining his perspective on the UN operations in the Congo to the General Assembly in October 1960

UN officials across the board agreed that the Congo crisis, which unfolded shortly after the central African country gained independence from Belgium in the summer of 1960, presented the most difficult challenge that the world organization had faced to date. Yet they also saw it as the most significant opportunity to prove the UN's worth, in defusing a potential Cold War powder keg, but above all in managing decolonization. To UN officials, it was a make-or-break point in the organization's history, with the potential to usher in a new era for postcolonial countries.[1]

There is a vast amount of literature on the Congo crisis. While many accounts focus on the role of foreign interests, especially the Cold War superpowers, comparatively little attention has been paid to the United Nations, although, given its large-scale peacekeeping intervention from 1960 to 1964, the *Operation de Nations Unies au Congo* (ONUC), the organization was arguably a central player in the unfolding of the crisis.[2] Existing discussions of ONUC are primarily concerned with the

STATE-BUILDING MEETS PEACEKEEPING 199

high-level political and military decision-making of UN officials and how it was inflected by Cold War dynamics.³ This chapter shows how ONUC was crucially shaped by Secretary-General Dag Hammarskjöld's broader vision of the role that the UN should play in managing decolonization. Hammarskjöld thought that the UN was ideally suited to simultaneously manage and reform newly independent states by taking over the state bureaucracy and thus set them on the path to "proper" Western-style development. A UN commitment in the Congo, he thought, would serve the twin purpose of keeping the Cold War at a distance, while overcoming the vestiges of colonialism.

It is seldom noted that the UN's concern for the Congo predated the unfolding of the postindependence crisis. Hammarskjöld visited the Belgian colony on a tour through Africa in January 1960, five months before the scheduled independence date, and reportedly predicted an immense need for international assistance. In April, Congolese representatives approached the world organization in New York to explore possibilities for UN assistance in military matters. Secretariat officials reformulated the Congolese appeal as a request for "technical assistance in security administration" to prevent the involvement of the UN Security Council—the intergovernmental body officially responsible for matters of war and peace, which was largely paralyzed by Cold War tensions at the time. More importantly, the Secretariat offered to embed this UN assistance in "security administration" in a much broader program designed to manage and reform the newly independent state. In effect, Hammarskjöld sought to seize the Congo's rushed independence to showcase the world organization's ability to handle decolonization by providing high-level administrative and technical assistance in a broad number of fields in which it expected a modern state to engage, ranging from health to education, from public finance to judicature.

Hammarskjöld's original plans were, however, quickly overtaken by the multifaceted crisis that followed the Congolese declaration of independence on June 30, 1960. When the Armée Nationale Congolaise (ANC) mutinied a few days after the June celebrations, Belgium intervened militarily, and the province of Katanga, the Congo's economic powerhouse, announced its secession. These actions in turn prompted the Congolese government to officially request the dispatch of UN troops to the Congo, thus bringing the crisis before the Security Council. The council approved the Congolese request in a rare moment of Cold War agreement. Instead of seeing his original plans frustrated, Hammarskjöld then seized the Security Council–sanctioned UN military intervention as an opportunity to simultaneously launch a highly autonomous large-scale civilian operation intended to manage and develop the newly independent state.

The secretary-general expanded the world organization's goals in the Congo well beyond the policing function of previous UN peacekeeping missions. The UN presence would not simply allow for the retreat of foreign troops, as its forces had in the Suez Crisis.[4] What Hammarskjöld envisioned for the Congo was effectively a "transformative occupation" that would "modernize" the country with UN guidance.[5] By drawing on the combined strength of the "UN family" of programs and specialized agencies, ONUC sought to build up a parallel administrative structure to the Congolese state. The goal was to prevent famine, pestilence, and other humanitarian disasters; to maintain basic public services in such fields as health, education, transport, and communications, which the colonial government had previously provided; to reform the Congo's administration, legal system, and public services to suit a newly independent state; and to train a Congolese elite that could eventually take over "the government machinery."[6] In many ways, this UN civilian program was a culmination of the (largely unrealized) plans to manage national governments for the sake of development that the world organization had previously introduced in Libya and Bolivia and with the UN program for the provision of operational and executive personnel (OPEX).

ONUC pursued its hugely ambitious project in the Congo on a shoestring budget, with negligible intelligence about the country and, ultimately, against significant Congolese as well as international resistance. Critics—including some UN employees—accused the organization of practicing a new form of colonialism in central Africa.[7] When the fiction of an apolitical, technical UN operation was impossible to maintain, ONUC officials deployed a variety of arguments to legitimize autonomous UN action. In some cases, they rationalized circumventing the organization's mandate of noninterference and neutrality in the country's internal affairs by pointing to exceptional circumstances, such as looming humanitarian disaster or economic breakdown. In others, they simply claimed to be operating well within the established bounds of legal constraints and political directives given by the Security Council.

Ultimately, the UN did not exert an unchallenged expert rule over the Congo. Rather, ONUC's operations were dependent on international backing from UN member states, above all from the U.S., but also from Afro-Asian countries, as well as a shifting alliance with Congolese politicians. The latter relied on the international organization to provide some public services, most notably in the fields of health, education, transportation, and communications, while largely rejecting UN interference in such matters as state budgeting, security forces, and the judicature. By providing these services, the UN significantly affected the unfolding of the crisis, empowering one faction over another, contributing nationally to the rise of long-term dictator Joseph Mobutu and internationally to a privileged position by the United States in Congolese affairs. Controversies among member states about UN conduct in the crisis brought the organization close to political and financial collapse. As a result, no similar missions were mounted in the following two decades. Yet, ONUC anticipated the type of international developmental peacekeeping missions that would proliferate with the end of the Cold War.

The complexity of the UN intervention in the Congo deserves book-length coverage; this chapter will focus on the following aspects:[8] first, it offers an overview of the crisis. It then explains how UN personnel reframed an initial Congolese request for assistance in military matters as a *technical* issue to avoid Security Council involvement and how they planned an expansive assistance program that went well beyond the Congolese request. Next, it traces how the Secretariat—against considerable resistance from the Soviet Union, but also from elected Congolese politicians—build up a largely autonomous civilian operation to effectively manage the Congolese state in the shadow of the Security Council-sanctioned military intervention. A survey of UN operations in the various civilian fields testifies to the rather modest impact of UN activities in comparison to the organization's aspirations. A closer look at a UN civilian officer's work in one of the county's provinces illustrates how the task of supporting the Congolese state in ostensibly *technical* matters could hardly be separated from *political* questions. The next section of the chapter analyzes the various strategies that UN officials developed to legitimize their hands-on-involvement in the country's internal affairs, which clashed with the organization's official mandate to "not intervene in matters which are essentially within the domestic jurisdiction of any state."[9]

The final part discusses UN efforts to phase out their highly unusual, controversial operation in the country.

## CHRONOLOGY OF THE CRISIS

The Congo crisis unfolded largely as a result of the "crash nature" of Congolese independence, compounded by attempts of both national and international actors—the Cold War adversaries, European imperial powers, Western business interests, antiimperialist states—to shape the emerging African polity in their respective interests. The decision for the Congo to become a sovereign country on June 30, 1960 had been made only five months before. It represented a sudden about-face in Belgian colonial policy, as Brussels had long favored a mix of harshly repressive and selective, paternalistic welfare-oriented policies over even gradual emancipation of its African "subjects."[10]

The Belgian Congo was a vast country in central Africa of about 2,300,000 square kilometers, eighty times the size of Belgium. Aside from a small shoreline on the Atlantic Ocean, the Congo was surrounded by the soon-to-be-independent French colonial possessions in Equatorial Africa to the west and north (Republic of Congo or Congo-Brazzaville and the Central African Republic); independent Sudan to the northeast; the British protectorate of Uganda, the Belgian-administered UN trust territory Ruanda-Urundi, and the British-administered trust territory Tanganyika to the east; the semiautonomous federation of Rhodesia and Nyasaland to the southeast, and Portuguese Angola to the southwest. The Belgian colony had a complex and far-reaching administration and economy, in which fourteen million Congolese—comprising multiple linguistic and ethnic groups—were heavily implicated while being denied meaningful participation.

The Congo was exceedingly rich in resources, particularly minerals, and home to some highly developed industries, most importantly mining. The colonial state as well as foreign private investors (above all, British, American and French) were intimately involved in the business of resource extraction. Most of the industry was located in the northern province of Katanga.[11] On the eve of independence, close to 35 percent of working-age male Congolese were wage-earners.[12] A colonial bureaucracy administered by around 10,000 Belgian civil servants, the church, and private enterprises facilitated public services in fields such as primary education, health, and transportation, which could be compared to those of "metropolitan" Belgium.

Yet very few Congolese enjoyed more than a primary education.[13] Virtually none had been admitted to the higher rungs of administration. And the colonial government had only hesitantly permitted limited political organization and participation in government at the municipal level from 1957 onward.[14] This legacy presented numerous obstacles to the smooth functioning of a suddenly independent Congo. To make matters worse, the newly independent state would inherit a hefty budget deficit and an enormous public debt, accrued through misguided Belgian development policies and a fall in primary product prices in previous years. In the spring of 1960, a quarter of the state's total budget, around $90 million, had to be allocated for debt service.[15] Belgian attempts to seek financial assistance for the Congo from the U.S. government prior to independence had been rebuffed.[16] With Congolese sovereignty impending, Belgian companies operating in the colony were moreover allowed to register their offices in Brussels, thus depriving the Congo's already strained treasury of a vast amount of tax revenue.[17]

When independence failed to yield improved status and benefits, soldiers of the Congolese army mutinied only five days later. The violence caused a mass exodus among Belgian residents of the Congo, which in turn resulted in the rapid dissolution of the Congolese state bureaucracy, as well as the collapse of large parts of the country's economy. Without the express permission of the Congolese government, Brussels responded by deploying Belgian soldiers across the Congo for the express purpose of protecting its remaining citizens and "restoring order." To counter this intervention, newly elected Congolese president Joseph Kasavubu and prime minister Patrice Lumumba approached the U.S. ambassador and asked for military assistance.[18] Wary of being involved in another postcolonial conflict that might result in a Cold War proxy war, the U.S. embassy redirected their request to the UN. The next day, on July 11, Moïse Tshombe, the governor of Katanga, Congo's mineral-rich economic powerhouse, declared the province's secession with the support of Belgian troops.[19]

On July 14, in a rare instance of superpower agreement, the Security Council authorized the UN secretary-general to arrange for the deployment of troops under UN command to police the country and thus deprive Brussels of the argument that a Belgian presence in the Congo was necessary for the maintenance of law and order and the protection of civilians. Though the Soviet Union was suspicious of a pro-Western bias, Moscow saw an advantage in handling the crisis through the UN. Doing so allowed the Soviet Union to position itself as antiimperialist, while protecting itself from too much involvement.[20] Britain and France opposed UN involvement in decolonization, but—like the Republic of China (Taiwan)—abstained from voting on the military intervention rather than using their veto power.

Following the Security Council authorization, Hammarskjöld arranged with remarkable swiftness for the dispatch of troops from African countries under UN auspices. They arrived the next day and were transported by U.S., British, and Soviet military aircraft.[21] The Africans were later joined by troops from Asian countries, Canada, Sweden, and Ireland.[22] At their peak strength, the UN troops numbered nearly 20,000. This was by far the largest military deployment in the organization's history to that date, but for a country more than three times the size of France, a rather slim presence. By comparison: in 1946, U.S. Occupation forces in West Germany numbered about 290,000.[23] Though ONUC's Security Council mandate was to police the country, Hammarskjöld also built up by far the largest UN development program—the UN civilian operations—in tandem with the world organization's military operation in the Congo.

While the Belgian military soon withdrew from most of the country, its continued presence in secessionist Katanga led the Congolese government to demand more forceful action on the part of the UN to protect the country's territorial integrity. When such assistance failed to materialize, the UN relationship with Prime Minister Lumumba rapidly deteriorated and, with logistical support from the Soviet Union, he deployed Congolese troops to fight the two secessionist provinces. (South Kasai had followed Katanga's lead in declaring autonomy on August 8, 1960.[24]) Hammarskjöld perceived the resultant civilian casualties and refugee crisis as coming very close to genocide and authorized UN troops to intervene, despite complaints that the UN was thus interfering in an internal civil conflict and acting against the wishes of the elected government of the Congo. In early September, with Belgian and U.S. backing, President Kasavubu used Lumumba's military campaign as a pretext to announce the prime minister's dismissal from office. Lumumba reciprocated by announcing Kasavubu's discharge. Andrew Cordier, the U.S. executive assistant to successive secretaries-general, who was then temporarily in charge of ONUC in Leopoldville, actively supported Kasavubu. Cordier ordered the city's radio station and airport closed and thus prevented Lumumba from rallying support.[25] The Congolese Parliament, however, expressed confidence in the prime minister.

In the midst of this standoff, known the "constitutional crisis," Joseph Mobutu, who had recently been appointed head of the Congolese army and was a frequent visitor to the UN headquarters in Leopoldville, stepped forward and—with support from Belgian intelligence and the U.S. Central Intelligence Agency (CIA)—carried out his first coup d'état on the evening of September 14.[26] Mobutu then expelled all Soviet diplomatic personnel and announced that a civilian "Council of Commissioners," a board of young Congolese technocrats, would henceforth administer national policy—an arrangement that strikingly resembled the structure of ONUC's civilian operations. Rather than working closely with the UN, however, Mobutu's regime relied heavily on Belgian advisors. A general "reflux" of Belgian civilian personnel began. Mobutu's relationship with the UN, meanwhile, cooled off considerably.[27] While the UN never officially recognized Mobutu and his commissioners as legitimate authorities in the Congo, ONUC personnel nevertheless cooperated with them on a daily basis in the name of keeping the country from further disintegration. Kasavubu carried on as the nominal head of state, while Lumumba entered UN "protective custody"—a house arrest to prevent his capture by Mobutu's forces.

At the fall session of the 1960 General Assembly in New York, the Soviet Union fiercely attacked the UN Operations in the Congo as neocolonial and the secretary-general as partisan. A majority of UN member states, though critical of the organization's biased role in the constitutional crisis and its failure to end Katanga's Belgian-supported secession, expressed their general support for Hammarskjöld personally and a UN role in the Congo more generally.[28] While a number of African envoys in Leopoldville sought to bring about reconciliation between Kasavubu and

Lumumba to end Mobutu's *regime d'exception*, Western officials hoped to appease "international opinion" by establishing a new parliament-approved but Western-friendly government without Lumumba.[29] Perhaps aware of multiple assassination plans directed against him, the elected prime minister escaped the UN's protective custody in late November. He was soon captured by Mobutu's forces and later—with U.S. complicity—transferred to Katanga, where he and his associates were brutally murdered by local gendarmerie and Belgian officials.[30]

News of Lumumba's death in February 1961 caused widespread Congolese mourning and international protests. It also resulted in a strengthened Security Council mandate sponsored by Afro-Asian states:[31] the UN was to prevent civil war by use of force, if necessary; discipline the Congolese army (whose "unruly behavior" the UN had earlier described as a major obstacle to its objectives in the Congo); evacuate all foreign military personnel; and restore the country's parliamentary institutions.[32] Congolese officials interpreted the resolution as a call to turn the country into a UN trust territory, and—in an unprecedented agreement—the de facto authorities in Leopoldville and the secessionist provinces decided to pool their respective military resources *against* the UN if need be. An anti-UN press campaign followed, as well as numerous assaults on UN personnel. Indian diplomat Rajeshwar Dayal, who had assumed ONUC's lead after Cordier, but quickly fell out of favor with Congolese officials and Western powers because of his outspoken critique of their policies, discontinued his UN service.[33] A three-man UN appeasement mission dispatched to the Congo in March ultimately managed to find common ground with and among Congolese leaders (save for Tshombe in Katanga) in the goals of restoring public services, reconvening parliament, reorganizing the Congolese army, and ejecting foreign military personnel.

On August 2, 1961, under pressure and direction from both UN and U.S. officials, the Congolese Parliament elected a new civilian government, headed by prime minister Cyrille Adoula.[34] Despite earlier promises to the contrary, Katanga refused to work with the new government and to comply with the Security Council mandate. In late August, UN troops on the ground resorted to a show of force in the province, capturing and deporting foreign military personnel in the hope of convincing the secessionist government to cooperate. While "Operation Rum Punch" reinvigorated the trust among Afro-Asian states in the world organization, it caused outrage among Western European governments, which saw in Tshombe's government a strong and prosperous regime and, more importantly, a pro-Western bastion in the Congo. When Hammarskjöld set out to negotiate a cease-fire between UN and Katangese forces on September 18, he perished in a plane crash under mysterious circumstances.[35]

Hammarskjöld's successor as secretary-general, the Burmese diplomat U Thant, initially tried to find a political solution for the problem of Katanga; not least because of great American reluctance to support the renewed use of UN force against the secessionist province.[36] When Tshombe continued to violate promises for cooperation throughout 1962, however, ONUC responded to an attack on peacekeeping forces in Katanga with a retaliatory offensive that ultimately secured the defeat and surrender of the secessionist province in January 1963. Tshombe, as well as large parts of his provincial military, fled the country.

After ending Katanga's secession, Thant was anxious to phase out the UN's highly controversial military operation. In addition to causing a political controversy, ONUC had thrown the UN into serious financial difficulties. The cost of the military operation was immense: in 1960 alone the bills reached $50 million, $120 million in 1962. The regular budget of the world organization in 1962, by contrast, amounted to $70 million. Because of their objections to UN policy in the Congo, some member states, most notably the Soviet Union and France, refused to pay their allotted share for ONUC. Though the UN was ultimately able to cover unpaid assessments by issuing bonds, which were later paid off by the organization's regular income, the financial difficulties provided an important reason for Thant to wrap up the organization's involvement in the Congo after 1963.[37]

The U.S. administration and Adoula's government in Leopoldville, by contrast, opposed a UN retreat, given several anti-Western opposition movements that were gaining strength in large parts of the country.[38] As a compromise solution, UN troop withdrawal was scheduled for the summer of 1964. But on the eve of this military retreat, Adoula was dismissed by President Kasavubu, who invited Tshombe to return from exile and assume the Congo's leadership. Although the new regime received support from mercenaries, the CIA, and Belgium, Congolese opposition movements persisted with (limited) support from the Soviet Union, China, and Cuba—despite a decisive blow masked as a humanitarian rescue operation in late 1964 ("Operation Dragon Rouge").[39] In November 1965, Mobutu staged a second coup d'état, promising a new era of prosperity and stability after five years of chaos.

## REFRAMING THE CONGOLESE REQUEST FOR UN ASSISTANCE

Prior to independence, Congolese leaders recognized the need for foreign assistance to maintain the state and lessen its dependence on Belgium. In April 1960, future president Joseph Kasavubu's Abako party sent a mission to the United States to consult with American, UN, World Bank, and International Monetary Fund (IMF) officials. The Congolese mission, led by Joseph Yumbu, was above all concerned with the Belgian military presence in the Congo. Belgian officers headed the Congolese army, the Force Publique, while Belgian troops were to be stationed at bases in Kamina, in the mineral-rich southern province of Katanga, and in Kitona, close to the country's short Atlantic Ocean coastline.[40] The Yumbu mission hoped that the UN might dispatch a police force, or at least send an observer team to oversee the behavior of the foreign troops. They further wanted a UN advisor to participate in the negotiations to determine the legal status of the Belgian military presence on Congolese soil. Finally, they asked the world organization to provide an international commander in chief for the Force Publique and help "Africanize" its officer corps. Yumbu also invited the UN to supervise the upcoming national elections and asked for the provision of unspecified technical assistance.[41]

The UN refused this initial Congolese appeal for help, arguing that the organization could not legally become involved in a country's military matters in the absence of a threat to world peace.[42] The Secretariat would be happy to provide conventional technical assistance to the Congo, but could only respond to formal requests for help from member states. Because the Congo was not yet independent, such requests would have to come from Belgium, which to date had shown "little enthusiasm" for involving the UN in colonial questions. In fact, Brussels had never requested the services of UN technical experts for the Congo. In 1953,

Belgium ceased to participate in the General Assembly's Committee on Information from Non-Self-Governing Territories (discussed in chapter 1), which reviewed reports on the economic, educational, and social conditions in UN member states' colonies.[43] While Secretariat officials were thus barred from taking any official action in response to the Yumbu mission, they nevertheless made sure to have a "UN presence" in Leopoldville in June 1960 to provide assistance as soon as the colony became a newly sovereign state.

At that point, Hammarskjöld had already been experimenting with the dispatch of a high-level special representative to assist newly independent African countries in managing their novel, rapidly achieved sovereign status. In 1957, Guinea's electorate voted for immediate independence from France and the French withdrew "lock, stock and barrel" the next year. Hammarskjöld dispatched Adrian Pelt (the former UN commissioner for Libya, who had overseen the territory's transition to independence in 1950 and 1951) to Conakry, to help see that the country's limited resources were put to the best possible use.[44] Similarly, Hammarskjöld had sent Pier Pasquale Spinelli (the former director of the Italian administration of the trust territory of Somaliland, who went on to become the head of the UN's European office) as his special representative to Togo in early 1960, as a deterrent against Ghana's rumored designs on the former French-administered trust territory.[45]

On May 19, 1960, David Owen, the British chairman of the UN Technical Assistance Board, the interagency body coordinating the technical assistance work of the UN and the specialized agencies, approached the secretary-general with "particular urgency" about the Congo, proposing a similar appointment of a high-level UN official "before, during, and for a short time after the celebration of independence" in Leopoldville.[46] On his tour through Africa half a year earlier, Hammarskjöld himself had visited the Belgian Congo and, given the lack of preparation for independence as well as the country's size and natural wealth, reportedly foresaw a series of extraordinary problems ahead.[47] "Ralph Bunche," Owen continued in his letter to Hammarskjöld, "with all that he symbolises for Africa, as well as the UN, might be a factor of great weight" at such a sensitive time for the Congo.

As noted in the first chapter, Bunche had traveled to Africa to compare French administration in the League of Nations mandate Togoland

and the colony Dahomey for his doctoral dissertation in political science at Harvard. As a postdoctoral project, Bunche set out to examine how Africans perceived the impact of colonial rule and Western culture. To prepare for this research, he studied cultural anthropology with Bronisław Malinowski at the London School of Economics, where he mingled with African students, some of whom—like Jomo Kenyatta—would play an important role in the independence struggles of the postwar period.[48] For his "field research," Bunche then traveled to South Africa, Kenya, Uganda, and, briefly, the Belgian Congo.[49] During World War II, Bunche joined the State Department, where he became an important contact for emerging African leaders and (as discussed in chapter 1) was involved in the American planning effort for the UN trusteeship system.[50]

After the war, Bunche directed the UN's Trusteeship Division, but was soon absorbed by mediation efforts in the former League of Nations mandate Palestine. In 1950, he was the first person of color to win the Nobel Prize, for having arranged a cease-fire between Israel and its Arab neighbors.[51] When Hammarskjöld assumed the UN secretary-generalship in 1953, he set out to reorganize the Secretariat and, in the process, created a new position for Bunche as undersecretary for special political affairs to deal with high-level problems.[52] In that capacity, Bunche was involved in solving the 1956 Suez Crisis, during which he helped establish the first UN peacekeeping force. Two years later, Bunche helped install a UN military observer mission in Lebanon to stave off a potential confrontation in that country between the United States and the Soviet Union.[53] In early 1960, Bunche had joined Hammarskjöld for the second leg of his tour through Africa.[54]

Bunche's political mission to the Congo, the Secretariat decided, was to be supplemented by a UN technical assistance coordinator, a so-called resident representative, who would oversee the world organization's long-term assistance to the country. Hammarskjöld had already offered this position to Sture Linnér, a Swedish classicist turned business executive, in late 1959, after seeing him in Liberia a few months earlier.[55] The two were not close friends, but knew each other from their academic years in Uppsala. According to Linnér, Hammarskjöld foresaw "great trouble" in the Congo when they met and asked his compatriot to coordinate UN assistance to the country. At first, Linnér was hesitant to agree, by his own account not knowing the first thing about the UN and not being particularly fond of this huge bureaucracy. Hammarskjöld, however, insisted that he was interested in Linnér precisely because he would not be hampered by "the usual civil servant caution," but would do what needed to be done. This, Linnér suggested, ultimately convinced him to take the job.[56]

Bunche arrived in the Congo in late June and Linnér in early July of 1960. Two other UN Secretariat officials joined them: F. T. Liu, a former Chinese diplomat working in the UN Trusteeship Department, and the German émigré economist Henry S. Bloch. Liu had grown up in Paris and often served as interpreter to Bunche, whose French—according to their colleague Brian Urquhart—was rather shaky.[57] Bloch had emigrated from Germany to the U.S. in 1937 and taught at the University of Chicago. He had joined the UN Secretariat in 1946, after a brief stint in the U.S. Treasury Department.[58] Ominously—given the impending military emergency in the Congo—Bloch had published on "The Economics of Military Occupation" and was billed as "a well-known specialist in war finance and economy."[59]

When Bunche and Liu arrived bright and early at Ndijili airport outside of Leopoldville on June 25, there were no Belgian representatives or Congolese politicians to receive them. Instead, they were "rescued" by a member of the American consulate, "who had been sent just in case"—foreshadowing the close UN–U.S. cooperation in the Congo.[60] Though Bunche might have taken this breach of etiquette as a deliberate message of disrespect on the part of the Belgian authorities, to his surprise, he soon found himself impressed with their seriousness and seemingly enthusiastic support for UN involvement in independent Congo.[61] He was also introduced to "the principal players in Congolese politics" in the days leading up to the independence day, but mainly mingled with Belgian officials.[62] The latter expressed hope that the Congolese would "listen" to UN representatives, implying that the world organization alone stood in the way of the Congo's being taken by Moscow.[63]

The threat of a Soviet takeover was certainly exaggerated. As Lise Namikas suggests, although the USSR indeed took a persistent interest in the Congo (not least because of Sino–Soviet competition in the "Third World"), Soviet decision-makers had no interest in escalating the postindependence crisis. Ultimately, Moscow's leverage was limited, its aid small and often used ineffectively.[64] Nevertheless, Carole Collins has argued that the core issue for both Hammarskjöld and his American executive assistant Andrew Cordier "was always the maintenance of global peace in a world deeply split by the Cold War." Both feared that a conflict in the Congo might intensify East–West tensions and ultimately spark a nuclear showdown.[65] Cordier, who would briefly replace Bunche as head of ONUC in early September 1960 and was otherwise part of Hammarskjöld's informal group of advisors known as the "Congo Club," believed that the Soviets' fundamental aim was "the destruction of Western civilization" and collaborated freely with U.S. officials on Congo policy.[66] Hammarskjöld and Bunche's positions, it seems, were less extreme.

The secretary-general had unsuccessfully, but earnestly, tried to establish a personal relationship with Soviet leader Nikita Khrushchev when he visited Sochi the previous year, where the Soviet first secretary had taken him on solitary rowing trips.[67] Bunche, who had been sympathetic to Marxist thought in the 1930s, had become a prominent target of the McCarthy-era witch-hunt for "concealed" communists in 1954.[68] He ridiculed the American obsession with the possibility of a communist takeover in the Congo.[69] Bunche was initially hopeful that the difficulties the UN would face in the country would be largely formal and manageable.[70] Rajeshwar Dayal, who succeeded Bunche in directing ONUC, also suggested that because Belgium had allowed little news to percolate from its giant colony, "[it] was generally thought that Belgian rule was beneficent and ... that Belgium was leading the country in an orderly way towards self-government."[71]

Others were less optimistic. Indeed, the more informed observers predicted that chaos would follow the transfer of sovereignty, given the rushed nature of the independence process, the previously repressive Belgian colonial policies, and the multiple competing interests in the country. Political scientist David Apter, for example, who belonged to the circle of influential U.S. modernization theorists of the 1960s, by his own account, was among those who expected the country "to explode in shambles" upon independence. At the time, Apter was studying the role of mass nationalist movements in colonies' transition to sovereign statehood. He stayed in the Congo for eight weeks prior to independence and, expecting a "bloodbath," slipped over the border to Uganda a day before the Congo became a sovereign country.[72]

The independence ceremonies, where newly elected prime minister Patrice Lumumba famously responded to King Baudouin's rosy portrayal of Brussels' record in the Congo with a speech that harshly indicted Belgian colonialism, are usually portrayed as the overture to the subsequent tragedy.[73] Serious trouble started five days later, when soldiers of the Force Publique, who desired advancement, better pay, and less racism, but were frustrated by their seemingly unchanged postindependence status, mutinied. Some lashed out against white civilians. The violence caused a mass panic among Belgian residents of the Congo. Some estimates suggest that close to 30,000 of about 100,000 Belgian citizens left the country between July 6 and 17.[74] The panic was most obvious among Belgians in the administration, which resulted in the rapid dissolution of the Congolese state bureaucracy and public services.[75] For example, of 100 Belgian technicians in civil aviation, only "a handful" were left after independence; all of the 542 agricultural engineers left in July; of 175 Belgians holding "responsible positions" in the postal service, all but one withdrew; and only about 200 of 760 medical doctors remained.[76] Belgians in private firms, who had no promise of reemployment in the "metropole," were more likely to stay put.[77]

On July 10, without the Congolese government's permission, Brussels deployed Belgian soldiers across the Congo to protect white residents. The same day, the U.S. ambassador to the Congo referred a Congolese request for American military assistance to the UN and Bunche met with the Congolese cabinet in the afternoon. According to Brian Urquhart—Bunche's British assistant, who joined him in Leopoldville in late July—the Congolese "urgently wanted help, but had no clear idea what was needed, nor what could reasonably be expected" of the UN.[78] Both President Kasavubu and Prime Minister Lumumba wished to "Africanize" the Congolese army, rechristened the Armée Nationale Congolaise (ANC), but recognized the need for outside assistance in security matters. Bunche explained at length the possibilities and limitations of UN assistance, which was officially confined to "technical" matters unless the Security Council were to be involved. The Council's decision-making, however, was usually paralyzed by Cold War superpower rivalry, he told them. Kasavubu and Lumumba thus asked the UN for "technical assistance of military nature," to help prepare the national army "for the twin purposes of national defense and the maintenance of law and order."[79] But while the Congolese government was very much concerned with *external* threats, Bunche proposed to focus UN assistance on the maintenance of the Congo's *internal* public order. He envisioned dispatching UN advisors and instructors, such as police experts trained in the nonviolent handling of riotous crowds. Moreover, he thought it essential to fly in other UN specialists "to keep the vital technical services going."[80]

In a phone call that night, Bunche summarized his discussions with Congolese officials for Hammarskjöld, who was in Geneva. The secretary-general proposed to frame the requested UN involvement in Congolese military matters as "technical assistance in the field of security administration," a novel category that he thought should be part of a much broader UN assistance program in the field of administration.[81] Bunche was to draw up a formal request along these lines, which Thomas Kanza, the Congolese designate ambassador to the UN, could then officially submit to the organization. The resultant request, signed by Prime Minister Lumumba, asked the UN to provide the Republic of Congo with "technical assistance for creating leaders in all areas [by] means of international experts and technicians." This UN assistance was meant to help the government reorganize the army in order to ensure national security and maintain public order and respect for the law.[82]

Hammarskjöld's plan, upon his return to New York, was to informally report on this rather unconventional "technical" assistance to representatives of the African member states of the UN, which then comprised Ethiopia, Ghana, Guinea, Liberia, Libya, Morocco, Sudan, Tunisia, and the United Arab Republic.[83] The secretary-general intended to get African backing on the matter and thus be in a stronger position when presenting the matter, again *informally*, to the members of the Security Council the next day. Hammarskjöld told the African delegates that, contrary to press reports, he did *not* want to involve them in any responsibility in the Congo, but merely hear their reactions and advice on his unusual plans for the country.[84]

He first spoke of Bunche's mission and his consultations with Congolese officials on the possibilities of UN assistance. As a result, he said, an official request from the government was expected to arrive via cable later that day. The request, Hammarskjöld predicted, would concentrate on technical assistance in "general administration," with an understanding that the most immediate "administrative" need was the reestablishment of security. In response, the secretary-general intended to dispatch a UN peacekeeping presence to the Congo (he thought, of army instructors and "experts with a police background") recruited from earlier UN observer missions, which the Security Council had sent to the Middle East.

The secretary-general conceded that one might see the problem in the Congo as one of a need for peace and security, which would have to be decided by the Security Council. This, he claimed, was something that the government of the Congo was carefully trying to avoid: given Cold War tensions, the Council would unlikely reach a unanimous decision on the matter. Hammarskjöld's statement, of course, squarely contradicted Bunche's and Urquhart's claims that the Congolese government did not understand what could reasonably be expected of the organization. "My line," Hammarskjöld continued, more to the point, "is that there should be no question before the Security Council on the basis of this approach as it is one in the civilian field and it is one of technical assistance." The secretary-general admitted that "Naturally," developments in the Congo would be of great interest to the Security Council and that he would keep its members informed of any UN action—not in order to involve them in any decision-making, but "simply to get on the record what we do on the Secretariat side."[85]

What Hammarskjöld had mind for the Congo, he admitted, was in some sense a military intervention. It would depart significantly from earlier peacekeeping missions, however, not only in its framing as a technical or civilian operation, but also in its broad understanding of what it took to assist a people in preserving their country's territorial integrity and independence. Just as crucial as military experts, Hammarskjöld determined, were measures in the civilian field "to *indirectly* protect the integrity of the country."[86] In front of his African audience, the secretary-general did not spell out what kind of civilian measures he had in mind, but referred to the UN program for the provision of operational and executive personnel (OPEX), which, as the New York Times put it simplistically that day, was supposed to supply "governmental experts to under-developed countries."[87]

A third unprecedented aspect of Hammarskjöld's intended assistance to the Congo related to funding. The secretary-general had asked for a $2,500,000 allocation from the regular UN budget to finance the operation he envisioned. It was up to the General Assembly to approve the organization's budget at its upcoming session in September, but "personally," Hammarskjöld noted, "I do not hesitate to run into the red in anticipation of the General Assembly decision."[88] He maintained that this would not be unconstitutional, merely "a very free interpretation of my rights." Independence and "the ensuing transitional needs of newly independent states," the secretary-general argued, resulted from political developments, which although not initiated or led by the UN, were nevertheless associated with the organization. He was quick to insist that even though these special transitional needs derived from political developments, they were not in themselves political. Because of their temporary, yet urgent nature, Hammarskjöld argued that these needs should be covered by the regular UN budget (composed of membership contributions), rather than await the slow allocation of voluntary funds through the regular technical assistance channels.[89]

Hammarskjöld's designation of matters as political or technical was thus rather flexible and utilitarian: to divest the Security Council of a decision-making role, he presented UN military assistance to the Congo as technical; to legitimize using the regular UN budget to finance such aid, he pointed to political developments that had given rise to the need for UN assistance. Hammarskjöld recognized that the UN assistance he envisioned for the Congo would be novel in kind, even "a complete innovation," but he also asserted that it would be "absolutely within the framework of what is reasonable assistance from the UN in the technical field." The secretary-general thus effectively tried to both have his cake and eat it. "We are not in here in deep waters," he reassured his African audience. To the contrary, if UN action in the Congo would be regarded as a precedent, it would be a good precedent. In a telling choice of words, he noted that Bunche was elaborating a broad program, and the UN was "fitting in" "as well as we can" the requests of the Congolese government.[90]

The establishment of a technical assistance office in Leopoldville under the direction of Sture Linnér, the secretary-general said, would be announced later that day. What was needed now was to get "people" into the Congo as soon as possible, drawing on the Secretariat's own personnel resources of neutral, UN member states–approved civil servants. "We do not impose anything," Hammarskjöld concluded, "we only respond as intelligently and as quickly as we can within the framework that we have."

The secretary-general hoped for the African delegates' support on the matter, saying that if "we would all go together on [this] important question, it would give an added moral background to whatever we do." He further urged the delegates' discretion with regard to their meeting, so as not to embarrass the government of the Congo.[91]

In the ensuing conversation—of which only contributions in English were recorded—the representative of Sudan worried that, as a result of the crisis and perhaps also given the far-reaching nature of the envisioned UN intervention, the world might infer that the Congo, and perhaps other African countries too, were "not worthy of being a nation."[92] The Ethiopian representative wondered about the possibility of finding an African, regional solution to the problem.[93] Hammarskjöld promised that the UN operation would not compete with any such initiative: "[W]e are not there to stay, but just to fill a gap," he insisted, "we are your organization." Finally, the Ethiopian representative highlighted two problems contributing to crisis in the Congo: the government's weakness in maintaining law and order and the breach of international law committed by Belgium with the deployment of its troops. The latter issue, Hammarskjöld noted, was an "entirely different problem" from the one the UN was currently prepared to address. It would require a further initiative of the Congolese government for the UN to do something about the Belgian military maneuvers.[94]

## READJUSTING THE UN PLANS IN VIEW OF THE SECURITY COUNCIL'S INVOLVEMENT

After Hammarskjöld left the meeting, such an initiative was indeed forthcoming: a new cable from Lumumba and Kasavubu now asked for direct UN military assistance to counter the Belgian aggression.[95] This request substantially altered the nature of UN assistance to the Congo and brought the matter under the purview of the Security Council, which Hammarskjöld had tried to avoid. The previous day, on July 11, Moïse Tshombe, the governor of Katanga, had declared the province's secession from the Congo (after having consulted Bunche on the matter a few days earlier and displaying an "unhealthy interest" in the federalist history of the

United States).⁹⁶ When Prime Minister Lumumba and President Kasavubu personally tried to negotiate with Tshombe, a Belgian commander denied them permission to land in Katanga's capital, Elisabethville. The Congolese leaders inferred that Brussels stood behind the secession of the Congo's economic powerhouse.⁹⁷ The Belgian Navy's shelling of the strategic port city of Matadi, from which almost all Belgians had already been evacuated, further confirmed their suspicions that the military intervention was not meant to assist the Congolese government in restoring order, or simply to protect Belgian citizens, but that it constituted an invasion and occupation of their country.⁹⁸ In response to the renewed, explicit Congolese request for military assistance, and for the first time in UN history, Hammarskjöld used his prerogative as secretary-general to bring a matter before the Security Council. An official meeting was convened the next day, on July 13.

Yet, Hammarskjöld did not drop his previously elaborated plans for expansive technical assistance. Rather, he sought to build on them and incorporate them into the requested UN military operation. His proposal to the Security Council was threefold: first, the UN would provide "technical assistance in security administration," to help maintain the country's internal order. Second, the organization would dispatch troops to render the Belgian "security presence" superfluous. And third, the United Nations Children Emergency Fund (UNICEF) would organize an emergency food supply.⁹⁹ The Council members discussed the matter all night and reached an agreement in the small hours of the next day.

As noted above, the resulting Security Council resolution represented a rare instance of Cold War superpower agreement. It called upon Belgium to withdraw its troops from the Congo and authorized the secretary-general "to provide the Government with such military assistance as may be necessary until, through the efforts of the Congolese Government with the technical assistance of the United Nations, the national security forces may be able, in the opinion of the Government to meet fully their tasks."¹⁰⁰ In other words, the Council approved of direct UN military assistance to the Congolese government, as well as technical assistance to the national security forces. The resolution said nothing about assistance in government administration or other civilian fields (aside from the provision of food), which, as described in the previous chapter, was anathema to the Soviet Union. Hammarskjöld, however, willfully chose to

FIG. 13  UN Food Aid to the Congo (1960)

Source: UN Photo, UN7771414

interpret the Security Council mandate expansively and led the UN to embark on the biggest civilian operation in the organization's history. Acting on the Security Council mandate, the secretary-general arranged for the dispatch of troops, which quickly took control of essential parts of the transportation system, as well as telecommunication and postal services. Maurice Pate, the American cofounder and executive director of UNICEF organized an emergency food relief program.[101]

Apart from providing these essential services, Hammarskjöld, driven by his vision for a technocratic management of decolonization, envisioned a much larger UN civilian effort—on equal or even higher standing than the military intervention. Indeed, he saw the essential, long-term contribution of the UN to the Congo as being in the civilian field.[102] To establish lasting order, he thought, the organization needed to do much more than simply police the country and maintain a minimum of communication and transport services. Rather, the UN needed to prevent disasters and epidemics, maintain the public services that the colonial administration had previously provided, reorganize the governmental administration, legal system, and public services so that they would suit a newly independent state, and train the Congolese in the use of their "government machinery."[103] Much to the disappointment of UN Secretariat officials, this mammoth civilian effort never received as much publicity as the military operation. Bunche even received letters suggesting that the UN take action in the Congo *beyond* its policing role, when such efforts were already well underway.[104]

Even though Hammarskjöld's vision for the Congo very much resembled the plans that UN economist Benjamin Higgins had drawn up for newly independent Libya (see chapter 2), there was no prior UN effort that ONUC's civilian personnel saw as a precedent for designing their operation.[105] The job of figuring out the scale and nature of civilian needs was largely left to the men on the spot, namely Bunche, Linnér, and Bloch, as well as Secretariat officials at the New York headquarters, who regularly gathered informally over lunch and dinner in so-called "Congo Club" meetings. Unsurprisingly, no Eastern European UN officials ever attended these meetings. According to Dayal, Hammarskjöld had little respect for the Soviet undersecretary for special political affairs, G. P. Arkadiev (Bunche's official equal in rank). The main "members" of the "Congo Group" (as it was called in UN memos) were Hammarskjöld, Andrew Cordier, Heinz Wieschoff, Bunche (after he returned from Leopoldville in August 1960), and Indian general Indar Jit Rikhye, Hammarskjöld's military advisor.[106]

Apparently, what all these UN officials had in common was that they operated on strikingly inadequate intelligence. In a 1986 interview, Hammarskjöld's American legal advisor Oscar Schachter recalled regretfully: "what was . . . astounding, . . . was how ignorant we all were."[107] According to Schachter, the Secretariat informally appointed Heinz Wieschoff their "Congo expert," even though Wieschoff's knowledge of the region was outdated at best. He was born in 1906 in Hagen, Germany. A student of ethnologist Leo Frobenius, Wieschoff submitted his dissertation on Rhodesia at the University of Frankfurt in 1933. In 1936, he immigrated to the U.S. and worked as curator of an African collection at the University of Pennsylvania. During World War II, he assisted the Office of Strategic Services on questions relating to Africa and joined the UN Trusteeship Department shortly after the war. According to Schachter, Wieschoff had visited the Congo during his "scholarly period." No outside expert, it seems, ever briefed the "Congo Club" members.[108]

Curiously, several UN officials found Henry Bloch's expertise with regard to the U.S. occupation of postwar Japan to be of "significant help" in establishing the civilian operations of ONUC.[109] Yet, the UN position in the Congo was, of course, fundamentally different from the American one in postwar Japan. The UN did not have authority over the country; its mandate depended on the consent of the Congolese government and/or the goodwill of the wildly at-odds members of the Security Council. In addition, the UN Secretariat had far fewer resources than the U.S. in terms of personnel, intelligence, enforcement, and financial means. As Brian Urquhart pointed out, under such circumstances, the overnight launching of an emergency multinational military expedition with a large civilian component into a vast, unfamiliar tropical country some 6,000 miles away from the UN headquarters was no easy feat.[110] "If we pull this thing out of the fire," Bunche wrote to his wife on August 4, 1960, "it will be the closest thing to a miracle I've ever seen."[111] Hammarskjöld, by contrast, did not seem daunted by the task, but rather, according to the U.S. ambassador to the UN, "intrigued by the creative role thrust upon him."[112]

On July 20, Bloch submitted a first assessment of the situation in the Congo. ONUC was still in the reconnoitering stage, as large parts of the country had not yet been visited by UN military, civilian, or Congolese government personnel. Nevertheless, it was possible to assess some immediate needs. Food supply and distribution, Bloch thought, were mainly a problem of reestablishing transportation. To maintain public health, the UN would have to find replacements for the departed Belgian doctors and continue mosquito spraying, inoculations, and water control. To keep electricity, communications, and the transport system going, the organization would have to recruit numerous foreign technicians. In some cases, Bloch noted, Belgian professionals might return to work, if their protection was assured.[113]

Taking a step back from immediate priorities, Bloch considered the overall nature of the task ahead. Normally, the UN planned for a *developing* economy. In the Congo, the world organization had to make arrangements for a *declining* economy on a "stop loss" basis, until ascendancy could resume—an assessment quite similar to the one that UN economists made in Libya and Somaliland on the eve of independence (see chapters 2 and 3).[114] At that point, Bloch noted, the economy itself had not been seriously damaged and the infrastructure was still intact. Even commercial and industrial establishments, as well as the transport and communication system, were not severely damaged; they had simply come to a standstill. Bloch asserted that rapid action could "save the patrimony of the state." To bridge the gap until the eventual return of stability, he recommended that the UN establish a transitional "crash program with a minimum of advisers and a maximum of managers"—essentially, making use of OPEX services "on an exceptionally large scale."[115]

To implement such a program, Bloch envisioned resident representative Sture Linnér as head of operations and serving the all-encompassing "purpose of assisting [the Congolese government] in planning its production, supply, distribution, as well as general economic, social and administrative activities." Linnér was, moreover, to advise the government on how to request aid from the UN and other sources. He would be assisted by a "consultative group," a team of high-level "multi-purpose" experts—ideally "with African experience"—who were to be drawn from or recruited by the various UN specialized agencies, such as the WHO, UNESCO, the FAO, the International Telecommunications Union (ITU), and the International Labor Organization (ILO). The Secretariat would provide overall direction to the civilian efforts and finance all posts through a "Congo account" established for that purpose by the secretary-general from the regular UN budget.[116]

The UN consultants, Hammarskjöld later explained, although not directly attached to or incorporated into governmental ministries, were to take care of "activities on a higher level of administrative responsibilities."[117] They could also advise the Congolese government on an ad hoc basis. He never spelled out precisely what relationship these consultants would have with the Congolese state. The novel arrangement, he argued, would allow the UN to establish "an undertaking that would go beyond the normal scope of technical assistance as provided by the UN to other countries," without infringing on the sovereignty of the Congo or hampering the development of the country's national administration. Each consultant would oversee a group of UN experts, covering one of the fields of "basic importance": public administration, transport and communications, natural resources, power, agriculture, industry, education, health, labor, social welfare and relief, budget and finance, trade and distribution, judicature, and civil aviation.[118] No distinction would be made between regular advisory and OPEX-type managerial services.[119]

In the name of noninterference and the maintenance of order, ONUC thus built up a parallel administrative structure to the state that could presumably, if necessary, operate autonomously from Congolese directions. At the very top of the hierarchy stood the secretary-general, who assumed "intense personal direction" over the civilian operation, effectively micromanaging the UN intervention in the Congo.[120] The fact that the Secretariat regarded ONUC's civilian operations as of equal importance to the military intervention was reflected in the fact that both Linnér and General Carl von Horn, the Swedish supreme commander of the UN Force, answered to a UN political officer, the personal representative of the secretary-general in Leopoldville (Bunche in the early days).[121] Both sides of the operation, moreover, had a liaison officer at the New York headquarters to provide immediate access to Hammarskjöld. Crucially, and in contrast to regular UN technical assistance, the UN civilian operations in the Congo, much like the UN troops, answered to the United Nations, or more precisely to the secretary-general, rather than to the Congolese government.[122]

This is not to say that Hammarskjöld completely bypassed Leopoldville on civilian matters. The first Congolese request, which was drafted by Bunche but signed by Lumumba and Kasavubu, had asked the UN for the provision of "general technical assistance for creating leaders in all areas [by] means of international experts and technicians ... [to] ensure national security, maintain public order and respect for law."[123] In late July, Lumumba toured North America (and later North Africa) to seek international assistance for his government and, while in New York, met with Hammarskjöld three times. According to the Secretariat, the conversations went well and they reached a preliminary understanding with regard to the UN's civilian operations, although the exact parameters of UN activities remained to be worked out by Congolese and UN officials in Leopoldville.[124] Lumumba voiced some complaints with regard to the preponderance of Europeans among top UN officials in the Congo, but he agreed to the creation of a UN consultative group and, in the eyes of the Secretariat, thus recognized the UN as his country's primary, if not exclusive source of assistance.[125]

Lumumba's principal aim in meeting Hammarskjöld, however, was not the discussion of civilian assistance, but getting the secretary-general to authorize the entry of UN troops into secessionist Katanga. Though he found Lumumba's request reasonable, Hammarskjöld refused to act on it, not wishing to risk a confrontation between UN and Belgian military. Lumumba then proceeded to Washington, DC, where he was again disappointed when seeking support for the use of force against Katanga. Severely frustrated, Lumumba told American reporters that the Soviet Union was the only superpower that truly supported the Congolese independence struggle.[126] He also complained to the press about those who thought of the Congolese as incapable of self-government and in need of UN guardianship. His government, the prime minister insisted, would secure aid from wherever it wished.[127] Hammarskjöld's subsequent attempts to find a diplomatic solution with Tshombe and his disregard of an ultimatum set by Lumumba led the latter to break relations with the secretary-general and his representatives in Leopoldville. Six weeks into his mission in the Congo, Bunche felt that his utility was exhausted because of his personal difficulties with the prime minister. In mid-August, he wrote to his wife, "The madman Lumumba is recklessly on the attack now—and most viciously—against Dag and the UN . . . it looks as though this greatest of international efforts will be destroyed by the insane fulminations of one reckless man."[128] Subsequent attempts by fellow African statesmen to mediate and bring about reconciliation between Lumumba and the UN did not succeed.[129]

It was amid this troubling situation that Hammarskjöld first reported on ONUC's civilian operations to the Security Council on August 11. He argued that the Council itself had conceived of "the civilian and military part as interrelated and mutually supporting elements of ONUC's operations."[130] According to Hammarskjöld, the organization's mandate for the UN civilian operations came from the Security Council, though he also pointed to a formal agreement with the Congolese government. If looked at closely, however, the Security Council document cited as evidence had very little to say about civilian operations and nothing about the specifics of the program.[131] Yet, Hammarskjöld argued that the Security Council had provided him with broad authority and therefore it was for him to determine the shape of the civilian operations.

Hammarskjöld's presentation and plans did not go unchallenged. The Soviet Union charged that the proposal for technical assistance would lead to the establishment of a "UN administration with wide powers," independent of the government of the Congo, and rejected it as "entirely unacceptable."[132] Such a program would limit the Congo's sovereignty, the Soviets argued, and in effect, turn the country into a trust territory. (At internal meetings, U.S. officials later approvingly concurred.[133]) The Soviet delegate stated that the UN consultants would possess the powers of ministers and thus be in a position to determine the future policy of the Congo, which, given the predominance of the United States and its allies in the UN Secretariat, would no doubt "be conducted along lines satisfactory to the U.S."[134] The whole plan violated both the Charter's provision of noninterference in domestic matters of member states and the Security Council's resolution, which provided "only for the rendering of assistance to the Government of the Congo," he insisted. Implementing the plan proposed by the secretary-general "would mean nothing other than . . . the establishment of a new form of colonial enslavement of the Congolese people under cover of the United Nations flag."[135] Representatives of the Congolese government (Deputy Prime Minister Antoine Gizenga and UN Ambassador Thomas Kanza) joined the Soviet criticism. To them, Hammarskjöld's initiative also smelled of neocolonialism, and they denounced his plan as illegal. Gizenga, however, noted that there was still room for cooperation between the Congolese government and the UN, if in the future the latter would rely on nonaligned states for policy advice rather than on Washington.[136]

In the ensuing Security Council debate, Hammarskjöld conceded that after "five very hectic weeks," the distribution of staff in terms of geographic background was "not satisfactory."[137] As the Soviet representative had noted, of sixty-five UN officials in the Congo, twenty-one were American citizens, who, moreover, occupied posts of key significance.[138] But after previously tracing his mandate to the Security Council resolution (presumably to circumvent the need for Congolese approval), the secretary-general now rejected the Council's authority. Because the whole civilian operation was basically a technical assistance operation, he argued, ECOSOC or the General Assembly would have to deal with the matter. The consultant arrangement itself was a question of how the Secretariat organized its work in the Congo and thus, "for good or for bad," the secretary-general's responsibility.[139] To counter the charge of neocolonialism, Hammarskjöld suggested that because the consultants were merely "internal administrators for the United Nations operation," their status vis-à-vis the Congolese national administration was actually weaker than that of conventional technical assistance experts (a contradiction of his earlier claim of UN consultants assuming "higher level administrative responsibilities"). Further at variance with his earlier statements, the secretary-general continued that because the consultants provided "regular technical assistance" to the government, "these men could not and would not have any executive authority or responsibility."[140]

Mongi Slim, the UN representative of Tunisia, strongly supported Hammarskjöld and, according to Urquhart, provided a rallying point for African countries in a reasoned and eloquent speech. Without directly addressing the Soviet criticism, he insisted that disinterested technical and administrative assistance was vitally important for the fledgling Congolese republic, and that the UN, though imperfect, was still generally the best available option for newly independent states in need of external assistance.[141] Similarly, Claude Corea of Ceylon expressed his support for the secretary-general.[142] Hammarskjöld had sought precisely such "Third World" backing for his Congo plans when he consulted African member states before the Security Council got involved. To build on this support—and probably also to manage potential criticism behind closed doors, rather than in the public arena of the General Assembly—Hammarskjöld created a UN Advisory Committee on the Congo, composed of representatives of troop-contributing countries, mostly from the "Global South," which would meet at regular intervals in New York to discuss UN Congo policy.[143] Despite continued Soviet attacks on Hammarskjöld and ONUC at the General Assembly sessions later that year (which culminated in Khrushchev's infamous call to replace the office of the secretary-general with a troika of officials from the East, the West, and the nonaligned world), a majority of UN member states ultimately expressed their confidence in the secretary-general and—by extension—in the UN operations in the Congo.[144]

## A SURVEY OF UN CIVILIAN ACTIVITIES

The first days of the civilian operation was characterized as a "hasty assemblage" of UN personnel in Leopoldville. The Secretariat reasoned that there was no need for individual Congolese approval of staffing, if UN employees were dispatched who had served or were currently serving the organization to the satisfaction of member states.[145] UN officials leaving for the Congo were gripped by a sense of adventure and uncertainty. "A breeze of expectancy swept through the Secretariat building," the wife of one UN official later recalled, when UN personnel found themselves, with surprising suddenness, thrust from their uneventful, routine life in New York into the heart of Africa. "Individuals with special knowledge of the subject, experts in technical and professional fields, specialists in various branches of administration," she wrote, and really "any others who could be spared," were "wafted" to the Congo at the shortest notice.[146] Never before had the demand been made for so many UN employees for the same project at the same time.

Linnér saw the Congo as a "panorama of disaster" and understood UN action in various fields as "fire-brigade" or "first-aid measures" that had to be executed independent of specific Congolese requests or cooperation.[147] Accordingly, some of the first assignments were taken on the UN Secretariat's own initiative. Transport, telecommunications, air services, meteorological services, and water supplies, according to one journalist's account, were repaired with exceptional speed by rushing in experts from all over the world with the help of the UN specialized agencies.[148] In a next step, ONUC arranged for the ITU, the World Meteorological Organization, and the International Civil Aviation Organization to train Congolese telephonists, telegraphists, radio operators, weather forecasters, and air traffic controllers.[149]

Another emergency measure of first priority was the dispatch of medical teams to keep the country's basic health services going. The World Health Organization invited twenty-four Red Cross teams from twenty nations, including Japan, several Eastern European countries, Egypt, India, Iran, and Pakistan, to staff the Congo's main hospitals and dispatched its own health experts to assist the Congolese Ministry of Health on such issues as sanitation, water supply, and disease control.[150] Breaking with its tradition of merely supplying health experts in advisory capacities, the WHO eventually replaced these emergency medical teams and supplied between 100 and 200 doctors to the Congo during each year of ONUC's operations.[151] Because the Congo had lost about 600 Belgian doctors, however, the UN was unable to maintain the pre-independence level of health services.[152]

FIG. 14 Ethiopian Nurses Serving ONUC in Stanleyville (Kisangani)

Red Cross nurses Aster Ayana (left) and Zenawit Ayele leaving the UN Headquarters in Stanleyville in Orientale Province (1960).

Source: UN Photo, UN7660623

The same was true for public works, another priority of ONUC's civilian operations.[153] UN officials perceived the unemployed as a significant threat to order and stability.[154] In early September, they dispatched international engineers to the Congo's five provinces to survey public works projects, which had been suspended before independence. In consultation with local officials, they selected seven projects that offered the "possibility of employing the largest number of workers with the least capital outlay."[155] About 4,000 Congolese workers were engaged in projects ranging from drainage of residential areas and swamps (to reclaim land for agricultural purposes) to road construction.[156] Although it is hard to define unemployment in the context of the Congolese colonial economy, official statistics counted 33,000 unemployed residents in 1959, before the disruptions that followed independence sent rates spiraling upward.[157] UN-initiated public works projects were thus hardly more than a drop in the bucket. In addition to these relief projects, twenty-five to thirty experts

STATE-BUILDING MEETS PEACEKEEPING 229

FIG. 15 Anti-Malaria Campaign on the Congo River near Leopoldville (Kinshasa)

With support from the WHO, ONUC deployed hand-operated sprayers as well as a special "fog-laying device" fitted to helicopters to combat mosquitos with an "oil solution" in the Congo's capital and its environs. Unnamed spray-operators with Sargent Fasasi-Ayeni of ONUC (1961).

Source: UN Photo, UN7664476

from the ILO conducted surveys and made policy recommendations on unemployment and wage policy, participated in the government's negotiations with Belgium on the transfer of social security schemes to the Congo, and trained labor officials and workers' representatives.[158] Social welfare experts engaged in community development services, training schemes, and sports and youth programs—the latter, again, intended "to combat the aggregation of unemployed."[159]

Under the banner of "social welfare" work, ONUC also launched a large-scale relief effort to combat famine among displaced members of the Baluba ethnic group, who had sought refuge in the secessionist province of South Kasai, where Albert Kalonji had followed Tshombe's lead in declaring independence on August 8, 1960. In late November, after being alerted to famine conditions, UN civilian operations launched and

FIG. 16 UN "Self-Help" Projects in Luluabourg (Kananga)

ONUC initiated community development projects "to encourage the rural populace to better their living conditions" through mutual aid. Children watch *animateurs ruraux* paint a new home in Luluabourg in Kasai Province (1963). Sixteen new homes (each with three bedrooms, a living room, a kitchen, and a bathroom) were completed in the town through "self-help" methods.

Source: UN Photo, UN7666579

coordinated a massive relief effort, drawing on the support of churches and nongovernmental organizations and bilateral assistance. The effort in many ways prefigured the type of international "humanitarian intervention" that historians have traced to Biafra's attempted secession in the Nigerian civil war in the latter half of the 1960s.[160]

Apart from emergency aid, high-level administrative assistance had been central to Hammarskjöld's vision of what was needed in the Congo. This entailed not only the provision of policy advice to individual ministries, but also the development of the governmental administration itself. ONUC asked Ghanaian economist Robert Gardiner to develop the Congolese administrative structure by examining its existing ministries for necessary organizational changes and creating new ministries.[161] Gardiner

FIG. 17  Public Works in Kivu Province

A bulldozer levels an access road to Kamanyola in Kivu Province (1965).

Source: UN Photo, UN7694725

outlined state officials' responsibilities, including those of the president and prime minister, drew up organizational charts for the various ministries, and created channels for intergovernmental communications. To what extent his recommendations were put into effect is unclear. ONUC, moreover, offered a two-month crash course in administrative organization, constitutional law, statistics, finance, and French for some 300 Congolese government officials and, with support from the Ford Foundation, set up a National School of Law and Administration in Leopoldville that offered four years of instruction to future Congolese civil servants.[162]

But ONUC also went far beyond the provision of high-level administrative assistance. As in the case of health, other branches of the UN civilian operations in the Congo engaged in large-scale "operational" assistance. In the field of education, UNESCO ran by far the largest civilian operations program in terms of personnel.[163] Starting with sixty-four Haitian teachers who arrived in the Congo in 1960, UNESCO supplied

FIG. 18 National School of Law and Administration in Leopoldville (Kinshasa)

Unnamed students in a mathematics class with UN expert Jean Reynalds of Haiti at the *École Nationale de Droit et d'Administration* (1962). ONUC established the school in early 1961 to train Congolese to fill judicial and administrative positions. Two years of "general background" studies were followed by two years of specialized studies and one year of practical training.

Source: UN Photo, UN7736444

about 800 educators by the end of 1963.[164] Much like the WHO, UNESCO was initially reluctant to provide such operational personnel when advisory assistance had been the international norm, but both UN agencies changed their policies in response to the Congo crisis and Hammarskjöld's lobbying. In addition to operating and staffing schools, UNESCO also advised the central and provincial ministries of education, assisted the government in adapting its educational plan to the needs of an independent country (rather than a colony), and set out to train Congolese staff to take charge of the educational system. One study suggests that UNESCO's main impact was the expansion of secondary education in the Congo. However, of the 30,000 students entering secondary education in 1961, a

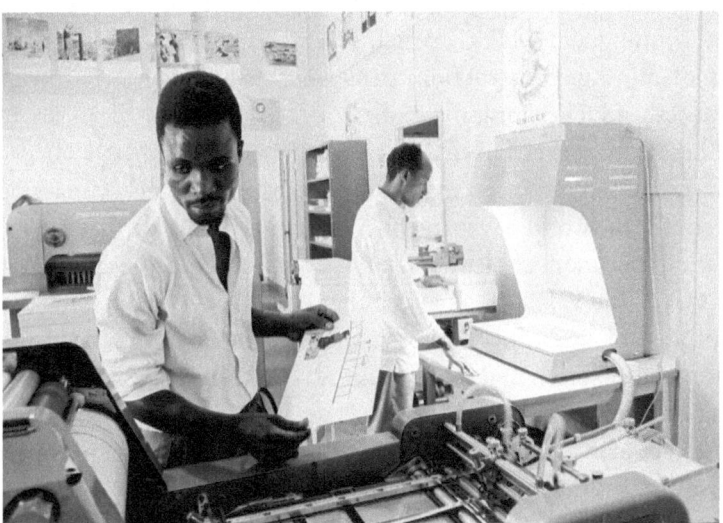

FIG. 19 New Printing Plant near Leopoldville (Kinshasa)

Together with the UNESCO, UNICEF, and the Congolese Ministry of Education, ONUC set up a printing plant outside of Leopoldville to produce "educative instruction sheets." Haitian UN expert Roger Ade (right) supervises the printing plant with four Congolese trainees, including Pierre Yenga (left) (1963).

Source: UN Photo, UN7736446.

mere 4,000 graduated, as most students were unable to remain in school for six continuous years during a period of severe economic hardship and political dislocation.[165]

In addition to basic education, on-the-job training was a major general goal of the UN's civilian operations in the Congo—in theory. In reality, the combination of a thin-stretched UN team with a high turnover rate, a multitude of tasks, and a lack of Congolese whom UN personnel considered sufficiently qualified, resulted in the de facto neglect of counterpart training. Fellowships that specialized agencies provided to enable Congolese to study abroad were not necessarily more effective: "It is rather pathetic, as most [applicants] have no qualifications at all, but think that six months abroad will equip them to be judges, chief administrators etc.," wrote one UN official.[166] Accordingly, the UN also supported specialized long-term education within the country. The WHO sent six to ten professors to the Lovanium Medical School in Leopoldville for additional training and ONUC created several educational institutes in the fields of mining, construction, pedagogy, meteorology, civil aviation, and postal and telecommunications.[167]

Whereas most specialized agencies eagerly supported ONUC's efforts, the international financial institutions refused to join Hammarskjöld's experiment in "world government."[168] The IMF "decided that the nature and scale of economic disorders in the Congo precluded its participation in ONUC." The World Bank stated that it was "not equipped to respond to this kind of emergency—to offer special personnel who could restrict economic devolution and make eventual bank lending possible sooner." In the latter case, it is more likely that the bank feared the Congo would default on a loan and did not want to cause a potential Belgian–American controversy over its participation in ONUC. In early 1960, the bank had already granted the soon-to-be-independent Congo a $40 million dollar loan, backed by a Belgian guarantee, but had never started disbursements. Had the Bank joined ONUC, the pressure to change course would surely have increased.[169]

ONUC thus recruited its own economic personnel in such fields as budget, accounting, treasury, taxation, and customs. Before independence, about 400 Belgian civil servants had run the financial affairs of the colonial state. After independence, sixteen "expatriates" continued to work in the Ministry of Finance.[170] Thirteen UN technical assistance experts joined them to continue basic administrative tasks and to conduct fact-finding missions into the former colonial fiscal and parastatal agencies, the public debt, and the "government portfolio" (a package of shares that the colonial government had accrued in companies as a payment for granting concessions, for example with regard to mining).[171] By the end of 1963, thirty UN experts were attached to the Ministry of Finance, most working in customs.[172] This minimal staff had to manage public disbursements for the army, politicians, and civil servants; juggle expenditures with declining revenues (due to secession, disruptions to businesses, gaps in tax collection, and the proliferation in tax evasion, corruption, and smuggling in the absence of law enforcement); and regulate the Congo's foreign trade.

But even the basic services provided by this staff were highly controversial. For example, on September 10, at the height of the constitutional crisis, in which President Kasavubu and Prime Minister Lumumba dismissed the other's legitimacy, Cordier, as temporary head of ONUC, authorized the disbursement of $1 million to unpaid Congolese soldiers. Even though the money was officially intended to prevent the troops from looting, it also bolstered Mobutu as the head of the Armée Nationale Congolaise: he assumed a prominent place in the payment ceremonies and staged his first coup d'état four days later.[173] The "colorful and unruly use of expenditures" by the Congolese government, on the other hand, "provided headaches for the international civil servants, who sought to impose financial discipline and yet stay out of internal politics," according to an early study of civilian operations.[174] ONUC's real success in the economic field, its author argued, was its ability to make arrangements for outside financial and commodity assistance.[175]

The FAO officially joined the UN effort in the Congo, but reportedly showed "callous disregard" for Hammarskjöld's initiative.[176] This attitude probably resulted in part from Director-General B. R. Sen's general skepticism toward international operational assistance and his desire to wait until the chaotic political situation in the Congo stabilized.[177] Farming was by far the major occupation of the Congolese population and in the pre-independence period, agricultural products accounted for one-third to one-half of the Congo's export earnings.[178] The Belgian Congo had employed close to 16,000 people in agricultural research and "management"—a highly euphemistic term that included the supervision of forced labor, as well as large-scale relocations of Congolese farmers, often away from fertile areas.[179] With independence, the administrative agricultural superstructure largely collapsed. Overall agricultural production, however, save for export-oriented farming, was apparently not much affected by the crisis until the outbreak of rebellions in several provinces in 1964.[180] The FAO ultimately sent about thirty agricultural specialists, who reportedly stood out for their patronizing, colonialist attitudes, inability to speak French, and lack of fervor. Ultimately, they failed even at the limited task that the organization set for itself: to advise the Ministry of Agriculture.[181]

In terms of revenue and foreign exchange earnings, mining was more important to the Congolese economy than agriculture. The UN consultant in the field of natural resources and industries had initially delineated ambitious goals for ONUC: to accelerate the training of Congolese at all technical levels, establish a detailed inventory of natural resources, standardize rules relating to mining-company dues and royalties, create mixed

Congolese and foreign mining enterprises, and curb the illicit traffic in precious metals and stones—as if the Congo's mineral treasure troves Katanga and South Kasai had never seceded. It is hardly surprising that ONUC's impact on mining was negligible. The first UN experts did not arrive until 1962. They conducted some surveys of natural resources, but largely failed to provide advice at the governmental level and were, in any case, outnumbered by Belgian and French bilateral advisors attached to the Congolese Department of Mines, the Geological Service, and the Mining Research Center.[182]

Given ONUC's explicit mandate to assist the Congo in the maintenance of law and order, its impotence in the field of domestic security institutions was even more striking. The original UN goal had been to help the Congolese government establish the Ministry of Defense, assist with the organization of a National General Staff for the army, train new combat units, and reorganize the ANC's gendarmerie.[183] An army-retraining program, which officially started in August 1960, suffered from high absenteeism on the part of Congolese soldiers.[184] It was discontinued after Mobutu's seizure of power. The general showed no interest in letting the UN create a powerful body atop the security forces that had enabled his coup, nor in letting ONUC single out individual ANC officers for further training. Nevertheless, UN officials continued to express hope of influencing Mobutu and his security forces "in the right direction." When Cyrille Adoula came to power in 1963, he signed bilateral training agreements for the armed forces with Belgium, Israel, and Italy, the costs of which the U.S. paid the lion's share.[185]

Similarly, although UN officials described their mandate in the Congo as one of restoring "law and order," the country's judicial system received only tardy, stopgap attention by the world organization.[186] Upon his arrival in September 1960, J. Grossen, the Swiss UN consultant for judicature "found a complete disruption of courts and suspension of legal activities," except for a modest number of "customary courts" that continued to operate.[187] Of some 400 Belgians who had exercised legal functions in the Congo, only 15 to 20 remained in the country beyond independence. Grossen set out to recruit foreign lawyers and judges, arrange for the accelerated training of Congolese judicial personnel, and—crucially—initiate a revision of the colonial legal system.[188] However, judges were not recruited until 1962 and even then, the forty-seven foreign magistrates were only just able to keep the highest trial courts open, as well as about half of the thirty-one district courts. Ultimately, UN assistance helped hold together the main parts of the urban judicial system and operated with gross inefficiency in the rest.[189] In 1964, ONUC's bare-bones judicial management system ended for lack of funds; any UN pretensions of bringing a "rule of law" to the Congo died along the way.[190] The most important contribution that UN legal experts made to the Congo, perhaps, was their assistance in drafting the 1964 "Luluabourg Constitution" for the new state, though its actual impact on affairs in the country is another question.[191]

All in all, ONUC's civilian operations thus engaged in emergency aid in the fields of famine relief, transportation, communication, and public works; high-level administrative and advisory assistance to any government branch that was receptive to advice; large-scale operational assistance in the fields of health, education, civil aviation, and policing; and a plethora of short- and long-term training schemes. By the end of 1963, its civilian operations counted almost 1,500 employees from 47 countries (including 800 teachers); most were from France and French-speaking countries such as Haiti and Switzerland.[192] This was, of course, minimal when compared to the number of Belgian administrators and professionals who had left the country after independence, but extraordinary when compared to the total number of 1,400 UN technical assistance experts employed in the rest of the world in 1966. Nothing in the original Congolese request for assistance, or in the Security Council resolutions relating to ONUC, had pointed to such an expansive civilian program. Regardless of size, the operations' impact on its various fields was mostly modest. Yet, it fundamentally remade the practice of peacekeeping and pushed international development assistance away from advisory services into a more operational direction.

## A CLOSER LOOK AT THE ELUSIVE TASK OF STATE-BUILDING

While the fields of operation for the UN specialized agencies were more or less clearly delineated, the overall task of pulling things together in an integrated effort of state-building was the Secretariat's responsibility—or so its officials thought. To realize this task, a UN political representative was dispatched to each of the six Congolese provinces, supported by individual technical assistance advisors and a small staff.[193] Most UN Secretariat officials arrived in Leopoldville without knowing exactly what their assignments would be. "It was a classic grumble among 'Onusiens,' as ONUC personnel came to be known in the Congo," the wife of one Secretariat official wrote, "that they had to drop whatever work they [were] doing in New York, probably work which had nothing to do with the Congo, to be rushed to Africa at a week's notice."[194] Once they arrived, there were no instructions or rules to guide the civilian personnel's conduct.[195] Beyond the fragmentary maintenance of the colonial state's infrastructure, the overall task of developing a new state, or transforming the existing one, proved elusive.

The assignment of British Secretariat official Antony Gilpin, who arrived in the Congo in October 1960 to help set up the provincial government services in the nonsecessionist northern part of Kasai, is illustrative in many ways.[196] A British Quaker born in 1913, Gilpin had studied modern languages and economics at Cambridge and worked in international refugee relief in Paris during World War II, before joining the UN Secretariat's Department of Economic Affairs in 1952. Gilpin admitted that for setting up the provincial government in Kasai, he had "no technical qualifications whatsoever!" He was quick to add, "Since it will be starting from scratch, perhaps that won't matter."[197] Although to some degree aware of his limitations, Gilpin thus accepted state-building as a field of technical expertise. In his eyes, it was not his ignorance of Kasai politics or his position as an international civil servant that disqualified for him the job of setting up a provincial government, but his lack of general *technical* qualifications. His immediate superior, the forceful, yet diplomatic Frenchman Francis Veillet-Lavallée, who ordinarily served as chief of language services of the UN in Geneva, did not appear more qualified for the task.[198]

According to Gilpin, ONUC's two-person civilian office in Luluabourg served various purposes. Above all, it was "a consulting room" for members of the provincial government, who dropped in at all hours. Veillet-Lavallée and Gilpin also assisted the UN troops in mediating between warring factions in the province and in gaining acceptance for the UN policing role in the region more generally. ONUC's civilian office was the

STATE-BUILDING MEETS PEACEKEEPING  239

contact point for any Congolese, mostly politicians, who sought protection by UN troops, UN military intervention on their behalf, or, in some cases, an airlift. Finally, the two UN civilian officers helped coordinate local, UN-directed relief programs for refugees and the unemployed and allocated UN fellowships. In a letter to his wife, Gilpin described a typical day at the office when he filled in for Veillet-Lavallée, which is worth quoting at length to illustrate the turbulent day-to-day business of the UN civilian operations:

> It starts with the first of our inter-agency meetings (WHO, ICAO, Public Works and ourselves). Very encouraging, as it shows how inter-related our work is and how we can help each other. Slight distraction by American woman journalist for a medical magazine who wanders round photographing us. Meeting ends at 10 a.m. and I get a little quiet dictation to our new French-Canadian male stenographer... Then things start moving. The Director of the water supply phones to say he must have full supplies from Port-Franqui or there will be no water or electricity in Luluabourg in a few days time. I ring the railway and find the matter is already in hand. Enter the Administrator of Dibaya. Can we help find nine persons arrested in September by the ANC disguised as UN [Liberian troops]? Can we also get payment from the [real UN Liberian troops] for goods supplied to them? Enter two young men wanting UN transport to their homes in Kamina—recommended by the Secretary-General of the Provincial Assembly; against the rules, but I stick out my neck with misgivings. Phone call from a very loquacious member of the President's cabinet. What is the UN doing about air shipments of munitions from Brazzaville... to the Kalonjists in Bakwanga... he had heard mysterious planes flying over Sunday night.... Another phone call on the same subject. Enter the Vice-President of the Provincial Assembly. Can we secure the release of a member of the Assembly and another man who have been arrested by the Kalonjists when their plane force-landed in Bakwanga? He fears for their safety. Enter later the Belgian representative of 'Cotonoo' who proves to have been arrested at the same time but was released the next day with profuse apologies from the Kalonjists. And so it goes. I refer some of these problems to Major Roach of the [Ghanaian UN troops], who signals the UN troops in Bakwanga as necessary. Phone call from the railway manager (Belgian) who wants UN

protection to go down the line to investigate an accident in which a women has been killed. I begin to wonder how Veillet-Lavallée has carried all this for months rather than one day.[199]

In practice, Gilpin found it hard, if not impossible, to draw a line between civilian affairs on the one hand and political or military matters on the other. This led to tensions with the UN leadership in Leopoldville. On a visit to the province, Linnér criticized the Luluabourg office "for yielding to the glamour of political and military matters" and not paying enough attention to the civilian side. According to Gilpin, Veillet-Lavallée "hit the ceiling" in response, crashed his glass on the table, and shouted that he was fed up with the Congo and happy to be sent back to Europe. Gilpin, himself "trembling with rage," pointed out that he and Veillet-Lavallée could rarely spend ten minutes on civilian matters without political questions, usually urgent, being forced on them. Again, Gilpin's response suggests that he accepted the theoretical division of neutral civilian affairs, and political questions—though he never attempted to define which was which.

One episode recorded by Gilpin illustrates clearly that the two could hardly be separated in practice and also testifies to the disagreement among UN staff over the proper course of action in potentially controversial cases.[200] In late November 1960, the provincial government of Kasai informed Veillet-Lavallée and Gilpin that they were planning to negotiate a trade agreement with secessionist Katanga. "The political delicacy," Gilpin later noted, "was obvious," for a trade agreement might imply recognition of Katanga's government. However, given Kasai's poor economic situation, the advantages of restoring commercial exchanges with wealthy Katanga were also obvious. Because it seemed that the Kasai provincial government would undertake the negotiations with or without UN help, Veillet-Lavallée decided that Gilpin should go along "to help reduce the risk of Kasai being exploited politically into treating Katanga as an independent country." They informed the UN headquarters in Leopoldville of their intention, but received no response from Linnér.[201] Gilpin thought that "quite a good agreement" emerged from the negotiations.[202] When he later reported on the matter to Leopoldville, Dayal and Linnér reacted with alarm. Gilpin dryly commented: "[The UN command in] Leo has now expressed grave doubts 'politically, legally and economically' about the trade agreement—which doesn't leave much room for other doubts!"[203] Even if the UN was more observer than initiator, Gilpin's presence threatened to imply UN recognition of the secessionist regime in Elisabethville. For Veillet-Lavallée and Gilpin, however, the "civilian" economic needs of Kasai trumped the need to stay aloof from the Congo's internal politics.

## THE POLITICS OF NON-INTERFERENCE: OF "SCRUPULOUS NEUTRALITY," "PRACTICAL WORKING ARRANGEMENTS," AND EXCEPTIONAL CIRCUMSTANCES

The impossibility of remaining, in the words of one UN document, "scrupulously neutral" vis-à-vis the Congo's internal politics became most dramatically clear during the constitutional crisis in September 1960, when President Kasavubu dismissed Prime Minister Lumumba and Mobutu staged his first coup d'état.[204] In the name of law and order, Mobutu had announced that the army would "neutralize" both of the country's leaders and close the houses of parliament.[205] Until a clear constitutional order could be established, a civilian Collège des Commissaires, a board of young Congolese technocrats, would administer national policy.[206] As mentioned above, this council strikingly resembled ONUC's organization, or more specifically its unofficial "shadow cabinet," the so-called UN consultative group. The UN never officially recognized Mobutu and his Commissaires as legitimate. Yet, in the name of keeping the country from further disintegration, ONUC officials did cooperate with his regime.[207] Dayal initially expressed misgivings, worrying that cooperation with an illegitimate government would pose a "political risk" to the UN. He ultimately decided, however, that certain UN civilian programs simply could not be put on hold, and that ONUC thus had to deal with "whatever authority it found in the ministerial chairs."[208] After all, the logic of UN technical assistance demanded that experts had to remain in contact with *somebody* Congolese, who was in a position to give *some kind* of orders.[209]

A November 1960 UN report stated that the early "attempt to dissociate civilian operations from the confusion of the political situation" had ended with "the realization that scrupulous neutrality [could not] create the operational basis for a technical assistance program where a genuinely effective government is lacking." UN technical assistance was designed to serve acting governments neutrally. Where there was no government, or rather, where there were competing claims to authority, "scrupulous neutrality" impeded the UN from carrying out its work. Civilian operations, the report continued, had "made the most of its routine ministry contacts to work out practical arrangements." Working with de facto authorities, the Secretariat asserted, was "free of political connotations." After all, so the argument went, UN civilian operations were engaged in *technical* assistance, not politics.[210]

To uphold this fiction, Hammarskjöld himself elaborated a specific protocol for UN civilian personnel. The UN would not enter into official agreements with Mobutu's Collège des Commissaires, which in either form or substance would imply recognition. "On the other hand, specific working arrangements may be made with individual *Commissaires* (or where appropriate with two or more *Commissaires* acting jointly) who have de facto administrative authority in [a] particular area concerned."[211] Such working arrangements were to be recorded in the form of an initialed memorandum and described as "interim arrangements" that were subject to approval and modification by a constitutionally established government later on. Hammarskjöld thus rather arbitrarily decided that, while signed agreements with the Collège as an entity implied UN recognition of Mobutu's regime, initialed interim working arrangements with individual or a small group of Commissaires were permissible.[212]

In some instances, ONUC's civilian personnel refrained altogether from securing the veneer of a Congolese directive or approval and simply took the initiative or refused Congolese requests. "We should not anticipate or assume the Government's wishes," one Secretariat memo of November 8, 1961 noted, "except in a situation of such emergency that we would be inviting an administrative or economic break-down if we did not accept responsibility for unilateral action." The memo pointed to the UN's interim acceptance of a U.S. offer of $12.95 million for importing American merchandise to the Congo. The offer would have lapsed before the constitution of a new parliament-approved government, which should have decided the matter. The UN initiative on behalf of the incoming government, the memo argued, was legitimate in view of the Congo's enormous economic troubles.[213]

Another example of a legitimate autonomous action on the part of the UN, the memo suggested, was ONUC's relief work in response to the famine among Baluba refugees in secessionist South Kasai. In this case, the enabling argument was less the danger of an administrative or economic breakdown than the specter of a humanitarian catastrophe. In such a situation, the memo stated, "we would prefer to accept responsibility rather than operate on the request of a Congolese authority of doubtful competence." In other words, UN solo initiatives were commendable not just in emergency cases where expedient action was called for that could not await Congolese direction or approval, but also where ONUC officials deemed Congolese decision-making of "doubtful competence."[214]

The same logic applied in the negative sense: Congolese "requests had to be refused in areas where we could not operate without complete assurance of legality," such as "the provision of magistrates and judges" and "association in negotiating a public debt and portfolio settlement."[215] It remains unclear why UN participation in negotiating the Congo's public debt and portfolio settlement was deemed more legally sensitive than, for example, the negotiations with Belgium relating to the transfer of social security provisions in which UN experts participated. Nevertheless, the memo reveals the range of narratives of exception that ONUC officials established to rationalize their own decision-making powers. Emergencies demanded a speedy executive response, humanitarian catastrophes allowed ONUC to override Congolese decision-making of "doubtful competence," and requests for assistance that were deemed "legally questionable" were simply rejected.[216]

## PHASING OUT AND PASSING ON THE TORCH

Congolese–UN relations reached a particularly low point in late 1960 and early 1961. In his official "progress" report of November 2, 1960, Rajeshwar Dayal had issued a scathing indictment of Congolese leaders, particularly Mobutu, as well as of Belgian meddling in Congolese affairs. The report also questioned the assumption—promoted in Western countries—that Lumumba had incited a civil war or engaged in genocide.[217] Western powers resented Dayal's advocacy on behalf of Lumumba, who had been confined to his house under UN "protective custody" since Mobutu had tried to arrest him in early October. Supporters of Lumumba, however, saw his subsequent murder, after he escaped UN supervision, as a failure on part of the world organization. A February 1961 Security Council resolution sponsored by Afro-Asian states, issued in the wake of Lumumba's death, nevertheless strengthened the UN mandate, calling for, among other things, the reorganization and discipline of Congolese army units. In the Congo, the resolution was received as a call to turn the country into a UN trust territory, and the leaders in Leopoldville, Elisabethville (Katanga) and Bakwanga (South Kasai)—in unprecedented agreement—agreed to join forces *against* the UN if necessary.[218]

In early March, Hammarskjöld replaced Dayal with the Sudanese diplomat Mekki Abbas and dispatched a three-man appeasement mission to the Congo composed of African UN representatives: Robert Gardiner of Ghana (who had earlier advised ONUC on the Congolese bureaucracy), Nigerian civil servant Francis Nwokedi, and Tunisian diplomat Mahmoud Khiari (who would succeed Linnér as chief of civilian operations in September 1961).[219] In their discussions with Congolese leaders, the three UN representatives acknowledged ONUC's shortcomings in respecting Congolese sovereignty. With the governments in Leopoldville, Bakwanga, and Stanleyville (where Antoine Gizenga, Lumumba's deputy prime minister, claimed to represent the central government), the UN mission managed to find common ground in the goals of restoring public services, reconvening the parliament, reorganizing the Congolese army, and ejecting the Belgian forces. They also drafted a revised and expanded technical assistance agreement. The long-term goal of the agreement was "Africanization," yet, for the time being, it said that Belgian civilian personnel should be allowed to remain in the Congo.[220] At the same time, ONUC officials hoped to achieve "a maximum integration" of UN personnel into the Congolese state administration and, in particular, to replace the remaining high-level Belgian political advisors with UN employees.[221]

On August 2, 1961, under pressure from both UN and U.S. officials, the Congolese Parliament elected a new civilian government, headed by Prime Minister Adoula, to take over from Mobutu. There was hope among UN officials that the existence of a legitimate, cooperative Congolese government would allow ONUC's civilian operations to leave the confused state of permanent exception behind, phase out its operational assistance, and shift to more regular, advisory technical assistance activities.[222] One memo specified, "Doctors, teachers, civil aviation and telecommunication technicians, even judiciary should not only be borne by the Congolese budget, but should also be servants of the Congolese Government." Special projects such as relief work would be subject to Congolese priorities. What would remain, UN officials hoped, was "a hard core of [UN] advisers and senior administrative personnel in Central and Provincial Ministries," ready to assist where needed, but with the intention to get themselves as well as other foreigners out of the county as quickly as was feasible. The "objective should be 'decolonization' in practical, unsentimental terms," the most rapid development of the Congo's administrative, political, and technical manpower through which alone truly national policies of the state could be achieved.[223]

Instead of contracting, however, ONUC's civilian activities significantly expanded in the following years. When Adoula was elected, there were 336 civilian UN experts; by the end of 1961, there were 426, a year later 520, and at the end of 1963, the number had risen to 631. (This did not include some 600 to 800 teachers who were recruited by UNESCO in 1962 and 1963.[224]) Naturally, none of the problems that the UN consultants had originally identified in their respective fields immediately went away with the election of the new Congolese government. ONUC officials hoped, moreover, that more constructive work could be realized in cooperation with a government that owed allegiance to the United Nations. And because UN officials perceived Adoula as a bulwark against radical Congolese politicians, they had an increased incentive to support his government with the help of civilian operations.

As noted above, the eventual phasing out of ONUC that followed the end of the Katangan secession in January 1963 had little to do with accomplishing the original goal of the UN mission to the Congo—the restoration of law and order. Political and financial pressures led U Thant, who succeeded Hammarskjöld as secretary-general after the latter's death on 18 September 1961, to reassess the UN mission in the Congo. Being accused of wrongdoing from all sides, many senior UN officials had personally had enough of the Congo.[225] The United States, meanwhile, lobbied for the UN to remain "to hold the country together," at least until the ANC had been "retrained." U.S. officials pointed out that Tshombe was "still hankering after secession" and that he maintained mercenaries and military equipment in northern Rhodesia and Angola. According to historian Arthur Schlesinger, the threat of another secession ultimately convinced Thant to keep UN troops in the Congo until the summer of 1964. Bunche credited the unified support of African member states in the General Assembly for the favorable response to Adoula's appeal.[226] The last UN troops withdrew by the end of June 1964, and ONUC's operations thus officially ended.

The new secretary-general had originally envisioned a yearlong phase-out of UN civilian operations to follow the troop withdrawal.[227] But with several opposition movements gaining strength across the country, security in the Congo was at a low ebb in 1964. Leaving behind a large civilian assistance program somewhat eased the consciences of those concerned about quitting the country militarily in the face of violent unrest.[228] "There is very, very much still to be done in the Congo," Bunche noted in 1964, "particularly in the realm of civilian assistance."[229] Forcing a rapid reduction in this area, many feared, would only cause further dislocations.[230] Officially, the UN civilian operations in the Congo were transformed into a regular UN technical assistance program in 1964. In terms of size, funding, and operations, however, UN technical assistance to the Congo continued to be far from conventional.

Until the end of 1963, ONUC's civilian operations had been financed by voluntary contributions by member states to the Congo Fund, which was established by the General Assembly in September 1960.[231] ONUC's military operations, by contrast, were financed through the fixed shares each UN member state was supposed to pay. When ONUC ceased to exist, part of the UN civilian assistance to the Congo, about $2.7 million, began to be covered through conventional UN technical assistance financing. However, the lion's share of the total costs, about $17 million, was financed through nonconventional funding, of which the U.S. shouldered about $11.5 million.[232] As of 1964, the UN rewarded the outsized U.S. contribution with regular reports on its operations to the United States Agency for International Development (USAID), as well as discussion sessions on staffing and disbursement of funds with USAID officials.[233] As one study put it, after 1964, UN technical assistance to the Congo became an internationally sanctioned program that the organization administered on behalf of the U.S..[234]

Because the UN regularly claimed that multilateral assistance was superior to bilateral in that it did not foster dependence on a single country, UN officials grew increasingly uncomfortable with the U.S.-sponsored Congo program. Similarly, USAID officials grew tired of convincing Congress each year of the value of their exceptional arrangement with the UN for multilateral assistance to the Congo.[235] In 1966, working groups of both USAID and the UN began a dialogue to downsize their extraordinary assistance to the level of a large, but regular UN development program.[236] The Congolese government reportedly was a mostly passive observer in this process.[237] Mobutu, who had staged a second coup in November 1965, only intervened personally to maintain a comparatively large UN presence in the health sector upon learning that some hospitals might have to be closed as a result of downsizing the international presence in the country.[238] By 1970, there were still "some vestiges" of non-conventionally financed posts, but with 250 experts, the UN technical assistance program to the Congo was less than a third of what it had been when the troops withdrew in 1964.[239] In the words of Arthur House, "'Stable'—rightly or wrongly—became in 1970 the common description of the Congolese economy and administration."[240] With Mobutu firmly in place and USAID securely established in the Congo, the UN considered the emergency there to be over, or at least the world organization's responsibility for it.

ONUC's breach or, rather, its subjective interpretation of the principal of noninterference in the internal affairs of the Congo, has been discussed elsewhere with regard to the UN command's high-level political and military decisions.[241] The sheer absurdity of clinging to the idea of noninterference at a time when ONUC was essentially building a parallel administrative structure in the country has not been discussed in the scholarly literature. It has been argued that the UN's priorities in the Congo shifted from enabling development to securing law and order and, ultimately, to prioritizing order over law.[242] As this chapter has shown, the maintenance of order was—at the request of the Congolese government—a UN priority from the start. It was not so much that the stated mission morphed from enabling development to securing order. Rather, in thinking about the Congo, Hammarskjöld and his staff dramatically expanded the definition of what peacekeeping or the maintenance of order entailed in a newly independent state: peacekeeping in the context of decolonization meant not just a policing function for UN troops, but the maintenance and reorganization of health, education, agriculture, finances, judicature, and other state services. In other words, order was above all to be achieved through expertise-driven technical assistance. This was certainly no apolitical task, but involved choosing sides or, more precisely, counterparts, and thus empowering some actors over others.[243]

At the outset of the Congo crisis, UN officials had been eager to demonstrate their worth as pioneers of peacekeeping and state-building. Yet, the organization's intervention—even more, perhaps, than the other missions covered in this book—proved to be a sobering experience. Some UN officials involved argued that it had made the best of an impossible situation, preserving the Congo's territorial integrity, maintaining a minimum of state public services, and keeping the Cold War (really the Soviets) out of the country and thus preventing an armed superpower confrontation in central Africa.[244] Others thought that the UN had simply taken on a job far too big for it.[245]

Still other officials wondered whether the problem went beyond the issue of insufficient resources and was really a question of authority. Critical politicians, academics and relief practitioners charged that many newly independent states were "fictions," that it was "unrealistic to regard them as entities in any sense."[246] They were essentially colonies, "if not of some traditional power ... then of the United Nations itself."[247] Yet the UN—hampered by the principle of noninterference in internal affairs—had, in effect, too little power: it was in the position of "a bicycle rider who is riding without the chain: he cannot ride uphill or on level ground, but only downward."[248]

UN officials began to wonder: "[S]hould the United Nations accept responsibility in a newly independent state where governmental institutions are still in a primitive state of development without making it a condition that it will assume such responsibility as is necessary for it to discharge its mandate, even to the extent of temporarily taking over some aspects of government?"²⁴⁹ Should states be allowed to "parade sovereign rights so as to emasculate the police authority of the international force?" "Must there not be an element . . . of trusteeship in any UN peacekeeping operation?"²⁵⁰ The snag about UN peacekeeping, another critic wrote in 1965, was that it simply "sterilized" or froze conflicts without solving them. Once in, the UN was there to stay indefinitely, or if it did get out, it usually left things worse off. The world was becoming littered with UN forces, which did not dare to withdraw, but could not afford to stay—a rather odd statement for the 1960s, given the scarcity of its peacekeeping efforts then, in comparison to the 1990s.²⁵¹

In fact, UN peacekeeping during the Cold War was never again as expansive as it had been during the Congo crisis. Nor did the organization embark on another large-scale operation to manage decolonization.²⁵² Along with the secretary-general himself, Hammarskjöld's vision for the premier role that the UN might play in handling postcolonial transformations died in the Congo crisis. UN officials realized that they had taken on a job far too big for them and the UN as a whole, and that large-scale international administrative and technical assistance did not, in fact, provide the necessary "elbow room" to establish truly independent states, as Hammarskjöld had hoped it would.²⁵³ Nevertheless, the UN intervention in the Congo had significant repercussions. With the large-scale provision of teachers, doctors, and technicians (in the field of civil aviation, for example), ONUC pushed international development assistance from an emphasis on advisory services into an operational direction. It established a range of narratives of exception, allowing international officials to circumvent the principle of noninterference and thus render state sovereignty a less meaningful barrier against outside intervention. Finally, ONUC significantly expanded the meaning of peacekeeping to signify not only a policing operation but, in effect, a kind of developmental "international territorial administration," engaged in any number of fields that had previously been considered the prerogatives of the state.²⁵⁴

After the end of the Cold War, this practice of international territorial administration enjoyed an unprecedented revival as a means to take care of states that were perceived as weak, failed, or vanquished—from Kosovo to East Timor to Iraq.²⁵⁵ In fact, forty years after the first UN mission to the Congo, blue helmets returned to the country to keep peace. In 2015, the *Mission de l'Organisation des Nations Unies pour la Stabilisation en*

FIG. 20  MONUSCO Peacekeepers in North Kivu

Indian peacekeepers with the UN mission in the Democratic Republic of the Congo (MONUSCO), deployed to the country's North Kivu Province (2012).

Source: UN Photo, UN7324335.

*Republique Democratique du Congo* (MONUSCO) counted around 20,000 military and close to 900 civilian UN employees.[256] At this writing, the UN presence in the Democratic Republic of Congo (DRC) consists of a peacekeeping mission and twenty-two programs, funds, and specialized agencies, working together and alongside the Congolese government for the stabilization and development of the DRC while providing humanitarian assistance to the needy.[257] Although MONUSCO is thus strikingly similar in objectives and challenges to ONUC, the 1960s UN intervention in the Congo seems, by and large, forgotten history.[258]

# EPILOGUE

How can we account for the strange triumph of state sovereignty on a global scale in the second half of the twentieth century?[1] While some scholars have argued that the Cold War superpower competition led to the rapid spread of the sovereign-state model of political organization in the postwar period, this book suggests that one must also take seriously the active role played by the United Nations.[2] The world organization supported the proliferation of independent states after 1945, while also changing the meaning of state sovereignty in the process. Whereas the road to statehood previously led through political negotiations, the UN pioneered a new form of state-building through development assistance. Member states initially sought out international assistance to determine on what basis they might endure or be strengthened, while UN officials increasingly offered technical assistance as an answer to that question. In doing so, they framed the sovereign nation-state as the logical outcome of decolonization and the prime agent of development, whose success, however, depended on the continued supply of foreign assistance.

In trying to ensure both self-determination and development, UN officials placed considerable emphasis on establishing or strengthening national administrations. Administrative capacity was presented as crucial for development to ensure the best use of available resources and outside assistance. Successful development, in turn, was perceived as necessary for true sovereignty and self-determination. More importantly, given the organization's comparatively limited resources as well as its mandate of noninterference in internal politics, UN officials conceived of administration as the ideal place for effective outside intervention: one that allowed significant influence on national politics while remaining respectful of state sovereignty. Politicians would decide policy, while international administrators would carry out and manage their decisions. They would engage in governance, not politics. Administration was presented as a science or skill and thus a legitimate terrain for non-state actors, an idea that lives on today in the ubiquitous invocation of "good governance" in development agendas.

Benjamin Higgins' chief economist plans for Libya, Hugh Keenleyside's administrative assistant scheme for Bolivia, Dag Hammarskjöld's proposal for an International Administrative Service, and ONUC's civilian operations, all of which proposed the dispatch of managers in some form or another, pushed what was considered acceptable international development assistance from advisory services toward more operational and paternalist practices. Instead of merely receiving counsel that could be taken or rejected, UN member states could increasingly call upon international experts to get work done on their behalf. While these member states would set in motion, own, and, if necessary, veto decisions, capable foreign experts would manage national development. Although far from uncontested, this was not a story of a neocolonial imposition by the UN on "developing countries," but rather a negotiated process in which the tension between international trusteeship in the name of expertise and national self-determination in the name of state sovereignty were continuously renegotiated.

The UN operations in the Congo (ONUC) in the 1960s proved in many ways to be a turning point in the organization's history. This was by far the most expansive UN effort to manage decolonization through technical assistance, an attempt to take over and reform a newly independent state bureaucracy. Invoking the pressures of an emergency situation, the UN operated autonomously from national decision-making in the Congo. This approach raised a host of questions about the basis of UN authority in the country, its claim to impartiality and neutrality, and its capacity to deliver on the promise of managing decolonization, providing security, and ensuring development in the postcolonial world. Controversies over UN conduct in the Congo brought the organization to the brink of political and financial collapse. The Secretariat, as well as UN member states, subsequently shied away from any similar international endeavors to manage decolonization.

The closest comparable UN initiative was initiated while ONUC was still in operation. From 1962 to 1963, for seven months, the UN temporarily assumed official authority in West New Guinea, formerly a Dutch colonial territory, to which Indonesia laid claim. The UN interim administration was intended as a buffer between the Dutch retreat and the transfer of the territory to Indonesia, which the two countries had agreed upon in 1962 (without consulting the Papuan inhabitants of the territory), after a period of prolonged fighting. Yet, the UN administration was never genuinely international, except at the most senior level. For a month or two, West New Guinea was staffed mostly by Dutch personnel; thereafter, it became predominantly Indonesian. Unlike under ONUC, the costs for the UN administration were not borne by all member states, but shared by the Dutch and Indonesians.[3] More importantly, the UN Temporary Executive Authority, or UNTEA, as the operation there was officially called, never pursued such expansive transformative ambitions as ONUC. The main goal of the brief UN regnum in West New Guinea was to prevent administrative collapse and enable the transfer of the territory from former colonial power (the Netherlands) to another former colony (Indonesia) without disruptions or controversy.[4]

It was only with the end of the Cold War that ONUC-style peacekeeping enjoyed an unexpected comeback, as the UN concept of security became ever more expansive. In the 1990s, the UN officially adopted a broader understanding of possible threats to peace, including "non-military sources of instability in the economic, social, humanitarian, and ecological fields."[5] This placed seemingly unprecedented peacekeeping demands on the organization and the scale of international executive action increased dramatically. The number of peacekeepers deployed by the UN worldwide went from around 10,000 at the end of 1990 to more than 78,000 by 1993.[6] During that decade, UN administrators assumed public authority in Cambodia, Croatia, Kosovo, and East Timor.[7] Rather than simply ensuring the absence of violence, the 1990s UN peacekeeping missions sought to eliminate the root causes of conflict by remaking the territories in question, much as the organization had tried in the Congo in the 1960s.[8]

Naturally, the problems posed by this executive rule and the concomitant questions about UN authority, neutrality, and capacity that had been raised during the Congo crisis did not disappear. These new post–Cold War experiments in "international territorial administration," one observer noted, were largely characterized by "the unwillingness or inability of the UN to conceive of its governing responsibilities as state-like public authority, requiring institutional checks and balances and mechanisms of accountability."[9] Yet, as Anne Orford has pointed out, much of the scholarly literature on the topic approaches UN government of places and peoples as a series of projects from which lessons can be learned and coherent policies developed.[10] Much international legal scholarship, for example, is dedicated to the goal of subjecting global governance to distinctive administrative law principles.[11] Orford, by contrast, rightly questions the legal basis and indeed the desirability of global managers, who enjoy broad immunities and privileges due to their status as international civil servants, to determine national policies and choose the ends of government abroad. She suggests that the work of law is central to the task of making international territorial administration comprehensible and thus amenable to political action.[12] Recovering the history of international governance, this book suggests, is just as important.

This is not to say that the United Nations has no role to play in the resolution of contemporary intrastate conflicts. To the contrary, recovering the history covered in this book also demonstrates the very direct responsibility and involvement of UN member states in creating a range of ostensible "failed states"—as well as the parallel reflex of divesting themselves of significant financial and political commitments in order to help these polities prosper.[13] In the 1940s and 1950s, not enough attention had been paid to the material and administrative basis on which newly independent states might endure. More recently, the pendulum seems to have swung too far in the other direction as state- or peace-building efforts were approached as technocratic challenges for international managers. It might thus be useful to review earlier UN operations, such as those in Somaliland and Libya, and devise similar, though more muscular local and national "political filters" to let inhabitants of the countries in question determine any peace-building process, while being mindful of the outsized international responsibility to see these efforts succeed.

# ACKNOWLEDGMENTS

This book is mostly a culmination of my time at New York University. I owe a great deal to the NYU History Department and faculty for teaching me how to read, think, and write like a historian. Above all, I thank my advisor, Mary Nolan, for her unflinching support, her straightforward, constructive criticism, and her committed encouragement throughout my studies and beyond. I owe special thanks to the late Marilyn Young and Frederick Cooper for critically engaging and encouraging this book from its inception and for their open doors for many stimulating conversations. I am grateful to Daniel Speich of the University of Lucerne and Mark Mazower of Columbia University for having helped me think through the project. I found NYU's graduate workshop in European history an inspiring forum for its commitment to rigorous scholarship and critical discussions of work beyond narrowly confined geographical fields, providing me an intellectual home—despite my eventually "straying from the path" and writing a history of international organization.

During my time as a PhD candidate, I benefited greatly from taking classes at Columbia University on the politics of humanity and development and continuing conversations on these topics with Sam Moyn and Michele Alacevich thereafter.

Participating in the final round of the National History Center's annual Decolonization Seminar under the direction of Roger Louis, Marilyn

Young, Sudhir Pilarisetti, Philippa Levine, Dane Kennedy and Jason Parker (whose introduction to the U.S. National Archives at College Park was truly invaluable) was a great experience intellectually and personally (a shout-out to Team 2015!), and I feel fortunate for having been able to join this broader history of decolonization community.

I greatly appreciate having received financial support from NYU, the Society for Historians of American Foreign Relations, and Harvard and Cambridge Universities' History Project for New Economic Thinking as well as, crucially, Yale University, where I spent academic year 2015–2016 as a Smith Richardson predoctoral fellow in International Security Studies (ISS). Paul Kennedy and Amanda Behm encouraged a serious commitment to making historical research relevant to current affairs and my cohort of fellows, Rebecca Lissner, Ian Johnson, and James Cameron, have been wonderful company and an important source of support.

At a very early stage of this project, Nils Gilman took considerable time to constructively challenge the whole premise of writing a history of UN development efforts and pushed me to define a clear narrative arc, which I hope to have managed. I am greatly indebted to Sinclair Thomson and Thomas Field for critically engaging my chapters on Bolivia and helping me navigate the field. Stephan Malinowski (who introduced me to development as history), John Shovlin (from whom I learned so much about teaching and the broader history of the elusive concept of an international order), Tom Bender (who guided me in teaching my own course on the history of development), Stef Geroulanos (who offered invaluable help with the dreadful art of writing grant proposals), Stephen Gross, Susan Pedersen, Patricia Clavin, Richard Jolly (who generously shared his chocolate bar as well as an unpublished memoir of a UN official that, alas, never made it into the final manuscript), Davide Rodogno, Sandrine Kott (who facilitated a last-minute visit to the Archives of the International Labor Organization), Małgorzata Mazurek, Miguel Bandeira Jerónimo, and Jennifer Welsh all kindly took the time to discuss my project at different stages of the research and writing.

I am forever thankful to my fellow graduate students at NYU, above all Sarah Griswold and Alexandra Steinlight for their patience reading the umpteenth version of various drafts of this work and for providing invaluable critical feedback, moral support, and diversion. Geoffrey Traugh, Rachel Kantrowitz, Beatrice Wayne, Samuel Misteli, Carmen Soliz,

Annalisa Urbano, Katrin Armborst, Jan Lüdert, and especially Jess Pearson have also provided immensely helpful thoughts on individual chapters and related material.

I benefited greatly from the multidisciplinary scholarly community at the European University Institute in Florence as a postdoctoral fellow and discussing my work and development and international history more broadly with Corinna Unger (an inspiring and supportive mentor throughout the year), Federico Romero, and the program's PhD candidates and postdoctoral fellows. The postdoc history writing group organized by Laurie Anderson was especially helpful: it included Giula Bonazza, Sinem Casale, Audrey Gillet, Jonathan Greenwood, Alexandra Chadwic, Andrej Milivojevic, Marta Musso, Mate Rigo, Katalin Straner, Veronika Pehe, and José Juan Pérez Meléndez. So were the discussions in the "Europe in the World" research seminar organized by Ulrich Krotz and Richard Maher.

I found temporary, but wonderful academic community in the Global History program at Freie University, Berlin, where Sebastian Conrad, Michael Goebel, Christoph Kalter, Valeska Huber, Nadin Heé, Susanne Schmidt, Fabian Steininger, Minu Haschemi, Tim Nunan, and especially Franziska Exeler (in our informal two-person workshop) provided valuable feedback on the project.

Workshops on the "Histories of International Organizations" and the "North–South Conflict" at Leiden and Leipzig Universities, organized by the "Rethinking Disability Team" as well as Jürgen Dinkel, Frank Reichherzer, and Steffen Fiebrig, as well as the Colloquium in Global History at Munich University offered me the welcome opportunity to present and discuss my research (and receive especially helpful comments from Corinne Pernet).

The 2018 International Research Award in Global History, sponsored by Roland Wenzlhuemer, Madeleine Herren-Oesch, and Glenda Sluga and organized by Susanne Hohler, allowed me to convene a workshop on international organizations and decolonization with a number of wonderful scholars, including Anne-Isabelle Richard, Jennifer Foray, Stella Krepp, Angela Loschke, Giuliano Garavini, Alanna O'Malley, Simon Stevens, Susan Pedersen, Meredith Teretta, Bastiaan Bouwman, Pamela Ballinger, William Caruthers, Sue Lin Lewis, Noelle Turtur, Brian McNeil, and Emily Baughan, who all helped me situate my project in the broader history on this topic. I have also learned a lot from working with a small team, including Cindy Ewing, Bogdan Iacob, Disha Jani, Elisabeth Leake and Giorgio Potì, supported by Heidi Tworek, on a publication on the topic.

A fellowship at Bern University in 2019 (as well as my youngest daughter's staying put beyond her official due date) allowed me to finalize the manuscript for submission while also exploring a new project on the history of international organizations. My colleagues at Vienna University, where I found a more permanent academic home in the Department of Development Studies in 2020, including Katharina Kreuder-Sonnen, Lucile Dreidemy, and Johannes Knierzinger, helped me with the final revisions.

I am grateful to Tim Nunan, Caelyn Cobb, Monique Briones, and Marisa Lastres at Columbia University Press for "adopting" the project and for helping me navigate the review and production process. I greatly appreciate the anonymous reviewers for their constructive, insightful feedback, which I have tried to address as best as I could, as well as Katherine Harper's thorough copyedits and June Sawyer's indexing work.

Of course, I could not have written this book without the help of the archivists at the United Nations Archives and Records Management Section, where Paolo Casini gave a wonderful introduction to the archives and Neshanta Karunanayake has been immeasurably helpful with regard to specific inquiries. I am grateful to the archivists at Oxford University's Bodleian Library, UCLA's Charles E. Young Library, the University of Maryland's George Meany Memorial Archives, Stanford University's Hoover Institution, the Archives of the International Labor Organization in Geneva, the Library and Archives Canada, the U.S. National Archives at College Park, Columbia University's Rare Book and Manuscript Library, Princeton's Seeley G. Mudd Library, and the United Nations Archives in Geneva. Stacy Williams and Carol Arnold-Hamilton of the Elmer Holmes Bobst Library have been an invaluable help for accessing NYU's United Nations and International Documents Collection.

I am more than grateful to the late Tony Judt for making history inspiring and relevant, encouraging me to pursue a graduate degree, and helping me navigate the U.S. application process.

Finally I would like to thank my parents, especially my mom, to whom I dedicate this project. They have been more than supportive. Christoph and our children, Emma, Hans, and Mona, provided a much needed counterpoint to academia—and also made nonfiction and archival papers look appealing again after multiple rounds of reading *Cars and Trucks and Things that Go* and *Conni geht zum Zahnarzt*.

Although I could not have completed this book without the incredibly generous help and support I have received, any potential errors or omissions are, naturally, my own.

# NOTES

## INTRODUCTION

1. Jean de la Roche, "The Objectives of International Trusteeship," 23 September 1946, Ralph Bunche papers (RB), Box 83, Folder 2, Charles E. Young Research Library, University of California (UCLA). For further biographical information on de la Roche, see chapter 1.
2. See "Growth in UN membership, 1945-present," https://www.un.org/en/sections/member-states/growth-united-nations-membership-1945-present/index.html, last accessed 30 October 2020.
3. Mark Mazower uses the phrase "strange triumph" to describe a strengthening of the principle of state sovereignty with the new human rights regime underwritten by the UN in 1945. See Mark Mazower, "The Strange Triumph of Human Rights, 1933–1950," *The Historical Journal* 47, no. 2 (June 1, 2004): 379–98. Susan Pedersen suggests that our current world order of formally independent states can be traced back to the mandates system of the UN predecessor body, the League of Nations. See Susan Pedersen, *The Guardians: The League of Nations and the Crisis of Empire* (Oxford: Oxford University Press, 2015), 13, 403–4.
4. For different political imaginaries at the time, from visions of "Eurafrica" to federalism, see, e.g., Michael Collins, "Decolonisation and the 'Federal Moment,'" *Diplomacy & Statecraft* 24, no. 1 (2013): 21–40; Frederick Cooper, *Citizenship between Empire and Nation: Remaking France and French Africa, 1945–1960* (Princeton: Princeton University Press, 2014); Gary Wilder, *Freedom Time: Negritude, Decolonization, and the Future of the World* (Durham, NC: Duke University Press, 2015); Adom Getachew, *Worldmaking after Empire: The Rise and Fall of Self-Determination* (Princeton: Princeton University Press, 2019); and Lydia Walker, "Decolonization in the 1960s: On Legitimate and Illegitimate Nationalist Claims-Making," *Past & Present* 242, no. 1 (2019): 227–64.
5. To call attention to the problematic implication of developmental hierarchies, I use the term "developing countries" in quotation marks.
6. Guy Fiti Sinclair, *To Reform the World: International Organizations and the Making of Modern States* (Oxford: Oxford University Press, 2017), 22. For the role of international

organizations in defining statehood and shaping its agenda, also see Connie McNeely, *Constructing the Nation-State: International Organization and Prescriptive Action* (Westport, CT: Greenwood, 1995).

7. For a similar argument, see Karuna Matena, "Popular Sovereignty and Anti-Colonialism," in *Popular Sovereignty in Historical Perspective*, ed. Richard Bourke and Quentin Skinner (New York: Cambridge University Press, 2016), 297–319; Getachew, *Worldmaking after Empire*. For Afghanistan as a laboratory for postcolonial sovereign statehood, see Timothy Nunan, *Humanitarian Invasion: Global Development in Cold War Afghanistan* (New York: Cambridge University Press, 2016); for an analysis of NGOs performing functions of sovereignty in the Sahel, see Gregory Mann, *From Empires to NGOs in the West African Sahel: The Road to Nongovernmentality*, African Studies Series 129 (New York: Cambridge University Press, 2015).

8. For the co-constitution and intersection between internationalism and imperialism, see Miguel Bandeira Jerónimo and José Pedro Monteiro, eds., *The Pasts of the Present: Internationalism, Imperialism and the Formation of the Contemporary World* (London: Palgrave Macmillan, 2017); and Susan Pedersen, "Foreword," in *The Institution of International Order: From the League of Nations to the United Nations* (London: Routledge, 2018). For the UN's own take on the organization's role in decolonization, see https://www.un.org/en/decolonization/ (last accessed 15 August 2019).

9. Mark Mazower, *No Enchanted Palace: The End of Empire and the Ideological Origins of the United Nations* (Princeton: Princeton University Press, 2009); Pedersen, *The Guardians*.

10. The Charter stipulated that colonial trusteeship should lead to self-government (*not necessarily independence*). See UN Charter, Chapter XI: Declaration Regarding Non-Self-Governing Territories, https://www.un.org/en/sections/un-charter/chapter-xi/index.html (last accessed 24 June 2019).

11. Following Vijay Prashad, I use the term "Third World" to denote a common political project. Evan Luard, *A History of the United Nations: The Age of Decolonization, 1955–1965*, vol. 2 (New York: St. Martin's Press, 1989); Vijay Prashad, *The Darker Nations: A People's History of the Third World* (New York: The New Press, 2008); Mark Mazower, *Governing the World: The History of an Idea* (New York: Penguin Press, 2012); Ryan Irwin, "Imagining Nation, State, and Order in the Mid-Twentieth Century," Rethinking Cold War History in Southern Africa, *Kronos* 37 (2011): 12–22; Getachew, *Worldmaking after Empire*. Also see footnote 31 for histories of self-determination.

12. Getachew, *Worldmaking after Empire*; also see Ryan Irwin, "A Wind of Change? White Redoubt and the Postcolonial Moment, 1960–1963," *Diplomatic History* 33, no. 5 (2009): 897–925. Also see Cindy Ewing, "'With a Minimum of Bitterness': Decolonization, the Arab-Asian Group and Postcolonial Internationalism at the United Nations," *Journal of Global History*, forthcoming.

13. Sunil Amrith and Glenda Sluga, "New Histories of the United Nations," *Journal of World History* 19, no. 3 (2008): 260.

14. Mazower, *No Enchanted Palace*, 27; David MacKenzie, *A World beyond Borders: An Introduction to the History of International Organizations* (Toronto: University of Toronto Press, 2010), 57.

15. For recent introductions to UN histories, see Amrith and Sluga, "New Histories"; Amy Sayward, *The United Nations in International History* (London: Bloomsbury, 2017); Elisabeth Röhrlich, "State of the Field Essay on the History of the United Nations and Its Organizations," *H-Diplo*, 2018, http://tiny.cc/E153; for a focus on the UN Secretariat, see John Toye and Richard Toye, *The UN and Global Political Economy: Trade, Finance,*

and Development, United Nations Intellectual History Project Series (Bloomington: Indiana University Press, 2004); Craig Murphy, *The United Nations Development Programme: A Better Way?* (Cambridge: Cambridge University Press, 2006); Daniel Speich Chassé, "Der Blick von Lake Success: Das Entwicklungsdenken der Frühen UNO als 'Lokales Wissen,'" in *Entwicklungswelten—Globalgeschichte der Entwicklungszusammenarbeit*, ed. Hubertus Büschel and Daniel Speich Chassé, vol. 6: *Globalgeschichte* (Frankfurt am Main: Campus, 2009), 143–74; David Webster, "Development Advisors in a Time of Cold War and Decolonization: The United Nations Technical Assistance Administration, 1950–59," *Journal of Global History* 6, no. 2 (2011): 249–72.

16. Alanna O'Malley similarly distinguishes between three dimensions of UN history: the UN as a public stage, the UN as an actor; and the UN as a socializing space. Writing about the League, Susan Pedersen understands international organizations as "force fields" made up of shifting alliances, networks, and institutions, which a host of different actors entered and thought to exploit. Alanna O'Malley, *Diplomacy of Decolonisation: America, Britain and the United Nations during the Congo Crisis 1960–64* (Manchester: Manchester University Press, 2018), 2–3; Pedersen, *The Guardians*, 5.

17. For a focus on Hammarskjöld and decolonization, see Henning Melber, *Dag Hammarskjöld, the United Nations and the Decolonisation of Africa* (London: Hurst & Company, 2019). The secretaries-general of the organization, and particularly Hammarskjöld, have indeed received scholarly attention; for biographies of Hammarskjöld, see Brian Urquhart, *Hammarskjold* (New York: Knopf, 1972); Manuel Fröhlich, *Political Ethics and the United Nations: Dag Hammarskjöld as Secretary-General* (London: Routledge, 2008); Roger Lipsey, *Hammarskjöld: A Life* (Ann Arbor: University of Michigan Press, 2013); for renewed attention to international public administrations, see Karen Gram-Skjoldager, Haakon A. Ikonomou, and Torsten Kahlert, eds., *Organizing the 20th-Century World: International Organizations and the Emergence of International Public Administration, 1920–1960s* (London: Bloomsbury Academic, 2020).

18. Karen Gram-Skjoldager and Haakon A. Ikonomou, "The Making of the International Civil Servant c. 1920–60: Establishing a Profession," in Gram-Skjoldager, Ikonomou, and Kahlert, *Organizing the 20th-Century World*, 215–30; also see David MacFayden et al., *Eric Drummond and His Legacies: The League of Nations and the Beginnings of Global Governance* (Cham: Palgrave Macmillan, 2019).

19. The International Court of Justice, though officially also a principal organ of the UN, is not serviced by the Secretariat in New York because it is located in the Hague. Initially, the principal units were: the Department of Security Council Affairs, the Department of Economic Affairs, the Department of Social Affairs, the Department of Trusteeship and Information from Non-Self-Governing Territories, the Department of Public Information, the Legal Department, Conference and General Services, and Administrative and Financial Services. (The Department of Economic Affairs and the Department of Social Affairs were merged in 1955.) See *Yearbook of the United Nations 1946–1947* (New York: United Nations, 1947), 614.

20. While the Secretariat in New York counted around 1,000 staff members in 1956, it nearly tripled in size over the next decade. In 1966, for example, it counted approximately 6,100 staff members, of whom 3,600 served at the UN headquarters in New York, while the remainder worked "in the field," including at other headquarters, such as the one in Geneva. In addition to these permanent staff members, there were about 1,400 temporarily employed UN technical assistance experts in 1966. See A/C.5/689 Composition of the Secretariat: report of the Secretary General, 7 December 1956, and information

provided with the photograph "United Nations Secretariat" (UN7768049), UN Photo Digital Asset Management System, https://dam.media.un.org/, last accessed 8 February 2021. Today the number is closer to 40,000. See https://ask.un.org/faq/14626, last accessed 9 August 2021.

21. Welsh civil servant David Owen, who served as deputy to the British executive secretary of the UN Preparatory Commission, Gladwyn Jebb, and then to the first UN secretary-general, Trygve Lie, played an important role in staffing the world organization. Toye and Toye, *The UN and Global Political Economy*, 61; Murphy, *The UNDP*, 75; Owen's personal papers are available at Columbia University's Rare Book and Manuscript Library. For biographical information, see Box 35 and 36 and Murphy, chapter 3; Sixten Heppling, *UNDP: From Agency Shares to Country Programmes, 1949–1975* (Stockholm: Ministry of Foreign Affairs, 1995), 20. Also see Chapter 5 on Owen.

22. On the League Secretariat, see Gram-Skjoldager and Ikonomou, "The Making of the International Civil Servant"; on British experiences in the UN civil service, see Amy Limoncelli, "Great Britain and International Administration: Finding a New Role at the United Nations, 1941–1975" (doctoral dissertation, Boston College, 2016); on Soviet approaches to international bureaucracies, see Louis H. Porter, "Cold War Internationalisms: The USSR in UNESCO, 1945–1967" (PhD dissertation, University of North Carolina, 2018).

23. Twenty-five posts were held by nationals from the U.S., fourteen from the UK, nine from France, five each from Sweden, Canada, and China, four from India, and three each from Mexico, the USSR, Poland, and Yugoslavia. See A/C.5/689 Composition of the Secretariat: report of the Secretary General, 7 December 1956.

24. Similarly, Martha Finnemore has argued that international organizations are producers of knowledge that structures the articulation of the interest of its member nations. Martha Finnemore, *National Interests in International Society* (Ithaca, NY: Cornell University Press, 1996).

25. For histories of the UN and development emphasizing ideas rather than practice, see the various contributions to the UN Intellectual History Project, which were written mainly by political scientists and economists based on the official publications by the organization: Richard Jolly, *UN Contributions to Development Thinking and Practice* (Bloomington: Indiana University Press, 2004); Devaki Jain, *Women, Development, and the UN: A Sixty-Year Quest for Equality and Justice* (Bloomington: Indiana University Press, 2005); Yves Berthelot, ed., *Unity and Diversity in Development Ideas: Perspectives from the UN Regional Commissions* (Bloomington: Indiana University Press, 2004); Thomas Weiss, *UN Voices: The Struggle for Development and Social Justice* (Bloomington: Indiana University Press, 2005); Olav Stokke, *The UN and Development: From Aid to Cooperation* (Bloomington: Indiana University Press, 2009); similarly based on the published records of the organization is: Digambar Bhouraskar, *United Nations Development Aid: A Study in History and Politics* (New Delhi: Academic Foundation, 2007). Archive-based accounts of the UN and development include Toye and Toye, *The UN and Global Political Economy*; Murphy, *The UNDP*; Webster, "Development Advisors in a Time of Cold War and Decolonization"; also see Daniel Speich Chassé, *Die Erfindung des Bruttosozialprodukts: globale Ungleichheit in der Wissensgeschichte der Ökonomie* (Göttingen: Vandenhock & Ruprecht, 2013). There is, however, a proliferating literature on the work of the various UN agencies and programs abroad, see https://www.histecon.magd.cam.ac.uk/unhist/research/bibliographies/technical_agencies.html.

26. Anne Orford and Guy Fiti Sinclair similarly point out that UN practice evolved not by formal amendments to the organization's Charter, but through "experiments" abroad.

Anne Orford, *International Authority and the Responsibility to Protect* (Cambridge: Cambridge University Press, 2011); Sinclair, *To Reform the World*; for an early emphasis on the importance of practical development experiences, see Monica Van Beusekom, *Negotiating Development: African Farmers and Colonial Experts at the Office du Niger, 1920–1960* (Portsmouth: Heinemann, 2002).

27. For the need of writing multilocal global histories of international organizations, see Simon Jackson and Alanna O'Malley, eds., *The Institution of International Order: From the League of Nations to the United Nations* (London: Routledge, 2018).

28. While historians have become increasingly interested in the history of international organizations in their own right since at least the 2000s, the study of their international public administrations has received comparatively scant attention. See Karen Gram-Skjoldager, Haakon A. Ikonomou, and Torsten Kahlert, "Introduction," in idem, *Organizing the 20th-Century World*, 2–3.

29. Erez Manela, *The Wilsonian Moment: Self-Determination and the International Origins of Anticolonial Nationalism* (New York: Oxford University Press, 2007).

30. For recent overviews, see Martin Shipway, *Decolonization and Its Impact: A Comparative Approach to the End of the Colonial Empires* (Malden, MA: Blackwell, 2008); Jan Jansen and Jürgen Osterhammel, *Dekolonisation: Das Ende der Imperien* (Munich: C.H. Beck, 2013); Dane Kennedy, *Decolonization: A Very Short Introduction* (New York: Oxford University Press, 2016); Martin Thomas and Andrew Thompson, eds., *The Oxford Handbook of the Ends of Empire* (Oxford: Oxford University Press, 2018).

31. On the history of self-determination, see Manela, *The Wilsonian Moment*; Bradley Simpson, "Self-Determination, Human Rights, and the End of Empire in the 1970s," *Humanity* 4, no. 2 (2013): 239–60; idem, *The First Right: Self-Determination and the Transformation of Post-1941 International Relations* (New York: Oxford University Press, forthcoming); Joseph Massad, "Against Self-Determination," *Humanity* 9, no. 2 (2018); Getachew, *Worldmaking after Empire*; Walker, "Decolonization in the 1960s."

32. Frederick Cooper, "Writing the History of Development," *Journal of Modern European History* 8, no. 1 (2010): 15. For further introductions to the topic, see idem, *Africa since 1940: The Past of the Present* (Cambridge: Cambridge University Press, 2002); idem, *Citizenship between Empire and Nation*.

33. Susan Pedersen, "Getting Out of Iraq—in 1932: The League of Nations and the Road to Normative Statehood," *The American Historical Review*. 115, no. 4 (2010): 975; Pedersen, *The Guardians*.

34. John Darwin, "Decolonization and the End of Empire," in *The Oxford History of the British Empire*, vol. 5: *Historiography* (Oxford: Oxford University Press, 2001), 541–58.

35. For a discussion of the entangled histories of decolonization and international organizations more generally see Eva-Maria Muschik, "Special Issue Introduction: Towards a Global History of International Organizations and Decolonization," *Journal of Global History*, forthcoming.

36. The UN Website's page "Decolonization," for example, reads: "The wave of decolonization, which changed the face of the planet, was born with the UN and represents the world body's first great success." See https://www.un.org/en/sections/issues-depth/decolonization/, last accessed 18 November 2020.

37. Wm. Roger Louis, *Imperialism at Bay: The United States and the Decolonization of the British Empire, 1941–1945* (New York: Oxford University Press, 1978); Stephen Wertheim, "Instrumental Internationalism: The American Origins of the United Nations, 1940–3," *Journal of Contemporary History* 54, no. 2 (2019): 265–83; idem, *Tomorrow, the World: The Birth of U.S. Global Supremacy* (Cambridge, MA: Harvard University Press, 2020).

38. Marika Sherwood, "'There Is No New Deal for the Blackman in San Francisco': African Attempts to Influence the Founding Conference of the United Nations, April–July, 1945," *The International Journal of African Historical Studies* 29, no. 1 (1996): 71–94; Getachew, *Worldmaking after Empire*, chapter 3.
39. For a concise introduction, see Luard, *The Age of Decolonization*; for strategic trust territories, see Ganeshwar Chand, "The United States and the Origins of the Trusteeship System," *Review (Fernand Braudel Center)* 14, no. 2 (1991): 171–230.
40. See UN Charter Chapter XI: Declaration Regarding Non-Self-Governing Territories, https://www.un.org/en/sections/un-charter/chapter-xi/index.html, last accessed 18 November 2020.
41. Jessica Pearson, "Defending Empire at the United Nations: The Politics of International Colonial Oversight in the Era of Decolonisation," *The Journal of Imperial and Commonwealth History* 45, no. 3 (May 31, 2017): 525–49.
42. Yassin El-Ayouty, *The United Nations and Decolonization: The Role of Afro-Asia* (The Hague: Martinus Nijhoff, 1971); Getachew, *Worldmaking after Empire*. Also see Cindy Ewing, "'With a Minimum of Bitterness'; and Elisabeth Leake, "States, Nations, and Self-Determination: Afghanistan and Decolonization at the United Nations" (forthcoming).
43. To call attention to the problematic implication of dependence, I use the term in quotation marks. For a reflection on the disciplining nature of IO vocabulary, see Susan Pedersen, "An International Regime in an Age of Empire," *American Historical Review* 124, no. 5 (2019): 1676, 1679; for a much stronger condemnation, see Sean Andrew Wempe, "A League to Preserve Empires: Understanding the Mandates System and Avenues for Further Scholarly Inquiry," *American Historical Review* 124, no. 5 (2019): 1728.
44. Luard, *The Age of Decolonization*, vol. 2, 176–79; Pearson, "Defending Empire at the UN," 541.
45. Getachew, *Worldmaking after Empire*, 90.
46. For the anticolonial campaign, see El-Ayouty, *The UN and Decolonization*; Luard, *The Age of Decolonization*; Prashad, *The Darker Nations*; Irwin, "Imagining Nation, State, and Order in the Mid-Twentieth Century"; Melber, *Hammarskjöld, the UN*; Getachew, *Worldmaking after Empire*; for the 1960 Declaration, also Alessandro Iandolo, "Beyond the Shoe: Rethinking Khrushchev at the Fifteenth Session of the United Nations General Assembly," *Diplomatic History* 41, no. 1 (2017): 128–54; on the Special Committee, see Oliver Turner, "'Finishing the Job': The UN Special Committee on Decolonization and the Politics of Self-Governance," *Third World Quarterly* 34, no. 7 (2013): 1193–1208.
47. Matthew Connelly, *A Diplomatic Revolution: Algeria's Fight for Independence and the Origins of the Post–Cold War Era* (New York: Oxford University Press, 2002).
48. On Namibia, see Henning Melber, "Liberating Namibia: The Long Diplomatic Struggle between the United Nations and South Africa," *Journal of Modern African Studies* 50, no. 4 (2012): 733–34; Molly McCullers, "'The Time of the United Nations in South West Africa Is Near': Local Drama and Global Politics in Apartheid-Era Hereroland," *Journal of Southern African Studies* 39, no. 2 (2018): 371–89; on South Africa at the UN, see Ryan Irwin, *Gordian Knot: Apartheid and the Unmaking of the Liberal World Order* (New York: Oxford University Press, 2012).
49. Emma Kluge, "West Papua and the International History of Decolonization, 1961–69," *The International History Review*, 2019, https://doi.org/10.1080/07075332.2019.1694052; Walker, "Decolonization in the 1960s"; Getachew, *Worldmaking after Empire*.
50. Prashad, *The Darker Nations*; Getachew, *Worldmaking after Empire*.

51. For a similar dynamic, see Jessica Pearson, *The Colonial Politics of Global Health: France and the United Nations in Postwar Africa* (Cambridge, MA: Harvard University Press, 2018).
52. Elizabeth Borgwardt, *A New Deal for the World: America's Vision for Human Rights* (Cambridge, MA: Belknap Press of Harvard University Press, 2005); Mazower, *No Enchanted Palace*; Wertheim, "Instrumental Internationalism"; idem, *Tomorrow, the World*. Also see Alanna O'Malley, H-Diplo Article Review 882 on Wertheim "Instrumental Internationalism," 2019, https://networks.h-net.org/node/4689090/pdf, last accessed 28 November 2020.
53. On UN hiring practices, see Toye and Toye, *The UN and Global Political Economy*, 61; Murphy, *The UNDP*, 13, 72; For an in-depth discussion of UNESCO recruiting, which in many ways was certainly comparable, see Porter, "The USSR in UNESCO."
54. Stokke, *The UN and Development*, 74; on continuities between colonial and international development efforts in terms of personnel, see Joseph Hodge, "British Colonial Expertise, Post-Colonial Careering and the Early History of International Development," *Journal of Modern European History* 8, no. 1 (2010): 24–46; Jennifer Gold, "The Reconfiguration of Scientific Career Networks in the Late Colonial Period: The Case of the Food and Agriculture Organization and the British Forestry Service," in *Science and Empire: Knowledge and Networks of Science across the British Empire, 1800–1970*, ed. Brett Bennett and Joseph Hodge (Basingstoke: Palgrave Macmillan, 2011), 297–320; Martin Rempe, *Entwicklung im Konflikt: Die EWG und der Senegal, 1957–1975* (Cologne: Böhlau, 2012); Véronique Dimier, *The Invention of a European Development Aid Bureaucracy: Recycling Empire* (London: Palgrave Macmillan UK, 2014); Eva-Maria Muschik, "The Art of Chameleon Politics: From Colonial Servant to International Development Expert," *Humanity* 9, no. 2 (2018): 219–44.
55. Toye and Toye, *The UN and Global Political Economy*, 76; Porter, "The USSR in UNESCO," chapter 3.
56. While the efforts of Third World countries in staffing international organizations have yet to be examined in closer detail, Porter suggests that, despite considerable efforts, the Soviets never quite managed to "catch up." For an informative introduction, see Urquhart, *Hammarskjold*, chapter 19. For the failed Soviet attempt to "catch up," see Porter, "The USSR in UNESCO," 218; apparently, there were similar initiatives with regard to the League Secretariat in the 1920s, which—similarly to the UN—bore increasing fruit once great powers retreated from the organization in the 1930s: see Gram-Skjoldager and Ikonomou, "The Making of the International Civil Servant," 222.
57. Sara Lorenzini, *Global Development: A Cold War History* (Princeton: Princeton University Press, 2019).
58. Evan Luard, *A History of the United Nations*, vol. 1: *The Years of Western Domination, 1945–1955* (New York: St. Martin's Press, 1982); MacKenzie, *World beyond Borders*; Mazower, *Governing the World*; Irwin, *Gordian Knot*.
59. See also Wertheim's suggestion that the U.S. displayed an instrumental attachment to the UN since 1945, using it when convenient and bypassing it when necessary. Wertheim, "Instrumental Internationalism," 282.
60. "How to Win the Cold War" by Paul Hoffman, Andrew Cordier papers (AC), B96, Folder H, Rare Book and Manuscript Library, Columbia University (RBML). For a brief discussion, see chapter 5.
61. For an argument about Cold War paralysis, see MacKenzie, *World beyond Borders*, 57; for the argument that the end of the Cold War brought new challenges into the realm

of peacekeeping, see Christopher O'Sullivan, *The United Nations: A Concise History* (Malabar: Kriegler, 2005), 81.

62. General Assembly resolution "Technical Assistance for Economic Development," 4 December 1948, A/RES/200(III).
63. On the campaign for a Special UN Fund for Economic Development (SUNFED), see Toye and Toye, *The UN and Global Political Economy*, 172; Murphy, *The UNDP*, 57.
64. The five UN regional commissions that were set up in the 1940s and 1950s, most prominently the UN Economic Commission for Latin America (ECLA) in 1948, represented an early repudiation of the national approach. For the creation of ECLA as an "act of audacity," see Toye and Toye, *The UN and Global Political Economy*, 137–38.
65. Toye and Toye, chapter 5.
66. Urquhart, *Hammarskjold*, 374.
67. For UNCTAD, see Toye and Toye, *The UN and Global Political Economy*; Prashad, *The Darker Nations*. For the NIEO, see Nils Gilman, "The New International Economic Order: A Re-Introduction," *Humanity* 6, no. 1 (2015): 1–16 as well as other contributions to this special issue; Samuel Moyn, *Not Enough: Human Rights in an Unequal World* (Cambridge, MA: Harvard University Press, 2018); Getachew, *Worldmaking after Empire*.
68. For a similar focus on small-scale assistance projects in the 1950s and '60s, see Daniel Immerwahr, *Thinking Small: The United States and the Lure of Community Development* (Cambridge, MA: Harvard University Press, 2015).
69. For two recent overviews, see Corinna Unger, *International Development: A Postwar History* (London: Bloomsbury Academic, 2018); Lorenzini, *Global Development*.
70. On the League's social work, see Margherita Zanasi, "Exporting Development: The League of Nations and Republican China," *Comparative Studies in Society and History* 49, no. 1 (2007): 143–69; Magaly Rodríguez, Liat Kozma, and Davide Rodogno, eds., *The League of Nations' Work on Social Issues: Visions, Endeavours and Experiments* (New York: United Nations Press, 2016). On the history of the ILO, see Daniel Maul, *Human Rights, Development and Decolonization: The International Labour Organization, 1940–70* (New York: Palgrave Macmillan, 2012); Sandrine Kott and Joëlle Droux, eds., *Globalizing Social Rights: The International Labour Organization and Beyond* (New York: Palgrave Macmillan, 2013); Sandrine Kott, "Fighting the War or Preparing for Peace? The ILO during the Second World War," *Journal of Modern European History* 12, no. 3 (2014): 359–76; Daniel Maul, *The International Labour Organization: 100 Years of Global Social Policy* (Berlin: DeGruyter, 2019).
71. The Harvard-based "UN History Project" offers useful bibliographies on the UN and its specialized agencies; see https://www.histecon.magd.cam.ac.uk/unhist/research/bibliographies.html (last accessed 15 August 2019).
72. Eric Helleiner argues that the Cold War, the American business community, and the bank's conservative leadership quickly diluted Washington's commitment to turn the IBRD into the premier international development agency. Eric Helleiner, *Forgotten Foundations of Bretton Woods: International Development and the Making of the Postwar Order* (Ithaca, NY: Cornell University Press, 2016); for the Bank's actual development activities, see Michele Alacevich, *The Political Economy of the World Bank: The Early Years* (Stanford, CA: Stanford University Press, 2009); Patrick Sharma, *Robert McNamara's Other War: The World Bank and International Development* (Philadelphia: University of Pennsylvania Press, 2017).
73. See UN Charter, Preamble and Chapter IX: "International and Economic Cooperation." https://www.un.org/en/about-us/un-charter/full-text, last accessed 23 April 2020.

74. Bhouraskar, *United Nations Development Aid*; Stokke, *The UN and Development*.
75. A/RES/200(III), 4 December 1948.
76. Regardless of the internationalist rhetoric, the U.S. bilateral assistance budget was still far larger than the American commitment to multilateral assistance. For Truman's speech, see, e.g., https://www.bartleby.com/124/pres53.html (last accessed 30 August 2019). For overviews of U.S. development activities, see David Ekbladh, *The Great American Mission: Modernization and the Construction of an American World Order* (Princeton: Princeton University Press, 2010); Michael Latham, *The Right Kind of Revolution: Modernization, Development, and U.S. Foreign Policy from the Cold War to the Present* (Ithaca, NY: Cornell University Press, 2011).
77. Stokke, *The UN and Development*, 73; also see Harold Jacobson, *The USSR and the UN's Economic and Social Activities* (Notre Dame, IN: University of Notre Dame Press, 1963). On the Soviet turn to the UN technical assistance, see Porter, "The USSR in UNESCO," 454–58. On Soviet aid more generally, see, e.g., Roger Kanet, *The Soviet Union, Eastern Europe and the Third World* (Cambridge: Cambridge University Press, 1987); Jeremy Friedman, "Soviet Policy in the Developing World and the Chinese Challenge in the 1960s," *Cold War History* 10, no. 2 (2010): 247–72; David Engerman, "The Second World's Third World," *Kritika: Explorations in Russian and Eurasian History* 12, no. 1 (2011): 183–211; Sara Lorenzini, "The Socialist Camp and the Challenge of Economic Modernization in the Third World," in *The Cambridge History of Communism*, ed. Norman Naimark, Silvio Pons, and Sophie Quinn-Judge (Cambridge: Cambridge University Press, 2017), 341–63; Artemy Kalinovsky, *Laboratory of Socialist Development: Cold War Politics and Decolonization in Soviet Tajikistan* (Ithaca, NY: Cornell University Press, 2018); James Mark, Artemy Kalinovsky, and Steffi Marung, eds., *Alternative Globalizations: Eastern Europe and the Postcolonial World* (Bloomington: Indiana University Press, 2020).
78. The FAO received 29 percent, the UN Secretariat 23 percent, the World Health Organization (WHO) 22 percent, the UNESCO 14 percent, the ILO 11 percent, and the International Civil Aviation Organization (ICAO) 1 percent. Later, the Universal Postal Union (UPU), the International Telecommunication Union (ITU), and the World Meteorological Organization (WMO) and International Atomic Energy Agency (IAEA) would join the program. The World Bank and the IMF did not automatically receive money through EPTA, but dispatched their own expert missions. For EPTA, see Stokke, *The UN and Development*, 57; Yonah Alexander, *International Technical Assistance Experts: A Case Study of the UN Experience* (New York: Praeger, 1966); Heppling, *UNDP*; Murphy, *The UNDP*; Bhouraskar, *United Nations Development Aid*. On the Bretton Woods institutions, see Alacevich, *The Political Economy of the World Bank*; Aldwin Roes, "World Bank Survey Missions and the Politics of Decolonization in British East Africa, 1957–1963," *International Journal of African Historical Studies* 42, no. 1 (2009): 1–28; Helleiner, *Forgotten Foundations of Bretton Woods*.
79. The TAA was initially led by Hugh Keenleyside, who figures prominently in chapter 3 as head of the UN technical assistance mission to Bolivia. On the TAA, see Alexander, *International Technical Assistance Experts*, 24–25; Webster, "Development Advisors in a Time of Cold War and Decolonization." For Keenleyside's own account of the UN assistance machinery, see Hugh Keenleyside, *International Aid: A Summary (with Special Reference to the Programmes of the United Nations)* (New York: James H. Heineman, 1966).
80. See Unger, *International Development*, chapters 4 & 5.
81. Walter Sharp, *International Technical Assistance: Programs and Organization* (Chicago: Public Administration Service, 1952), 67; Guy Fiti Sinclair, "The United Nations,

Public Administration and the Making of Postcolonial States," paper presented at the Technologies of Stateness: International Organizations and the Making of States workshop, European University Institute, Florence, 15–16 September 2016, 8.

82. Alden Young, *Transforming Sudan: Decolonization, Economic Development and State Formation* (Cambridge: Cambridge University Press, 2018); Priya Lal, "Decolonization and the Gendered Politics of Developmental Labor in Southeastern Africa," in *The Development Century: A Global History*, ed. Stephen Macekura and Erez Manela (New York: Cambridge University Press, 2018), 173–96.

83. James Ferguson, *The Anti-Politics Machine: "Development," Depoliticization, and Bureaucratic Power in Lesotho* (New York: Cambridge University Press, 1990).

84. For idealists' accounts, see, e.g., Amy Sayward, *The Birth of Development: How the World Bank, Food and Agriculture Organization, and World Health Organization Changed the World, 1945–1965* (Kent, OH: Kent State University Press, 2006); Murphy, *The UNDP*. For neocolonialist interpretations, see Antony Anghie, *Colonialism, Sovereignty, and the Making of International Law* (New York: Cambridge University Press, 2004); Gilbert Rist, *The History of Development: From Western Origins to Global Faith*, 3rd ed. (New York: Zed Books, 2008).

85. Greg Mann similarly finds that NGOs did not "muscle" their way into newly independent African states uninvited. Mann, *From Empires to NGOs in the West African Sahel*.

86. Writing about the International Monetary Fund, the World Bank and USAID, the Washington-based agencies that became increasingly active across the postcolonial world, Timothy Mitchell, too, suggests that "they were seldom able to impose new policies, still less control the outcome when their interventions were successful. Where they did achieve results, however, was in the monopoly of their expertise." Timothy Mitchell, *Rule of Expert: Egypt, Techno-Politics, Modernity* (Berkeley: University of California Press, 2002), 211; for further arguments about the triumph and tyranny of development experts, see Joseph Hodge, *Triumph of the Expert: Agrarian Doctrines of Development and the Legacies of British Colonialism* (Athens: Ohio University Press, 2007); William Easterly, *The Tyranny of Experts: Economists, Dictators, and the Forgotten Rights of the Poor* (New York: Basic Books, 2013).

87. Daniel Speich Chassé, "Decolonization and Global Governance: Approaches to the History of the UN-System" (Lecture HION, Geneva, 2013).

88. Pelt to Broadley, 4 September 1950, and Broadley to Pelt, 13 September 1950, S-0655-0002-04, UNARMS.

89. For a discussion of international territorial administration, see the epilogue.

90. See contributions to the workshop "Technologies of Stateness: International Organizations and the Making of States," European University Institute, Fiesole, Italy, 15–16 September 2016.

91. For political roads to statehood, see, for example, Susan Pedersen, "Getting Out of Iraq—in 1932,"; and also the UN's first case of decolonization: David Webster, *Fire and the Full Moon: Canada and Indonesia in a Decolonizing World* (Vancouver, BC: UBC Press, 2009).

92. Stephen Browne similarly notes that while semantically "aid" turned into "cooperation," in practice, development took a paternalist turn. Stephen Browne, *The United Nations Development Programme and System* (New York: Routledge, 2012), 12.

93. For a twenty-first-century review of the literature on international territorial administration, see Anne Orford, "Book Review Article: 'International Territorial Administration and the Management of Decolonization,'" *International and Comparative Law Quarterly* 59 (2010): 227–50.

94. For a similar argument, see Inis Claude, *Swords into Plowshares: The Problems and Progress of International Organization* (New York: Random House, 1956), 370.

## 1. THE UN AND THE COLONIAL WORLD

1. Stephen Wertheim, *Tomorrow, the World: The Birth of U.S. Global Supremacy* (Cambridge, MA: Harvard University Press, 2020).
2. Translation of "The Colonial Question after World War II," *Pravda* 7 August 1947, Ralph Bunche Papers (hereafter RB), Charles E. Young Library, University of California, Los Angeles (hereafter UCLA), B86, F10.
3. It is unclear at what point overseas possessions, which the League of Nations Covenant, for example, still referred to as "colonies," became "dependent territories" in international parlance. It is likely an American euphemism, designed to account for imperial holdings such as Guam or Hawaii, that allowed the U.S. to maintain its anticolonial self-image, which gained wider currency through the U.S.-led wartime discussions about the future role of international organization in the colonial world. Wearing the newly agreed-upon teleological understanding of colonies on its sleeve, the UN Charter would ultimately settle for the cumbersome term "Non-Self-Governing Territories."
4. Susan Pedersen, *The Guardians: The League of Nations and the Crisis of Empire* (Oxford: Oxford University Press, 2015).
5. On British positions, see Wm. Roger Louis, *Imperialism at Bay: The United States and the Decolonization of the British Empire, 1941–1945* (New York: Oxford University Press, 1978). On the French, see Jessica L. Pearson, "Defending Empire at the United Nations: The Politics of International Colonial Oversight in the Era of Decolonisation," *The Journal of Imperial and Commonwealth History* 45, no. 3 (May 31, 2017): 525–49; Jessica L. Pearson, "The French Empire Goes to San Francisco: The Founding of the United Nations and the Limits of Colonial Reform," *French Politics, Culture & Society* 38, no. 2 (2020): 35–55. For general overviews, see Kenneth J. Twitchett, "The Colonial Powers and the United Nations," *Journal of Contemporary History* 4, no. 1 (1969): 167–85; Evan Luard, *A History of the United Nations*, vol. 2: *The Age of Decolonization, 1955–1965* (New York: St. Martin's Press, 1989). Spain and Portugal only joined the UN in 1955 and even then continued to evade UN oversight. On Portugal at the UN, see Miguel Bandeira Jerónimo and José Pedro Monteiro, "The Inventors of Human Rights in Africa: Portugal, Late Colonialism, and the UN Human Rights Regime," in *Decolonization, Self-Determination, and the Rise of Global Human Rights*, ed. Dirk Moses, Marco Duranti, and Roland Burke (New York: Cambridge University Press, 2020), 285–315.
6. For an abbreviated, slightly revised version of this chapter, see Eva-Maria Muschik, "The Trusteeship System, Decolonization and (the Limits of) UN Agency," in *The United Nations Trusteeship System: Legacies, Continuities, and Change*, ed. Julius Heise, Maria Ketzmerick, and Jan Lüdert (London: Routledge, forthcoming).
7. UN trust territories included: *British Togoland*, which, united with the British Gold Coast, achieved independence in 1957 as Ghana; *Somaliland* under Italian Administration, which, united with the British Somaliland Protectorate, formed the independent state of Somalia in 1960; *French Togoland*, which became independent Togo in 1960; *French Cameroons*, which gained independence as Cameroon in 1960; *British Cameroons*, whose northern part joined Nigeria, while the southern part joined Cameroon in 1961; *British Tanganyika*, which gained independence in 1961 and, in union with the former British Protectorate of Zanzibar, became Tanzania in 1963; *Belgian Ruanda-Urundi*, which a plebiscite divided into the two sovereign states of Rwanda

and Burundi in 1962; *Western Samoa*, which gained independence from New Zealand as Samoa in 1962; *Nauru*, administered by Australia, which became independent in 1968; Australian *New Guinea*, which, together with the Australian colony of Papua, formed the independent State of Papua New Guinea in 1975; as well as the U.S. *Trust Territory of the Pacific Islands*, comprising the Federated States of Micronesia, the Republic of the Marshall Islands, the Commonwealth of the Northern Mariana Islands, and, last, Palau, which became "fully self-governing in free Association with the United States" in 1990 and 1994, respectively. "Trust Territories That Have Achieved Self-Determination," http://www.un.org/en/decolonization/selfdet.shtml, (last accessed 18 July 2016). The League's Middle-Eastern mandates—Syria, Lebanon, Palestine, Transjordan, and Mesopotamia (Iraq)—as well as South West Africa, which was administered by South Africa, did not become UN trust territories.

8. Ruth Russell, *A History of the United Nations Charter: The Role of the United States, 1940–1945* (Washington, DC: Brookings Institution, 1958); Louis, *Imperialism at Bay*.
9. Brian Urquhart, *Ralph Bunche: An American Life* (New York: W.W. Norton, 1993), 122.
10. Neta Crawford, "Decolonization through Trusteeship: The Legacy of Ralph Bunche," in *Trustee for the Human Community: Ralph J. Bunche, the United Nations, and the Decolonization of Africa*, ed. Robert A. Hill and Edmond J. Keller (Athens: Ohio University Press, 2010), 102; also see Herschelle S. Challenor, "The Contribution of Ralph Bunche to Trusteeship and Decolonization," in *Ralph Bunche: The Man and His Times*, ed. Benjamin Rivlin (New York: Holmes & Meier, 1990), 143. For a mixed assessment of the effects of the Trusteeship System on the decolonization of an individual territory, see Ullrich Lohrmann, *Voices from Tanganyika: Great Britain, the United Nations and the Decolonization of a Trust Territory, 1946–1961* (Berlin: Lit, 2007). For a general overview of literature on the UN and decolonization, see the introduction to this book.
11. Louis, *Imperialism at Bay*, 117.
12. For a discussion of calls for the return of trusteeship, see Crawford, "Decolonization through Trusteeship," 94; Paul Kennedy, *The Parliament of Man: The Past, Present, and Future of the United Nations* (New York: Random House, 2006), 262–63.
13. Twitchett, "The Colonial Powers and the United Nations"; Yassin El-Ayouty, *The UN and Decolonization: The Role of Afro-Asia* (The Hague: Martinus Nijhoff, 1971); Luard, *The Age of Decolonization*; Jan Lüdert, "Conditions Apply: Non-State Actors Challenging State Sovereignty through Intergovernmental Organizations: An Analysis of National Liberation Movements and Indigenous Peoples at the United Nations," doctoral dissertation, University of British Columbia, 2016; Pearson, "Defending Empire at the UN."
14. Julius Heise, Maria Ketzmerick, and Jan Lüdert, eds., *The United Nations Trusteeship System: Legacies, Continuities, and Change* (London: Routledge, forthcoming).
15. See, for example, Lu-Yu Kiang, "The Development and Operation of the Method of Supervision in the United Nations Trusteeship System," PhD thesis, New York University, 1955; Will Joseph Selzer, "The Trusteeship Council of the United Nations and Self-Government, with Particular Reference to British East Africa, 1947–1951," PhD thesis, University of Pennsylvania, 1959; Edward Rowe, "The Effects of the United Nations' Trusteeship System," PhD thesis, University of California Berkeley, 1966; Giuliano Ferrari-Bravo, "The Development of International Trusteeship at the United Nations with Particular Reference to British Reactions: 1944–1960," PhD thesis, University of Cambridge, 1976; Adebisis Oluwatoyin Adebiyi, "The Role of the United Nations Visiting Missions in the Decolonisation of East Africa, 1948–1960," MLit thesis, University of Oxford, 1985; Catherine Burke, "The Great Debate: The Decolonization Issue at

the United Nations, 1945–1980," DPhil thesis, University of Oxford, 1986; Cherifa Belhabib, "The United Nations Trusteeship System, 1945–1961," PhD thesis, University of Cincinnati, 1991.

16. Lohrmann, *Voices from Tanganyika*; Meredith Terretta, "'We Had Been Fooled into Thinking That the UN Watches over the Entire World': Human Rights, UN Trust Territories, and Africa's Decolonization," *Human Rights Quarterly* 34, no. 2 (2012): 329–60. Lohrmann initially repeats Louis's assessment of the trusteeship system's strength, but then goes on to show at length how the few results of UN oversight quickly turned inhabitants' high expectations into anger and disillusionment.

17. For a review of recent literature on the topic, see Anne Orford, "Book Review Article: 'International Territorial Administration and the Management of Decolonization,'" *International and Comparative Law Quarterly* 59 (2010): 227–50.

18. Mark Mazower, *Governing the World: The History of an Idea* (New York: Penguin Press, 2012), 254.

19. On Bunche, see Peggy Mann, *Ralph Bunche, UN Peacemaker* (New York: Coward, McCann & Geoghegan, 1975); Benjamin Rivlin, *Ralph Bunche, the Man and His Times* (New York: Holmes & Meier, 1990); Urquhart, *Ralph Bunche*; Charles P. Henry, *Ralph Bunche: Model Negro or American Other?* (New York: New York University Press, 1999); Carol Elaine Anderson, *Eyes off the Prize: The United Nations and the African American Struggle for Human Rights, 1944–1955* (Cambridge; New York: Cambridge University Press, 2009); Robert Hill and Edmond Keller, eds., *Trustee for the Human Community: Ralph J. Bunche, the United Nations, and the Decolonization of Africa* (Athens: Ohio University Press, 2010); also see discussions in Pedersen, *The Guardians*; Robert Vitalis, *White World Order, Black Power Politics: The Birth of American International Relations*, Ithaca, NY: Cornell University Press, 2017, and forthcoming work by Christopher Dietrich.

20. Lawrence Finkelstein, "Bunche and the Colonial World: From Trusteeship to Decolonization," in Rivlin, *Ralph Bunche: The Man and His Times*, 114–24.

21. On moving beyond the success/ failure narrative, see Susan Pedersen, "Back to the League of Nations," *The American Historical Review* 112, no. 4 (October 2007): 1090–1117.

22. Pandit led a "counter-delegation" to San Francisco to the one that the British had handpicked for India. Manu Bhagavan, India and the Quest for One World: The Peacemakers (New York City: Palgrave Macmillan, 2013), 44.

23. For a discussion of self-determination as a counterrevolutionary Wilsonian concept meant to preserve international racial hierarchy, see Adom Getachew. *Worldmaking after Empire: The Rise and Fall of Self-Determination* (Princeton: Princeton University Press, 2019), chapter 2.

24. In her 2019 essay on the mandates system, Pedersen suggests that it still remains to be seen whether her claim that the publicity and contestation that the mandates system entailed did more to destabilize the imperial order than to legitimize it. Pedersen, *The Guardians*; eadem, "An International Regime in an Age of Empire,"*American Historical Review* 124, no. 5 (2019): 1680.

25. Louis, *Imperialism at Bay*, 225, 538. In "Tomorrow, the World," Stephen Wertheim shows that despite the anticolonial rhetoric, U.S. policymakers briefly considered forming a collaborative "Anglo-American Imperium" in 1941. Also see Thomas M. Meaney, "The American Hour: U.S. Thinkers and the Problem of Decolonization, 1948–1983," doctoral dissertation, Columbia University, 2017.

26. Mark Mazower, *No Enchanted Palace: The End of Empire and the Ideological Origins of the United Nations* (Princeton: Princeton University Press, 2009), 16.

27. Stephen Wertheim, "Instrumental Internationalism: The American Origins of the United Nations, 1940–3," *Journal of Contemporary History* 54, no. 2 (2019): 265–83.
28. Louis, *Imperialism at Bay*; also see Russell, *A History of the United Nations Charter*; Twitchett, "The Colonial Powers and the United Nations."
29. The 9th conference of the Institute of Pacific Relations in Hot Springs, Virginia, in early 1945 seems to have been an important informal discussion setting prior to San Francisco. Pearson, "Defending Empire at the UN," 36, 46.
30. El-Ayouty, *The UN and Decolonization*; Marika Sherwood, "'There Is No New Deal for the Blackman in San Francisco': African Attempts to Influence the Founding Conference of the United Nations, April–July, 1945," *The International Journal of African Historical Studies* 29, no. 1 (1996): 71–94; Lüdert, "Conditions Apply."
31. For the Covenant, see, for example, https://avalon.law.yale.edu/20th_century/leagcov.asp (last accessed 30 August 2019). On development in the mandates, see Simon Jackson, "Transformative Relief: Imperial Humanitarianism and Mandatory Development in Syria-Lebanon, 1915–1925," *Humanity* 8, no. 2 (2017): 247–68. On continuities from the League to the UN, see Simon Jackson and Alanna O'Malley, *The Institution of International Order: From the League of Nations to the United Nations* (London: Routledge, 2018); specifically on the transition from the mandates to the trusteeship system, see Pedersen, *The Guardians*, conclusion.
32. For the charter text, see, for example, http://avalon.law.yale.edu/wwii/atlantic.asp (accessed 2 April 2016); Louis, *Imperialism at Bay*, 122; Wertheim, "Tomorrow, the World," chapter 3; Bradley Simpson, "The Atlantic Charter and the Imagined Future of Self-Determination and Decolonization, 1941–1945," paper presented at Challenging the Liberal World Order: The History of the Global, Decolonization and the United Nations, 1955–2000, Leiden University, 2018.
33. See, for example, Sherwood, "There Is No New Deal," 72–73.
34. Louis, *Imperialism at Bay*, 121–22, 126–28.
35. Louis, *Imperialism at Bay*, 134–35, 154–55.
36. Louis, *Imperialism at Bay*, 134,140; Frederick Cooper, "Writing the History of Development," *Journal of Modern European History* 8, no. 1 (2010): 9.
37. Russell, *A History of the United Nations Charter*, 84.
38. In the president's view, international trusteeship would not only be confined to "minors" of the international community, but could also be applied to lead "adult nations . . . back into a spirit of good conduct." Louis, *Imperialism at Bay*, 148, 165–66.
39. Pedersen, *The Guardians*.
40. Russell, *A History of the United Nations Charter*, 86; Wertheim, "Tomorrow, the World," 24–25. Author's emphasis.
41. Twitchett, "The Colonial Powers and the United Nations," 173.
42. Louis, *Imperialism at Bay*, 188.
43. Russell, *A History of the United Nations Charter*, 87–88.
44. Lawrence Finkelstein, "Castles in Spain: United States Trusteeship Plans in World War II," PhD thesis, Columbia University, 1970, 52.
45. Louis, *Imperialism at Bay*, 197. On the views of the British Left, see Twitchett, "The Colonial Powers and the United Nations." By referring to "dependent" rather than "colonial" peoples, the British left the door open for a further twist: namely, that the commissions might have as much—or as little— of a say with regard to "colonial subjects" as they would with regard to "dependent peoples" *within* sovereign states, such as Native Americans. The Canadians feared as much. See Louis, *Imperialism at Bay*, 406.
46. Russell, *A History of the United Nations Charter*, 88.

## 1. THE UN AND THE COLONIAL WORLD   275

47. Louis, *Imperialism at Bay*, 232, 246; also see Twitchett, "The Colonial Powers and the United Nations," 174–75.
48. Russell, *A History of the United Nations Charter*, 88.
49. Russell, *A History of the United Nations Charter*, 77.
50. Russell, *A History of the United Nations Charter*, chapter XX, "The Stimson Memo."
51. Finkelstein, "Castles in Spain," 9.
52. Pearson, "French Empire Goes to San Francisco," 46.
53. Lüdert, "Conditions Apply."
54. The strategic trust territories have received comparatively little attention. John Maki, "U.S. Strategic Area or UN Trusteeship," *Far Eastern Survey* 16, no. 15 (August 13, 1947): 175–78; Earl Pomeroy, *Pacific Outpost American Strategy in Guam and Micronesia* (Stanford, CA: Stanford University Press, 1951); Finkelstein, "Castles in Spain"; Wm. Roger Louis, *National Security and International Trusteeship in the Pacific* (Annapolis: Naval Institute Press, 1972); Ganeshwar Chand, "The United States and the Origins of the Trusteeship System," *Review (Fernand Braudel Center)* 14, no. 2 (1991): 171–230. Also see Elisa Leclerc, "Nuclear Testing on the Strategic Trust Territory of the Pacific Islands—How the U.S. Became an Imperial Power in the Region of Micronesia," in *The United Nations Trusteeship System: Legacies, Continuities, and Change*, ed. Julius Heise, Maria Ketzmerick, and Jan Lüdert (London: Routledge, forthcoming).
55. For the larger argument about American designs to graft UN universalism atop a U.S. power base, see Wertheim, "Tomorrow, the World," 24–25; for a history of U.S. overseas expansion, see Daniel Immerwahr, "The Greater United States: Territory and Empire in U.S. History," *Diplomatic History* 40 (2016): 373–91; idem, *How to Hide an Empire: A History of the Greater United States* (New York: Farrar, Strauss and Giroux, 2019).
56. Russell, *A History of the United Nations Charter*, 808.
57. Russell, *A History of the United Nations Charter*, 819.
58. The French, too, were apparently uninformed about the American plans, and feared that Washington might pressure them to give up all overseas territories or that the principle of UN trusteeship might be applied to all colonies. Finkelstein, "Bunche and the Colonial World," 124; Pearson, "Defending Empire at the UN," 528.
59. Pearson, "The French Empire Goes to San Francisco," 48.
60. Twitchett, "The Colonial Powers and the United Nations," 181.
61. For anticolonial calls for oversight mechanisms, see Sherwood, "There Is No New Deal"; Lüdert, "Conditions Apply."
62. For League Covenant, Article 23 b), see https://avalon.law.yale.edu/20th_century/leagcov.asp#art23; for UN Charter, Article 73, see https://www.un.org/en/sections/un-charter/chapter-xi/index.html.
63. Pearson, "Defending Empire at the UN."
64. Russell, *A History of the United Nations Charter*, 816.
65. Sherwood, "There Is No New Deal"; Lüdert, "Conditions Apply"; also see Roger Normand and Sarah Zaidi, *Human Rights at the UN: The Political History of Universal Justice* (Bloomington: Indiana University Press, 2008); and Carol Anderson, *Eyes off the Prize: The United Nations and the African American Struggle for Human Rights, 1944–1955* (Cambridge: Cambridge University Press, 2009).
66. Sherwood, "There Is No New Deal," 84.
67. Sherwood, "There Is No New Deal," 91.
68. Finkelstein, "Castles in Spain."
69. UN Charter, Chapter XII: International Trusteeship System, Article 76, b.

70. Lüdert, "Conditions Apply."
71. The Charter also left the door open for colonial powers to place other territories under UN supervision, though even the most optimistic among the internationalist postwar planners did not think this likely to happen.
72. Jean de la Roche, "Objectives of Trusteeship," 23 September 1946, RB, B83, F2, UCLA.
73. De la Roche, "Objectives of Trusteeship."
74. See undated CV, RB, B92, F15, UCLA.
75. Jean Gottmann and Jean de la Roche, *La Fédération Française: Contacts et Civilisation d'Outre Mer* (Montréal: Editions de L'Arbre, 1945), 17.
76. For a discussion of the book, see António Ferraz de Oliveira, "Territory and Theory in Political Geography, c.1970s–90s: Jean Gottmann's *The Significance of Territory*," *Territory, Politics, Governance* (2020), 8–9.
77. De la Roche, "Objectives of Trusteeship."
78. De la Roche thus welcomed the vagueness of the term "self-government" as wide enough to accommodate "national political autonomy" as well as interdependence.
79. De la Roche, "Objectives of Trusteeship."
80. For a wider discussion of these issues in French government circles, see Frederick Cooper, *Citizenship between Empire and Nation: Remaking France and French Africa, 1945–1960* (Princeton: Princeton University Press, 2014).
81. De la Roche, "Objectives of Trusteeship."
82. De la Roche, "Objectives of Trusteeship."
83. The Secretariat's Trusteeship Department, or more specifically Bunche, was nevertheless heavily involved in the discussions about the future fate of Palestine. For Bunche's role in the Arab-Israeli conflict, see Rivlin, *Ralph Bunche, the Man and His Times*, part III; Urquhart, *Ralph Bunche*, chapters 11–16. On South West Africa, see Chris Saunders, "The Role of the United Nations in the Independence of Namibia," *History Compass* 5, no. 3 (May 2007): 737–44.
84. Finkelstein, "Bunche and the Colonial World," 126. The territories for which the first trust agreements were submitted to the General Assembly included New Guinea, administered by Australia; Ruanda-Urundi, administered by Belgium; Togoland and Cameroons, administered by France; Western Samoa, administered by New Zealand; and Tanganyika, Togoland and Cameroons, administered by the United Kingdom. See *Yearbook of the United Nations 1946-1947* (New York: United Nations, 1947), 576.
85. Luard, *The Age of Decolonization* vol. 2, 121.
86. Twitchett, "The Colonial Powers and the United Nations," 179.
87. Lawrence Finkelstein, "The Trusteeship System: An Analysis: A Study and Interpretation of the Steps Leading to the Conclusion of the First Nine Trusteeships," Master's essay, Columbia University, 1948, Columbia University, Rare Book & Manuscript Library; Charmian Edwards Toussaint, *The Trusteeship System of the United Nations* (New York: Praeger, 1956), chapter 5; Gordon Morrell, "A Higher Stage of Imperialism? The Big Three, the UN Trusteeship Council, and the Early Cold War," in *Imperialism on Trial*, ed. R.M. Douglas, Michael D. Callahan, and Elizabeth Bishop (Lanham, MD: Lexington, 2006), 111–37; Twitchett, "The Colonial Powers and the United Nations," 180.
88. Finkelstein, "Bunche and the Colonial World," 122. Julius Lewin, "The Squalid Farce of Trusteeship," *The Nation* 31 July 1948: 119–20.
89. Lewin, "Squalid Farce of Trusteeship."
90. The United States, though in charge of "strategic trust territories," which came under the purview of the Security Council, did not count as an "administering power" on the

Trusteeship Council the first year. Somaliland became a UN trust territory under Italian administration in 1950, even though Italy would only join the UN as a member state five years later. Until then, Italy participated in the Council deliberations without the right to vote. *Yearbook of the United Nations 1946–1947* (New York: United Nations, 1947), 577; *Yearbook of the United Nations 1950* (New York: United Nations, 1951), 105.

91. The provisional questionnaire used until 1952 was based on drafts submitted by France, the United Kingdom, the United States, and the Secretariat. The "administering authorities," the Economic and Social Council and its subsidiary bodies, and the specialized agencies were invited to suggest changes. *Yearbook of the United Nations 1952* (New York: United Nations, 1952), 81.
91. Several states argued—ultimately unsuccessfully—for a simplification of the universal questionnaire or, rather, for its adaption to each trust territory. See *Yearbook of the United Nations 1953* (New York: United Nations, 1953), 655.
92. "Confidential Resumé of a General Discussion between Representatives of Belgium, France and the United Kingdom on Future Policy towards the Trusteeship Council," Ministère des Colonies. Direction des Affaires politiques, 1AFFPOL/3316/3, Archives Nationales d'Outre-Mer, Aix-en-Provence (ANOM). I thank Julius Heise for this reference.
93. Lewin, "Squalid Farce of Trusteeship."
94. Luard, *The Age of Decolonization*, vol. 2, 127.
95. Ilya Gaiduk, *Divided Together: The United States and the Soviet Union in the United Nations, 1945–1965* (Stanford, CA: Stanford University Press, 2012), 248.
96. Alan Burns, *In Defense of Colonies: British Colonial Territories in International Affairs* (London: Allen & Unwin, 1957), 16–17, cited in Pearson, "Defending Empire at the UN," 538.
97. See unofficial translation of the letter in the *Literary Gazette* of the USSR 11 October 1947, RB, B71, F15, UCLA.
98. Unofficial translation of *Literary Gazette* letter.
99. Gaiduk, *Divided Together*, 248; Lawrence Finkelstein, *Somaliland under Italian Administration: A Case Study in United Nations Trusteeship.* (New York: Woodrow Wilson Foundation, 1955), 32; Alvin Rubinstein, *The Soviets in International Organizations: Changing Policy toward Developing Countries, 1953–1963* (Princeton: Princeton University Press, 1964).
100. "Confidential Resumé of a General Discussion."
101. Luard, *The Age of Decolonization*, 2:127.
102. Pedersen, *The Guardians*.
103. Lüdert, "Conditions Apply."
104. See, e.g., Lohrmann, *Voices from Tanganyika*; Terretta, "We Had Been Fooled." Also see Julius Heise, "Right to Petition vs. Rules of Procedure," in *The United Nations Trusteeship System: Legacies, Continuities, and Change*, ed. idem, Maria Ketzmerick, and Jan Lüdert (London: Routledge, forthcoming).
105. Anecdotal evidence suggests that individual Secretariat members approached missions for their personal advancement—to increase their per diems and consolidate their respective positions within the UN bureaucratic hierarchy. "Preliminary Study Regarding the Organization of Visits" [n.d.]. RB, B83, F7, UCLA. See Mona Yung-Ning Hoo, *Painting the Shadows: The Extraordinary Life of Victor Hoo* (London: Eldridge & Co., 1998), 158.
106. Luard, *The Age of Decolonization*, vol. 2, 126.
107. Lohrmann, *Voices from Tanganyika*, 78.

278   1. THE UN AND THE COLONIAL WORLD

108. The Fourth Committee is one of the six Main Committees of the General Assembly that correspond to the major fields of responsibility of the General Assembly. Luard, *The Age of Decolonization*, vol. 2, 127; Jan Lüdert shows that the General Assembly's Third Committee on Social, Humanitarian and Cultural Issues also provided a site for contesting colonial sovereignty, arguing that as a comparatively unknown committee, it offered a "sheltered venue" from great power pressure that allowed smaller states to take the lead. See Lüdert, "Conditions Apply."
109. Hoo's personal papers are available at the Hoover Institution Archives at Stanford University. In 1989, seventeen years after her father's death, Hoo's daughter set out to write a biography, which was published nine years later: Hoo, *Painting the Shadows*.
110. A/C.4/29, para 24-35, cited in Lüdert, "Conditions Apply."
111. Hoo, *Painting the Shadows*, 168.
112. Speech given by Hoo in honor of Bunche winning the Nobel Prize on 12 October 1950, Victor Hoo papers (hereafter VH), B5, F5.6 "Speeches and Writings, General, 1950," Hoover Institution Archives, Stanford University (hereafter HIA). See Broadcast manuscript, 16 November 1946, VH, B5, F5.1 "Speeches and Writings, General, 1946," HIA.
113. On Bunche, see note 20 above.
114. Ralph Bunche, "The International Implications of Far Eastern Colonial Problems" Council on World Affairs, Cleveland, OH, 3 February 1945, quoted in Urquhart, *Ralph Bunche*, 115.
115. Urquhart, *Ralph Bunche*, 62; chapter 4.
116. Ralph Bunche, *A World View of Race* (Washington DC: Association in Negro Folk Education, 1936), 39; cited in Martin Kilson, "Ralph Bunche's Analytical Perspective on African Development," in Rivlin, *Ralph Bunche: The Man and His Times*, 85–86.
117. Ralph Bunche, "French Administration in Togoland and Dahomey," PhD thesis, Harvard University, 1934; also see Pedersen, *The Guardians*, 321–22.
118. Getachew. *Worldmaking after Empire*, 7.
119. Bunche, "French Administration in Togoland and Dahomey," 388; cited in Kilson, "Ralph Bunche's Analytical Perspective on African Development," 87–88.
120. Bunche, "French Administration in Togoland and Dahomey," 41–42; cited in Nathan Huggins, "Ralph Bunche the Africanist," in Rivlin, *Ralph Bunche: The Man and His Times*, 78.
121. Bunche, "French Administration in Togoland and Dahomey," 425; cited in Huggins, "Ralph Bunche the Africanist," 73.
122. Daniel Maul, *Human Rights, Development and Decolonization: The International Labour Organization, 1940–70* (New York: Palgrave Macmillan, 2012), 85.
123. Finkelstein, "Bunche and the Colonial World," 121.
124. Crawford, "Decolonization through Trusteeship," 102. Citing Peggy Mann, W. Ofuatey-Kodjoe writes: "In the final analysis, there can be no more fitting comment about Ralph Bunche than this: 'It must be remembered that in his UN role as director of the Department of Trusteeship, Bunche did more than any single man in setting out the guidelines which helped the nations of Africa reach independence.'" W. Ofuatey-Kodjoe, "Ralph Bunche: An African Perspective," in Rivlin, *Ralph Bunche: The Man and His Times*, 106; Mann, *Ralph Bunche, UN Peacemaker*, 333.
125. Finkelstein, "Bunche and the Colonial World," 114–24.
126. Ramendra N. Chowdhuri, *International Mandates and Trusteeship Systems: A Comparative Study* (Dordrecht: Springer, 1955), 51.
127. Urquhart, *Ralph Bunche*, 119–20.
128. Bunche to his wife Ruth, 17 June 1945, cited in Urquhart, 121.

## 1. THE UN AND THE COLONIAL WORLD 279

129. Lüdert, "Conditions Apply," 83–84.
130. Finkelstein, "Bunche and the Colonial World," 124ff.
131. Finkelstein, "Bunche and the Colonial World," 124–25.
132. UN Charter, Chapter XI, Declaration Regarding Non-Self-Governing Territories, Article 73 e).
133. Pearson, "The French Empire Goes to San Francisco."
134. "Report on the Work of the Non-Self-Governing Territories Division for the Month of January 1949," S-0504-0001-08, UNARMS.
135. Twitchett, "The Colonial Powers and the United Nations," 183.
136. Benson to Hoo, 1 July 1950, "Monthly Report on the Division"; "Report on the Work of the Non-Self-Governing Territories Division for the Month of January 1949.".
137. Initially there were eight "administering powers" on the Committee: France, Great Britain, Belgium, the United States, Australia, Denmark, the Netherlands, and New Zealand. While Portugal and Spain joined the UN in 1955, Spain refused to submit information to the Committee until 1960 but Portugal did so consistently, as did South Africa. Pearson, "Defending Empire at the UN"; for a summary, see Luard, *The Age of Decolonization*; for Portugal at the UN, see Bandeira Jerónimo and Monteiro, "The Inventors of Human Rights in Africa."
138. Benson to Hoo, 22 August 1947, S-0504-0001-08, UNARMS.
139. Luard, *The Age of Decolonization*, 176–79.
140. Pearson, "Defending Empire at the UN," 541.
141. Finkelstein, "Bunche and the Colonial World," 127.
142. Urquhart, *Ralph Bunche*, 140.
143. Urquhart, *Ralph Bunche*, 154.
144. Urquhart, *Ralph Bunche*, chapters 11–16.
145. Taylor Shore to Bunche, "1950 on 1951," RB, B468, F2, UCLA.
146. General Assembly Resolution 58, "Transfer to the UN of the advisory social welfare functions of UNRRA," 14 December 1946, A/RES/58(I). Also see Jessica Reinisch, "Internationalism in Relief: The Birth (and Death) of UNRRA," *Past & Present* 210, Supplement 6 (2011): 258–89.
147. Craig Murphy, *The United Nations Development Programme: A Better Way?* (Cambridge: Cambridge University Press, 2006), 53.
148. Digambar Bhouraskar, *United Nations Development Aid: A Study in History and Politics* (New Delhi: Academic Foundation, 2007), 24. For a discussion of development issues at Bretton Woods, see Eric Helleiner, *Forgotten Foundations of Bretton Woods: International Development and the Making of the Postwar Order* (Ithaca, NY: Cornell University Press, 2016).
149. Economic and Social Council Resolution, "Expert Assistance to Member Governments," 26 March 1947, E/RES/51(IV).
150. On the symbolism of sending the first comprehensive mission to Haiti, see Sunil Amrith and Glenda Sluga, "New Histories of the United Nations," *Journal of World History* 19, no. 3 (2008): 263–64.
151. *UN Mission of Technical Assistance to Haiti: Report* (Lake Success: United Nations, 1949).
152. Bhouraskar, *United Nations Development Aid*, 33.
153. General Assembly Resolution, "Technical Assistance for Economic Development," 4 December 1948, A/RES/200(III).
154. For a broader argument to see Truman's speech and U.S. development initiatives more generally as a response to demands from the Global South, see Christy Thornton,

"'Mexico Has the Theories': Latin America and the Interwar Origins of Development," in *The Development Century: A Global History*, ed. Stephen Macekura and Erez Manela (New York: Cambridge University Press, 2018), 263–82.
155. In fact, EPTA was directed by a three-layered steering structure: the UN Secretariat's Technical Assistance Administration (TAA), which carried out the day-to-day work of the program; the Technical Assistance Board (TAB), where the heads of the specialized agencies came together to consult about the services rendered; and the Technical Assistance Committee (TAC), composed of government representatives, which was supposed to supervise and guide the UN program.
156. Benson to Hoo, 18 April 1949, "European Mission," S-0504-0001-08, UNARMS.
157. "Brief Memorandum on the Role of the Trusteeship Council and of the Trusteeship Department in the Programme of Technical Assistance for Economic Development of the Under-developed Countries"; "Technical Assistance for Economic Development and the Trust Territories," no date, S-1564-0000-0020, UNAMRS.
158. "Technical Assistance for Economic Development and the Trust Territories."
159. For a similar argument, see Jessica L. Pearson, *The Colonial Politics of Global Health: France and the United Nations in Postwar Africa* (Cambridge, MA: Harvard University Press, 2018).
160. Benson to Hoo, 23 June 1947, "Report to Dr. Victor Hoo on the Work of the Department for the Week Ending 21 June," S-0504-0001-02, UNARMS.
161. Benson to Hoo, "Note on Technical Assistance for Trust and Non-Self-Governing Territories," 4 January 1950, S-0504-0001-08, UNARMS.
162. Luard, *The Age of Decolonization*, vol. 2, 141.
163. The Committee of 24 (initially the Committee of 17) was established by the General Assembly in 1961 to see to the implementation of its 1960 Declaration on the Granting of Independence to Colonial Peoples. In contrast to the other two committees, the Committee of 24 did not feature an equal number of colonial and noncolonial powers and quickly became a year-round source of critiques of imperialism. On the Committee of 24, see Luard, *The Age of Decolonization*, 187–95. On the Committee on Information from Non-Self-Governing Territories, see El-Ayouty, *The UN and Decolonization*; and Pearson, "Defending Empire at the UN." On the Fourth Committee, see, e.g., Miguel Bandeira Jerónimo, "Competing Developments: Intercolonial Organisations and Colonial Education (1940s-1970s)," in *Education and Development in Colonial and Postcolonial Africa: Policies, Paradigms, and Entanglements, 1890s–1980s*, ed. Damiano Matasci, Miguel Bandeira Jerónimo, and Hugo Gonçalves Dores (London: Palgrave, 2020), 237–62. On the Third Committee, see Lüdert, "Conditions Apply."
164. Luard, *The Age of Decolonization*, 2:197.

## 2. HOW TO BUILD A STATE?

1. Mark Karp, *The Economics of Trusteeship in Somalia* (Boston: Boston University Press, 1960), 13.
2. For similar arguments about the emergence of new understandings of sovereignty, see, for example, Timothy Nunan, *Humanitarian Invasion: Global Development in Cold War Afghanistan* (New York: Cambridge University Press, 2016); Guy Fiti Sinclair, *To Reform the World: International Organizations and the Making of Modern States* (Oxford: Oxford University Press, 2017); Getachew, *Worldmaking after Empire: The Rise and Fall of Self-Determination* (Princeton: Princeton University Press, 2019).

3. Scott Bills, *The Libyan Arena: The United States, Britain, and the Council of Foreign Ministers, 1945–1948* (Kent, OH: Kent State University Press, 1995); Saul Kelly, *Cold War in the Desert: Britain, the United States, and the Italian Colonies, 1945–52* (New York: St. Martin's Press, 2000); Awni al-Ani, "Libyen, Tochter der UNO," in *Libyen*, ed. Fritz Edlinger (Vienna: Promedia, 2011), 102–23. For broad historical overviews, see Ioan Lewis, *A Modern History of Somalia: Nation and State in the Horn of Africa* (Boulder, CO: Westview Press, 1988); Geoffrey Simons, *Libya and the West: From Independence to Lockerbie* (Oxford: Centre for Libyan Studies, 2003); Dirk Vandewalle, *A History of Modern Libya* (Cambridge: Cambridge University Press, 2017); Ronald Bruce St. John, *Libya: From Colony to Revolution* (London: Oneworld, 2017).
4. Wm. Roger Louis, "Libya: The Creation of a Client State," in *Decolonization and African Independence: The Transfers of Power 1960–1980*, ed. Wm. Roger Louis and Prosser Gifford (London: Yale University Press, 1988), 503–28; Kelly, *Cold War in the Desert*.
5. Paolo Tripodi, *The Colonial Legacy in Somalia: Rome and Mogadishu: From Colonial Administration to Operation Restore Hope* (Basingstoke: Macmillan, 1999); Annalisa Urbano, "Imagining the Nation, Crafting the State: The Politics of Nationalism and Decolonisation in Somalia (1940–60)," PhD dissertation, University of Edinburgh, 2012; Antonio Morone, "How Italy Returned to Africa: From the Loss of the Colonies to African Independence," in *Colonialism and National Identity*, ed. Bartella Farnetti and C. Dau Novelli (Newcastle upon Tyne: Cambridge Scholars, 2015), 126–44; Antonio Morone, "Somali Independence and Its Political Connections with Nasser's Egypt," in *The Horn of Africa since the 1960s: Local and International Politics Intertwined*, ed. Ylonen Aleksi and Jan Zahorik (Basingstoke: Routledge, 2017), 109–22. Also see Francesco Tamborini, "The United Nations, the Italian Decolonization and the 1949 Bevin-Sforza Plan: A Victory for Neo-Colonialism?" and Alessia Tortolli, "The Trust Territory of Somaliland, 1950–1960: Trusteeship or Colony?" in *The United Nations and Decolonization*, ed. Nicole Eggers, Jessica L. Pearson, and Aurora Almada e Santos (New York: Routledge, 2020).
6. Official UN documents include meeting records of the main UN organs and their subsidiary bodies, as well as reports submitted to these forums. These published UN documents are available at "UN depository libraries" across the world. The world organization distinguishes these official UN documents from general UN publications, which may be available at regular libraries.
7. The chapter also draws on the records of the UN Technical Assistance Board (which brought together the heads of the UN specialized agencies to oversee the UN technical assistance program) at the UN archives in Geneva, as well as select personal papers of UN employees, including Ralph Bunche, director of the UN Secretariat's Trusteeship Division, and Carter Goodrich, who led the first technical assistance mission to Libya. While the reviewed papers alone warrant follow-up in-depth individual studies, the intergovernmental discussions at the General Assembly, the Economic and Social Council, the Trusteeship Council, and the various subsidiary bodies with regard to the transitory period of Libya and Somaliland before independence have yet to be examined more closely. The personal papers of UN Commissioner for Libya Adrian Pelt, which are held by the United Nations archives in Geneva, provide another interesting source base. More importantly, Libyan and Somali voices, some of which were recorded in petitions and oral presentations to the Trusteeship Council, have yet to receive the scholarly attention they deserve.
8. Bills, *The Libyan Arena*, preface.
9. Urbano, "Imagining the Nation," chapter 4.2.

10. See Benjamin Rivlin, *The United Nations and the Italian Colonies* (New York: Carnegie Endowment for International Peace, 1950), 2. Rivlin worked for the State Department during the war and then for the UN Trusteeship Department in the 1940s. In 1950, he taught Political Science at Brooklyn College. His book on the Italian colonies was based on his 1949 Harvard dissertation on the topic.
11. Rivlin suggests that the Italian colonies were also an issue in the 1948 American elections. Rivlin, *The United Nations and the Italian Colonies*, 2.
12. For the case of Somaliland, Annalisa Urbano suggests that the major concern of the commission was not so much to investigate local aspirations as to establish the extent of opposition to a restoration of Italian rule. Urbano, "Imagining the Nation," 94–95; for an examination of the work of the Commission, see Bills, *The Libyan Arena*.
13. Bills, *The Libyan Arena*, 111.
14. Though submitted to the General Assembly in September 1948, examination of the matter was deferred until the second part of the Assembly's third session in April and May of 1949. Rivlin, *The United Nations and the Italian Colonies*, 14.
15. Kelly, *Cold War in the Desert*, 116.
16. Awni S. al-Ani suggests that the Haitian delegate, who decided to vote against his government's directives at the very last moment, was decisive for the rejection of the Bevin-Sforza plan. Al-Ani, "Libyen, Tochter der UNO," 104–5. Also see Cindy Ewing, "'With a Minimum of Bitterness': Decolonization, the Arab-Asian Group and Postcolonial Internationalism at the United Nations" (forthcoming).
17. The fullest, albeit dated, account is given in Rivlin, *The United Nations and the Italian Colonies*; more recent accounts include Kelly, *Cold War in the Desert*, chapter 5; al-Ani, "Libyen, Tochter der UNO."
18. General Assembly resolution, "Question of the Disposal of the Former Italian Colonies," 21 November 1949, A/Res/289(IV).
19. Pelt received twenty-six out of fifty-six votes. The two other nominees were José Arce of Argentina, who received twenty votes, and Muhammad Zafrullah Khan of Pakistan, who received three votes. (There were three abstentions.) Adrian Pelt, *Libyan Independence and the United Nations: A Case of Planned Decolonization* (New Haven, CT: Yale University Press, 1970), 111.
20. A/Res/289(IV), 21 November 1949, section A.
21. Evan Luard notes that the General Assembly decision to merge Eritrea with Ethiopia—taken in total disregard of the express wishes of Eritreans for self-government or independence, with no safeguards for the maintenance of Eritrean autonomy or special economic assistance—was an easy way for UN member states to dispose of an awkward problem. Rivlin, *The United Nations and the Italian Colonies*; Gordon Morrell, "A Higher Stage of Imperialism? The Big Three, the UN Trusteeship Council, and the Early Cold War," in *Imperialism on Trial*, ed. R. M. Douglas, Michael D. Callahan, and Elizabeth Bishop, 111–37 (Lanham, MD: Lexington Books, 2006); Evan Luard, *A History of the United Nations*, vol. 2: *The Age of Decolonization, 1955–1965* (New York: St. Martin's Press, 1989), 134–39.
22. A Jewish minority "of ancient standing" had likewise greatly decreased by emigration to Israel since 1948 from close to 35,000 people to 8,000. Some 2,000 Maltese and around 500 Greeks were living in Tripoli and Benghazi. John Lindberg, *A General Economic Appraisal of Libya* (New York: United Nations Technical Assistance Administration, 1952), 4–5, https://catalog.hathitrust.org/Record/001320335. (Hereafter Lindberg, *Lindberg Report Libya*.)
23. Lindberg, *Lindberg Report Libya*; Vandewalle, *A History of Modern Libya*, chapter 1.

24. See Vandewalle, *A History of Modern Libya*, 24–30.
25. Cyrenaica had long provided the backbone of resistance to Italian rule. Relations between it and Tripolitania had been acrimonious at times, at least since the Sanusi Order of Cyrenaica had attempted to extend its power into eastern Tripolitania by force during World War I. Yet when Rome acquiesced to Cyrenaican autonomy under Idris in the aftermath of the war, some Tripolitanian leaders asked the Sanusi leader to extend his rule to Tripolitania to avoid Italian domination. Vandewalle suggests that the outward appearance of unity masked deep divisions and distrust that persisted between the two provinces. Vandewalle, *A History of Modern Libya*, 27–30.
26. Vandewalle suggests that the nation's first encounter with modern statehood under Italian rule—an experience of exclusion and subjugation—contributed to a lasting Libyan nostalgia for a pre-bureaucratic, stateless society. Vandewalle, *A History of Modern Libya*, 3, 32–33.
27. St. John, *Libya: From Colony to Revolution*, chapter 5 (Kindle Position 2317).
28. British foreign secretary Anthony Eden merely promised that Cyrenaica would not come under Italian domination again. Vandewalle, *A History of Modern Libya*, 36.
29. The Sanusiyya or Sanusi Order was an Islamic movement established in Cyrenaica by the mid-nineteenth century, which advocated the return to a more pristine, scriptural form of religion. It rapidly built a network in the region, while its core support remained among Cyrenaican tribes. The movement established a rudimentary structure of governance—through tax collection, by providing social services, and by maintaining peace among different tribes—and a sense of identification. It met with little resistance from the Ottomans, but provided an important source of resistance to Italian rule. During World War I, the leader of the Sanusiyya, Sayyid Idris al-Sanusi, formed a tacit alliance with the British. In the brief, relatively peaceful interlude that followed the war, Italians acquiesced to the relative autonomy of the Sanusiyya in Cyrenaica, while some Tripolitanian leaders asked Idris to extend his rule to their territory to avoid Italian domination. Vandewalle, *A History of Modern Libya*, 18–19, 28–29, 38.
30. Several authors have claimed that a UN trusteeship would not have allowed the Western powers to maintain bases in Libya. This is not entirely accurate: as discussed in the previous chapter, the UN trusteeship system also comprised *strategic* trust territories, which allowed for the maintenance of military facilities and were supervised by the Security Council rather than the Trusteeship Council. However, the Soviet Union would not likely have agreed to such an arrangement for Libya. St. John, *Libya: From Colony to Revolution*, chapter 4, section "United Nations Decides" (Kindle Position 2141).
31. Vandewalle, *A History of Modern Libya*, 39.
32. A/Res/289(IV), section A, paragraph 9. Also see Pelt, *Libyan Independence*, 682.
33. Geoffrey Simons, *Libya and the West: From Independence to Lockerbie* (Oxford: Centre for Libyan Studies, 2003); St. John, *Libya: From Colony to Revolution*; Vandewalle, *A History of Modern Libya*.
34. Pelt, *Libyan Independence*.
35. Louis, "Libya: The Creation of a Client State."
36. Pelt, *Libyan Independence*, 111.
37. Andrew Cordier, the U.S. executive assistant to the secretary-general, in turn, had suggested Pelt's name to Trygve Lie. Pelt, *Libyan Independence*, 111–12.
38. Contrary to standard procedure, Pelt was allowed to select his own staff and would successfully stave off budget cuts and even expand the mission staff later on. Pelt, *Libyan Independence*, 118, 414–16.

39. Pelt, *Libyan Independence*, 113–14. Royal Institute of International Affairs, *The International Secretariat of the Future* (London: Oxford University Press, 1944).
40. Pelt, *Libyan Independence*, 117.
41. Tom Power was born in 1916 and received a PhD from Columbia University in 1942. His book *Jules Ferry and the Renaissance of French Imperialism* was published in 1944. Upon graduation, he joined the U.S. State Department as a research specialist and became specialist for Dependent Area Affairs in 1945. He was part of the international secretariat that supported the San Francisco Conference on International Organization in 1945 and joined the permanent U.S. mission to the UN thereafter. He stayed in Libya beyond independence as the UN's technical assistance resident representative and served in various UN posts in Geneva, Iran, Egypt, and Pakistan thereafter. For biographical information, see Pelt, *Libyan Independence*, 120 fn. 9; for a full staff list, see 974–75.
42. "Juridical Egyptian: Dr. Omad Loufti," *New York Times* 8 November 1956: 8.
43. Power's deputy was the Colombian diplomat Alberto González-Fernández. Next in the hierarchy came four political officers: Christopher Burney from the UK, Paul Cremona from Malta, Albert Grand from France, and Saleh Hahmoud from Egypt. Most of the initial staff appointments were made in February and March of 1950, so that the Secretariat was ready to support the Council when it convened for the first time in April. Later appointments included Jerome Pintos as deputy principal secretary for economic and social affairs, as well as the on-staff advisors Syed H. Ahmed (budget and administration), Albert J. P. L. Bel (agriculture), Johann P. Mensing (land claims), and Marc Schreiber (law). Aside from these staff members paid through the regular UN budget, Pelt was supported by numerous short-term technical assistance experts. Pelt, *Libyan Independence*, 122–23.
44. Pelt, *Libyan Independence*, 124–26. Pelt to Lie, 2 March 1950, S-0655–0014–07, United Nations Archives and Records Management Section, New York City (hereafter UNARMS).
45. Pelt, *Libyan Independence*, 178–80. For short biographies of the Council representatives, see 204–6.
46. See Pelt to Power, 16 January 1950, S-0660–0002–02, UNARMS. Pelt, *Libyan Independence*, 124–25, 202–4.
47. Pelt to Lie, 7 January 1950, S-0655–0014–05, UNARMS. Pelt, 115–16, 125–26.
48. Pelt, *Libyan Independence*, chapter 4.
49. Pelt, *Libyan Independence*, 220. Pelt to Lie, 2 March 1950, S-0655–0014–07, UNARMS.
50. Vandewalle, *A History of Modern Libya*, 45–46.
51. Kelly, *Cold War in the Desert*, chapter 6.
52. With highly unequal population numbers in the three territories, the question of proportional versus equal representation was a major bone of contention throughout the negotiations. Pelt, *Libyan Independence*, 221.
53. Pelt, *Libyan Independence*, chapter 3.
54. Vandewalle, *A History of Modern Libya*, 48; Pelt, *Libyan Independence*, 723–24.
55. Pelt, *Libyan Independence*, 298; also see Kelly, *Cold War in the Desert*, chapter 6.
56. Pelt, *Libyan Independence*, 461, 487–89. Cairo's role in Libya's transformation seems well worth looking into further: its public diplomacy at the General Assembly, on the Council for Libya, and in the Arab League; its cooperation with Pakistan; its support for Tripolitanian nationalists; its press campaign against the constitution of the Libyan National Assembly; its compliant stance on the monetary issues at the Meeting of Experts convened by Pelt in early 1951; and its hands-on assistance/ influence through the dispatch of teachers (who, in Cyrenaica, according to a UN memo, were nearly all

drawn from Egypt.) See "Conference with Mr. Cordier," 26 June 1950, S-0655-0001-04, UNARMS.

57. Pelt, *Libyan Independence*, 610. Cable to Pelt/UN Tripoli (from Power?), 10 April 1951, S-0655-0007-0; Pelt to Lie, 12 April 1951, S-0655-0014-05, UNARMS.
58. Pelt, *Libyan Independence*, 611.
59. Pelt to Lie, 2 March 1950, S-0655-0014-07, UNARMS.
60. Pelt to Lie, 8 August 1950, S-0655-0014-05, UNARMS.
61. Secretary-General private meeting, 8 October 1950, David Owen papers (hereafter DO), Box 10, Folder 3, Rare Book and Manuscript Library, Columbia University, New York City (hereafter RBML).
62. Pelt, *Libyan Independence*, 217–19, 397–99.
63. Pelt, *Libyan Independence*, 413–14, 899.
64. Pelt, *Libyan Independence*, 399, 415.
65. Pelt, *Libyan Independence*, 399–401. Power wrote to Goodrich in July 1950 that the WHO experts' visit was "more coincidental than in answer to our request." Public health never became a central concern for the UN mission in Tripoli, even though an early UN memo noted that Italian doctors would likely "pull out" of Libya in 1951, and that their absence would present a serious problem, even though the people "were accustomed" to few health services. Power to Goodrich, 8 July 1950, S-0655-0001-04; "Conference with Mr. Cordier" by Dean, 26 June 1950, S-0655-0001-04, UNARMS.
66. Pelt to Lie, 8 August 1950, S-0655-0014-05, UNARMS; Pelt, *Libyan Independence*, 399.
67. "Conference with Mr. Cordier" by Dean, 26 June 1950, S-0655-0001-04, UNARMS.
68. "Missions Coordination Committee," Special Meeting held on 23 May to consider technical assistance needs of Libyan Mission, Carter Goodrich papers (hereafter CG), B44, F11, RBML.
69. "Reflexiones sobre el Provenir Economico de Bolivia," speech given by Goodrich at Bolivia's First National Sociology Congress, 14 July 1952, CG, B42, F6, "Bolivia Mission History," RBML. With regard to his academic publication, see, e.g., *Government promotion of American canals and railroads, 1800–1890* (New York: Columbia University Press, 1960). For his ILO work, see Daniel Maul, *Human Rights, Development and Decolonization: The International Labour Organization, 1940–70* (New York: Palgrave Macmillan, 2012), 52.
70. Owen to Goodrich, 6 July 1950, CG, B44, F13; "Report of the UN Preparatory Mission on Technical Assistance to Libya," 24 August 1950, CG, B44, F11; Goodrich to Thorp, no date, CG, B44, F12, RBML.
71. Though Pelt does not specify the names of the Libyan interlocutors of the UN mission in his book, they are listed in Goodrich's report. Pelt, *Libyan Independence*, 405. "Report of the UN Preparatory Mission on Technical Assistance to Libya," 24 August 1950, CG, B44, F11, RBML.
72. The IMF expert G. Blowers, for example, found his interviews with local officials generally "not particularly helpful." Blowers to Pelt, 16 October 1950, S-0655-0006-09, UNARMS.
73. Pelt, *Libyan Independence*, 405.
74. Pelt, *Libyan Independence*, 406.
75. Pelt, *Libyan Independence*, 410. For a similar effect of World Bank survey missions to British East Africa ten years later, see Aldwin Roes, "World Bank Survey Missions and the Politics of Decolonization in British East Africa, 1957–1963," *International Journal of African Historical Studies* 42, no. 1 (2009): 1–28. For Sudanese policymakers' struggles with the question of what it might mean to administer a sovereign postcolonial

286  2. HOW TO BUILD A STATE?

economy, see Alden Young, *Transforming Sudan: Decolonization, Economic Development and State Formation* (Cambridge: Cambridge University Press, 2018).

76. "Report of the UN Preparatory Mission on Technical Assistance to Libya," 24 August 1950, CG, B44, F11, RBML. Also see Pelt, *Libyan Independence*, 399, 668.
77. Pelt, *Libyan Independence*, 441.
78. Pelt, *Libyan Independence*, 441.
79. Pelt to Broadley, 4 September 1950, and Broadley to Pelt, 13 September 1950, S-0655-0002-04, UNARMS. For UN "administrative assistance" in Bolivia, see next chapter.
80. Dean to Goodrich, 18 September 1950, Memo by Myrdal, 25 August 1950; Dean to Goodrich, 31 August 1950; Goodrich to Owen, 4 September 1950, CG, B44, F10, RBML.
81. "Report of the UN Preparatory Mission on Technical Assistance to Libya," 24 August 1950, CG, B44, F11, RBML.
82. Goodrich to Dean, 28 September 1950, and Goodrich to Dean 24 October 1950, CG, B44, F10, RBML.
83. Pelt had appealed to the British and French authorities to request a UN developmental survey of Libya as early as March 1950. Pelt, *Libyan Independence*, 399.
84. Power to Goodrich, 30 March 1951, S-0655-0001-05, UNARMS.
85. Pelt, *Libyan Independence*, 411–13.
86. Pelt, *Libyan Independence*, 668. Power to Goodrich, 30 March 1951, S-0655-0001-05, UNARMS.
87. Pelt, *Libyan Independence*, 408. A February UN memo similarly noted that members of the Council preferred simple, concrete projects to a general ambitious development plan. "Minutes of the Meeting of Technical Assistance to Libya" No. 2, 1 February 1951, S-0655-0002-01, UNARMS.
88. Pelt, *Libyan Independence*, 407.
89. Pelt, *Libyan Independence*, 412.
90. Pelt, *Libyan Independence*, 408–9.
91. Pelt, *Libyan Independence*, 869.
92. Pelt, *Libyan Independence*, 413.
93. For biographical information on Lindberg, see Pelt, *Libyan Independence*, 664n4.
94. Dean to Goodrich, 5 July 1951, CG, B44, F11, RBML. For Lindberg's role in Bolivia, see chapter 4.
95. Pelt, *Libyan Independence*, 674; Lindberg, *Lindberg Report Libya*.
96. Libyan Higgins to Rice, 16 August 1951, S-0655-0001-12; Higgins to Fried, 16 October 1951, S-0655-0002-03, UNARMS.
97. After Lindberg gravely criticized an early draft of their report on Libya's balance of payments in January, the IMF experts delayed sharing their balance of payments study until April 1951. Lindberg to Pelt, 29 January 1951 and 1 February 1951, S-0655-0002-02; Lindberg to Keenleyside, 5 March 1951, S-0655-0001-09; Lindberg to Pintos, 13 Mar 1951, S-0655-0001-01, Lindberg to Pintos, 21 March 1951, S-0655-0002-02; Lindberg to Keenleyside, 1 April 1951, S-0655-0001-09; Lindberg to Pintos, 18 April 1951, S-0655-0002-02, UNARMS.
98. Ten years later, London would similarly try to prevent international judgments regarding its monetary arrangements in East Africa. Roes, "World Bank Survey Missions." For the establishment of a Sudanese national currency and its relation to the Sterling Bloc, see Alden Young, "A Currency for Sudan: The Sudanese National Economy and Postcolonial Development," in *The Development Century: A Global History*, ed. Stephen Macekura and Erez Manela (New York: Cambridge University Press, 2018), 130–49.

## 2. HOW TO BUILD A STATE? 287

99. For a list of pros and cons as summarized by Pelt, see "Suggested Opening Remarks by the Commissioner for Meeting of Experts on Libyan Financial, Monetary and Development Problems," second session, Geneva, 20 April 1951, S-0655-0007-01, UNARMS.
100. Lindberg to Pelt, 1 February 1951, S-0655-0002-02, UNARMS.
101. Pelt, *Libyan Independence*, 747, fn.33. Pelt to Bey, 19 August 1950, S-0655-0006-09, UNARMS.
102. Both Blowers and McLeod subsequently worked for the Saudi Arabian Monetary Agency, while McLeod would become governor of the Central Bank of Guyana. Pelt, *Libyan Independence*, 687. Pelt to Bey, 19 August 1950, S-0655-0006-09, UNARMS.
103. See Power to Pelt, 8 September 1950; Blowers to Pelt, 16 October 1950; Blowers to Lie, 21 November 1950, S-0655-0006-09, UNARMS.
104. Blowers and McLeod to Pelt, 31 October 1950; Blowers to Lie, 21 November 1950, S-0655-0006-09, UNARMS.
105. Pelt, *Libyan Independence*, 873.
106. Pelt, *Libyan Independence*, 355, 683, 873-75.
107. Lindberg's successor Benjamin Higgins later agreed that the Blowers-McLeod report should have received much further criticism before being circulated and suggested that his own team had prepared greatly improved balance-of-payments figures. Higgins did not think that the proposed monetary system would create problems "from a technical point of view." Lindberg to Pelt, 29 January 1951; Lindberg to Pelt, 1 February 1951, S-0655-0002-02; Lindberg to Pelt, 22 June 1951, S-0655-0002-02; Higgins to Keenleyside, 11 August 1951, S-0655-0001-12. For McLeod's position on the Sterling area question and Lindberg's report, see: McLeod to Power, 7 August 1951, S-0655-0001-12, UNARMS.
108. Lindberg to Keenleyside, 8 June 1951, S-0655-0001-09. Also see 0655-0007-01, UNARMS.
109. Pelt, *Libyan Independence*, 702-4.
110. Pelt, *Libyan Independence*, 702-3, 706.
111. Pelt, *Libyan Independence*, 702-3.
112. Pelt also noted that the arguments for and against membership in the Sterling area were parallel in many ways to those for and against imperial preferences and customs union: "Members of the group contend that they are applying the principles of multilateralism as far as they can in practice, whereas non-members complain that the members are discriminating against them." See "Suggested Opening Remarks by the Commissioner," second session, Geneva 20 April 1951, S-0655-0007-01, UNARMS.
113. Pelt writes that, although it was initially not referred to as "rent," a tie between foreign financial assistance and base rights did, of course, exist. Pelt, *Libyan Independence*, 705.
114. Pelt, *Libyan Independence*, 702-4. For criticisms in the General Assembly, see chapter 11. Also see Secret Memorandum of Conversation, Stewart, Power, McLeod, 18 April 1951, S-0655-0007-01, UNARMS.
115. For initial disagreements, see Pelt, *Libyan Independence*, 702-4; Louis, "Libya: The Creation of a Client State"; Kelly, *Cold War in the Desert*, chapter 6.
116. Pelt, *Libyan Independence*, 712.
117. Pelt, *Libyan Independence*, 713.
118. Louis, "Libya: The Creation of a Client State," 179-80; also see Kelly, *Cold War in the Desert*, chapter 6.
119. Delegates of the Tripolitanian National Congress accused British authorities of expelling their advisor, Dr. Shoukri. Memo Regarding the Lindberg Report Presented on

Behalf of the Tripolitanian National Congress, 18 August 1951, S-0655-0001-02, UNARMS.
120. Kirkor to Lindberg, 24 July 1951, S-0655-0001-09; McLeod to Power, 17 August 1951, S-0655-0001-12, UNARMS.
121. Power to Goodrich, 31 July 1951, S-0655-0001-05, UNARMS; Dean to Goodrich, 5 July 1951, CG, B44, F11, RBML.
122. Power to Lie, 14 October 1951, S-0655-0001-11, UNARMS; Pelt, *Libyan Independence*, 674.
123. Pelt, *Libyan Independence*, 676. Regardless of the somber economic outlook, the UN Relief and Works Agency for Palestine Refugees in the Near East began exploring the possibilities of large-scale resettlement of Palestinian refugees in Libya around the same time. See Keen to Power, 25 July 1951, S-0655-0009-15, UNARMS.
124. For Italian faith in agricultural improvement, see Vandewalle, *A History of Modern Libya*, 32.
125. Lindberg, *Lindberg Report Libya*.
126. Pelt, *Libyan Independence*, 681.
127. Pelt, *Libyan Independence*, 672.
128. MacDonald to Power, 20 September 1951, S-0655-0001-07, UNARMS. From 1959 to 1967, Higgins served as a professor of economics at the University of Texas, then became head of Department of Economics at the University of Montreal. Pelt, *Libyan Independence*, 664–65; David Webster, "Development Advisors in a Time of Cold War and Decolonization: The United Nations Technical Assistance Administration, 1950–59," *Journal of Global History* 6, no. 2 (2011): 249–72.
129. Higgins to Keenleyside, 17 October 1951, S-0655-0001-01, UNARMS.
130. Minutes of Inter-Departmental Meeting to Discuss Technical Assistance to Libya, 19 September 1950, S-0655-0001-01, UNARMS.
131. Health Report for Libya for the Time of March–June 1951, S-0655-0001-10, UNARMS.
132. Technical Assistance Mission in Libya: Monthly Progress Report, July 1951, S-0655-0001-09, UNARMS.
133. Power to Martínez-Cabañas, 16 March 1951, S-0655-0001-09; Kirkor to Higgins, 10 December 1951, S-0655-0001-13, UNARMS.
134. Health Report for Libya for the Time of March, June 1951, S-0655-0001-10, UNARMS.
135. Health Report for Libya for the Time of March, June 1951, S-0655-0001-10, UNARMS.
136. Memo on Relations with Officials and Private Individuals in Libya for Guidance of Technical Assistance Personnel, 19 September 1951, S-0655-0001-07; Power to Wheatley, 30 June 1951, S-0655-0001-09, UNARMS.
137. Higgins to Keenleyside, 11 August 1951, S-0655-0001-12, UNARMS.
138. As noted above, Pelt considered it vitally important "to associate" Libyan leaders as closely as possible with the UN technical assistance work from early on, as did Lindberg. Pelt, *Libyan Independence*, 688. Lindberg to Power, 19 March 1951, S-0655-0001-01, UNARMS.
139. Benjamin Higgins, *The Economic and Social Development of Libya* (New York: United Nations Technical Assistance Administration, 1953). See also "Libya: Economic and Social Development: Extracts from Report of Chief Economist, Technical Assistance Commission Dr. Benjamin Higgins, Part VIII: Conclusions, Goals Scope and Nature of the Plan" (TAB/INF/R.94, 18 January 1952), GX 26/14, Box 2597, Jacket 7, United Nations Archives at Geneva (hereafter UNOG).
140. For example, Walt Whitman Rostow noted, "Marx was a city boy," whereas Americans understood that the path to modernity ran through the countryside. See David

Engerman and Corinna Unger, "Introduction: Towards a Global History of Modernization," *Diplomatic History* 33, no. 3 (2009): 383.
141. Higgins, *Higgins Report Libya*.
142. For a similar emphasis on the show effect of the so-called "miracle rice" during the Green Revolution, see Nick Cullather, "Miracles of Modernization: The Green Revolution and the Apotheosis of Technology," *DIPH Diplomatic History* 28, no. 2 (2004): 227–54.
143. Higgins, *Higgins Report Libya*.
144. For a similar dynamic in postcolonial Tanzania and Zambia, see Priya Lal, "Decolonization and the Gendered Politics of Developmental Labor in Southeastern Africa," in *The Development Century: A Global History*, ed. Stephen Macekura and Erez Manela (New York: Cambridge University Press, 2018), 173–96.
145. Pelt, *Libyan Independence*, 679.
146. Pelt, *Libyan Independence*, 407. Cable by Ali Jerbi to the Prime Minister of Cyrenaica, 29 November 1950, S-0655-0011-15, UNARMS.
147. Higgins, *Higgins Report Libya*.
148. Health Report for Libya for the Time of March, June 1951, S-0655-0001-10; "Subsistence Allowances for Technical Assistance Experts in Libya," 12 June 1951, S-0655-0011-10, UNARMS.
149. The service was established by an agreement among the U.S., the UK, and France on 15 June 1951. Power to Goodrich, 30 March 1951, S-0655-0001-05; Power to UN European Office, 16 August 1951, S-0655-0011-10, UNARMS.
150. Higgins, *Higgins Report Libya*.
151. Power to Lie, 31 December 1951, S-0655-0001-13, UNARMS.
152. Pelt, *Libyan Independence*, 695.
153. Pelt, *Libyan Independence*, 696, 700–1. In *World without Want* (New York: Harper & Row, 1962), 107, Paul G. Hoffmann writes that several bilateral programs in Libya, particularly the American one, were larger than the UN one. For Libyan wishes for UN technical assistance after independence, and specifically the appointment of a UN technical assistance resident representative, see Pelt to Owen, 16 September 1951, S-0655-0004-04, UNARMS.
154. Hoffmann, *World without Want*, 107.
155. Higgins to Keenleyside, 17 October 1951, S-0655-0001-11, UNARMS. Pelt, *Libyan Independence*, 719–20. Both sets of statutes were revised to accommodate British wishes.
156. Pelt, *Libyan Independence*, 698, 858 fn.9.
157. Pelt, *Libyan Independence*, 701–3.
158. Vandewalle, *A History of Modern Libya*, 48; Pelt, *Libyan Independence*, 723–24.
159. "Memorandum on Relations with Officials and Private Individuals In Libya for the Guidance of Technical Assistance Personnel," A/AC.32/TA.10, 19 September 1951, S-0655-0001-07, UNARMS.
160. See correspondence in S-0655-0009-15-18; and Power to Goodrich, 8 July 1950, S-0655-0001-04; Memo of Telephone Conversation, Adiseshiah and Power, 14 August 1950, S-0655-0010-01; Myrdal to Laugier, Owen, Pelt, Goodrich, 25 August 1950, S-0655-0001-03, UNARMS.
161. Blackley to Pelt, 9 October 1951, S-0655-0004-04; also see Higgins to Keenleyside, 11 August 1951 and Memo, 18 August 19551, S-0655-0001-12; 17 October 1951, S-0655-0001-11, UNARMS. Pelt, *Libyan Independence*, 723–24.
162. In 1953, the British government secured strategic rights in a twenty-year treaty in return for paying £3,750,000 a year for economic development and budgetary assistance. For

the maintenance of its military bases, the U.S. government agreed to pay the Libyan government $4,000,000 a year from 1954 to 1960, then $1,000,000 a year until 1975. Additionally, the U.S. provided Libya with military and grain supplies. Though the French wished to secure similar base rights, they were merely granted air and surface transit rights in return for the equivalent of $U.S. 1,000,000 of development aid in 1955, because of Libyan hostility to French policies in North Africa. Kelly, *Cold War in the Desert*, 141–44.

163. Secretary-General private meeting, 8 May 1952, DO, B10, F5 "1952," RBML.
164. Secretary-General private meeting, 8 May 1952, DO, B10, F5 "1952," RBML. For French and British fears of Libya's setting a precedent, see Louis, "Libya: The Creation of a Client State."
165. Secretary-General private meeting, 8 May 1952.
166. Secretary-General private meeting, 8 May 1952.
167. Gilbert Ware, "Somalia: From Trust Territory to Nation, 1950–1960," *Phylon* 26, no. 2 (1965): 173–85.
168. Hoffmann, *World without Want*, 108; for Hoffmann's role at the UN, see Craig Murphy, *The United Nations Development Programme: A Better Way?* (Cambridge, MA: Cambridge University Press, 2006), 62.
169. Pelt, *Libyan Independence*, 875.

## 3. IF TEN YEARS SUFFICE FOR SOMALILAND . . .

1. Mark Karp, *The Economics of Trusteeship in Somalia* (Boston: Boston University Press, 1960), 11; Lawrence Finkelstein, "Castles in Spain: United States Trusteeship Plans in World War II," PhD thesis, Columbia University, 1970, 504.
2. In 1945, when the United States first entertained the idea of restoring the colonies to Italian authority under UN supervision, Ralph Bunche drafted a trusteeship agreement for Libya, Thomas Power one for Somaliland, and Lawrence Finkelstein one for Eritrea. Finkelstein wrote later that "none [of them] was especially expert with respect to any of the territories, and little help was to be anticipated on the Labor Day weekend," on which they were given the task. Lawrence Finkelstein, "Bunche and the Colonial World: From Trusteeship to Decolonization," in *Ralph Bunche: The Man and His Times*, ed. Benjamin Rivlin (New York: Holmes & Meier, 1990), 125.
3. Benjamin Rivlin, *The United Nations and the Italian Colonies* (New York: Carnegie Endowment for International Peace, 1950), 71.
4. Rivlin, *The United Nations and the Italian Colonies*, 74.
5. The UN staff in Mogadishu kept a detailed, though naturally biased record of this crucial period. To date, however, there has been no published scholarship on Somali history that draws on the fairly extensive UN archival sources reviewed for this chapter. The official records of the organization regarding Somaliland (the deliberations in the General Assembly, the Trusteeship Council, the Economic and Social Council, and so on, as well as reports submitted to those organs), available at any UN depository library around the world, have also yet to be examined. Most fruitful, perhaps, would be an analysis of the manifold petitions that Somalis sent to the UN; those that were officially accepted by the Trusteeship Council also became part of the official published record of the UN.
6. Taylor Shore to Bunche, 23 September 1951, Ralph Bunche Papers (hereafter RB), B86, F15, University of California, Los Angeles (hereafter UCLA).
7. Goro Deeb to Bunche, 19 May 1952, S-0723-0001-12, United Nations Archives and Records Management Section, New York City (hereafter UNARMS).

3. IF TEN YEARS SUFFICE FOR SOMALILAND . . .   291

8.  See, e.g., Bunche to Jean de la Roche, 3 November 1953, S-0723-0001-13; Aleksander to de la Roche, 5 January 1954, S-0723-0002-01, UNARMS.
9.  Alphonso Castagno, *Somalia* (New York: Carnegie Endowment for International Peace, 1959); Ioan Lewis, *A Modern History of Somalia: Nation and State in the Horn of Africa* (Boulder, CO: Westview Press, 1988); Paolo Tripodi, *The Colonial Legacy in Somalia: Rome and Mogadishu: From Colonial Administration to Operation Restore Hope* (Basingstoke: Macmillan, 1999).
10. French Somaliland was a colony from 1896 to 1946 and a French overseas territory until 1967, when it gained independence as Djibouti. Charles de Gaulle's policies of "turning Somalis into Frenchmen" and alleged repression of political freedom were protested in Italian Somaliland by crowds of some 5,000 demonstrators. British Somaliland—which Secretariat officials described as "miserable" in comparison to poor Italian Somaliland—gained independence on 26 June 1960. It was then merged with, or rather swallowed by Italian Somaliland as the independent Somali Republic on 1 July 1960.
11. Castagno, *Somalia*, 345. For the Investigative Commission as a survey of local opinion, see chapter 6 in Scott Bills, *The Libyan Arena: The United States, Britain, and the Council of Foreign Ministers, 1945-1948* (Kent, OH: Kent State University Press, 1995). See also note 12 to chapter 2.
12. At the time, some sixty-eight people died and close to 100 were wounded. Antonio Morone, "How Italy Returned to Africa: From the Loss of the Colonies to African Independence," in *Colonialism and National Identity*, ed. Bartella Farnetti and C. Dau Novelli (Newcastle upon Tyne: Cambridge Scholars, 2015), 362. For Italian sponsorship of the Conferenza, see Urbano, "Imagining the Nation."
13. Lewis, *A Modern History of Somalia*; Paolo Tripodi, "Back to the Horn: Italian Administration and Somalia's Troubled Independence," *Journal of Modern African Studies* 32, no. 2/3 (1999): 359-80; Saul Kelly, *Cold War in the Desert: Britain, the United States, and the Italian Colonies, 1945-52* (New York: St. Martin's Press, 2000); Morone, "How Italy Returned to Africa."
14. Morone, "How Italy Returned to Africa," 136-37. AFIS officials, in turn, resented the appointment of career diplomats rather than colonial officers as chief administrators of the territory. De la Roche to Bunche, 29 December 1952, RB, B86, F16, UCLA.
15. Lewis, *A Modern History of Somalia*, chapter 7; Urbano, "Imagining the Nation," 134.
16. A secretariat official thought the Italians, or rather the local police, had only themselves to blame for the incident, because they refused to grant the SYL an interview with the acting administrator on his visit to town. See Shore to Bunche, 1 September 1952, RB, B93, F13, UCLA.
17. Shore to Bunche, 1 September 1952, S-0723-0001-12, UNARMS.
18. Tripodi, "Back to the Horn"; Urbano, "Imagining the Nation," 134-35; Morone, "How Italy Returned to Africa."
19. Cary to Bunche, 29 May 1950, RB, B86, F16, UCLA.
20. For further information, see Tamara Rachbauer, *Egon Ranshofen-Wertheimer—Chronologie eines bewegten Lebens* (Munich: Grinn, 2008).
21. "Summary record of meeting between the Secretary-General and the principal secretaries of UN field missions," 8 October 1950, DO, B10, F3, Rare Book and Manuscript Library, Columbia University, New York City (hereafter RBML).
22. UNACS A/AC.33/PV.1 15 October 1951 (Verbatim Record of 14th Meeting, 10 October 1951); Lucas to Cordier and Bunche, 11 October 1951, RB, B86, F15, UCLA.

23. Shore reported that Lucas looked like "Death warmed over," that he spent more time in the bathroom than out of it and battled with occasional bouts of asthma. Shore to Bunche, 15 April 1951, RB, B93, F13, UCLA.
24. "Data relating to Complaints of the Italian Administration in Somaliland against Mr. Carpio," RB, B86, F15, UCLA.
25. Shore to Bunche, 1 May 1952; Deeb to Bunche, 11 May 1952, S-0723-0001-12, UNARMS.
26. For Shore's personal descriptions of Carpio, see Shore to Bunche 15 April 1951, 25 August 1951, 3 November 1951, 17 November 1951, 1 December 1951; for official accounts, see Shore to Bunche, 3 November 1952; De la Roche to Bunche, 1 December 1952, S-0723-0001-12, UNARMS. De la Roche to Bunche, 29 December 1952, RB, B86, F15, UCLA.
27. Shore to Bunche, 23 September 1951, RB, B86, F15, UCLA.
28. Shore to Bunche, 17 November 1951, RB, B93, F13, UCLA.
29. According to Shore, Castello's look ("protruding eyes," "thin as a rail") owed to his alcoholism, and he had become a social nuisance, arriving late and overstaying his welcome at cocktail parties. Shore to Bunche, 15 April 1951, 25 August 1951, 3 November 1951, 1 September 1952, RB, B93, F13, UCLA.
30. Shore to Bunche, 21 September 1952, RB, B86, F15, UCLA.
31. Shore to Heinz Wieschoff and B. Cohen, 5 May 1958, S-0723-0001-15, UNARMS.
32. Shore to Bunche, 15 April 1951, RB, B93, F13, UCLA.
33. Shore to Bunche, 19 November 1951, RB, B93, F13, UCLA.
34. Shore to Bunche, 25 November 1951, RB, B93, F13, UCLA.
35. De la Roche to Bunche, 26 October 1954, RB, B86, F15, UCLA; De la Roche to Cohen, 5 November 1955, S-0723-0222-01, UNARMS. Apparently, Egyptian "campaigning" intensified with the arrival of Kamal al din-Salah in 1954. When Salah was murdered in April 1957, Hagi Mohamed Hussein, a founding member and former president of the ruling nationalist party, the Somali Youth League (who was on a fellowship in Cairo at the time), presented the assassination as a Western plot and denounced Italian, French, British, and especially American interference in Somalia in speeches and articles. He subsequently outpolled the pro-Italian "moderate" faction of the SYL and was reelected president of the party on July 28, 1957. His rhetoric alarmed the Western powers, who supported his ouster from the party by "moderate" SYL politicians. See Antonio Morone, "Somali Independence and Its Political Connections with Nasser's Egypt," in *The Horn of Africa since the 1960s: Local and International Politics Intertwined*, ed. Ylonen Aleksi and Jan Zahorik (Basingstoke: Routledge, 2017), 109–22.
36. Provisional Record of the 46th Meeting of the Advisory Council, 28 November 1951, RB, B86, F15; Shore to Bunche, 23 September 1951, RB, B86, F15; Shore to Bunche, 21 January 1952, RB, B86, F15; "Problems Concerning the Advisory Council's Functioning," RB, B86, F16, UCLA.
37. J.J. Cebe-Habersky to Protitch and Wieschoff, 17 October 1958, S-0723-0002-03, UNARMS.
38. De la Roche to Aleksander, 24 December 1953, S-0723-0001-13, UNARMS.
39. De la Roche to Bunche, 11 June 1953, S-0723-0001-13, UNARMS.
40. Shore to Wieschoff and Cohen, 2 March 1957, S-0723-0002-01, UNARMS.
41. Cebe-Habersky to Protitch and Wieschoff, 19 September 1958; Cebe-Habersky to Protitch and Wieschoff, 13 November 1958, S-0723-0002-03, UNARMS.
42. UN Advisory Council: Observations of the Advisory Council concerning the New Draft Law on Political Elections, 22 November 1958; Cebe-Habersky to Protitch and Wieschoff, 27 November 1958, S-0723-0002-03, UNARMS.

3. IF TEN YEARS SUFFICE FOR SOMALILAND ... 293

43. Cebe-Habersky to Protitch and Wieschoff, 24 October 1958, S-0723-0002-03, UNARMS.
44. On the new electoral law, see Urbano, "Imagining the Nation," 147–51.
45. Cebe-Habersky to Wieschoff, 22 January 1959, S-0723-0002-03, UNARMS.
46. Roche to Bunche, 31 January 1953, S-0723-0001-13; Cebe-Habersky to Syrovy, 10 July 1959, S-0723-0002-02; Shore to Wieschoff and Cohen, 2 February 1957, S-0723-0002-01, UNARMS.
47. De la Roche to Bunche, 24 August 1953, S-0723-0001-13, UNARMS.
48. For Shore's account of the incident, see Shore to Bunche, 13 April 1952; for Deeb's work see, e.g., Shore to Bunche, 17 November 1951, RB, B93, F13, UCLA.
49. To prove his point about Somalis, Shore recounted that a local recruit, "a young Somali rascal," who was influential in the SYL, had propositioned "the wife of one of our white guards." "Naturally," Shore wrote, "we fired him," which the SYL protested. Shore to Bunche, 3 November 1951, RB 93, F13, UCLA.
50. Shore to Bunche, 15 April 1951, 6 November 1952, RB, B93, F13, UCLA.
51. C. K. Robinson to Bunche, 29 May 1950, RB, B85, F16, UCLA; Shore to Bunche, 3 March 1952, S-0723-0001-12; De la Roche to Bunche, 3 January 1953, S-0723-0001-12; De la Roche to Bunche, 7 January 1954, S-0723-0001-13; de la Roche to Bunche, 1 December 1952, S-0723-0001-12, UNARMS.
52. "Problems Concerning the Advisory Council's Functioning," RB, B86, F16, UCLA.
53. Rules governing the Co-operation of the United Nations Advisory Council for the Trust Territory of Somaliland under Italian Administration in Matters of Petitions, 20 October 1950, RB, B86, F16, UCLA.
54. Earlier, de la Roche had appealed to headquarters to appoint Lakhdari as acting principal secretary during his own leave, writing that "he is exactly the kind of man the Somali population would like to see with us." De la Roche to Aleksander, 30 December 1953, S-0723-0001-13; De la Roche to Bunche, 1 December 1952, S-0723-0001-12, UNARMS.
55. Shore to Wieschoff and Cohen, 5 May 1958, S-0723-0001-15, UNARMS.
56. Castagno, *Somalia*, 349.
57. The initial appointees were twenty-one clan leaders, seven representatives of political parties (four from members of the pro-Italian umbrella association *Conferenza per la Somalia* and three from the Somali Youth League), two from the commercial class, two of the Italian community, two of the Arab/Yemeni community, and one from the Indo-Pakistani community. Urbano, "Imagining the Nation," 142–43.
58. Lawrence Finkelstein, *Somaliland under Italian Administration: A Case Study in United Nations Trusteeship*. (New York: Woodrow Wilson Foundation, 1955), 14.
59. Urbano, "Imagining the Nation," 147–51.
60. Castagno, *Somalia*; Urbano, "Imagining the Nation," 144.
61. Castagno, *Somalia*; Urbano, "Imagining the Nation."
62. Finkelstein, *Somaliland under Italian Administration*, 22.
63. For Italy's international repositioning in the postwar years, see Silvia Salvatici, "Between National and International Mandates: Displaced Persons and Refugees in Postwar Italy," *Journal of Contemporary History* 49, no. 3 (2014): 514–36.
64. Michele Alacevich, "Postwar Development in the Italian Mezzogiorno: Analyses and Policies," *Journal of Modern Italian Studies* 18 (2013): 90–112.
65. Tripodi, *The Colonial Legacy in Somalia*, 61.
66. Memo, "Technical Assistance to Somaliland under Italian Administration," 16 February 1951, RB, B86, F16, UCLA.
67. "Technical Assistance to Somaliland under Italian Administration."

68. "Dean, William H. (1910–1952)" at http://encyclopedia.jrank.org/articles/pages/4202/Dean-William-H-1910-1952.html (last accessed 3 April 2016).
69. Sunil Amrith and Glenda Sluga, "New Histories of the United Nations," *Journal of World History* 19, no. 3 (2008): 251–74. Also see chapter 1 of this book for a brief discussion of the Haiti mission.
70. Carter Goodrich to David Weintraub, 8 August 1950, CG, B44, F11; Goodrich to David Owen, 29 August 1950, CG, B44, F10, RBML.
71. A public health expert had been added to the originally envisioned three economists. Dean to Caustin, 28 May 1951, RB, B85, F8, UCLA.
72. Dean to Caustin, 28 May 1951, RB, B85, F8, UCLA.
73. Dean to Goodrich, 5 July 1951, CG, B44, F11, RBML.
74. Dean's mission included the following members: W. Bond, an agronomist from FAO; Dr. V. Caffari, a public health expert from WHO; G. Feral, an expert in social development and nomadic questions; A. Fielding-Clarke, an "educationalist" from UNESCO; J. Pechanec, an expert in livestock and range management from FAO and D. Johnston, the only women on the team, as administrative assistant and secretary. See "United Nations Advisory Council for the Trust Territory of Somaliland under Italian Administration: Draft Report of the Advisory Council for the Period of 1 April 1951 to 31 March 1952." RB, B86, F15, UCLA.
75. Dean, Somaliland: First Progress Report, 19 September 1951, ST/TAA/F/Somaliland/R.1, GX 26/14, B2596, J4, UNOG.
76. De la Roche to Bunche, 10 December 1953, S-0723-0001-13, UNARMS.
77. Dean, Somaliland: First Progress Report, 19 September 1951, ST/TAA/F/Somaliland/R.1, GX 26/14, B2596, J4, UNOG.
78. Dean, Somaliland: Second Progress Report, 24 October 1951, ST/TAA/F/Somaliland/R.2, GX 26/14, B2596, J4, UNOG.
79. Shore to Bunche, 23 September 1951, RB, B86, F15, UCLA. Ten years later, on the eve of Somali independence, Bunche himself would feel no more sympathy than Dean toward the Italian administration and described the administrator with the following words: "Di Stefano is a fat, fatuous, unpleasant civilian, who is generally regarded as a tragedy for Somaliland." Brian Urquhart, *Ralph Bunche: An American Life* (New York: W. W. Norton, 1993), 300.
80. Shore also noted that, for some reason, Dean and principal secretary Lucas "didn't hit it off too well together either," speculating, without going into further details, that this might have had to do with "protocol." Shore to Bunche, 23 September 1951, RB, B86, F15, UCLA.
81. Dean, Somaliland: Second Progress Report, 24 October 1951, ST/TAA/F/Somaliland/R.2, GX 26/14, B2596, J4, UNOG.
82. Dean, Somaliland: Second Progress Report, 24 October 1951, ST/TAA/F/Somaliland/R.2, GX 26/14, B2596, J4, UNOG.
83. Castagno, *Somalia*, 379.
84. They discussed possible support from the International Bank (of Reconstruction and Development), the Bank of Italy, the Bank of Naples, and the Currency Board. Dean, Somaliland: Second Progress Report, 24 October 1951, ST/TAA/F/Somaliland/R.2, GX 26/14, B2596, J4, UNOG.
85. In a letter to Shore, Bunche described Dean's death as a terrible tragedy, but in a sense inevitable, because he had never learned to unwind. Bunch to Shore, 23 January 1952, RB, B93, F13, UCLA. No other reasons for Dean's suicide were provided in the press or his obituaries. See, e.g., "Channing Tobias' Son in Law, William Dean Commits

Suicide," *Jet* 24 January 1952. W. M. Brewer, "William Henry Dean," *The Journal of Negro History* 38, no. 1 (1953): 134–36.

86. *The Trust Territory of Somaliland under Italian Administration: Report* (hereafter *Dean Report Somaliland*) (New York: United Nations Technical Assistance Administration, 1952).
87. *Dean Report Somaliland.*
88. *Dean Report Somaliland*; Annalisa Urbano, "A 'Grandiose Future for Italian Somalia': Colonial Developmentalist Discourse, Agricultural Planning, and Forced Labor (1900–1940)," *International Labor and Working-Class History* 92 (2017): 69–88.
89. Tripodi, *The Colonial Legacy in Somalia.*
90. Castagno, *Somalia*, 351. Shore to Wieschoff and Cohen, 7 January 1957, S-0723-0001-01, UNARMS.
91. Castagno, *Somalia*; Lewis, *A Modern History of Somalia*; Tripodi, *The Colonial Legacy in Somalia.* According to UN documents, it was only in August 1957 that Rome assured Mogadishu of its continued support until 1960. Chudson to Wieschoff, 13 August 1957, S-0723-0003-05, UNARMS.
92. Castagno, *Somalia*, 364.
93. Castagno, *Somalia*, 364.
94. Castagno, *Somalia*, 366. Comments on UNESCO report, 24 October, S-1559-0000-01; also see Wieschoff to Shore, 22 October 1956, S-0723-0003-05, and Shore to Wieschoff and Cohen, 5 November 1956, S-1559-0000-01, UNARMS.
95. Castagno, *Somalia*, 373.
96. Syrovy to Cebe-Habersky, S-0723-0018-10, 30 June 1959, UNARMS.
97. Wieschoff to Shore, 8 October 1956, S-0723-0003-05; "Trip through Mudugh and Midjertain Regions, 29 January—6 February 1959," S-0723-0002-03; Cebe-Habersky to Wieschoff and Protitch, 14 April 1959, S-0723-0002-03, UNARMS.
98. Cohen to Owen, 30 November 56, S-1559-0000-01; Shore to Wieschoff, 5 November 1956, S-0723-0002-01, UNARMS.
99. Chudson to Shore, 3 March 1958, and Shore to Wieschoff, 3 July 1958, S-0723-0001-15, UNARMS.
100. See "United Nations Mission to Trust Territories in East Africa, 1954: Report on the Trust Territory of Somaliland," S-1563-0000; Karakacheff to Cohen, 1 August 1956, S-0723-0002-01; Chudson to Wieschoff and Cohen, 3 September 1957, S-0723-0001-15; Shore to Wieschoff and Cohen, 2 October 1957, S-0723-0001-15; Shore to Wieschoff, 3 July 1958, S-0723-0001-15, UNARMS.
101. Tripodi similarly suggests that Italian developmental policies were marked by confusion and improvisation rather than a strategy to restore the prewar situation. Tripodi, "Back to the Horn."
102. De la Roche to Aleksander, 2 December 1953, S-0723-0001-13. The 1954 UN visiting mission to Somaliland drew a similar conclusion. See United Nations Mission to Trust Territories in East Africa, 1954: Report on the Trust Territory of Somaliland," S-1563-0000, UNARMS.
103. De la Roche to Aleksander, 27 November 1953, S-0723-0001-13, UNARMS.
104. Finkelstein, *Somaliland under Italian Administration*, 22.
105. De la Roche to Bunche, 17 September 1953; de la Roche to Aleksander, 27 November 1953, S-0723-0001-13, UNARMS.
106. De la Roche to R. Bunche, 17 September 1953; de la Roche to B. Aleksander, 27 November 1953, S-0723-0001-13, UNARMS.
107. Tripodi, "Back to the Horn," 372.

108. As a "face-saving measure," the Advisory Council received the report a few days before the Trusteeship Council did. De la Roche to Aleksander, 20 April 1954, S-0723-0002-01, UNARMS.
109. Mark Karp maintains that it is unclear to what degree Malagodi's study influenced the plan, despite official claims, as some of Malagodi's principal recommendations were not included. Karp suggests that the ICA played an important role in determining the priorities of the plan. Karp, *The Economics of Trusteeship in Somalia*, 124.
110. Karp, *The Economics of Trusteeship in Somalia*, 123–25.
111. Unfortunately, there is very little information about Walton. When she passed away in August 1955, principal secretary de la Roche showered her with praise, while conceding that she had caused irritation in some quarters. "United Nations Visiting Mission to Trust Territories in East Africa, 1954: Report on the Trust Territory of Somaliland," chapter 3, "Economic Advancement: Economic Development," S-1563-0000; de la Roche to Cohen, 9 August 1955, S-0723-0002-01, UNARMS.
112. Bunche to de la Roche, 22 September 1953, S-0723-0001-13, UNARMS.
113. Karp, *The Economics of Trusteeship in Somalia*.
114. Karp, *The Economics of Trusteeship in Somalia*.
115. See statements made by the Administering Authority of Somaliland and the two vice-presidents of the Territorial Council in *Official Records of the Trusteeship Council, Fourteenth Session*, 528th and 530th meetings. Also see Territorial Council's motion of 4 January 1954 T/1116, annex.
116. See General Assembly resolution "Financing of the economic development plans of the Trust Territory of Somaliland under Italian Administration," 14 December 1954, A/Res/855(IX); and Trusteeship Council resolution "Financing the economic development plans of the Trust Territory of Somaliland under Italian Administration," 7 July 1954, T/Res/1001(XIV).
117. Castagno, *Somalia*, 379, 383. IBRD, *The Economy of the Trust Territory of Somalia*, Report of January 1957, paragraph 210. Reproduced as United Nations Trusteeship Council, *Official Records* (TCOR): 20th Sess., Annexes, Agenda item 11.
118. A predecessor of today's *Milwaukee Journal Sentinel*, the *Milwaukee Journal* established itself as a leading voice of Midwestern liberalism beginning in the late 1930s and its articles won several Pulitzer Prizes during that period. At its peak in the early 1960s, the journal sold between 400,000 and 600,000 copies daily.
119. The article was first published in the *Milwaukee Journal* and then reprinted in the Paris edition of the *New York Herald Tribune* before it was picked up by the *Corriere della Somalia*. In Italian, the final quote reads: „La Somalia e l'esempio perfetto dei ridicoli estremi ai quali l'irragionavole culto practico nel Santuario del nazionalismo sta trascinando il mondo moderno." See "Tenativo di creare una nazione dove non esiste nazione," *Corriere dell Somalia* clipping; Chudson to Wieschoff & Cohen, 3 September 1957, S-0723-0001-15, UNARMS.
120. "A proposito della 'poverta' della Somalia" clipping from *Corriere della Somalia* Anno VII—Numero 192, no date, S-0723-0001-15, UNARMS.
121. "A proposito della 'poverta' della Somalia" clipping.
122. The reference likely referred to a recent article in the *Journal of Middle Eastern Affairs*, which, according to UN officials, was said to advocate Somali federation with Ethiopia. Chudson to Wieschoff and Cohen, 3 September 1957, S-0723-0001-15, UNARMS.
123. Morone, "Somali Independence and Its Political Connections," 115.
124. The exact figures of Italian foreign assistance are somewhat contradictory: UN documents suggest that Italy promised $1,500,000 to pay for 150 Italian technicians as well as 80 to 100 scholarships to Italy, and $500,000 as a budget contribution. Morone

suggests that Italy promised 250 technicians, 80–100 scholarships, and $2 million. Tripodi suggests that Italy offered $1.5 million for 300 Italian experts, $200,000 for scholarships, and $300,000 as a budget contribution. Cebe-Habersky to Protitch and Wieschoff, 17 October 1958, S-0723-0002-03; Tripodi, *The Colonial Legacy in Somalia*; Morone, "Somali Independence and Its Political Connections with Nasser's Egypt," 116.

125. The Secretariat reported that the British were also concerned about the Soviet Union as well as Egypt gaining influence through UN technical assistance. Shore to Protitch and Wieschoff, 8 August 1958, S-0723-0001-15; Shore to Wieschoff, 29 August 1958, S-0723-0003-05, UNARMS. For Egyptian interests in Somaliland, see Morone, "Somali Independence and Its Political Connections"; for the late 1970s and early 1980s, see Donna Jackson, *Jimmy Carter and the Horn of Africa: Cold War Policy in Ethiopia and Somalia* (Jefferson, NC: McFarland, 2006); Donna Jackson, "The Carter Administration and Somalia," *Diplomatic History* 31, no. 4 (2007): 703–21.
126. Cebe-Habersky to Wieschoff and Protitch, 24 October 1958, S-0723-0002-03, UNARMS.
127. Secretariat officials, by contrast, considered slowing down the transfer of power. Cebe-Habersky to Protitch, 7 April 1959, S-0723-0002-03, UNARMS.
128. Anthony Reyner, "Somalia: The Problems of Independence," *The Middle East Journal* 14, no. 3 (1960): 247.
129. Reyner, "Somalia: The Problems of Independence," 255.
130. Alphonso Castagno, "Review of 'The Economics of Trusteeship' by Mark Karp," *Middle East Journal* 15, no. 4 (1961): 171.
131. On a Fulbright grant in 1949–1950, Castagno studied the history of the former Italian colonies at the University of Florence. In 1957 and 1958 he spent eighteen months in the Somali regions of the Horn of Africa on a Ford Foundation grant. In 1959, Castagno worked as a lecturer in the Department of Public Law and Government at Columbia University. He later became director of the African Studies Center at Boston University.
132. Castagno, "Review of 'The Economics of Trusteeship'"; on Rostow and modernization theory, see Nils Gilman, *Mandarins of the Future: Modernization Theory in Cold War America* (Baltimore: Johns Hopkins University Press, 2003).
133. Ioan Lewis, "Review of 'The Economics of Trusteeship' by Mark Karp,'" *Journal of the International African Institute* 31, no. 2 (1961): 190; Jan M. Haakonsen, "In Memory of I. M. Lewis," *Nomadic Peoples* 18, no. 2 (2014): 1–9. For UN officials' reference to Lewis's work, see Comments on UNESCO report, 24 October, S-1559-0000-01, UNARMS.
134. Castagno, *Somalia*.
135. Alex de Waal, "The Wrong Lessons," *Boston Review* 1 December 2003. http://bostonreview.net/world/alex-de-waal-wrong-lessons; Urbano, "Imagining the Nation," 4–5.
136. Urbano, "Imagining the Nation," 4–13. For a similar argument with regard to the scholarly lack of attention to postcolonial state-building and, in particular, administrative and economic histories, see Alden Young, *Transforming Sudan: Decolonization, Economic Development and State Formation* (Cambridge: Cambridge University Press, 2018).
137. For a similar description, see Gregory Mann, *From Empires to NGOs in the West African Sahel: The Road to Nongovernmentality* (New York: Cambridge University Press, 2015).

## 4. MOVING BEYOND ADVICE

1. Dag Hammarskjöld to Carter Goodrich, 30 September 1953, Carter Goodrich Papers (hereafter CG), B42, F1 "Bolivia since Return," Rare Book and Manuscript Library, Columbia University, New York City (hereafter RBML).

2. Goodrich to David Owen, 29 July 1953, CG, B42, F1 "Bolivia since Return," RBML.
3. Glenn Dorn, *The Truman Administration and Bolivia: Making the World Safe for Liberal Constitutional Oligarchy* (University Park: Pennsylvania State University Press, 2011), 96.
4. Memo by Ansgar Rosenborg, 1 October 1949, CG, B43, F11 "1949 Mission," RBML.
5. Appendix 4, Notes on Interviews; UN Preparatory Mission—Bolivia, Nov 1949, CG, B43, F11 "1949 Mission," RBML.
6. For U.S. opposition to the UN, see Stephen Schlesinger, *Act of Creation: The Founding of the United Nations: A Story of Superpowers, Secret Agents, Wartime Allies and Enemies, and Their Quest for a Peaceful World* (Boulder, CO: Westview, 2003).
7. For interpretations of international development efforts as neocolonialist, see Antony Anghie, *Colonialism, Sovereignty, and the Making of International Law* (New York: Cambridge University Press, 2004); Gilbert Rist, *The History of Development: From Western Origins to Global Faith*, 3rd ed. (New York: Zed Books, 2008).
8. For arguments about the rule, triumph, and tyranny of experts, see Timothy Mitchell, *Rule of Expert: Egypt, Techno-Politics, Modernity* (Berkeley: University of California Press, 2002); Joseph Hodge, *Triumph of the Expert: Agrarian Doctrines of Development and the Legacies of British Colonialism* (Athens: Ohio University Press, 2007); William Easterly, *The Tyranny of Experts: Economists, Dictators, and the Forgotten Rights of the Poor* (New York: Basic Books, 2013).
9. See, for example, Kevin Young, "Purging the Forces of Darkness: The United States, Monetary Stabilization, and the Containment of the Bolivian Revolution," *Diplomatic History* 37, no. 3 (2013): 509–37; Thomas Field, *From Development to Dictatorship: Bolivia and the Alliance for Progress in the Kennedy Era* (Ithaca, NY: Cornell University Press, 2014).
10. For brief discussions of the Haiti mission, see chapter 1 as well as Sunil Amrith and Glenda Sluga, "New Histories of the United Nations," *Journal of World History* 19, no. 3 (2008): 251–74.
11. Memo by Alva Myrdal, 5 October 1949, CG, B43, F11 "1949 Mission," RBML.
12. Memo by Rosenborg, 1 October 1949, CG, B43, F11 "1949 Mission," RBML.
13. Memo by Rosenborg, 1 October 1949, CG, B43, F11 "1949 Mission," RBML.
14. Memo by Rosenborg, 1 October 1949, CG, B43, F11 "1949 Mission," RBML.
15. Myrdal moved on to UNESCO in 1955 and won the Nobel Peace Prize for her disarmament advocacy in 1982. She was married to development economist Gunnar Myrdal, another early Secretariat official and eventual Nobel laureate. Glenda Sluga, "The Human Story of Development: Alva Myrdal at the UN, 1949–1955," in *International Organizations and Development, 1945–1990*, ed. Corinna Unger, Marc Frey, and Sonke Kunkel (London: Palgrave Macmillan, 2014), 46–74.
16. Memo by Myrdal, 5 October 1949, CG, B43, F11 "1949 Mission," RBML.
17. "Technical Assistance to Bolivia—Note on Meeting Held on 6 October 1949 in the Office of the Assistant Secretary-General for Economic Affairs," S-0369-0022-09, United Nations Archives and Records Management Section, New York City (hereafter UNARMS).
18. "Technical Assistance to Bolivia."
19. Manuel Pérez-Guerrero to Martin Hill et al., 17 August 1949, S-0369-0022-09, UNARMS.
20. It is not clear how Goodrich was chosen for this task. His involvement with the ILO, as well as his physical proximity to the UN headquarters, must surely have factored into his appointment. For further information on Goodrich, see Chapter 2.

21. Kenneth Iverson, "The 'Servicio' in Theory and Practice," *Public Administration Review* 11, no. 4 (1951): 223–28; Kenneth Lehman, *Bolivia and the United States: A Limited Partnership* (Athens: University of Georgia Press, 1999), 127.
22. Memo by Goodrich to Myrdal, Rosenborg, Duran, Silva [n.d.], CG, B43, F13 "Bolivia Miscellaneous," RBML.
23. Dorn, *The Truman Administration and Bolivia*, 8.
24. Dorn, 8; Glenn Dorn, "Pushing Tin: U.S.–Bolivian Relations and the Coming of the National Revolution," *Diplomatic History* 35, no. 2 (2011): 205–6.
25. Paul Drake, *The Money Doctor in the Andes: The Kemmerer Missions, 1923–1933* (Durham, NC: Duke University Press, 1989), 182.
26. Dorn, "Pushing Tin," 206.
27. Kenneth Lehman writes that Villaroel was more interested in co-opting progressive movements than in supporting their agendas and found himself under constant attack from a strange alliance of enemies, including both the tin barons and the pro-Stalinist left wing. While the military was divided in their alliances, the U.S. further undermined Villaroel's government by maintaining a tough stance on the tin price. Lehman, *Bolivia and the United States*, 93–94.
28. Drake, *The Money Doctor in the Andes*, 177–81.
29. Drake, *The Money Doctor in the Andes*, 175–76. On U.S. dollar diplomacy more generally, see Emily Rosenberg, *Financial Missionaries to the World: The Politics and Culture of Dollar Diplomacy, 1900–1930* (Durham, NC: Duke University Press, 2007). On the Kemmerer mission, also see James Siekmeier, *The Bolivian Revolution and the United States, 1952 to the Present* (University Park: Pennsylvania State University Press, 2011), 16.
30. Drake, *The Money Doctor in the Andes*.
31. Lehman, *Bolivia and the United States*, 78.
32. Lehmann, *Bolivia and the United States*, 81-82.
33. Quoted in Lehman, *Bolivia and the United States*, 81. La Paz, Magruder reported, was skeptical of the newfound U.S. interest in Bolivian welfare, expecting to be "dropped ... like a hot cake" after the war. Joint-Bolivian–American Labor Commission 1943, Dossier No/File No Z 3/8/1, Dossier Connexes, Req. file MI 1/8., Magruder to Hull, 22 March 1943, International Labour Organization Archives, Geneva.
34. Goodrich to David Weintraub, 5 December 1949, CG, B43, F11 "1949 Mission," RBML.
35. Appendix 4, Notes on Interviews; UN Preparatory Mission—Bolivia, Nov 1949, CG, B43, F11 "1949 Mission," RBML.
36. According to Goodrich, Urriolagoitia, after taking office, had himself asked for a confidential social and economic survey of the country. Goodrich to David Weintraub, 5 December 1949, CG, B43, F11 "1949 Mission," RBML. According to a U.S. embassy dispatch, Goodrich's visit received little attention in the local press. In two newspapers it was mentioned briefly, but favorably. Embassy dispatch No. 675, 25 November 1949, RG84, B224, United Nations, The National Archives at College Park, Maryland (hereafter NAII).
37. Carter Goodrich, "Bolivia in Time of Revolution," in *Beyond the Revolution: Bolivia since 1952*, ed. Richard Thorn and James Malloy (Pittsburgh: University of Pittsburgh Press, 1971), 7.
38. Miscellaneous handwritten notes, CG, B43, F13 "Bolivia Miscellaneous," RBML. The Haiti mission was composed of experts in the fields of agricultural development, tropical agriculture, development of fisheries, combined resource development, industrial development, finance and credit organization, public finance, fundamental education, and tropical public health organization. See *UN Mission of Technical Assistance to Haiti: Report* (Lake Success, NY: United Nations, 1949).

39. While the UN recognized the tin industry as the central motor of the Bolivian economy, in Haiti, primary emphasis was placed on improving agricultural and forest resources. *UN Mission of Technical Assistance to Haiti: Report*.
40. Goodrich, "Bolivia in Time of Revolution," 7.
41. "Tentative lists of possible fields for the mission," CG, B43, F11 "1949 Mission," RBML.
42. Goodrich, "Bolivia in Time of Revolution," 7.
43. Department of Economic Affairs, Inter-Divisional Committee on Technical Assistance, Minutes of 14th Meeting, December 1, 1949, handwritten notes, CG, B42, F5 "Bolivia—Materials," RBML.
44. When the UN approached Keenleyside in 1949 to head the comprehensive mission to Bolivia, he was commissioner of the Northwest Territories.
45. Clipping, "A Canadian at the UN: Keenleyside Report on Bolivia Likely to be Amazingly Frank," Hugh L. Keenleyside Fonds, Volume 8, Folder 2, "Bolivia—United Nations Mission of Technical Assistance" (2 of 2), Library and Archives Canada (hereafter LAC).
46. "A Canadian at the UN."
47. Hugh Keenleyside, *Memoirs of Hugh L. Keenleyside.*, vol. 2 (Toronto: McClelland and Stewart, 1981), 326–27.
48. The experts were J. Houston Angus of South Africa, a UN consultant on power problems, as electric-power expert; David Blelloch of the UK, a former staff member of the ILO, as labor expert; Leon H. E. Coursin of France, director general of public works of the French Ministry of Overseas Affairs, as transportation expert; Carl Fritzle of Switzerland, Technical Consultant of the FAO, as tropical crops expert; Donald W. Gillifan of the U.S., technical consultant to the FAO, as irrigation expert; Richard Goode of the U.S., assistant professor of economics at the University of Chicago, as taxation expert; Henry S. Kernan of the U.S., forestry consultant to U.S. government agencies, as forestry expert; Albert Lepawsky of the U.S., professor of public administration at the University of Alabama, as fiscal expert; John Lindberg of Sweden, professor of economics at Princeton University, as expert on the standard of living; Helge Lorentzen of Denmark, under-secretary of the Ministry of Labor and Housing of Denmark, as social welfare expert; G. C. Monture of Canada, chief of the mineral resources division of the Department of Mines and Technical Surveys of Canada, as mining expert; Lucas Ortiz Benítez of Mexico, chief of rural education in the Mexican Ministry of education, as education expert; Theodore R. Seldenrath of the Netherlands, professor of mining at the Delft Institute of Technology, as mining expert; and R. Earl Storie of the U.S., of the division of soils at the University of California, as soils expert. See Albert Lepawsky, *The Bolivian Operation: New Trends in Technical Assistance* (New York: Carnegie Endowment for International Peace, 1952), 115. Keenleyside Fonds, Volume 8, Folder 2, LAC.
49. Keenleyside, *Memoirs*, 2:328. For press clippings, see Keenleyside Fonds, Volume 8, Folder 2, LAC
50. As mentioned in the introduction, Truman's emphasis on working through the UN has received scant attention. For Truman's speech, see: "Inaugural Address of Harry S. Truman," 20 January 1949, The Avalon Project, https://avalon.law.yale.edu/20th_century/truman.asp [last accessed 28 April 2021]. For a discussion of the Point IV speech, see Michael Latham, *The Right Kind of Revolution: Modernization, Development, and U.S. Foreign Policy from the Cold War to the Present* (Ithaca, NY: Cornell University Press, 2011), 31–32.
51. Keenleyside, *Memoirs*, 2:329.
52. "Bolivia—United Nations Mission of Technical Assistance" (1 of 2), UN Mission of Technical Assistance to Bolivia, Minutes of 1st meeting in the field, Arequipa, Peru, April 22, 1950, Keenleyside Fonds, Volume 8, Folder 1, LAC.

4. MOVING BEYOND ADVICE   301

53. Keenleyside, *Memoirs*, 2:331.
54. Keenleyside, "Travel Diary—UN Mission to Bolivia—1950," entry 29 April 1950, Keenleyside Fonds, Volume 30, Folder 12, LAC.
55. Keenleyside, "Travel Diary," 10 May 1950.
56. Keenleyside, "Travel Diary," 3 May 1950.
57. Keenleyside, "Travel Diary," 21 April 1950.
58. Keenleyside, "Travel Diary," 28 April 1950.
59. Keenleyside, *Memoirs*, vol. 2, 333.
60. Memorandum of Conversation, 1 September 1950, Keenleyside, Edward Miller, King, RG59, B2, NAII.
61. Keenleyside, "Travel Diary," 19 May 1950.
62. Keenleyside, "Travel Diary," 19 May 1950; Keenleyside, *Memoirs*, 2:338.
63. Keenleyside, "Travel Diary," 9 May 1950.
64. Memorandum of Conversation, 1 September 1950.
65. Keenleyside, *Memoirs*, 2:336.
66. In 1952, Blelloch returned to Bolivia as the ILO expert for the UN Indigenous Population Project, a concerted effort to improve the socio-economic conditions of the indigenous population of the Andean highlands by overcoming the subsistence economy. Touching the lives of around eight million people, it was by far the largest program carried out by the ILO and an exception to the otherwise small-scale approach of ILO technical assistance. Personnel File Blelloch, ILO Archives, Geneva. Keenleyside, *Memoirs*, vol. 2, 336; Maul, *Human Rights, Development and Decolonization*, 142; Jef Rens, *Le Programme Andin. Contribution de l'OIT a Un Projet-Pilote de Coopération Technique Multilatéral* (Brussels: E. Bruylant, 1987).
67. In 1943, Blelloch and colleagues pondered the idea of establishing mechanisms to inspect countries to see to what extent they followed established legal codes. Letter to Blelloch of April 13, 1943, MI 1, Jacket No. 2, 01/1943–05/1946, "Missions—David Blelloch," ILO Archives, Geneva.
68. See *Yearbook of the United Nations 1947–1948* (New York: United Nations, 1948), 652.
69. Faqir Muhammad, "United Nations Technical Assistance in Public Administration with Special Reference to the Provision of Operational and Executive Personnel" (Dissertation, Syracuse, Syracuse University, 1960), 107–9. Also see the following chapter for a more detailed discussion of the General Assembly debates regarding public administration.
70. "Technical Assistance in Public Administration," 1 November 1949, CG, B43, F13 "Bolivia Miscellaneous," RBML.
71. Patricia Clavin, *Securing the World Economy: The Reinvention of the League of Nations, 1920–1946* (Oxford: Oxford University Press, 2013), 26–33; also see Nathan Marcus, *Austrian Reconstruction and the Collapse of Global Finance, 1921–1931* (Cambridge, MA: Harvard University Press, 2018). Regarding the case of Austria, Marcus writes that the League commissioner had very little de facto control, but served as a useful scapegoat for the Austrian government when it came to laying blame for economic hardships.
72. Adom Getachew, *Worldmaking after Empire: The Rise and Fall of Self-Determination* (Princeton: Princeton University Press, 2019), 60.
73. Keenleyside, "Travel Diary," 18 May 1950.
74. "Technical Cooperation with Bolivia," Dispatch No 646, 26 May 1950, RG 59, B4606, F3, NAII.
75. In his diary, Keenleyside mentioned Arce of the Social Democrats, Unsaga de la Vega of the Falange, and Elio of the Liberals. "Travel Diary," 30 and 31 May and 7 June 1950.

76. Keenleyside, "Travel Diary," 17 June 1950; Oral Memoirs of Richard B. Goode, Baylor University Institute for Oral History & Department of Economics, Oral History Memoir, Interviewee: Richard B. Goode, Date: 6 March 1998, Interviewer: H. Stephen Gardner; accessible at: http://digitalcollections.baylor.edu/cdm/ref/collection/buioh/id/4684 [November 5, 2014].
77. 3rd Interview with President Urriolagoitia, June 8, 1950, Keenleyside, Vol. 8, Folder 1, LAC.
78. On 27 August 1949, militias of the MNR rose up. The government suppressed the outbreak in La Paz, but quickly lost ground elsewhere. The president's forces ultimately succeeded in "breaking the back" of the insurrection within weeks and defeated the rebels in late September. The war killed almost 600 Bolivians and resulted in another 600 captured and imprisoned. Dorn, *The Truman Administration and Bolivia*, 96–104.
79. Dorn, *The Truman Administration and Bolivia*, 108.
80. Dorn, *The Truman Administration and Bolivia*, 109.
81. 3rd Interview with President Urriolagoitia, June 8, 1950.
82. Keenleyside, "Travel Diary," 25 June 1950.
83. Keenleyside, "Travel Diary," 29 June 1950.
84. Keenleyside, "Travel Diary," 3 and 6 July 1950. For a discussion of FAO Director General Herbert Broadly's enthusiastic support of Keenleyside's proposal, see previous chapter.
85. Keenleyside, "Travel Diary," 11 July 1950.
86. The *La Razón* article was based on an a *New York Times* interview with Urriolagoitia, in which the president was quoted as saying that the plan envisioned "the employment on a long-term basis of international experts who would eventually occupy positions in various ministries with a view to coordinating the inefficient administration of the country." While the Bolivian Foreign Office later denied the accuracy of some quotes about unrelated matters, it did not retract the comments about the UN mission. "Interview of President Urriolagoitia by New York Times Correspondent—Politico-Economic Aspects" by William Hudson, 18 July 1950, RG59, B4606, F3, NAII. A monthly review of Bolivian economic matters by the U.S. embassy in La Paz also reported that "there [was] considerable hope locally that a serious and well-directed attack on Bolivia's basic problems will issue from [the recommendations of the UN mission]." "Monthly Economic Airgram—August 1950," 28 August 1950, RA59, B4606, F2, NAII.
87. Keenleyside, "Travel Diary," 11 July 1950. Emphasis in original.
88. "Bolivia Yesterday, Today and Tomorrow" by Florman, 14 July 1950, RG59, B4613, F2, NAII.
89. "Tin—the United Nations—the United States—Bolivia," Florman to Department of State, Dispatch 193, 25 August 1950, RG59, B4613, F2, NAII.
90. In addition to the UN expert, Florman listed Lindberg's friend and neighbor Albert Einstein, "the great scientist, philosopher, and cosmologist," as an example. Florman thought that Einstein had failed terribly "when he attempted to become an intellect in the field of diplomacy and politics. It is easily provable that practically all of Dr. Einstein's statements on current events have been wrong and misleading," he noted. As evidence, he cited "fiery speeches imploring American people to deprive their country of effective weapons [i.e., pursue nuclear disarmament] weeks prior to the Korean attack." "Tin—the United Nations—the United States—Bolivia."
91. "Tin—the United Nations—the United States—Bolivia."
92. Keenleyside, "Travel Diary," 24, 26, 28, 29 April 1950.

93. Florman described himself as an "outspoken opponent of monopolistic tin cartels [who] championed tin reform." See "Tin—the United Nations—the United States—Bolivia"; Dorn, *The Truman Administration and Bolivia*, 107–8.
94. Dorn, *The Truman Administration and Bolivia*, 120; Florman to Secretary, 29 August 1950, RG 59, 824.2544, NAII; "Tin—the United Nations—the United States—Bolivia."
95. In a review of Glen Dorn's research, Kenneth Lehman points out that, in addition to the contempt of his employees and superiors, Florman received "a TNT-filled two liter milk tin bomb, lined with concrete, left outside his office." The bomb was discovered and defused before it could detonate, but "Florman became increasingly paranoid and his dispatches to the State Department ever more bizarre. In April 1951, Florman wrote Truman directly, telling the president that he was convinced that there were agents within the embassy that wished to have him 'murdered by Communists.' Inexplicably, and fully supporting Dorn's thesis [of the low priority given to Bolivia by the U.S. Government], it took the State Department eight more months to remove him." Dorn, *The Truman Administration and Bolivia*, 122–23; Kenneth Lehman, "Review Article: Glen J. Dorn. 'Pushing Tin: U.S.-Bolivian Relations and the Coming of the National Revolution.' *Diplomatic History* 35:2 (April 2011): 233–258," *H-Diplo*, H-Diplo Article Reviews, no. 303 (May 5, 2011): 3, http://www.h-net.org/~diplo/reviews/PDF/AR303.pdf. Even before Florman's intervention with regard to the August 11 decree, assistant secretary Miller wrote to the ambassador that he was "disturbed . . . by [Florman's] telegrams and despatches . . . which were critical of the Department." Miller to Florman, 7 August 1950, RG 59, RASSLA Miller 1949–53, NAII.
96. Dorn, *The Truman Administration and Bolivia*, 120, fn. 10; Keenleyside, Hickerson, Bennett, Miller, et al., MC, 27 June 1951, RG 59, RASSLAA, 1949–53, NAII.
97. Telegram 8503, Acheson to Florman, 25 August 1950, RG59, B4613, F2, NAII.
98. Memorandum of Conversation on "Economic Assistance to Bolivia," 11 August 1950, O'Gara, Schaetzel, Malembaum, Bramble, Speigel, White, Cady, King, NAII, RG 59, B4606, F2, NAII.
99. Telegram 338, Acheson, State Department to King, Atwood, Embassy La Paz, 1 September 1950, RG59, B4606, F3; Memorandum of Conversation, 1 September 1950, Keenleyside, Miller, King, RG59, ASSLA, B2, NAII.
100. Telegram 338, Acheson, State Department to King, Atwood, Embassy La Paz, 1 September 1950, RG59, B4606, F3, NAII. Dorn refers to Bolivian newspaper articles reporting that the UN mission had called for nationalization, a reining-in of capital flight and massive infusions of foreign aid. Dorn, *The Truman Administration and Bolivia*, 121. Also see correspondence between Patino Enterprise and Assistant Secretary of State Miller. Miller wrote that the State Department had "high hopes" for the work of the UN: "[Keenleyside's] views appear to coincide closely with ours." Rovensky to Miller, 22 August 1950 and Miller to Rovensky, 14 September 1950, RG59, B2760, F1, NAII.
101. Memorandum of Conversation, 1 September 1950, Keenleyside, Miller, King, RG59, ASSLA, B2, NAII.
102. Martin Hill to Tryvge Lie, 20 November 1950, S-0369-0022-09, UNARMS.
103. Translation of a Memorandum from M. Laugier on the Report of Dr. Keenleyside on Bolivia, S-0369-0022-09, UNARMS.
104. Translation of a Memorandum from M. Laugier.
105. Translation of a Memorandum from M. Laugier.
106. Alexander Dallin, *The Soviet Union at the United Nations: An Inquiry into Soviet Motives and Objectives* (New York: Praeger, 1962); Alvin Rubinstein, *The Soviets in International Organizations: Changing Policy toward Developing Countries, 1953–1963* (Princeton:

Princeton University Press, 1964); Richard Mansbach, "The Soviet Union, the United Nations, and the Developing States," in *The Soviet Union and the Developing Nations* (Baltimore: Johns Hopkins University Press, 1974); Ilya Gaiduk, *Divided Together: The United States and the Soviet Union in the United Nations, 1945–1965* (Stanford, CA: Stanford University Press, 2012).

107. See, for example, the speech of the British delegate at the 1956 Economic and Social Council 22nd session, 942nd meeting.
108. The Technical Assistance Committee (TAC) was a subsidiary body of the UN Economic and Social Council (ECOSOC), which—like the General Assembly and the Security Council—is one of the main organs of the organization. At the TAC, representatives of UN member states were supposed to give broad policy direction to UN technical assistance activities. The TAC was furthermore charged with overseeing the planning, execution, and evaluation of technical assistance. It reported to ECOSOC, which in turn reported to the General Assembly. The Technical Assistance Board (TAB), by contrast, was composed of the executive heads of the UN specialized agencies (FAO, WHO, UNESCO etc.). It met three times a year to coordinate, supervise, and budget all aspects of the UN technical assistance program.
109. Translation of a Memorandum from M. Laugier.
110. Keenleyside, *Memoirs*, vol. 2, 369.
111. Martin Hill to Tryvge Lie, 20 November 1950, S-0369-0022-09, UNARMS; Webb, Department of State to U.S. Embassy La Paz, 25 September 1950, RG59, B4606, F3, NAII. The State Department appeared a bit disgruntled that it was given "no opportunity to see, study or comment on the report . . . prior to its submission in its final form to the Secretary-General" and that it could "do nothing more than hope that the recommendations of the mission [would] be in harmony with U.S. policies and objectives." But it was generally optimistic about the document.
112. Albert Lepawsky, *The Bolivian Operation: New Trends in Technical Assistance* (New York: Carnegie Endowment for International Peace, 1952), 117; *Report of the United Nations Mission of Technical Assistance to Bolivia* (hereafter *Keenleyside Report Bolivia*) (New York: United Nations Technical Assistance Administration, 1951).
113. *Keenleyside Report Bolivia*, iii.
114. Dorn, "Pushing Tin," 206.
115. In 1953, Singer wrote: "Development requires good administration, yet good administration is itself a result of economic development. It is not, of course, a necessary result, for some highly developed countries have very bad administrations. The difference is that once development has been achieved, bad administration can be afforded as a luxury . . ." Singer, a student of Joseph Schumpeter and John Maynard Keynes, is perhaps best known for the so-called Singer-Prebisch thesis on the terms of international trade being detrimental to countries reliant on the export of primary commodities. He was one of the first economists to join the UN Secretariat. Myrdal served as executive secretary of the UN Economic Commission for Europe from 1947 to 1957. His assistant in that position was none other than Walt Whitman Rostow, who would become the doyen of American Modernization Theory. *Keenleyside Report Bolivia*, 2. For the notion of a vicious cycle, see, e.g., Gunnar Myrdal, *Rich Lands and Poor: The Road to World Prosperity*. (New York: Harper, 1957); Hans Singer, "Obstacles to Economic Development," *Social Research* 20, no. 1 (1953): 19–31.
116. *Keenleyside Report Bolivia*, 2. For a history of U.S. modernization theory, see Nils Gilman, *Mandarins of the Future: Modernization Theory in Cold War America* (Baltimore: Johns Hopkins University Press, 2003).

117. *Keenleyside Report Bolivia*, 3.
118. *Keenleyside Report Bolivia*, 45.
119. *Keenleyside Report Bolivia*, 48.
120. *Keenleyside Report Bolivia*, 45, 48.
121. *Keenleyside Report Bolivia*, 47.
122. *Keenleyside Report Bolivia*, 49.
123. *Keenleyside Report Bolivia*, 49.
124. *Keenleyside Report Bolivia*, 53–54.
125. *Keenleyside Report Bolivia*, 57.
126. *Keenleyside Report Bolivia*, 119.
127. "Policy Statement Bolivia," 19 December 1951, Department of State, p. 8, RG 59, B2760, 611.24–611.26 (1950–54), F1, NAII.
128. "Report of the UN Mission of Technical Assistance to Bolivia," Miller to King, 14 December 1950, RG59, B4607, F1, NAII. "Technical Assistance—Bolivia," Memorandum of Conversation, 27 July 1951, Thatcher Winslow (ILO), Phillip Burnett (UNE), RG59, B4607, F1, NAII. The Director of the Washington, DC ILO branch noted that the specialized agencies were "being held in line on this matter with great difficulty" as they were all "eager to proceed in Bolivia." The State Department thought it wise to "avoid some possible future criticism" by following the line of the Agencies.
129. Dorn, *The Truman Administration and Bolivia*, 134.
130. "Junta Accepts UN Technical Mission Report in Principle," 31 July 1951, Maleady to State Department, RG59, B4607, F1, NAII.
131. "Bolivian Wishes with Regard to Formulation of a Convention with the UN for Technical Assistance and its Implications for the Point Four Program," D.A. de Lima to W. Hudson, 14 September 1951, RG59, B4607, F1, NAII. "Bolivian Dilemma," Embassy to State Department, 2 April 1952, ("major contribution" Galambos; "important contributions" Cobb and Amott; "lesser contribution" and signed by Maleady), RG59, B4606, F1, NAII.
132. The Commission was *ad-honorem* in character and consisted of Casto Rojas, a jurist and former head of the Central Bank, as president of the group; Alberto Crespo Gutiérrez, ex-minister of the economy, businessman, and one of the leaders of the small social democratic party PSD; Remberto Capriles Rico, chairman of the board of the National Social Security Fund and, according to Goodrich, "a Professor of social legislation and correspondent of the ILO"; Jaime Palenque Cevallos, professor of economy at San Andres University and secretary of the Chamber of Commerce; and Walter Montenegro, a "prominent journalist" and agent of Lloyd Aereo Boliviano. See "Bolivian Commission to Study Keenleyside Report," W. Cobb to State Department, 22 August 1951, RG84, B231, Folder "312 UN 1950–51," NAII; Report of the United Nations Technical Assistance Mission to Bolivia, September–October 1951 (Draft), CG, B42, F9 "September 1951 Negotiations," RBML.
133. "Bolivian Wishes with Regard to Formulation of a Convention with the UN for Technical Assistance and its Implications for the Point Four Program," D. A. de Lima to W. Hudson, 14 September 1951, RG59, B4607, F1, NAII.
134. Maleady to Hudson, 27 September 1951, RG 59, 824.00, B4606, F1, NAII.
135. Goodrich, "Bolivia in Time of Revolution," 11; "Report of the UN Mission to Bolivia on the Implementation of Technical Assistance," ST/TAA/F/Bolivia/R.1, 17 October 1951, B2596, J4, United Nations Archives at Geneva, Switzerland (hereafter UNOG).

306   4. MOVING BEYOND ADVICE

136. The Bolivian committee also did not think it necessary, for example, to position UN administrative assistants in the Ministries of Health and Education, because Bolivia already received U.S. assistance in these fields. Goodrich suggests that U.S. representatives would have welcomed such appointments in these ministries to support their own position vis-à-vis the Bolivians. The State Department, in fact, instructed the U.S. embassy in La Paz that the U.S. position was to "not (repeat not) oppose the placement [of] UN experts in these ministries." "Report of the UN Mission to Bolivia on the Implementation of Technical Assistance," ST/TAA/F/Bolivia/R.1, 17 October 1951, p.8, B2596, J4, UNOG; telegram of 14 September 1951, Acheson to U.S. Embassy La Paz, RG59, B4607, F1, NAII.
137. Report of the United Nations Technical Assistance Mission to Bolivia, September–October 1951 (Draft), CG, B42, F9, "September 1951 Negotiations," RBML.
138. Goodrich to Gustavo Martínez Cabañas, 29 September 1951, CG, B42, F9 "September 1951 Negotiations," RBML.
139. "Bolivia: Progress Report—Procedure for Implementation of the Special United Nations Agreement with Bolivia," TAB/ R.140, 4 December 1951, B2597, J6; "Agreement between the United Nations and the Government of Bolivia," TAB/R.131, 15 October 1951, Annex I, p. 11, B2596, J4, UNOG.
140. "Transmittal of the Technical Assistance Agreement between the Government of Bolivia and the UN," Cobb to Department of State, 5 October 1951, RG84, B231, NAII.
141. Transmittal of the Technical Assistance Agreement.
142. Dorn, "Pushing Tin"; Lehman, "Review Article: Dorn 'Pushing Tin.'"
143. "UN Mission to Bolivia, Comments of FONOFF Official," Maleady to State Department, 25 October 1951, RG59, B4607, F2; "Transmittal of the Technical Assistance Agreement."
144. "Transmittal of the Technical Assistance Agreement."
145. "Annual Audit for Bolivia," Hudson to Atwood, Miller, 9 January 1952, RG59, B4606, F1; "Transmittal of the Technical Assistance Agreement"; Maleady to Hudson, 27 September 1951, RG59, 824.00, B4606, F1; "Interview of President Urriolagoitia by New York Times Correspondent—Politico-Economic Aspects" by William Hudson, 18 July 1950, RG59, B4606, F3, NAII.
146. "Argentina Reaction to the UN Technical Mission to Bolivia," U.S. Embassy Buenos Aires to State Department, 28 December 1951, and "Editorial Appearing in O Mundo," U.S. Embassy Rio de Janeiro to State Department, 3 December 1951, RG84, B231, NAII. Some headlines of attached clippings read "Truman Pretende Ayuda los Pueblos Que Explota Wall Street: Hace Ensayos de un Supergobierno en Bolivia el Imperialismo Yanqui" ["Truman Pretends to Help the People Exploited by Wall Street: Yanqui Imperialism Tries out a Supergovernment in Bolivia"] (*La Epoca*, 8 December 1951); "El Plan Keenleyside se Ejecuta Contra la Argentina Peronista" ["The Keenleyside Report Is Directed against Peronist Argentina"] (*El Lider*, 10 December 1951); "Coincide la Presencia de Preconsules Yanquis en Bolivia con una Campaña Antiargentina de la Prensa Colonialista" ["The Presence of Yanqui Preconsules in Bolivia Coincides with an Anti-Argentina Campaign in the Colonialist Press"] (*La Epoca*, 7 Dec 1951).
147. Emphasis mine. "Bolivian Dilemma."
148. "Bolivian Wishes with Regard to Formulation."
149. "Bolivian Dilemma."
150. "Bolivian Wishes with Regard to Formulation."
151. As noted above, U.S. officials were worried about a conflation of the U.S. and the UN, and that potential political pushback against the UN program might be directed

unfairly at the U.S.. "Visit of Sr. Crespo and Mr. Goodrich," Hudson to Atwood, 14 January 1952, RG59, B4607, F2, NAII.
152. Goodrich to Burns, 23 November 1952, CG, B42, Folder 6 "Bolivia Mission History"; Handwritten Report to the UN TAB, 20 March 1953; Folder 2 "Lectures: Bolivia," "Bolivia: Test of Technical Assistance" by Goodrich, *Foreign Affairs*, April 1954, RBML.
153. Goodrich, "Bolivia in Time of Revolution," 12.
154. Confidential Interview with Mr. X, n.d., CG, B42, F6 "Bolivia Mission History," RBML; "Report of the Resident Technical Assistance Representative for the Month of June 1952," TAB/INF/E/Bolivia/R.5, 8 July 1952, B2600, J13, UNOG.
155. "Report of the Resident Technical Assistance Representative for the Month of May 1952," TAB/INF/E/Bolivia/R.4, 20 June 1952; also see "Report of the Resident Technical Assistance Representative for the Month of April 1952," TAB/INF/E/Bolivia/R.3, 13 May 1952, B2600, J13, UNOG.
156. Goodrich, "Bolivia in Time of Revolution," 14.
157. Goodrich, "Bolivia in Time of Revolution," 14. Goodrich's official report to the UN of September 1952 contradicts his recollections, suggesting that the Controller-General had assigned Mr. Escoube, the "able French" administrative assistant, "the important responsibility for proposing revision of relevant legislation." "Report of the Resident Technical Assistance Representative for the Month of August 1952," TAB/INF/E/Bolivia/R.7, 11 September 1952, B2601, J15, UNOG.
158. "Four Months of MNR Government, a Summary and Review," Edward Rowell, Deputy Chief of Mission U.S. Embassy La Paz to State Department, RG59, B4606, F1, NAII.
159. "Report of the Resident Technical Assistance Representative for the Month of May 1952," TAB/INF/E/Bolivia/R.4, 20 June 1952, B2600, J13, UNOG.
160. Goodrich's correspondence with Columbia University regarding an extension of his leave of absence, Goodrich to Burns, 23 November 1952; Goodrich to Minister of Foreign Relations Walter Guevara Arce [sic], 8 January 1953, CG, B42, F6 "Bolivia Mission History," RBML.
161. Dorn, *The Truman Administration and Bolivia*, 166; Alexander interview with Goodrich, La Paz, 15 August 1952, George Meany Memorial Archives, University of Maryland Libraries, Jay Lovestone Papers, Robert Alexander; for a description of the Robert Alexander interview collection, see John French, "The Robert J. Alexander Interview Collection," *Hispanic American Historical Review* 82, no. 2 (2004): 315–26.
162. *Asesor* can be translated as consultant or adviser. Columbia University, Memorandum of Understanding (Strictly Confidential Draft), 20 October 1952, CG B42, Folder 6 "Bolivia Mission History," RBML.
163. Goodrich, "Bolivia in Time of Revolution," 15.
164. Goodrich, "Bolivia: Test of Technical Assistance." Revised Agreement for Technical Assistance between the Government of Bolivia and the UN (Draft), March, 13, 1953; Report to TAB, 20 March 1953; Policy Comments in Headquarters Letters, 22 April to 2 June 1953, CG B42, Folder 6 "Bolivia Mission History," RBML.
165. Karasz cites labor disputes decided in favor of workers as well as job security and an increase in bureaucracy due to nationalization (while maintaining pre-MNR levels of corruption) as reasons for the decrease in productivity. Arthur Karasz, "Experiment in Development: Bolivia since 1952," in *Freedom and Reform in Latin America*, ed. Fredrick Pike (Notre Dame, IN: University of Notre Dame Press, 1959), 268–69; Dorn, *The Truman Administration and Bolivia*, 174–84.
166. Karasz, "Experiment in Development," 270–71.
167. Karasz, "Experiment in Development," 271.

308   4. MOVING BEYOND ADVICE

168. "Monthly Economic Summary—Bolivia—June," Charles Bridgett, Commercial Attaché, to State Department, 21 July 1953, RG 59, B4606, F3, NAII.
169. Lehman writes that the U.S. granted $9 million in food aid, $2 million for technical assistance, and another $2,400,000 for road construction to Bolivia. Dorn notes that Paz Estenssoro, due to pressure from Washington, eventually agreed to "some compensation" for the tin barons, without specifying its extent. Karasz, "Experiment in Development," 271; Lehman, *Bolivia and the United States*, 109; Dorn, *The Truman Administration and Bolivia*, 184.
170. Other conditions included that the tin barons had to be compensated and that the MNR needed to cut its relations with Eastern Bloc countries. Lehman, *Bolivia and the United States*, 110. "Memorandum presented on behalf of the UN Mission of Technical Assistance to Bolivia to Dr. Milton Eisenhower, Special Envoy of the President of the United States," 7 July 1953, CG, B43, Folder "Report and Basic Documents—Bolivia," RBML.
171. Karasz, "Experiment in Development," 271; Lehman, *Bolivia and the United States*, 112; Field, *From Development to Dictatorship*, 6.
172. Notes, "The Bolivian Revolution," 10 December 1953, CG, B42, F2 "Lectures: Bolivia," RBML.
173. Young, "Purging the Forces of Darkness," 513.
174. "Bolivian Dilemma."
175. Karasz to Goodrich, November 1, 1954. Emphasis in original. CG, B42, F4 "Cornell Lectures," RBML.
176. Harrington to Goodrich, n.d., CG, B43, F3 "Bolivian Chapter—Correspondence," RBML.
177. Rebecca Scott, "Economic Aid and Imperialism in Bolivia," *Monthly Review* 24, no. 1 (1972): 48–60.
178. Karasz to Goodrich, 1 November 1954, CG, B42, Folder 4 "Cornell Lectures," RBML.
179. Lehman, *Bolivia and the United States*, 119.
180. George Eder, *Inflation and Development in Latin America: A Case History of Inflation and Stabilization in Bolivia* (Ann Arbor: University of Michigan, 1968), 479.
181. Eder, *Inflation and Development in Latin America*, 477–79.
182. Eder, *Inflation and Development in Latin America*; cited in Young, "Purging the Forces of Darkness," 525–26.
183. Young, "Purging the Forces of Darkness," 529.
184. Lehman, *Bolivia and the United States*, 124.
185. Lehman, *Bolivia and the United States*, 127.
186. Karasz, "Experiment in Development," 277.
187. Karasz, "Experiment in Development," 277, fn. 22.

## 5. HAMMARSKJÖLD, DECOLONIZATION, AND THE PROPOSAL FOR AN INTERNATIONAL ADMINISTRATIVE SERVICE

1. "Address by Secretary-General Dag Hammarskjöld to International Law Association at McGill University, Montréal, Wednesday, 30 May 1956," UN Press Release SG/482 (hereafter "McGill Speech").
2. Sarah Stockwell, "Exporting Britishness: Decolonization in Africa, the British State and Its Clients," in *The Ends of European Colonial Empires: Cases and Comparisons*, ed. Miguel Bandeira Jerónimo and António Costa Pinto (London: Palgrave Macmillan UK, 2015), 148–77.

3. Brian Urquhart, *Hammarskjold* (New York: Knopf, 1972), 387.
4. "McGill Speech."
5. "McGill Speech."
6. As noted earlier, I follow Vijay Prashad in using the term "Third World" to describe a common political project. Vijay Prashad, *The Darker Nations: A People's History of the Third World* (New York: The New Press, 2008).
7. Anne Orford, by contrast, suggests that Hammarskjöld saw the state not as an agent for transformation, but as an arbiter between competing interests. Anne Orford, *International Authority and the Responsibility to Protect* (Cambridge: Cambridge University Press, 2011), 52.
8. As noted earlier, to call attention to the problematic implication of developmental hierarchies, I use the term "developing countries" in quotation marks.
9. Greg Mann asks a similar question: how and why did nongovernmental organizations begin to assume functions of sovereignty at a time when it was so highly valued? Mann, *From Empires to NGOs in the West African Sahel: The Road to Nongovernmentality* (New York: Cambridge University Press, 2015). Mark Mazower uses the phrase "strange triumph" to describe a strengthening of the principle of state sovereignty with the new Human Rights regime underwritten by the UN in 1945. Mark Mazower, "The Strange Triumph of Human Rights, 1933–1950," *The Historical Journal* 47, no. 2 (1 June 2004): 379–98.
10. Mark Mazower, *No Enchanted Palace: The End of Empire and the Ideological Origins of the United Nations* (Princeton: Princeton University Press, 2009); Susan Pedersen, *The Guardians: The League of Nations and the Crisis of Empire* (Oxford University Press, 2015).
11. Anne Orford similarly notes that administration became the principal means of governing in the postwar world. She distinguishes between *administrative* rule in industrialized states and *managerial* rule by international actors in the decolonized world. Orford, *International Authority*, 4.
12. It took the Security Council members several months to agree on a candidate, after Trygve Lie was forced to resign when he lost the support of the Soviet Union over the Korean War. Urquhart, *Hammarskjold*, 15; Henning Melber, *Dag Hammarskjöld, the United Nations and the Decolonisation of Africa* (London: Hurst & Company, 2019), 30.
13. Paul Kennedy, *The Parliament of Man: The Past, Present, and Future of the United Nations* (New York: Random House, 2006), 61.
14. Urquhart, *Hammarskjold*, 22, 369.
15. Anne Orford, "Hammarskjöld, Economic Thinking and the United Nations," in *Peace Diplomacy, Global Justice and International Agency Rethinking Human Security and Ethics in the Spirit of Dag Hammarskjöld*, ed. Carsten Stahn and Henning Melber (Cambridge: Cambridge University Press, 2014), 157; John Toye and Richard Toye, *The UN and Global Political Economy: Trade, Finance, and Development* (Bloomington: Indiana University Press, 2004), 101.
16. Orford, "Hammarskjöld, Economic Thinking," 163.
17. Toye and Toye, *The UN and Global Political Economy*, 101.
18. Urquhart, *Hammarskjold*, 370–71, 375; for a closer examination of Hammarskjöld's view of decolonization based on his statements and speeches, see Melber, *Hammarskjöld, UN, Decolonisation*.
19. In the 1960s and 1970s, the UN would become an important forum for "developing countries'" initiatives calling for fairer trade relations, first through the UN Conference on Trade and Development (UNCTAD) and later through the New International

Economic Order (NIEO).Urquhart, *Hammarskjold*, 374. For UNCTAD, see Toye and Toye, *The UN and Global Political Economy*; Prashad, *The Darker Nations*. For the NIEO, see Nils Gilman, "The New International Economic Order: A Re-Introduction," *Humanity* 6, no. 1 (2015): 1–16; also see other articles in this special issue on the topic.
20. Toye and Toye, *The UN and Global Political Economy*, 102.
21. Toye and Toye suggest that Hammarskjöld's emphasis on economic development of "underdeveloped countries" constituted a real shift from prior UN concerns about the international spread of depressions and the pursuit of full employment. See Toye and Toye, *The UN and Global Political Economy*, chapter 4.
22. Urquhart, *Hammarskjold*, 370, 376.
23. General Assembly resolution "Technical Assistance for Economic Development," 4 December 1948, A/RES/200(III).
24. Olav Stokke, *The UN and Development: From Aid to Cooperation* (Bloomington: Indiana University Press, 2009), 48.
25. Stokke, *The UN and Development*, 22.
26. Philip Glick, *The Administration of Technical Assistance* (Chicago: University of Chicago Press, 1957), 60–61.
27. Patricia Clavin, *Securing the World Economy: The Reinvention of the League of Nations, 1920–1946* (Oxford: Oxford University Press, 2013), 26–33; also see Nathan Marcus, *Austrian Reconstruction and the Collapse of Global Finance, 1921–1931* (Cambridge, MA: Harvard University Press, 2018). For Austria, see chapter 4, note 71. For information on Ethiopia and Liberia, see Adom Getachew, *Worldmaking after Empire: The Rise and Fall of Self-Determination* (Princeton: Princeton University Press, 2019), 20–26.
28. Margherita Zanasi, "Exporting Development: The League of Nations and Republican China," *Comparative Studies in Society and History: An International Quarterly* 49, no. 1 (2007): 143–69; Clavin, *Securing the World Economy*, 26–33; Nathan Marcus, *Austrian Reconstruction and the Collapse of Global Finance, 1921–1931* (Cambridge, MA: Harvard University Press, 2018).
29. Faqir Muhammad, "UN Technical Assistance in Public Administration with Special Reference to the Provision of Operational and Executive Personnel," PhD dissertation, Syracuse University, 1960, 107–9. My emphasis.
30. Muhammad, "UN Technical Assistance in Public Administration," 107–9.
31. See General Assembly Summary Records of the Administrative and Budgetary Committee (Fifth Committee), Meetings 126–165, 17 and 23 November 1948 (A/C.5/SR162–165). On Eastern European interest in importing capitalist management techniques through the UN system, see Sandrine Kott, "The Social Engineering Project: Exportation of Capitalist Management Culture to Eastern Europe (1950–1980)," in *Planning in Cold War Europe: Competition, Cooperation, Circulations (1950s–1970s)*, ed. Michel Christian, Sandrine Kott, and Ondrej Matejka (Berlin: De Gruyter, 2018), 123–42.
32. See A/C.5/SR162–165.
33. This rise also coincided and, to a degree, overlapped with the rise of (business) management training programs, as contributions to the workshop "World of Management: Transregional Approaches to Management Knowledge since 1945," University of Vienna, 14–16 April 2021 made clear. Public administration was one of seven categories of technical assistance activity for which the UN Secretariat assumed primary responsibility. The others were economic development, industrial development, transport and communications, public finance and fiscal questions, statistical services, and social development. For a survey of public administration in both practice and theory since

the late 19th century, see Guy Fiti Sinclair, "The United Nations, Public Administration and the Making of Postcolonial States," paper presented at the Technologies of Stateness: International Organizations and the Making of States workshop, European University Institute, Florence, 15–16 September 2016.; Guy Fiti Sinclair, *To Reform the World: International Organizations and the Making of Modern States* (Oxford: Oxford University Press, 2017).

34. "The Improvement of Public Administration" by F. Tickner, David Owen Papers (hereafter DO), B6, Folder "Dag Hammarskjold Correspondence 1953–61 (2)," Rare Book and Manuscript Library, Columbia University, New York City (hereafter RBML).
35. *The Contributions of the United Nations to the Improvement of Public Administration: A 60 Year History* (New York: United Nations, 2009).
36. Sinclair, "United Nations, Public Administration"; Sinclair, *To Reform the World*.
37. Muhammad, "UN Technical Assistance in Public Administration," 142–43, 145, 329.
38. Muhammad, "UN Technical Assistance in Public Administration," 146.
39. Muhammad, "UN Technical Assistance in Public Administration," 331.
40. Hammarskjöld to Carter Goodrich, 30 September 1953, Carter Goodrich Papers (hereafter CG), B42, Folder 1 "Bolivia since Return," RBML.
41. Following the pattern of its Bolivian program, the UN also staffed Indonesia's State Planning Bureau, which came into existence in the early 1950s. The idea for the Bureau originated with the Indonesian finance minister, Sumitro Djojohadikusumo, a Rotterdam- and London-trained economist, who had called for a centralized agency to handle economic planning in 1940, well before Indonesia achieved independence in 1949. As in the Bolivian model, Bureau personnel were recruited and paid by the UN, but directly responsible to the Indonesian government. Benjamin Higgins, who had previously led the comprehensive development survey mission to not-yet-independent Libya, served as chief economist at the Jakarta Bureau. (He would later join Walt Rostow and Paul Rosenstein-Rodan at the Massachusetts Institute of Technology.) According to David Webster, Indonesian fears that UN experts might be enabled "to run things themselves" proved unfounded. The Bureau was nevertheless influential in promoting technocratic attitudes toward modernization and providing a vital training center for the modernizing elite who would come to power under Suharto's U.S.-backed New Order regime in 1965–1966, following a brutal campaign against the Indonesian Left. Webster, "Development Advisors in a Time of Cold War and Decolonization: The United Nations Technical Assistance Administration, 1950–59," *Journal of Global History* 6, no. 2 (2011): 249–72; Brad Simpson, *Economists with Guns: Authoritarian Development and U.S.–Indonesian Relations, 1960–1968* (Stanford, CA: Stanford University Press, 2008).
42. Urquhart, *Hammarskjold*, 253, 255.
43. Urquhart, *Hammarskjold*, 259, 380. Also see "Mr. Hammarksjold, We Presume," *The Economist*, 2 January 2 1960.
44. Urquhart, 256, 380.
45. Robert Vitalis, "The Midnight Ride of Kwame Nkrumah and Other Fables of Bandung (Ban-Doong)," *Humanity* 4, no. 2 (2013): 261–88; Jeffrey James Byrne, "Beyond Continents, Colours, and the Cold War: Yugoslavia, Algeria and the Struggle for Non-Alignment," *The International History Review* 37, no. 5 (2015): 912–32.
46. Toye and Toye, *The UN and Global Political Economy*, 102.
47. When the UN's development activities were merged into the UN Development Program (UNDP) in 1965, Owen was appointed co-administrator, second-in-command to Paul Hoffman—a poor reward, as some complained, for having developed the UN's

technical assistance activities from the scratch. Owen left the UN in 1969 to serve briefly as general secretary of the International Planned Parenthood Federation before passing away the following year at age 65. Owen's personal papers are available at Columbia University's Rare Book and Manuscript Library. For biographical information, see DO, B35 and 36; Craig Murphy, *The United Nations Development Programme: A Better Way?* (Cambridge: Cambridge University Press, 2006), chapter 3; Sixten Heppling, *UNDP: From Agency Shares to Country Programmes, 1949–1975* (Stockholm: Ministry of Foreign Affairs, 1995), 20.

48. The draft referred to the "frustrations and disappointments which have inevitably attended a fundamental realignment of political power in the atomic age." McGill Speech Draft by David Owen, 18 May 1956, DO, B6, Folder "Dag Hammarskjold Correspondence 1953–61 (2)," RBML.
49. McGill Speech Draft by David Owen.
50. It is interesting to note that with regard to this sudden enlargement, Secretariat officials worried mainly about an increase in their workload and that the General Assembly proceedings would become unwieldy and cumbersome. In the future, a 1955 Secretariat memo on the topic suggested, the secretary-general might take a more active part in setting the Assembly's agenda. The impact on the organization's technical assistance programs was not expected to be significant, since all but three states that joined the organization in 1955 were already participating in the UN assistance programs either as contributor or recipient countries or both. See Secretary-General private meeting, 7 January 1955; Secretariat Working Paper "Implications of the Admission of New Members of the UN: Questions of Procedure and Working Methods of the General Assembly," 9 March 1956; B. Cohen to Hammarskjöld, 4 January 1956; Keenleyside to Cordier, 4 January 1956, S-1555–0000–0116; UNARMS.
51. Luard notes that of the fifty-one original UN members, only three had recently emerged from colonial rule or were about to do so (India, Lebanon, and Syria), while another four had been subjected to semicolonial status (Egypt, Iraq, China, and Iran). In 1955, Ceylon, Cambodia, Laos, Libya, and Jordan, as well as Albania, Bulgaria, Hungary, and Romania, became UN member states. In 1956, Morocco, Sudan, and Tunisia joined the organization. By 1960, another twenty-one former colonies had joined the organization and by 1965, nineteen more. See "Growth in United Nations Membership, 1945-present," https://www.un.org/en/sections/member-states/growth-united-nations-membership-1945-present/index.html (last accessed August 21, 2019); Evan Luard, *A History of the United Nations: The Age of Decolonization, 1955–1965*, vol. 2 (New York: St. Martin's Press, 1989), 2.
52. For alternative political projects, see, e.g., Michael Collins, "Decolonisation and the 'Federal Moment,'" *Diplomacy & Statecraft* 24, no. 1 (2013): 21–40; Frederick Cooper, *Citizenship between Empire and Nation: Remaking France and French Africa, 1945–1960* (Princeton: Princeton University Press, 2014); Gary Wilder, *Freedom Time: Negritude, Decolonization, and the Future of the World* (Durham, NC: Duke University Press, 2015); Getachew, *Worldmaking after Empire*.
53. McGill Speech Draft by David Owen.
54. McGill Speech Draft by David Owen.
55. McGill Speech Draft by David Owen.
56. McGill Speech.
57. McGill Speech Draft by David Owen.
58. McGill Speech.
59. McGill Speech.

60. For a useful discussion of the term, a prevalent trope at the time, see "Revolution of Rising Expectations," *International Encyclopedia of the Social Sciences, Encyclopedia.com*, https://www.encyclopedia.com/social-sciences/applied-and-social-sciences-magazines/revolution-rising-expectations (last accessed 28 April 2021).
61. "Transcript of the Secretary-General's Press Conference held at ICAO Headquarters, Montréal, 30 May 1956," 8 June 1956, DO, B6, Folder "Dag Hammarskjöld Correspondence 1953–61 (2)," RBML (hereafter Montréal Press Conference Transcript).
62. Montréal Press Conference Transcript. Henning Melber disagrees with this assessment: see Melber, *Hammarskjöld, UN, Decolonisation*, 62–64.
63. Hoffman initially led the so-called UN Special Fund for Development, which was established in 1959 to appease "developing countries'" decades-long call for a UN mechanism to finance development projects. The Fund, however, merely sponsored "pre-investment" projects. It was later merged with EPTA to form the UNDP. Also see chapter 2 for a brief introduction to Hoffman. "How to Win the Cold War" by Paul Hoffman, Andrew Cordier papers (hereafter AC), B96, Folder H, RBML. On the UN Special Fund, see Murphy, *The UNDP*, 57–65; Digambar Bhouraskar, *United Nations Development Aid: A Study in History and Politics* (New Delhi: Academic Foundation, 2007), chapter 7; Prashad, *The Darker Nations*, 298, fn. 35; Stokke, *The UN and Development*, 83–114.
64. Montréal Press Conference Transcript.
65. McGill Speech.
66. "Statement by Secretary-General Dag Hammarskjold before the Economic and Social Council on International Cooperation on Behalf of Former Trust Territories Which Have Become Independent," 14 April 1960, UN Press Release SG/908.
67. Hammarskjöld statement on former Trust Territories, 14 April 1960, UN Press Release SG/908.
68. Hammarskjöld statement on former Trust Territories. Author's emphasis.
69. Urquhart, *Hammarskjold*, 384–85.
70. Montréal Press Conference Transcript.
71. Montréal Press Conference Transcript.
72. Montréal Press Conference Transcript.
73. Urquhart, *Hammarskjold*, 384–85.
74. Unfortunately, Kirk-Greene does not mention when the services were created. Anthony Kirk-Greene, *Britain's Imperial Administrators, 1858–1966* (New York: St. Martin's Press, 2000), 162; Teresa Hayter, *French Aid* (London: Overseas Development Institute, 1966). On the Africanization of French colonial state bureaucracies, see Michelle Pinto, "Employment, Education, and the Reconfiguration of Empire: Africanization in Postwar French Africa," PhD dissertation, New York University, 2013. For self-reliance being a guiding ethos rather than a literal imperative in Tanzania, see Priya Lal, "Decolonization and the Gendered Politics of Developmental Labor in Southeastern Africa," in *The Development Century: A Global History*, ed. Stephen Macekura and Erez Manela (New York: Cambridge University Press, 2020), 173–96.. On the absorption of a number of French colonial servants into the emerging European aid bureaucracy, see Véronique Dimier, *The Invention of a European Development Aid Bureaucracy: Recycling Empire* (London: Palgrave Macmillan UK, 2014).
75. "Secure Jobs in Oversea Civil Service Guaranteed: Central Pool of Officers to Be Set Up—From Our Political Correspondent," *Manchester Guardian* 18 May 1956.
76. Kirk-Greene, *Britain's Imperial Administrators*, 264.
77. "Service Overseas," *Manchester Guardian* 18 May 1956.
78. Kirk-Greene, *Britain's Imperial Administrators*, 255.

314   5. HAMMARSKJÖLD AND DECOLONIZATION

79. Kirk-Greene, *Britain's Imperial Administrators*, 254.
80. Anthony Kirk-Greene, "Decolonization: The Ultimate Diaspora," *Journal of Contemporary History* 36, no. 1 (2001): 140.
81. Heinz Wieschoff to Robertson, 20 June 1957, S-0175-2295-0003, UNARMS.
82. Wieschoff to Robertson.
83. Wieschoff to Robertson. Emphasis in original.
84. Secretary General's Private Meeting No. 100, 1 June 1956, S-0847-0002-0004, UNARMS; "A World Civil Service," *New York Times* 23 June 1957.
85. The Administrative Committee on Coordination (ACC) was set up in 1949 to coordinate the work of the specialized agencies and the UN regional economic commissions. See *Yearbook of the United Nations 1948–1949* (New York: United Nations, 1950), 681.
86. Memo for Hammarskjöld, 28 August 1957, S-0175-2295-0004, UNARMS.
87. Even the Eastern European countries, which constituted the only unified voting block at the UN and opposed the initiative, showed some measure of independence. Poland, for example, expressed sympathy with the proposal but objected on financial grounds. Ilya Gaiduk suggests that Moscow did not issue strict orders to the UN delegations of its satellite states: that they were allowed "a normal amount of discretion," but themselves usually sought to coordinate their policies at the UN in advance with the Soviets. Ilya Gaiduk, *Divided Together: The United States and the Soviet Union in the United Nations, 1945–1965* (Stanford, CA: Stanford University Press, 2013).
88. General Assembly Summary Records of the Economic and Financial Committee (Second Committee), 553rd Meeting (A/C.2/SR.533), 24 October 1958; Hugh Keenleyside to Lind, 12 May 1958, S-0175-2296-0001, Matsch to Secretariat, 9 May 1958, S-0175-2296-0001, UNARMS.
89. A/C.2/13/SR.533, 24 October 1958.
90. Keenleyside to Lind, 12 May 1958, S-0175-2296-0001, Matsch to Secretariat, 9 May 1958, S-0175-2296-0001 UNARMS.
91. Economic and Social Council Summary Records, 942nd Meeting (E/SR.942), 24 July 1956.
92. Economic and Social Council, Technical Assistance Committee Summary Records, 146th meeting (E/TAC/SR.146), 19 July 1957.
93. A/C.2./SR.545, 6 November 1958.
94. A/C.2./SR.544, 5 November 1958.
95. For an in-depth look at the Soviet engagement with UNESCO, but also the UN system more generally, see Louis H. Porter, "Cold War Internationalisms: The USSR in UNESCO, 1945–1967," PhD dissertation, University of North Carolina, 2018.
96. Economic and Social Council Summary Records, 942nd meeting (E/SR.942), 24 July 1956.
97. Ullrich Lohrmann, *Voices from Tanganyika: Great Britain, the United Nations and the Decolonization of a Trust Territory, 1946–1961* (Berlin: Lit, 2007), 249.
98. Memo for the Secretary-General by Keenleyside, 28 August 1957, S-0175-2295-0004, UNARMS.
99. Keenleyside to Davidson, 23 May 1958, S-0175-2296-0001, UNARMS. On colonial powers' coordination at the UN, also see Jessica Pearson, "Defending Empire at the United Nations: The Politics of International Colonial Oversight in the Era of Decolonisation," *The Journal of Imperial and Commonwealth History* 45, no. 3 (May 31, 2017): 525–49.
100. Luker to Keenleyside, 14 May 1958, S-0175-2296-0001, UNARMS.
101. Ahmed to Keenleyside, 13 May 1958; Luker to Keenleyside, 14 May 1958; Keenleyside to Davidson, 23 May 1958, S-0175-2296-0001, UNARMS.

5. HAMMARSKJÖLD AND DECOLONIZATION  315

102. "Proposal for the Establishment of an International Administrative Service: Report by the Secretary-General," 19 May 1958, Economic and Social Council, Official Records (E/3121).
103. Memo for the Secretary-General by Keenleyside, 28 August 1957, S-0175-2295-0004, UNARMS.
104. Memo for the Secretary-General by Keenleyside, 28 August 1957.
105. Taylor to Keenleyside, 13 February 1958, S-0175-2296-0001, UNARMS.
106. B. R. Sen to Hammarskjöld, 19 February 1958, and Hammarskjöld to Sen, 10 March 1958, S-0175-2296-0001, UNARMS.
107. E/TAC/SR.163, 7 July 1958.
108. Hill to De Seynes, 6 May 1957, S-0175-2295-0003, UNARMS.
109. Caroline Pruden, *Conditional Partners: Eisenhower, the United Nations, and the Search for a Permanent Peace* (Baton Rouge: Louisiana State University Press, 1998), 194; Gaiduk, *Divided Together*, 2013.
110. Greg Poulgrain, by contrast, suggests that the Kennedy administration envisioned an important role for the UN and in particular the OPEX program in turning West New Guinea, the island territory claimed by both the Netherlands and Indonesia, into an independent state in the early 1960s. Poulgrain even suggests that Kennedy's and Hammarskjöld's vision for West New Guinea, which conflicted with former CIA director Allen Dulles' wish to transfer sovereignty to Indonesia, may have played a role in their untimely deaths. Greg Poulgrain, *The Incubus of Intervention: Conflicting Indonesia Strategies of John F. Kennedy and Allen Dulles* (Petaling Jaya [Malaysia]: Strategic Information and Research Development Centre, 2015), chapter 2; the book was republished in the U.S. as *JFK vs. Allen Dulles: Battleground Indonesia* (New York: W. W. Norton & Co., 2019).
111. Montréal Press Conference Transcript.
112. E/SR.945, 25 July 1956.
113. For shifting U.S. attitudes toward European colonialism, see Wm. Roger Louis and Ronald Robinson, "The Imperialism of Decolonization," *Journal of Imperial and Commonwealth History* 22, no. 3 (1994): 462–511; also see Matthew Connelly, "Taking Off the Cold War Lens: Visions of North-South Conflict during the Algerian War for Independence," *The American Historical Review* 105, no. 3 (2000): 739–69.
114. "Statement by Dr. R.A. Asmaun to the 23rd Session of ECOSOC," 24 April 1957, p. 4, S-0175-2295-0003, UNARMS.
115. "An International administrative service: Memorandum by the Secretary-General," 10 June 1957, E/3017.
116. Webster, "Development Advisors in a Time of Cold War." Also see note 41 above.
117. A/C.2/SR.530, 20 October 1958.
118. A/C.2/SR.544, 5 November 1958; "Programmes of Technical Assistance: Establishment of an International Administrative Service; Statement by the Secretary-General at the 539th meeting, on 30 October 1958," A/C.2/L.376, S-0369-0030-04, UNARMS.
119. Accounting for 54 percent of the total budget, the United States was by far the largest contributor to UN assistance programs, followed by the United Kingdom, with an 8 percent share, and Canada and France, with a 5 percent share each. Stokke, *The UN and Development*, 73; Alvin Rubinstein, *The Soviets in International Organizations: Changing Policy toward Developing Countries, 1953–1963* (Princeton: Princeton University Press, 1964).
120. Urquhart, *Hammarskjold*, 384.

316   5. HAMMARSKJÖLD AND DECOLONIZATION

121. De Selys Longchamps to Cohen, 20 January 1958, S-0175-2295-0004, UNARMS.
122. De Selys Longchamps to Cohen, 20 January 1958.
123. Goldschmidt to Luker, 29 March 1958, S-0175-2296-0001, UNARMS.
124. Goldschmidt to Luker, 29 March 1958.
125. The initial Iranian interest in the scheme, the local resident representative reported, had caused a considerable stir, as "the Bank people" naturally felt a certain resentment and senior Iranians—keenly aware that the plan organization was currently using a $75,000,000 loan from the bank—became uneasy, fearing their interest in Hammarskjöld's proposal might "rock the boat." Thomas Power to Cohen, 25 March 1958, S-0175-2296-0001, UNARMS.
126. Muhammad, "UN Technical Assistance in Public Administration," 273.
127. Muhammad, "UN Technical Assistance in Public Administration," 273.
128. "Technical Assistance in Public Administration: Provision of Operational, Executive and Administrative Personnel," report by the Secretary-General, 14 September 1959, General Assembly, Official Records (A/4212), S-0175-2296-0002; Review of OPEX for U.S. State Department, 11 December 1963, S-0175-2297-0002, UNARMS.
129. *Yearbook of the United Nations 1959* (New York: United Nations, 1960), 29.
130. General Assembly resolution "United Nations assistance in public administration: provision of operational, executive and administrative personnel," 15 December 1960, A/RES/1530(XV).
131. Cameroon, Central African Republic, Chad, Congo (Brazzaville), Congo (Leopoldville), Cyprus, Dahomey (Benin in 1974), Gabon, Ivory Coast, Malagasy Republic (Madagascar in 1975), Mali, Niger, Nigeria, Senegal, Somalia, Togo, Upper Volta (Burkina Faso in 1984). A *Life* magazine article described the newly admitted nations as a "rich new price waiting to be won," which could swing the majority in the General Assembly. "The Biggest Show on Earth: The United Nations," *Life* 3 October 1960: 34.
132. MacCabe to Gardiner, 19 October 1961, S-0175-2295-0005, UNARMS.
133. MacCabe to Gardiner, 19 October 1961.
134. Gardiner to Coates, 15 November 1961, S-0175-2295-0005, UNARMS. In 1963, the Secretariat still struggled with the reputation of OPEX appointments as "second-class." MacCabe to Luna, 18 March 1963, S-0175-2296-0004, UNARMS.
135. F. Tickner to De Seynes, 7 March 1962, S-0175-2295-0005, UNARMS.
136. For a discussion of the how the UN intervention in the crisis built on Hammarskjöld's OPEX idea, see the following chapter.
137. Symonds to Owen, 26 January 1962, S-0175-2295-0005, UNARMS.
138. MacCabe to Victor Hoo, 10 December 1963, S-0175-2297-0002, UNARMS.
139. Interoffice Memorandum, Luker to Malinowski, 23 January 1962; Luker to Malinowski, 21 May 1962, S-0175-2295-0005, UNARMS.
140. Luker to Malinowski, 23 January 1962, S-0175-2295-0005, UNARMS.
141. MacCabe to Mendez, 14 December 1964, S-0175-2297-0003, UNARMS.
142. Hill to Abbas, 8 November 1960, S- S-0175-2297-0001, UNARMS.
143. MacDiarmid to Owen, 3 July 1962, S-0175-2295-0005; MacDiarmid to Huyser (FAO), 8 November 1962, S-0175-2296-0003, UNARMS.
144. MacDiarmid to Owen, 3 July 1962, S-0175-2295-0005, UNARMS.
145. Note by Bapat on UNESCO proposal, 8 November 1960, S-0175-2297-0001, UNARMS.
146. Report on Commissioner's Meeting on 18 January 1963, 21 January 1963, S-0175-2296-0004; MacCabe to Emmerich, 2 July 1962, S-0175-2295-0005, UNARMS.
147. Symonds to Owen, 26 January 1962, S-0175-2295-0005, UNARMS.

148. "Policy Matters: Operational Assistance under the Technical Assistance Component," 1 December 1967, Report by the Administrator to Governing Council, UNDP, Official Records (DP/TA/L.15), 4.
149. "Policy Matters."
150. Frank Sutton (Nairobi, Ford Foundation), "Technical Assistance: An Article Prepared for the International Encyclopedia of the Social Sciences," 1965, DO, B20, RBML.
151. Sutton, "Technical Assistance." The study further cited the following numbers for technical assistance personnel dispatched to "developing countries," broken down by sending country or organization: France (including Algeria), 53,887; United Kingdom, 17,500; United States as well as the USSR "and other Sino-Soviet Bloc," around 8,500; United Nations, 4,542; Egypt, 3,700; Belgium, 3,336. Other countries such as Japan, Israel, and other Western European states sent fewer than 500 technical assistance experts abroad. The study noted elsewhere that while the U.S. was in the lead in overseas aid spending, its expenditure on technical assistance formed a considerably smaller part of the total.
152. MacCabe to Merghani, 3 August 1964, S-0175-2297-0003, UNARMS.
153. DP/TA/L.15, p.7.
154. Stephen Browne, *The United Nations Development Programme and System* (New York: Routledge, 2012), 15.
155. Amy Sayward, *The Birth of Development: How the World Bank, Food and Agriculture Organization, and World Health Organization Changed the World, 1945–1965* (Kent, OH: Kent State University Press, 2006).
156. For a similar argument, see Sinclair, *To Reform the World*.
157. See, e.g., Cooper, *Citizenship between Empire and Nation*; Wilder, *Freedom Time*.

## 6. STATE-BUILDING MEETS PEACEKEEPING

1. See, for example, "UN Broadcast," 1 January 1961, Hugh L. Keenleyside Fonds, Volume 28, Folder 48, Library and Archives Canada, Ottawa (hereafter LAC); Antony Gilpin, "Letters from the Congo," 25 and 26 October 1960, United Nations Career Records Project (hereafter UNCRP), MS.Eng.c.4674, 4/18/(256), Bodleian Library, Oxford University; Henning Melber, *Dag Hammarskjöld, the United Nations and the Decolonisation of Africa* (London: Hurst & Company, 2019), 98.
2. Early research focused, above all, on key Western nations, notably the U.S. and Britain. See, e.g., Stephen Weissman, *American Foreign Policy in the Congo, 1960–1964* (Ithaca, NY: Cornell University Press, 1974); Madeleine Kalb, *The Congo Cables: The Cold War in Africa from Eisenhower to Kennedy* (New York: Macmillan, 1982); Richard Mahoney, *JFK: Ordeal in Africa* (New York: Oxford University Press, 1983); David Gibbs, *The Political Economy of Third World Intervention: Mines, Money, and U.S. Policy in the Congo Crisis* (Chicago: University of Chicago Press, 1991); Alan James, *Britain and the Congo Crisis, 1960–1963* (New York: St. Martin's Press, 1996). For an emphasis on the Belgian perspective, see Ludo de Witte, *The Assassination of Lumumba* (London; Verso, 2001). More recent scholarship has brought valuable insights on the Soviet role in the crisis: see Sergei V. Mazov, *A Distant Front in the Cold War: The USSR in West Africa and the Congo, 1956–1964* (Stanford, CA: Stanford University Press, 2010); Lise Namikas, *Battleground Africa: Cold War in the Congo, 1960–1965* (Stanford, CA: Stanford University Press, 2013). On the position of middling powers, see Kevin Spooner, *Canada, the Congo Crisis, and UN Peacekeeping, 1960–64* (Vancouver: University of British Columbia Press, 2009); Michael Kennedy and Art Magennis, *Ireland,*

*the United Nations and the Congo: A Military and Diplomatic History, 1960–1* (Dublin: Four Courts Press, 2014). Other historians have focused on the Western powers' perspective: see John Kent, *America, the UN and Decolonisation: Cold War Conflict in the Congo* (London: Routledge, 2010); Emmanuel Gerard and Bruce Kuklick, *Death in the Congo: Murdering Patrice Lumumba* (Cambridge, MA: Harvard University Press, 2015), which provides a closer look at Belgian policies; and Alanna O'Malley, *Diplomacy of Decolonisation: America, Britain and the United Nations during the Congo Crisis 1960–64* (Manchester: Manchester University Press, 2018), which also pays attention to UN and Third World agency. For further emphasis on the latter, see Jitendra Mohan, "Ghana, the Congo, and the United Nations," *Journal of Modern African Studies* 7, no. 3 (1969): 369–406; Alanna O'Malley, "Ghana, India, and the Transnational Dynamics of the Congo Crisis at the United Nations, 1960–1," *International History Review* 37, no. 5 (2015): 970–90; Zoe LeBlanc, "'They Are All Lumumbas': Anti-Colonial Solidarities and Media Representations in the United Arab Republic during the Congo Crisis 1960–1," paper presented at the International Decolonization Capstone Conference, Washington, DC, 2016.

3. Ernest Lefever, *Crisis in the Congo: A UN Force in Action* (Washington, DC: Brookings Institution Press, 1965); Ernest Lefever, *Uncertain Mandate: Politics of the UN Congo Operation* (Baltimore: Johns Hopkins University Press, 1967); Georges Abi-Saab, *The United Nations Operation in the Congo, 1960–1964* (Oxford: Oxford University Press, 1978); Carole Collins, "The Cold War Comes to Africa: Cordier and the 1960 Congo Crisis," *Journal of International Affairs* 47, no. 1 (1993): 243–69; Anne Orford, *International Authority and the Responsibility to Protect* (Cambridge: Cambridge University Press, 2011); Melber, *Dag Hammarskjöld, the UN*. Notable exceptions that concern themselves with the nonmilitary, purportedly technical work of the organization include Harold Karan Jacobson, "ONUC's Civilian Operations: State-Preserving and State-Building," *World Politics* 17, no. 1 (1964): 75–107; Arthur House, *The UN in the Congo: The Political and Civilian Efforts* (Washington, DC: University Press of America, 1978). A terrific study of the first eight months of ONUC's operations is Hallen Korn, "Law or Order: The Politics of Development and Humanitarian Intervention in the Congo Crisis, 1960–61," undergraduate thesis, Columbia University, 2014; Aaron Rietkerk's PhD thesis similarly draws on heretofore unused UN archival material to examine the UN civilian operation in the Congo; see Aaron Rietkerk, "In Pursuit of Development: The United Nations, Decolonization and Development Aid, 1949–1961," PhD thesis, London School of Economics, 2015, http://etheses.lse.ac.uk/3158/. For an international law perspective on these activities,, see Guy Fiti Sinclair, *To Reform the World: International Organizations and the Making of Modern States* (Oxford: Oxford University Press, 2017), chapter 4. There are also numerous personal accounts of UN officials who were involved in the crisis: Conor Cruise O'Brien, *To Katanga and Back: A UN Case History* (New York: Simon and Schuster, 1963); Carl von Horn, *Soldiering for Peace* (New York: D. McKay, 1967); Brian Urquhart, *Hammarskjold* (New York: Knopf, 1972); Rajeshwar Dayal, *Mission for Hammarskjöld: The Congo Crisis* (Princeton: Princeton University Press, 1976); Brian Urquhart, *A Life in Peace and War* (New York: Harper & Row, 1987); Brian Urquhart, *Ralph Bunche: An American Life* (New York: W. W. Norton, 1993); Indar Jit Rikhye, *Military Adviser to the Secretary-General: UN Peacekeeping and the Congo Crisis* (London: Hurst, 1993); see also Larry Devlin, *Chief of Station, Congo: A Memoir of 1960–67* (New York: Public Affairs, 2007).

4. In 1948, the UN Truce Supervision Organization (UNTSO) was created as a buffer between Arab States and Israel. In 1951, the Security Council created the UN Military

Observer Group in India and Pakistan (UNMOGIP) to observe and report violations of the cease-fire. In 1956, the first United Nations Emergency Force (UNEF) was deployed in the Suez Crisis to allow for the withdrawal of British, French, and Israeli forces that had invaded Egyptian territory. Ilana Feldman argues that UNEF's ambitions were initially broader (for example, the UN force initially was to take over the administration of the contested Gaza Strip from Egypt for an undetermined time), but that they were quickly scaled back due to pushback on the ground. Ilana Feldman, "Ad Hoc Humanity: UN Peacekeeping and the Limits of International Community in Gaza," *American Anthropologist* 112, no. 3 (2010): 416–29; also see Manuel Fröhlich, "The 'Suez Story': Dag Hammarskjöld, the United Nations and the Creation of UN Peacekeeping," in *Peace Diplomacy, Global Justice and International Agency: Rethinking Human Security and Ethics in the Spirit of Dag Hammarskjöld*, ed. Carsten Stahn and Henning Melber (Cambridge: Cambridge University Press, 2014), 305–40.

5. For a helpful discussion of this and related terms, see Simon Jackson and Dirk Moses, "Introduction: Transformative Occupations in the Modern Middle East," *Humanity* 8, no. 2 (2017): 231–46; for the related concept of "constructive wars" or "transformative invasions," see Moritz Feichtinger and Stephan Malinowski, "Konstruktive Kriege? Rezeption und Adaption der Dekolonisationskriege in westlichen Demokratien," *Geschichte und Gesellschaft* 37, no. 2 (2011): 275–305; Moritz Feichtinger and Stephan Malinowski, "Transformative Invasions: Western Post-9/11 Counterinsurgency and the Lessons of Colonialism," *Humanity* 3, no. 1 (Spring 2012): 35–63.

6. Urquhart, *Hammarskjold*, 402.

7. According to one UN employee, when the first UN troops landed at Ndjili airport, a senior official of the world organization joked that "now the UN has its first colony." Antony Gilpin, "Letters from the Congo," UNCRP, Ms.Eng.c.4675 (2) [back].

8. See the forthcoming doctoral thesis by Katrin Armborst, "A Blue Penciled World: The United Nations' Take on Global Governance in the 1960s Congo Crisis," University of Freiburg.

9. UN Charter, chapter 1, article 2, paragraph 7, https://www.un.org/en/about-us/un-charter/full-text (last accessed 30 April 2021).

10. For a good summary of the sudden turn-around, see David Van Reybrouck, *Congo: The Epic History of a People* (London: Fourth Estate, 2014), chapter 6.

11. The three biggest mining companies were the Union Minière de Haut-Katanga (Union Minière or UMHK), the Société Internationale Forestière et Minière du Congo (Fominière) and the Compagnie du Chemin de Fer du Bas-Congo au Katanga (BCK). Half the UMHK's starting capital came from British investors, the other half from a Belgian holding company. Its primary product was copper, but it also extracted, among other materials, tin, cobalt, radium, uranium, zinc, silver, and gold. Before the UMHK was created in 1906, the Special Comité du Katanga—a semigovernmental organization run by the colonial state with public and private funding—enjoyed exclusive mining rights for half of Katanga, and also took care of the province's political administration. Fominière was set up with American capital and focused on diamond extraction. BCK was founded with French–Belgian capital for the purpose of railroad construction, but soon expanded into mining as well. Van Reybrouck, *Congo*, 120–21.

12. For a study of the change from forced labor to wage labor, see Julia Seibert, *In Die Globale Wirtschaft Gezwungen. Arbeit under kolonialer Kapitalismus im Kongo (1885–1960)* (Frankfurt am Main: Campus, 2016). Seibert argues that, paradoxically, the introduction of ostensibly free labor depended very much on coercion and violence.

13. Building on Herbert Weiss's scholarship, Margot Tudor has argued that the depiction of Congolese society at independence as uneducated by Western standards is misleading. See Margot Tudor, "'Now the UN has its first colony': Technical Assistance and Informal Trusteeship during the UN Peacekeeping Mission in Congo, 1960," in *The United Nations Trusteeship System: Legacies, Continuities, and Change, Global Institutions*, ed. Julius Heise, Maria Ketzmerick, and Jan Lüdert (London: Routledge, forthcoming). Tudor points to the Wilson Centre's "The Congo Crisis, 1960-1961: A Critical Oral History Conference" of 28 November 2011 for further information.
14. Jacobson, "ONUC's Civilian Operations"; House, *The UN in the Congo*; Van Reybrouck, *Congo*.
15. House, *The UN in the Congo*, 40–41.
16. Before the independence date had been set, Belgian policy makers approached U.S. officials to inquire about financial support, but were informed that Washington had no interest in "alleviating colonial problems." When the date was decided, U.S. officials proposed the establishment of an international financial consortium led by the IMF and supported by the U.S. and Belgium to provide assistance to the Congo after independence. Guy Vanthemsche writes that, although some critics argued that the Congo's miserable financial situation provided the real motivation for Belgium to relinquish its colony, there is no concrete evidence to support that claim. The budget deficit amounted to either around $50 or $150 million, depending on whether extraordinary public investments such as those under the Ten-Year Development Plan, launched in 1949, are included in the calculation. Public debt amounted to $740 million in 1959. The numbers are based on a 1960 UN memo. "Belgian Congo" by Ona B. Forrest, June 1960 (draft), Andrew Cordier papers (hereafter AC), Box 162, Folder "Reports—Miscellaneous," Columbia University; Guy Vanthemsche, *Belgium and the Congo, 1885–1980* (Cambridge: Cambridge University Press, 2012), 160–65.
17. Van Reybrouck, *Congo*, 260–63.
18. Joseph Kasavubu, a former teacher who had studied for the priesthood, was in his late forties when he assumed the presidency as leader of the *Alliance de Bakongo* (Abako), a Leopoldville Province party based on ethnic affiliation. Patrice Lumumba, who was thirty-five when he became prime minister, hailed from a small minority in the Kasai Province. He attended a Protestant mission school and worked as a brewery manager in Leopoldville while also writing for Congolese journals and newspapers. He was the first Congolese leader to establish a nationalist vision, appealing to people across the country in passionate speeches. His party, the *Mouvement National Congolais* (MNC), too, was based on regional support in the Equateur, Orientale, Kasai, and Kivu provinces. See Namikas, *Battleground Africa*, 36–38.
19. Moïse Tshombe, who was forty-one when the Congo gained independence, had enjoyed a comparatively privileged upbringing as a member of the Katanga royal family. He was educated at an American mission school, trained as an accountant, and worked as a manager of a chain of stores. He led the *Confederation des Associations Tribales du Katanga* (CONAKAT), which was financed by Belgian mining company UMHK. See Namikas, *Battleground Africa*, 44.
20. For the most comprehensive treatment of the Soviet role in the Congo crisis, see Namikas, *Battleground Africa*; also see Mazov, *A Distant Front in the Cold War*; Alessandro Iandolo, "Beyond the Shoe: Rethinking Khrushchev at the Fifteenth Session of the United Nations General Assembly," *Diplomatic History* 41, no. 1 (2017): 128–54. Namikas writes that Moscow sought to avoid a clash with the U.S. while improving its

standing at the UN among nonaligned states, particularly in view of its rivalry with the People's Republic of China (which was excluded from the UN until 1971).

21. Urquhart, *Hammarskjold*, 401. Namikas (*Battleground Africa*, 75) suggests that only the U.S. was in a position to render such logistical support.
22. The following countries contributed military personnel to ONUC: Canada, Ceylon, Ethiopia, Ghana, Guinea, India, Indonesia, Ireland, Liberia, Malaya, Mali, Morocco, Nigeria, Pakistan, Senegal, Sudan, Sweden, Tunisia, and the United Arab Republic.
23. For data on the U.S. occupation of Germany, see Earl Ziemke, *The U.S. Army in the Occupation of Germany, 1944–1946* (Washington, DC: U.S. Government Printing Office, 1975).
24. In contrast to Katanga, South Kasai did not explicitly declare full independence from the Congo; after a cease-fire was negotiated in September, UN troops were generally able to move freely around the province. Ethnic violence, however, persisted. Kalonji remained on relatively good terms with the government in Leopoldville after Lumumba's ouster. In April 1961, however, he was disavowed by a majority of South Kasai parliamentary representatives and, on a visit to Leopoldville, arrested in December 1961.
25. Cordier was born in Ohio in 1901 and educated at the University of Chicago and the Graduate Institute of Geneva. He worked at the U.S. Department of State before joining the UN Secretariat in 1946, where he eventually served both Trygve Lie and Dag Hammarskjöld as executive assistant. In 1962, he left the UN to become dean of the School of International Affairs at Columbia University and served as president of the university from 1968 to 1970. His personal papers are available at Columbia University's Rare Books and Manuscript Library (hereafter RBML).
26. Joseph Mobutu, who was thirty when the Congo gained independence, hailed from the northwest of the country. He was educated at a Catholic boarding school before serving the in the Force Publique, where he rose through the ranks to the highest position available to Africans. He trained as an accountant and dabbled in journalism, leaving the army in 1956. He subsequently befriended Lumumba and became his personal aide, as well as secretary of state in his first government, while likely also serving as an informer to Belgian intelligence. Namikas writes that the precise involvement of the CIA in Mobutu's first coup remains unclear. When it was announced over the radio, Mobutu was at the ONUC headquarters, a modern apartment complex in Leopoldville called the Royale. Two days earlier, the general had appeared at the Royale in civilian clothes, announcing his intention to resign as chief of the ANC. Dayal, who had replaced Bunche as head of ONUC shortly after the constitutional crisis, urged him to stay "for the good of the country." When his coup was announced, Dayal asked Mobutu to leave ONUC's premises so that the organization would not be associated with the putsch. Namikas, *Battleground Africa*, 54, 105; Urquhart, *Hammarskjold*, 450–51; Thomas Kanza, *Conflict in the Congo: The Rise and Fall of Lumumba* (Harmondsworth: Penguin, 1972), 303; Dayal, *Mission for Hammarskjöld*, 61–63, 90.
27. Dayal, *Mission for Hammarskjöld*, 90.
28. For a nuanced account of the role played by Kwame Nkrumah and Jawaharlal Nehru in pressuring Hammarskjöld to seek a political solution that would include Lumumba and take more vigorous action against Belgium, see O'Malley, "Ghana, India, and the Transnational Dynamics."
29. Dayal suggests that it was Mobutu who ended the month-long African effort at political pacification. Dayal, *Mission for Hammarskjöld*, 89. O on U.S. views of Lumumba, see Namikas, *Battleground Africa*, chapter 5. Urquhart suggests that Lumumba's decision to airlift the ANC into Kasai in late August and the subsequent massacres of the

Baluba changed Hammarskjöld's opinion of the Congolese prime minister: see Urquhart, *Hammarskjold*, 435. Bunche had apparently written off the possibility of a constructive relationship with Lumumba by mid-August; see Urquhart, *Ralph Bunche*, 328; also see Dayal, *Mission for Hammarskjöld*, chapter 1. O'Malley, however, suggests that, due to the pressure from Afro-Asian states, Hammarskjöld had come to the position that no solution to the Congo's political problems was possible without Lumumba. O'Malley, *Diplomacy of Decolonisation*, 51; also see O'Malley, "Ghana, India, and the Transnational Dynamics." Rajeshwar Dayal, Bunche and Cordier's successor in Leopoldville, similarly advocated reconciliation with Lumumba: see Dayal, *Mission for Hammarskjöld*; Namikas, *Battleground Africa*.

30. Witte, *The Assassination of Lumumba*; Namikas, *Battleground Africa*, 1–3.
31. For the role played by Nehru in overcoming internal divisions among Afro-Asian states and formulating a stronger mandate for the UN, see O'Malley, "Ghana, India, and the Transnational Dynamics," 13–15.
32. Security Council resolution "The Congo Question," 21 February 1961, S/RES/161 (1961). France and the Soviet Union abstained from voting.
33. In a recent roundtable review, Lise Namikas suggests that it is unclear whether Dayal resigned or was withdrawn. Dayal was an Indian diplomat born in 1909, who served as ambassador to Yugoslavia before being seconded to the UN Observation Group in Lebanon in 1958, which he later described as "the neatest and most successful peacekeeping enterprise." In September 1960, he succeeded Bunche as head of ONUC, after Cordier's brief intermittent tenure. Dayal's 1976 book *Mission for Hammarskjöld* provides his own view on the UN operations in the Congo. He also published on community development and food policy in India as well as an autobiography. See H-Diplo Roundtable Review XX-32 on the Diplomacy of Decolonization: America, Britain, and the United Nations during the Congo Crisis 1960–1964, 8 April 2019, http://www.tiny.cc/Roundatble-xx-32 (last accessed August 22, 2019), p. 12. Dayal, *Mission for Hammarskjöld*; Rajeshwar Dayal, *A Life of Our Times* (London: Sangam, 1998); Swapna Kona Nayudu, "'A Man of Supreme Patience': Rajeshwar Dayal, Hammarskjöld's Envoy," Wilson Center, April 23, 2018, https://www.wilsoncenter.org/blog-post/man-supreme-patience-rajeshwar-dayal-hammarskjolds-envoy; Swapna Kona Nayudu, "'In the very eye of the storm': India, the UN, and the Lebanon Crisis of 1958," *Cold War History* 18, no. 2 (2018): 221–37.
34. U.S. officials described the campaign to get Adoula elected as "really a U.S. operation but using outstanding UN personalities." Namikas argues that Adoula's election was a close call and that the Congolese representatives almost elected Antoine Gizenga, Lumumba's deputy prime minister and loyal follower. Roger Hilsman, *To Move a Nation; the Politics of Foreign Policy in the Administration of John F. Kennedy* (Garden City, NY: Doubleday, 1967), 251; William Mountz, "Americanizing Africanization: The Congo Crisis, 1960–1967," doctoral dissertation, University of Missouri, 2014, 65; Namikas, *Battleground Africa*, 147.
35. The suspicious circumstances of Hammarskjöld's death in a plane crash in near Ndola, in what was then Northern Rhodesia (Zambia today) has been subject to numerous investigations. In the summer of 2015, a UN-appointed "Independent Expert Panel" found that "new information relating to hijacking and sabotage had nil or weak probative value." Susan Williams' acclaimed 2001 historical study, by contrast, concluded: "Hammarskjöld may have been assassinated; or he may have been killed in a failed hijacking. But whatever the details, his death was almost certainly the result of a sinister intervention. It is most unlikely that [Hammarskjöld's plane] crashed as a result

6. STATE-BUILDING MEETS PEACEKEEPING    323

of pilot error" as claimed by previous investigations. Williams' list of potential culprits include the governments of Rhodesia, Katanga, the UK, and South Africa; western European business interests (mostly Belgian and French mining companies) that operated in Katanga; foreign mercenaries active in Katanga; rogue elements of the CIA or MI5; or likely, some combination of the above "supporters of continued white domination over southern Africa." "Secretary-General Conveys Report of Independent Expert Panel about Death in 1961 of Secretary-General Dag Hammarskjöld, 15 Companions | Meetings Coverage and Press Releases," accessed July 28, 2016, http://www.un.org/press/en/2015/sgsm16916.doc.htm; A. Susan Williams, *Who Killed Hammarskjöld?: The UN, the Cold War, and White Supremacy in Africa* (New York: Columbia University Press, 2011), 232. Philip Muehlenbeck, Review of Williams, A. Susan, *Who Killed Hammarskjöld?: The UN, the Cold War, and White Supremacy in Africa*. H-Diplo, H-Net Reviews. June, 2012, http://www.h-net.org/reviews/showrev.php?id=36031, last accessed July 28, 2016.

36. U Thant was born in 1909 to a moderately wealthy family of landowners and rice merchants. He studied history together with the future Burmese prime minister U Nu and worked as a teacher while also contributing to newspapers and magazines. When Burma won independence in 1948, Thant served in several government posts and as the prime minister's closest confidant and advisor. He participated in a number of international conferences, including in Bandung in 1955, and served as Burma's permanent representative to the UN from 1957 to 1961. His appointment as secretary-general, proposed by representatives of nonaligned states, was accepted unanimously by the Security Council powers and later by the General Assembly. Though Thant held the office for a record ten years, the secondary literature on his tenure is sparse. For biographical information, see Ramses Nassif, *U Thant in New York, 1961–1971: A Portrait of the Third UN Secretary-General* (New York: St. Martin's Press, 1988); Bernard Firestone, *The United Nations under U Thant, 1961–1971* (Metuchen, NJ: Scarecrow Press, 2001).

37. Evan Luard, *A History of the United Nations*, vol. 2: *The Age of Decolonization, 1955–1965* (New York: St. Martin's Press, 1989), chapter 17; Namikas, *Battleground Africa*, 120.

38. There were two main movements in opposition to the central government, one in the eastern regions of the province of Leopoldville, centered around Pierre Mulele, who had been minister of education in Lumumba's government. After traveling to China, Eastern Europe, and Egypt, Mulele set out to organize the Congolese peasantry into small, independent partisan cells, promising an equitable new society free from foreign exploitation. The second opposition movement, in the eastern provinces of Kivu and Orientale, the *Conseil National de Liberation*, claimed the anti-imperialist legacy of Lumumba and was led by Christophe Gbenye, Gaston Soumialot, and Laurent Kabila. Namikas, *Battleground Africa*, 188–90; Van Reybrouck, *Congo*, 321–23.

39. On operation "Dragon Rouge" and the continued rebel activity, see Namikas, *Battleground Africa*, chapters 12 and 13.

40. The day before independence, the Congolese government signed a Treaty of Friendship with Brussels, which granted Belgium sovereignty over the bases and the right to intervene militarily should the Congolese government request assistance. The Congolese parliament never ratified the treaty. Thomas Mockaitis, *Peace Operations and Intrastate Conflict: The Sword or the Olive Branch?* (Westport, CT: Praeger, 1999), 12.

41. Jef Van Bilsen, *L'indépendance du Congo* (Tournai: Casterman, 1962); Jacobson, "ONUC's Civilian Operations," 80–81; House, *The UN in the Congo*, 44–45.

42. Jacobson, "ONUC's Civilian Operations," 81; House, *The UN in the Congo*, 46.

43. Jacobson, "ONUC's Civilian Operations," 81. For a recent discussion of the work of the committee, see Jessica L. Pearson, "Defending Empire at the United Nations: The Politics of International Colonial Oversight in the Era of Decolonisation," *The Journal of Imperial and Commonwealth History* 45, no. 3 (May 31, 2017): 525–49.
44. Through Pelt and his successor, Ansgar Rosenborg, Hammarskjöld remained in close touch with the government in Conakry and celebrated Christmas there in 1959 during his African tour. According to Urquhart, president Ahmed Sékou Touré asked Hammarskjöld's advice on monetary, economic, and administrative reforms, which left the secretary-general both gratified and embarrassed. In Urquhart's telling, Hammarskjöld refrained from giving his advice by pointing out that big decisions needed to be made by national governments and their people. UN assistance could merely be concerned with the consequences and problems of application of whatever policies were adopted by the government. Urquhart, *Hammarskjold*, 378–80.
45. Peter Heller, *The United Nations under Dag Hammarskjöld, 1953–1961* (Lanham, MD: Scarecrow Press, 2001), 56; Connie Peck, "Special Representatives of the Secretary-General," in *The UN Security Council: From the Cold War to the 21st Century*, ed. David Malone (Boulder, CO: Lynne Rienner, 2004), 325–39.
46. Memo from Owen to SG, 19 May 1960, David Owen papers (hereafter DO), B6, Folder "Dag Hammarskjöld Correspondence," RBML.
47. Urquhart, *Hammarskjold*, 388.
48. Urquhart, *Ralph Bunche*, 62; chapter 4.
49. In addition to South and East Africa, Bunche also visited the Dutch East Indies. Ultimately his own research was put on hold because of his participation in Gunnar Myrdals' mammoth Carnegie-funded study *An American Dilemma: The Negro Problem and Modern Democracy*. Urquhart, *Ralph Bunche*, chapters 5 and 6.
50. Urquhart, *Ralph Bunche*, chapters 8–10; Benjamin Rivlin, "The Legacy of Ralph Bunche," in *Ralph Bunche: The Man and His Times* (New York: Holmes & Meier, 1990), 12.
51. Urquhart, *Ralph Bunche*, chapters 11–16.
52. In fact, Hammarskjöld created two such positions, one for Bunche and one for a Soviet counterpart. Both were initially referred to as Under-Secretaries without Portfolio, which, according to Urquhart, caused much hilarity in the Secretariat. Urquhart, *Hammarskjold*, 77; Urquhart, *Ralph Bunche*, 245.
53. Urquhart, *Ralph Bunche*, chapters 20 and 21.
54. On this trip, Bunche visited Liberia, Ghana, Nigeria, Uganda, Somaliland, Ethiopia, Sudan, Egypt, Tunisia, and Morocco. Hammarskjöld, who left the U.S. in late 1959, also visited Senegal, Guinea, French Togoland, French and British Cameroons, the French and the Belgian Congo, Ruanda-Urundi, Tanganyika, and Zanzibar. Urquhart, *Ralph Bunche*, 298–300.
55. Hammarskjöld visited Liberia on his tour of Africa. Linnér was then working in Monrovia for LAMCO, a Swedish-American mining company. Linnér had a rather unusual career. In 1943, he became an associate professor of Greek language and literature. That same year, he went to Nazi-occupied Gıreece to work for the International Red Cross. After the war, Linnér became chairman of the Italian subsidiary of the Swedish home appliance manufacturer Elektrolux.
56. Interview by Jean Krasno with Sture Linnér, 8 November 1990, UN Oral History Project, http://www.unmultimedia.org/oralhistory/2011/10/linner-sture/ (last accessed 29 April 2016).
57. Bunche himself had previously sneered at Francis Sayre, the first president of the Trusteeship Council, who pretended to know French while asking Bunche, as secretary of the Council, to take notes "on French discourses." Urquhart, *Ralph Bunche*, 134, 204.

6. STATE-BUILDING MEETS PEACEKEEPING   325

58. A 1988 *New York Times* obituary suggests that Bloch left the UN in 1962 to work for a New York investment bank. In R. V. A. Janssens' *"What Future for Japan?": U.S. Wartime Planning for the Postwar Era, 1942–1945* (Amsterdam: Rodopi, 1995), Bloch is listed as "an economist who specialized in colonial government." Bloch published works on international tax problems and the training of jurists for public administration, a book cowritten with Raúl Prebisch on problems of revenue policy relating to economic development, and a UN technical assistance program in Ghana in the fiscal and financial field.
59. Henry S. Bloch and Bert F. Hoselitz, *Economics of Military Occupation: Selected Problems* (Chicago: University of Chicago Press, 1944). Hoselitz, an Austrian emigrant to the U.S. and a former student of Ludwig Mises, also taught at the University of Chicago and is usually credited as one of the founding fathers of development economics. "Bloch, Mead Will Lecture," *The Harvard Crimson* 1 July 1942, http://www.thecrimson.com/article/1942/7/1/bloch-mead-will-lecture-phenry-s/ (last accessed 3 June 2016).
60. Urquhart, *Ralph Bunche*, 304.
61. Urquhart, *Ralph Bunche*, 306.
62. Urquhart, *Ralph Bunche*, 304. Interview with F. T. Liu by Sutterlin, 23 March 1990, UN Oral History Project, http://www.unmultimedia.org/oralhistory/2011/10/liu-f-t/ (last accessed 5 May 2016).
63. Urquhart, *Ralph Bunche*, 305.
64. Namikas, *Battleground Africa*, 11, 15–16.
65. Collins, "Cold War Comes to Africa," 253.
66. Collins, "Cold War Comes to Africa," 254; also see Kalb, *The Congo Cables*; Namikas, *Battleground Africa*, 81.
67. Urquhart, *Hammarskjold*, 467.
68. As discussed in chapter 1, Bunche's earliest publication was a Marxist interpretation of race. In *A World View of Race*, he hinted at revolutionary overthrow in the colonial world, suggesting that there was "no apparent peaceful means of transition to full self-control" for the oppressed and that it was "both logical and likely" for colonial peoples to turn to "the Soviet Union's principles of equality and humanitarianism." In the early 1950s, Bunche became a target of Joseph McCarthy's witch-hunt for communists. Following allegations of subversive action among members of the UN Secretariat, President Truman had ordered for all U.S. citizens serving international organizations to be subjected to loyalty investigations. Of 1,760 UN cases, only 32—including Bunche's—involved a hearing, which received much attention in the tabloid press. A case based on witness testimony, his early writings, and acquaintance with American communists was mounted against Bunche in 1954, accusing him of being a "concealed" communist. (Bunche commented that the charge "says in effect that 'Ralph Bunche is a communist because he is one.' . . . It does seem to me that if someone were to make an allegation, unsupported by evidence, that I am 'Stalin's aunt' I should not be called upon to disprove it.") He drafted a 100-page document in his defense and declared that the Communist Party, its tactics and revolutionary philosophy had always been repugnant to him. He conceded that "from todays perspective" it might have been wiser not to have done some of the things he did in the 1930s. "But [then] the common and urgent enemy of peace and freedom was Hitler and his Nazi creed. Today it is communism alone." Eisenhower's White House had reassured Bunche throughout the proceedings of its support and the investigative board unanimously reached the conclusion that there was no doubt of his loyalty to the U.S.. The two witnesses were later prosecuted for perjury. Nevertheless, "a combination of communist obsession, racial prejudice, and hatred of the UN," Urquhart suggests, ensured that the allegation against Bunche "continued to resound in the echo chamber of the extreme right for many years." Urquhart, *Ralph*

*Bunche*, 243–45; Ralph Bunche, *A World View of Race* (Washington, DC: Association in Negro Folk Education, 1936); Martin Kilson, "Ralph Bunche's Analytical Perspective on African Development," in *Ralph Bunche: The Man and His Times*, ed. Benjamin Rivlin (New York: Holmes & Meier, 1990), 84, 98.

69. Urquhart, *Ralph Bunche*, 307.
70. Urquhart, *Ralph Bunche*, 305.
71. Dayal, *Mission for Hammarskjöld*, 1.
72. Interview with David Apter by Sutterlin, 27 February 1991, UN Oral History Project, Dag Hammarskjöld Library. For a history of U.S. modernization theory, see Nils Gilman, *Mandarins of the Future: Modernization Theory in Cold War America* (Baltimore: Johns Hopkins University Press, 2003).
73. Urquhart, *Ralph Bunche*, 306.
74. House, *The UN in the Congo*, 75.
75. Catherine Hoskyns, *The Congo since Independence, January 1960–December, 1961* (London: Oxford University Press, 1965), 87–92, 102–3, as cited in House, *The UN in the Congo*, 51; also see p. 75.
76. House, *The UN in the Congo*, 189.
77. House, *The UN in the Congo*, 189.
78. Urquhart, *Hammarskjold*, 393. Brian Urquhart, born in England in 1919, was a longtime UN civil servant and a prolific, elegant writer. After assisting the Preparatory Commission of the UN, he became one of the world organization's first civil servants. During the 1956 Suez Crisis, Urquhart—as one of the few advisors to Hammarskjöld with military experience—was involved in setting up the first UN peacekeeping force alongside Bunche. He joined Bunche in Leopoldville shortly after the arrival of first UN troops and left the country in the last week of September. He returned to the Congo in November 1961 to replace Conor Cruise O'Brien as chief of civilian operations in Katanga, a position he would hold until March 1962. Urquhart published a comprehensive biography of Dag Hammarskjöld in 1972. After his retirement, he published an autobiography (*A Life in War and Peace*) in 1987 and a biography of Ralph Bunche in 1998. His other publications include *Decolonization and World Peace* (1989) as well as several tomes on UN reform, including *A World in Need of Leadership: Tomorrow's United Nations* (1990), *Towards a More Effective United Nations* (1991), and *Renewing the United Nations System* (1994).
79. Urquhart, *Hammarskjold*, 393.
80. Urquhart, *Ralph Bunche*, 310–11.
81. Urquhart, *Hammarskjold*, 394.
82. Kanza, *Conflict in the Congo*, 203.
83. Given its Apartheid regime, South Africa, though too a UN member state, was not considered part of the African group. Urquhart, *Hammarskjold*, 394.
84. "UN to Ask Africa for Help in Congo: 9 Nations to Hear Request by Hammarskjöld to Send Negro Officers There," *New York Times* 12 July 1960. Conversation of 12 July 1960, AC, B158, Folder "AWC: Congo: African Group, Meeting Jul-Aug 60," RBML.
85. Conversation of 12 July 1960, AC.
86. Conversation of 12 July 1960, AC.
87. "UN to Ask Africa for Help in Congo." As discussed in the previous chapter, OPEX was a new UN program established as a result of Hammarskjöld's initiative for an "International Administrative Service," which was intended to offer newly independent states high-level administrative personnel to manage government affairs until trained local personnel could take over. Ultimately, OPEX offered UN member states

operational personnel—that is experts, who carried out certain jobs on the spot—rather than the more conventional advisory assistance in any number of fields.

88. Conversation of 12 July 1960, AC.
89. Hammarskjöld argued that if technical assistance in this field happened to have "useful political consequences," that should be no argument against it. "We should not be such purists as to refuse to do things in technical assistance," he doubled down, "which have a political impact in the right direction." Conversation of 12 July 1960, AC.
90. Conversation of 12 July 1960, AC.
91. Conversation of 12 July 1960, AC.
92. Apparently, the UN Secretariat had lacked the resources or, more likely, the organizational skill to assign a secretary to the meeting who was able to transcribe the conversation in both English *and* French.
93. On the Organization of African Unity's response to the Congo crisis, see Catherine Hoskyns, *The Organization of African Unity and the Congo Crisis, 1964–65: Documents* (Dar-es-Salaam: Published for the Institute of Public Administration, University College Dar-es-Salaam, by Oxford University Press, 1969).
94. Conversation of 12 July 1960, AC.
95. The cable specified that the "aid asked [was] not for the purpose of re-establishing the internal situation of the Congo, but [for] protecting [the] national territory against aggression of metropolitan Belgian troops." Kanza, *Conflict in the Congo*, 206.
96. Urquhart writes that Tshombe had come to see Bunche two days before the secession. Bunche, who tried to dissuade Tshombe from secession, thought that the latter only seemed encouraged when he learned that the American Articles on Confederation had failed woefully to work. Urquhart, *Ralph Bunche*, 309.
97. Van Reybrouck suggests that Brussels was unpleasantly surprised by Tshombe's decision, but on the ground, Katangan leaders, Belgian soldiers, and Union Minière officials quickly developed rapport. Van Reybrouck, *Congo*, 295.
98. Van Reybrouck, *Congo*, 294–96.
99. It is unclear why Hammarskjöld thought that food relief was necessary. Bloch later noted that food scarcity was above all a problem caused by disruptions to transportation.
100. Security Council resolution "The Congo Question," 14 July 1960, S/RES/143 (1960).
101. In 1960, UNICEF's headquarters were located on the twenty-fourth floor of the UN Secretariat's building. When Hammarskjöld asked Maurice Pate for his assistance in the Congo, the latter volunteered to leave the next day. According to a coworker, Pate looked twenty years younger when he left Hammarskjöld's office that day. "He was happy to get out into the field again and set up a relief organization in a hurry. That's the thing he liked best." Pate arrived on the morning of July 18 and set up shop (together with International Red Cross workers) in a florist's boutique in a Leopoldville hotel. Ritchie Calder, *Agony of the Congo* (London: Gollancz, 1961), 39; John Charnow and UNICEF, *Maurice Pate: UNICEF Executive Director, 1947–1965* (New York: United Nations Children's Fund, 1989), 14.
102. "Memorandum by the Secretary-General on the United Nations Civilian Operation in the Republic of the Congo," 11 August 1960, Second Report by the Secretary-General on the Implementation of the Security Council Resolutions S/4387 of 14 July 1960 and S/4405 of 22 July 1960, Addendum No. 5, S/4417/Add.5.
103. Urquhart, *Hammarskjold*, 402.
104. See, e.g., Edward T. Hall, Washington School of Psychiatry, to Bunche, 14 September 1960; Joseph E. Jefferson, Philadelphia, to Bunche, 21 July 1960; Ralph Bunch papers, B280, F4, Charles E. Young Library, University of California Los Angeles.

105. For Higgins' plans, see chapter 2.
106. Other Secretariat officials who attended "Congo Group" meetings included the Scottish Sir Alexander MacFarquhar, who served as liaison officer for ONUC's civilian operations in New York; Hammarskjöld's assistant and compatriot Wilhelm Wachtmeister; Indian civil servant Chakravarthi V. Narasimhan, who assisted Bunche as under-secretary for special political questions; Ghanaian economist Robert Gardiner; Dayal, who succeeded Bunche as head of ONUC in September 1960; Nigerian Francis Nwokedi; Oscar Schachter, Hammarskjöld's American legal advisor; and Australian public information officer George Ivan Smith, who would briefly represent the UN in Katanga in 1961. According to Schachter, Henry Labouisse was also a member. Labouisse, previously a U.S. civil servant, had served as director of the UN Relief and Works Agency for Palestine Refugees (UNRWA) from 1954 to 1958. There were some discussions about his representing the UN in the Congo or, alternatively, reorganizing U.S. foreign aid for the Kennedy administration. Ultimately, he settled for a job at the World Bank before becoming director of UNICEF from 1965 to 1979. For the "Congo Group" luncheons, see AC, B58, Folder "Entertainment: 'Congo Club' luncheon meeting SG's conference room, 38th floor 1961," RBML; interview with Oscar Schachter by William Powell, 14 March 1986, UN Oral History Project, http://www.unmultimedia.org/oralhistory/2011/06/schachter-oscar/, (last accessed 7 June 2016). For Labouisse's correspondence on the Congo crisis, see Henry Labouisse papers, B16, F5, Seeley G. Mudd Library, Princeton University. Dayal, *Mission for Hammarskjöld*, 308–9.
107. Interview with Oscar Schachter by William Powell, 14 March 1986.
108. Interview with Oscar Schachter by William Powell, 14 March 1986.
109. House, *The UN in the Congo*, 79.
110. Urquhart, *Hammarskjold*, 400.
111. Urquhart, *Ralph Bunche*, 316.
112. Rietkerk, "In Pursuit of Development," 182 Telegram From the Mission at the United Nations to the Department of State, 18 July 1960, in *Foreign Relations of the United States (FRU.S.) 1958–1960*, Volume 14, no. 131; Dayal (*Mission for Hammarskjöld*, 11) also notes that "Hammarskjöld carried about him an aura of supreme confidence, the immensity of his responsibilities seeming only to exhilarate him."
113. "Technical Assistance to the Congo" by H.S. Bloch, 20 July 1960, AC, B162, Folder "Reports, miscellaneous," RBML.
114. See chapter 2.
115. For OPEX, see previous chapter. "Technical Assistance to the Congo" by H. S. Bloch, 20 July 1960, AC, B162, Folder "Reports, miscellaneous," RBML.
116. Memo "First Subject," 30 July 1960, AC, B162, Folder "Reports, miscellaneous," RBML.
117. S/4417/Add.5, 11 Aug 1960.
118. "Technical Assistance to the Congo" by H. S. Bloch.
119. Memo "First Subject," 30 July 1960.
120. House, *The UN in the Congo*, 74. According to his assistant, Liu, Bunche reported on every small detail to Hammarskjöld. Interview with F. T. Liu by Sutterlin, 23 March 1990.
121. Bunche was briefly replaced by Andrew Cordier as acting special representative of the secretary-general on August 28, 1960. Rajeshwar Dayal arrived in the Congo on September 5 and took over from Cordier on September 8. When Dayal left for New York in March 1961, his deputy, the Sudanese diplomat Mekki Abbas, became acting special representative. Abbas was replaced by Sture Linnér, who assumed the new title "officer-in-charge" when Dayal resigned in late May 1961. Linnér was replaced by Robert Gardiner from February 1962 to May 1963, who was succeeded by the Haitian Max H.

Dorsinville from May 1963 to April 1964, who was replaced by Bibiano F. Osorio-Tafall (Mexico) for ONUC's last three months, until June 1964.
122. House, *The UN in the Congo*, 78.
123. Kanza, *Conflict in the Congo*, 203.
124. According to Kanza, the joint Congolese UN communiqué issued on this occasion read: "[T]ogether [the prime minister and the secretary-general] considered the possibilities and scope of economic and technical aid which the UN could usefully and effectively offer the Republic. In consideration [of] both immediate needs, and those of the more distant future, they reached certain conclusions in regard to the immediate dispatch to the Republic of Congo House of technical assistance staff (to include personnel for administration and security)." Kanza, *Conflict in the Congo*, 239; also see House, *The UN in the Congo*, 82.
125. Catherine Hoskyns suggests that Haitian Jean David joined ONUC as Linnér's assistant in response to Lumumba's complaint. Linnér thought that David "did quite a good job" initially, "especially as liaison with the Congolese authorities, where his nationality ... stood him in good stead," and he was assigned to help Kasavubu reorganize his office. When David started to act as liaison between the president and Lumumba, Linnér asked him to report directly to Cordier and later Dayal, because his new "political function obviously had nothing to do with Civilian Operations." Yet, instead of closely reporting to his superiors in Leopoldville, David acted as a "rather freewheeling agent." For "playing politics," Linnér removed him to Bukavu in the province of Kivu, but David continued to irritate his ONUC colleagues there by making rash promises to the Provincial Government of UN payments to bring the Congolese army to heel and by criticizing the UN command in Leopoldville and New York, complaining about "excessive white influence" among the permanent staff of the organization. With Dayal's support, Linnér asked Hammarskjöld to recall David to New York, ostensibly "for consultation," "so as not to provoke ill-feelings amongst certain influential Congolese [e.g., president Kasavubu], who hold him in high esteem ... and who might otherwise use the racial issue as a convenient pretext for stirring up trouble." In his memoirs, Dayal, by contrast, suggests that Cordier encouraged David's efforts to bring about reconciliation between Kasavubu and Lumumba, giving him a free hand, and that David was released from his post in the Congo at his own request. Linnér to Hammarskjöld, 20 October 1960; Linnér to Hammarskjöld, 22 October 1960, AC, B162, Folder "Linner Correspondence," RBML. Hoskyns, *The Congo since Independence*, 156; Rietkerk, "In Pursuit of Development," 197; Dayal, *Mission for Hammarskjöld*, 57–58, 87.
126. Namikas, *Battleground Africa*, 82.
127. House, *The UN in the Congo*, 82; Rietkerk, "In Pursuit of Development," 193.
128. Urquhart, *Ralph Bunche*, 328.
129. At a conference of African foreign ministers in Leopoldville at the end of August, convened by Lumumba to rally support for a military campaign against Katanga without UN support, delegates urged the prime minister to mend fences with the world organization instead and even adopted a declaration that praised the secretary-general's efforts in the Congo. O'Malley, "Ghana, India, and the Transnational Dynamics," 8. For Lumumba breaking relations with Hammarskjöld, see Namikas, *Battleground Africa*, 87–89; for Bunche's relationship with Lumumba, see Urquhart, *Ralph Bunche*, 328; Dayal, *Mission for Hammarskjöld*, 8,13.
130. S/4417/Add.5, 11 Aug 1960.
131. The document was mainly concerned with the deployment of UN troops. As for civilian operations, it merely stated: "The foregoing provisions shall likewise be applicable, as

appropriate, to the non-military aspects of the United Nations operations in the Congo." See "First Report by the Secretary General on the Implementation of the Security Council Resolution S/4387 of 14 July 1960," Addendum No. 5, S/4389/Add.5, 29 July 1960.

132. "Letter Dated 20 August 1960 from First Deputy Minister for Foreign Affairs of the Union of Soviet Socialist Republics Addressed to the Secretary-General," S/4446, 20 August 1960. A subsequent KGB memorandum to the Central Committee reported that the activity of the U.S. and its allies in the Congo was far greater than expected and that Western advisors were all over the Congo. Namikas, *Battleground Africa*, 86.

133. Korn, "Law or Order," 26; Namikas, *Battleground Africa*, 89; Memorandum of Discussion at the 456th Meeting of the National Security Council, 18 August 1960, document 180, FRU.S., Vol. 14, 423.

134. S/4446, 20 August 1960.

135. The American response is worth quoting at length: "Something has to be said about the Americans who are employed in the United Nations technical assistance plan in the Congo.... I would like to say that they are working under a plan approved by the Secretary-General and Prime Minister Lumumba.... In any case, the few American experts cannot as Mr. Kuznetsov alleged, threaten the independence of the Congo. No one has ever been enslaved by the United States. These American experts are not under orders of the United States Government." See Security Council Verbatim Records (*proces-verbaux*), meeting 889 (S/PV.889), 21 August 1960, paragraphs 57–60.

136. Rietkerk, "In Pursuit of Development," 195; Kanza, *Conflict in the Congo*, 267–71; Namikas, *Battleground Africa*, 89. S/PV.887, 12 August 1960, 70, 90–95.

137. S/PV.888, 21 August 1960, 56.

138. Jacobson, "ONUC's Civilian Operations," 87.

139. S/PV.888, 21 August 1960, 56.

140. S/PV.888, 21 August 1960, 53.

141. Urquhart, *Hammarskjold*, 434. S/PV.888, 21 August 1960, 61–63.

142. Rietkerk, "In Pursuit of Development," 195.

143. Namikas suggests that the advisory committee was established as a result of an initiative from Afro-Asian UN member states. The Soviet Union opposed the creation, favoring a *supervisory* rather than *advisory* body. In addition to the Advisory Committee, the General Assembly also established a UN Conciliation Commission in September, which was composed of government representatives from Afro-Asian states and intended to help resolve the Congo's internal political conflicts. According to Dayal, the Conciliation Commission was ultimately more interested in conducting an inquiry into ONUC's "supposed inadequacies" than in the "sweaty task of negotiation." Namikas, *Battleground Africa*, 89, 270 fn. 58; Esref Aksu, *The United Nations, Intra-State Peacekeeping and Normative Change* (Manchester: Manchester University Press, 2018), chapter 5: "The UN in the Congo Conflict: ONUC"; Dayal, *Mission for Hammarskjöld*, 171, 174.

144. The roaring support that Hammarskjöld received from Afro-Asian countries in September 1960 would soon begin to crumble as various countries expressed their misgivings and threatened to withdraw their support because of the UN stance with regard to the constitutional crisis, the Belgian presence in Katanga, and the organization's failure to prevent Lumumba's murder. For a discussion of the debates at the General Assembly, and particularly the role of Afro-Asian countries in setting the UN agenda, see O'Malley, "Ghana, India, and the Transnational Dynamics"; O'Malley, *Diplomacy of Decolonisation*, chapter 2; and Dayal, *Mission for Hammarskjöld*. For a discussion of Khrushchev's vendetta against Hammarskjöld, see Iandolo, "Beyond the

Shoe"; Eva-Maria Muschik, "Article Review: 'Beyond the Shoe: Rethinking Khrushchev at the Fifteenth Session of the United Nations General Assembly,'" *H-Diplo* 718 (October 6, 2017), http://tiny.cc/AR718; Namikas, *Battleground Africa*, 101–3, 107–9.

145. "A Tentative Approach to Civilian Affairs—Draft" 23 July 1960, S-0845-0006-06-00001, UNARMS; Sinclair, *To Reform the World*, chapter 4.
146. "A Spectator in the Congo: Memories from the Diary of an Onlooker at the Violent Birth of the Democratic Republic of the Congo" by Winifred Tickner (1971), 127, 132, UNCRP, MS.Eng.c.4704, Bodleian.
147. Calder, *Agony of the Congo*, 36, 39.
148. Calder, *Agony of the Congo*, 39–40.
149. An early study deemed the UN's efforts in civil aviation particularly noteworthy: within two years of independence, air traffic almost doubled—though this was partly because ground transportation became more and more dangerous. ICAO not only managed an exponentially increased level of air traffic, but also trained sufficient Congolese to phase out all of its operational assistance by 1970. House, *The UN in the Congo*, 234–35, 294–323, 413.
150. Progress Report No. 2 on United Nations Civilian Operations in the Congo, 6 September 1960, p. 13–14, AC, B158, Folder "Report 2–9 1960–1961," RBML.
151. See previous chapter on the WHO's initial reluctance to provide operational assistance.
152. House, *The UN in the Congo*, 215.
153. *Yearbook of the United Nations 1960* (New York: United Nations, 1961), 117.
154. Calder, *Agony of the Congo*, 105–7.
155. *Yearbook of the United Nations 1960*, 117–18.
156. *Yearbook of the United Nations 1960*, 117–19.
157. House, *The UN in the Congo*, 21. By the end of 1960, a UN report counted more than 60,000 "idle" Congolese in Leopoldville alone. Leaving out structural unemployment, the report noted, the figure amounted to 24,500. According to the report, more Congolese were employed as houseboys (1,500) than in building and public works (900). Progress Report No. 9 on United Nations Civilian Operations in the Congo during February 1961, p. 10a, AC, B158, Folder "Report 2–9 1960–1961," RBML.
158. Together with UNESCO, the ILO was also working on turning the military base of Kamina into a technical and clerical training center. Progress Report No. 5 on United Nations Civilian Operations in the Congo, 5 November 1960, AC, B158, Folder "Report 2–9 1960–1961," RBML. Also see House, *The UN in the Congo*, 207.
159. House, *The UN in the Congo*, 213.
160. The Belgians had employed the Balubas, who originally hailed from Kasai, in Katanga's mines. Violence against these comparatively well-off migrants had driven close to 100,000 back into their prior homelands as early as October 1959. The interethnic violence further escalated after the withdrawal of Belgian authority following independence and culminated in a second wave of refugees, who sought refuge in South Kasai in the summer of 1960. On August 8, Albert Kalonji—a former supporter of Lumumba, who had lost out on a ministerial post in the new government—declared the secession of South Kasai and the creation of a Baluba homeland. Lumumba, with logistical support from the Soviet Union, sent in the ANC to quash the secession. When the poorly provisioned and disciplined ANC soldiers lashed out against civilians, Hammarskjöld framed their actions as of "genocidal character" and authorized UN troops to intervene in the civil war, despite being accused of taking sides in an internal conflict. For the UN-coordinated relief effort for refugees in Kasai, see UNCRP, Antony Gilpin papers (MS.Eng.c 4674, 4675), Bodleian; John King Gordon papers (MG 20, C241),

Vol. 30, File 11, LAC. For Biafra, see Marie-Luce Desgrandchamps, "Dealing with 'Genocide': Humanitarian and International Organizations during the Nigeria-Biafra War (1967–1970)," *Journal of Genocide Research* 16, no. 2–3 (2014): 281–97; Lasse Heerten, *The Biafran War and Postcolonial Humanitarianism: Spectacles of Suffering* (Cambridge: Cambridge University Press, 2017); Marie-Luce Desgrandchamps, *L'humanitaire en Guerre Civile. La Crise du Biafra (1967–1970)* (Rennes: PUR, 2018); Marie-Luce Desgrandchamps, "Du Congo au Biafra. Guerres Civiles et Actions Humanitaires dans les Relations internationales Postcoloniales," *Relations Internationales* 176, no. 4 (2018): 55–67.

161. House, *The UN in the Congo*, 196. For biographical information on Gardiner, see Samuel Misteli, "Gardiner, Robert Kweku," in *IO BIO, Biographical Dictionary of Secretaries- General of International Organizations*, ed. Bob Reinalda, Kent J. Kille, and Jaci Eisenberg, www.ru.nl/fm/iobio (last accessed 29 October 2018).
162. House, *The UN in the Congo*, 196–97.
163. House, *The UN in the Congo*, 218. Also see Garry Gullerton, *UNESCO in the Congo* (Paris: UNESCO, 1964).
164. House, *The UN in the Congo*, 189, 219; The UNESCO teachers recruited from Haiti are nowadays thought to have played a central role in the AIDS pandemic by exporting HIV to the Americas. Jacques Pepin, *The Origins of AIDS* (Cambridge: Cambridge University Press, 2011); David Quammen, *Spillover: Animal Infections and the Next Human Pandemic* (New York: W. W. Norton & Co., 2012). On the special role played by Haitians in the Congo, see Regine Jackson, "The Failure of Categories: Haitians in the United Nations Organization in the Congo, 1960–64," *Journal of Haitian Studies* 20, no. 1 (2014): 34–64; Chantalle F. Verna, "Haiti, the United Nations, and Decolonization in the Congo," in *The United Nations and Decolonization*, ed. Nicole Eggers, Jessica L. Pearson, and Aurora Almada e Santos (New York: Routledge, 2020).
165. House, *The UN in the Congo*, 219, 224.
166. Gilpin also noted that the application process could have amusing aspects: "The application form has one section, which requires a responsible person to state what job the applicant will occupy on completion of the fellowship. A persistent young man from the *Surete* [the civil police force] asked my advice on who should sign this for him, so I suggested his 'chef.' He looked a bit embarrassed, and then I noticed that he himself had written 'Administrateur en Chef de la Surete' as the job which he would take on his return." See "Letters from the Congo," UNCRP, Ms.Eng.c.4674 (282), Bodleian.
167. According to Dayal, training Congolese for "positions of responsibility in the country" was one of the most successful, though not eye-catching of ONUC's achievements. House, *The UN in the Congo*, 215, 228–30; Dayal, *Mission for Hammarskjöld*, 139.
168. Interestingly, George Martelli, who used the term "world government" in his 1966 book to characterize ONUC, said nothing about the UN's civilian operations. George Martelli, *Experiment in World Government: An Account of the United Nations Operation in the Congo, 1960–1964* (London: Johnson Publications, 1966).
169. House, *The UN in the Congo*, 327–28; also see Kanza, *Conflict in the Congo*, 285.
170. In 1965, fifty-one UN experts were attached to the ministry and in 1966, forty-two. House, *The UN in the Congo*, 330, 338.
171. The portfolio's market value, estimated at over $700 million in 1958, had been dropping dramatically since the independence negotiations. At the so-called roundtable discussions prior to independence, Congolese representatives had favored turning some of the shares into capital for economic development projects (instead of leaving the portfolio intact and using only its income). Belgian officials, in turn, resisted a

## 6. STATE-BUILDING MEETS PEACEKEEPING 333

break-up of the portfolio and its straightforward transfer to the future sovereign state. Instead, they proposed forming a joint Belgian–Congolese development company to manage the portfolio and handle public investments together. To make the arrangement more attractive, Brussels promised to match the portfolio's worth in Belgian contributions to the development company's assets. "Belgian Congo" by Ona B. Forrest, June 1960 (draft), AC; House, *The UN in the Congo*, 331.

172. House, *The UN in the Congo*, 339.
173. House, *The UN in the Congo*, 330; David Gibbs, "The United Nations, International Peacekeeping and the Question of 'Impartiality': Revisiting the Congo Operation of 1960," *The Journal of Modern African Studies* 38, no. 3 (2000): 359–82.
174. The distribution of import licenses was perceived as "a system of giving favors to relatives of powerful people in the government" and, according to House, caused considerable resentment among Congolese against ONUC, even though UN personnel did not determine who received import licenses. House, *The UN in the Congo*, 334, 341.
175. House, *The UN in the Congo*, 361.
176. House, *The UN in the Congo*, 279.
177. For Sen's skepticism with regard to operational assistance, see previous chapter; for his uneasiness to work in an unclear political situation, see Rietkerk, "In Pursuit of Development," 190.
178. House, *The UN in the Congo*, 244.
179. House, *The UN in the Congo*, 248–50.
180. House, *The UN in the Congo*, 265–67.
181. House, *The UN in the Congo*, 278–79.
182. When Mobutu nationalized the UMHK in 1966, no UN personnel took part in the negotiations. House, *The UN in the Congo*, 209–11.
183. Progress Report No. 5 on United Nations Civilian Operations in the Congo, 5 November 1960, p. 28, AC, B158, Folder "Report 2–9 1960–1961," RBML.
184. House, *The UN in the Congo*, 149; von Horn, *Soldiering for Peace*, 150–59. According to General von Horn's account, those who did show up often left with supplies.
185. General Indar Jit Rikhye, Hammarskjöld's military advisor, who was temporarily in charge of ONUC in November 1960, for example, believed that it was essential to maintain frequent contact with Mobutu to influence him: "He basically remains a good man . . . and we must support him." The civilian operations report of November noted that although progress had been disappointing in the field of military instruction, "the UN [had] intensified its efforts to advise on the necessary reorganization and training [of the Congolese security forces] and to encourage the professional spirit prerequisite to any real programme of instruction." Korn, "Law or Order," 59; Namikas, *Battleground Africa*, 160, 176–77. Progress Report No. 5 on United Nations Civilian Operations in the Congo, 5 November 1960, p. 28, AC, B158, Folder "Report 2–9 1960–1961," RBML.
186. House, *The UN in the Congo*, 204.
187. Progress Report No. 4 on United Nations Civilian Operations in the Congo, 15 October 1960, p. 19, AC, B158, Folder "Report 2–9 1960–1961," RBML.
188. There was no specialized agency dedicated to law. Instead, the UN consultant sought support from the International Commission of Jurists, an NGO founded in 1952, according to its website, to protect the rule of law. Progress Report No. 8 on United Nations Civilian Operations in the Congo during January 1961, p. 17, AC, B158, Folder "Report 2–9 1960–1961," RBML.
189. House, *The UN in the Congo*, 205.

190. House, *The UN in the Congo*, 206.
191. Namikas writes that earlier constitution-writing efforts were a joint U.S./UN exercise and that in 1964, Kasavubu appointed a commission to draft a new constitution that allowed him to dismiss Adoula's government and ask Tshombe to return and lead the country. As discussed in chapter 2, assistance in formulating the constitution had been the primary goal of the UN's very first state-building exercise in Libya. In the 1990s, constitution writing billed as technical or development assistance became more common. House, *The UN in the Congo*, 205; Sara Kendall, "'Constitutional Technicity': Displacing Politics through Expert Knowledge," *Law, Culture and the Humanities* 11, no. 3 (2015): 363–77. Also see the PhD project in political sociology "The Good Parliament" by Quentin Deforge at the Paris-Dauphine University. Namikas, *Battleground Africa*, 166, 191.
192. In December 1962, the countries most strongly represented among experts in the Congo (excluding teachers, who were recruited, above all, from Haiti) were the following: 112 from France, 60 from Haiti, 54 from Switzerland, 36 from Spain, 35 from Italy, 25 from Greece, and 22 each from the UK, the United Arab Republic, and Tunisia. Only 15 UN experts came from Belgium. Belgium's bilateral program, by contrast, counted 1,861 employees, of whom 1,212 were engaged in education. House, *The UN in the Congo*, 189–90, 193. On the special role of Haitian experts, see Jackson, "The Failure of Categories"; Verna, "Haiti, the United Nations, and Decolonization in the Congo."
193. Dayal, *Mission for Hammarskjöld*, 24.
194. "A Spectator in the Congo" by W. Tickner, p. 134, UNCRP.
195. Rietkerk notes that Linnér initially ordered ten copies of a tourist guidebook on the Congo to prepare his staff. By the end of September 1960, he had developed a twenty-page informational leaflet on the Civilian Operations for distribution to incoming personnel. House, *The UN in the Congo*, 187; Rietkerk, "In Pursuit of Development," 191–92.
196. After a postwar stint with the private British research group Political and Economic Planning (PEP), Gilpin was recruited by David Owen, a fellow PEP alumnus and one of the first UN Secretariat officials, to work for the establishment of the International Trade Organization (ITO) in 1947–1948. When the ITO failed to materialize, Gilpin joined the Secretariat of the UN Economic Commission for Asia and the Far East (ECAFE) in Shanghai, before joining the Department of Economic Affairs at the UN's New York headquarters in 1952. In 1957, he became deputy director of the Technical Assistance Bureau of the UN Secretariat. In the mid-1980s, Gilpin collected the letters he had written from the Congo, adding reflections and memories in the introductory chapters as well as footnotes, and donated the manuscript, alongside further recollections of his career, to Oxford University's UN Career Records Project. See Gilpin, "Letters from the Congo," UNCRP, Ms.Eng.c.4674 and 4675, Bodleian.
197. Gilpin, "Letters from the Congo," UNCRP, Ms.Eng.c.4674, (256), Bodleian. With regard to his position in the Congo, Gilpin wrote: "I think my title is 'Civilian Affairs Officer,' but I have seen so many different titles attached to my name that I am not quite sure. The one which amused me the most was 'M. Gilphyn [sic], Anthony [sic], Administrator of Schools and Hospitals' ... Clement, our Congolese office boy, addresses me as 'Chef' ... which is rather gratifying!" UNCRP, Ms.Eng.c.4674 (295), Bodleian.
198. Gilpin, "Letters from the Congo," UNCRP, Ms.Eng.c.4674 (256) [back], Bodleian. For a description of Veillet-Lavallée, see Gilpin, "Letters from the Congo," UNCRP, Ms.Eng.c.4674 (247), Bodleian.

6. STATE-BUILDING MEETS PEACEKEEPING    335

199. Gilpin, "Letters from the Congo," UNCRP, Ms.Eng.c4674 (262) [back], Bodleian.
200. Gilpin, "Letters from the Congo," UNCRP, Ms.Eng.c4674 (280), Bodleian.
201. In addition to Gilpin, the delegation consisted of Kasai's provincial minister of economic affairs, M. Maole; the Belgian manager of the local branch of the Central Bank, M. Marchand; and an Israeli businessman from Luluabourg, M. Simon Israel. In Elisabethville (today's Lubumbashi), the group expected to negotiate with three Katanga ministers and two "technicians." Instead, they found themselves confronted with eighteen Belgian businessmen and four Katangese, none apparently of ministerial rank, as counterpart negotiators. Gilpin, "Letters from the Congo," UNCRP, Ms.Eng.c.4674 (265) [back], Bodleian.
202. Gilpin, "Letters from the Congo," UNCRP, Ms.Eng.c4674 (265) [back], Bodleian. The Kasai delegation enjoyed "quite a round of entertaining." Gilpin was struck by the "extraordinarily normal Western atmosphere" in Elisabethville, Katanga's capital. "The shops are full of everything, the food is plentiful," he wrote his wife, "and yet you have to remember that . . . to the West (in South Kasai . . .), refugee children are dying every day of *starvation*."
203. Gilpin, "Letters from the Congo," UNCRP, Ms.Eng.c.4674 (267, 279), Bodleian.
204. Progress Report No. 5 on United Nations Civilian Operations in the Congo, 5 November 1960, p. 1, AC, B158, Folder "Report 2-9 1960-1961," RBML.
205. Whereas Mobutu ultimately allowed Kasavubu to stay on as president, Lumumba was placed under house arrest in his capital city residence.
206. Korn rightly points out: "With his *Collège des Commissaires*, Mobutu established precisely what the UN claimed to be: an apolitical group of technical experts charged with benevolently running the country until order could be restored. . . . The UN had defined a field of legitimate (a)politics, and Mobutu operated comfortably within that definition." Korn, "Law or Order," 60–61.
207. Korn, "Law or Order," 53–54. Dayal, Leopoldville to Secgen, New York, Outgoing Code, no. B-1204," 8 October 1960, in incoming and outgoing 1960 file, S-0736-0005-05, UNARMS.
208. Dayal, *Mission for Hammarskjöld*, 112; also see Korn, "Law or Order," 55. "Meeting No.9, United Nations Advisory Committee on the Congo, Meeting at the United Nations Headquarters" 5 November 1960 at 10am, S-0849-0001-02, UNARMS.
209. My italics. Korn, "Law or Order," 55.
210. Progress Report No. 5 on United Nations Civilian Operations in the Congo, 5 November 1960, p. 1, AC, B158, Folder "Report 2-9 1960-1961," RBML.
211. Emphasis in original. Cable No. 2564 from Hammarskjöld, 10 October 1960, quoted in "Situation Report on the Civilian Operation in the Congo," MacFarquhar to Secretary-General, 8 November 1961, AC, Folder "Report 2-9 1960-1961," RBML.
212. Interestingly, ONUC's somewhat arbitrary approach in choosing Congolese counterparts was not only challenged on the grounds that it empowered one faction over another. Rather, during a meeting with the UN Advisory Committee on the Congo (UNACC), composed of representatives of troop-contributing UN member states, the Pakistani delegate Mr. Hasan charged that "by dealing with almost everyone," the UN's deliberate policy of not building up certain "outstanding personalities" added to the confused state of Congolese politics." Korn, "Law or Order," 55. Meeting No.9, United Nations Advisory Committee on the Congo, Meeting at the United Nations Headquarters" 5 November 1960 at 10am, S-0849-0001-02, UNARMS.
213. "Situation Report on the Civilian Operation in the Congo," MacFarquhar to Secretary-General, 8 November 1961, AC, B158, Folder "Report 2—9 1960-1961," RBML.

336   6. STATE-BUILDING MEETS PEACEKEEPING

214. Situation Report on the Civilian Operation in the Congo," MacFarquhar to Secretary-General, 8 November 1961, AC, B158, Folder "Report 2—9 1960–1961," RBML.
215. The reference to the judiciary likely referred to a disagreement between ONUC and Mobutu's commissioner for justice with regard to the reappointment of Belgian judges. Journalist Ritchie Calder, who toured the Congo in 1960, noted that the commissioner, who had yet to graduate, drew on the advice of his Belgian professors, who promoted the return of the 122 Belgian magistrates. Calder suggested that ONUC opposed their return for fear of civil disturbances. The progress reports on civilian operations are notably quiet on the topic, merely noting in January 1961 that some twenty Belgian magistrates had returned at the request of the commissioner, "for whom the UN bore no responsibility." Calder, *Agony of the Congo*, 95. Progress Report No. 8 on United Nations Civilian Operations in the Congo during January 1961, AC, B158, Folder "Report 2–9 1960–1961," RBML.
216. "Situation Report on the Civilian Operation in the Congo," MacFarquhar to Secretary-General, 8 November 1961, AC, B158, Folder "Report 2–9 1960–1961," RBML.
217. Namikas, *Battleground Africa*, 116.
218. Rietkerk, "In Pursuit of Development," 209.
219. Officially, Abbas merely served the interim acting special representative for Dayal until Linnér took his place as officer-in-charge, on 25 May 1961 (and was again replaced with Gardiner by U Thant after Hammarskjöld's death in February 1962). Khiari took over Linnér's former job as chief of civilian operations in May 1961. Gilpin described Khiari, in contrast to Linnér, as "brilliant" and "highly political." *Yearbook of the United Nations 1961* (New York: United Nations, 1962), 731; Gilpin, "Letters from the Congo," UNCRP, MS.Eng.c.4675 (250), Bodleian.
220. Rietkerk, "In Pursuit of Development," 227–33; for Belgian advisors as a bone of contention between UN officials and Congolese politicians, see 198–201.
221. Memo from Gardiner to Secretary-General, 21 April 1961, AC, B158, Folder "Civilian Operations—Miscellaneous," RBML; also see correspondence between Linnér and MacFarquhar in the same folder.
222. House, *The UN in the Congo*, 144.
223. "Situation Report on the Civilian Operation in the Congo," MacFarquhar to Secretary-General, 8 November 1961, AC, B158, Folder "Report 2—9 1960–1961," RBML.
224. House, *The UN in the Congo*, 189.
225. House, *The UN in the Congo*, 159.
226. Ralph Bunche, "The United Nations Operation in the Congo," speech given at Columbia University 16 March 1964, in *The Quest for Peace: The Dag Hammarskjöld Memorial Lectures*, ed. Andrew Cordier and Wilder Foote (New York: Columbia University Press, 1965), 127; Arthur Schlesinger, *A Thousand Days: John F. Kennedy in the White House* (Boston: Houghton Mifflin, 1965), 484; House, *The UN in the Congo*, 165; Mountz, "Americanizing Africanization," 124.
227. Mountz, "Americanizing Africanization," 153.
228. House, *The UN in the Congo*, 174.
229. Bunche was concerned that troop withdrawal would undo the UN's achievements, posing the more general question: "how can a successfully functioning United Nations peace force ever be withdrawn without disastrous consequences?" Bunche, "The United Nations Operation in the Congo," 136.
230. House, *The UN in the Congo*, 371.
231. House, *The UN in the Congo*, 198. There were some exceptions to this arrangement, as salaries for some technicians in the fields of transportation and communications were covered by military expenditures.

6. STATE-BUILDING MEETS PEACEKEEPING   337

232. House, *The UN in the Congo*, 201–2. As the largest contributor to UN technical assistance programs more generally, the U.S. paid for about 50 percent of conventional funding.
233. House, *The UN in the Congo*, 380, 372. The U.S. thus ensured that no communist technicians would be sponsored by their contributions.
234. House, *The UN in the Congo*, 369, 428; Kanza, *Conflict in the Congo*, 304–5. Interpreting Mobutu's first coup, Kanza wrote: "In brief, the Congo had become an international, and more specifically an American colony. Having agreed to pay a third of the cost of the UN operation in the Congo, to say nothing of all the 'invisible' expenditure needed to keep the country within the Western sphere of influence, the Americans were in command. The Congo became rather like a business company in which the largest shareholder could determine how the governing board was to act. By paying most of the expenses involved in preserving order and peace in the Congo, the U.S.A thenceforth took it upon itself to behave as the major shareholder. Resolutions were voted in New York —whether in the Security Council or the General Assembly—only if approved by Washington, in consultation with its Western allies; and only the most meager concessions were made to the Afro-Asian nations to preserve appearances— for they were, after all, the people who had sent their troops to the Congo under the UN flag."
235. Whether UN officials were also troubled to support Mobutu's *regime d'execption* that followed his second coup on November 25, 1965 remains unclear. American officials were rather happy about the prospect that the dictator would ensure both "political stability" in the Congo and friendly relations with the U.S.. House, *The UN in the Congo*, 371–73; Mountz, "Americanizing Africanization," 197.
236. House, *The UN in the Congo*, 368–69; Stokke, *The UN and Development*, 198.
237. House, *The UN in the Congo*, 375–77.
238. House, *The UN in the Congo*, 397.
239. House, *The UN in the Congo*, 401. After August 1965, the Congo assumed direct responsibility for hiring expatriate teachers.
240. House, *The UN in the Congo*, 404.
241. For Hammarskjöld's position on Katanga's secession, see, e.g., Gibbs, "The United Nations, International Peacekeeping and the Question of 'Impartiality'; for the secretary-general's approach to the violence in South Kasai and a discussion of Cordier's decision to close the airport, see Korn, "Law or Order"; for the UN refusal to protect Lumumba, see Witte, *The Assassination of Lumumba*.
242. Korn, "Law or Order," 8.
243. Korn, "Law or Order," 8 draws a similar conclusion.
244. Urquhart, *A Life in Peace and War*, 195–96.
245. Gilpin, "Letters from the Congo," UNCRP, MS. 4674 (280) [back], Bodleian.
246. Review of King Gordon, *The United Nations in the Congo* by Smith Simpson, *The American Academy of Political and Social Science* 951 (Jan. 1964): 223, in John King Gordon papers (MG 20, C241), Vol. 30, File 11, LAC; speech "The United Nations: Game Over" by Robert Kaplan, First National Conference on Profit Sharing, Toronto, November 24, 1974, p. 6, KG, 23—18, LAC.
247. Kaplan, "The United Nations: Game Over." Kaplan continued, "What may be happening is that the United Nations may be creating enough of such mini-states to assure life to the organization, but the dynamics of the relationship are so frail in real world terms that if the real world abandons the UN, its mini-world must go down with it. I feel that if the UN serves only its mini-world, the real world should and will abandon it."
248. Urquhart, *A Life in Peace and War*, 164.

249. "Note Regarding the Insuperable Difficulty from the Nature of the Congolese Civil Service," KG, 30—4, LAC.
250. "The Congo" Outline for Alison, 31 January 1965, p. 6, KG, 33–4, LAC.
251. Martelli, *Experiment in World Government*, 12.
252. A parallel, if little-studied effort was the UN Temporary Executive Authority and the UN Security Force in West New Guinea, established in October 1962 to administer the transfer of the Dutch colony to Indonesia on 1 May 1963 (see epilogue.) In 1989, the UN Transition Assistance Group oversaw the withdrawal of South Africa from Namibia and the election of a new government.
253. Gilpin, "Letters from the Congo," UNCRP, Gilpin, MS. 4674 (280) [back], Bodleian.
254. For a brief discussion of the literature on international territorial administration, see epilogue.
255. Anne Orford, "Book Review Article: 'International Territorial Administration and the Management of Decolonization,'" *International and Comparative Law Quarterly* 59 (2010): 227–50.
256. "MONUSCO at a Glance, January 2015," http://monusco.unmissions.org/sites/default/files/global_factsheet._eng.pdf (last accessed 7 June 2016).
257. http://monusco.unmissions.org/en/un-drc (last accessed 7 June 2016).
258. Séverine Autesserre, *The Trouble with the Congo: Local Violence and the Failure of International Peacebuilding* (Cambridge: Cambridge University Press, 2010), 37.

# EPILOGUE

1. In *From Empires to NGOs in the West African Sahel: The Road to Nongovernmentality* (New York: Cambridge University Press, 2015), Gregory Mann asks a similar question: how and why did nongovernmental organizations begin to assume functions of sovereignty at a time when this was so highly valued?
2. Prasenjit Duara, "The Cold War and the Imperialism of Nation-States," in *The Oxford Handbook of the Cold War*, ed. Richard Immerman and Petra Goedde (Oxford: Oxford University Press, 2013); Jeffrey J. Byrne, "Africa's Cold War," in *The Cold War in the Third World*, ed. Robert J. McMahon (New York: Oxford University Press, 2013), 101–23.
3. Similar arrangements of voluntary payment were arranged for subsequent peacekeeping missions in Yemen and Cyprus. Evan Luard, *A History of the United Nations*, vol. 2: *The Age of Decolonization, 1955–1965* (New York: St. Martin's Press, 1989), 462.
4. Luard, *Age of Decolonization*, 327–47; John Saltford, "United Nations Involvement with the Act of Self-Determination in West Irian (Indonesian West New Guinea) 1968 to 1969," *Indonesia* 69 (2000): 71–92; John Saltford, *The United Nations and the Indonesian Takeover of West Papua, 1962–1969: The Anatomy of a Betrayal* (London: Routledge, 2003); also see Emma Kluge, "Decolonisation in the Pacific: West Papua, the United Nations and the Non-Aligned Movement," paper presented at the conference "Challenging the Liberal World Order: The History of the Global South, Decolonization and the United Nations, 1955–2000," Leiden University, 2018; Emma Kluge, "West Papua and the International History of Decolonization, 1961-69," *The International History Review* 42, no. 6 (2019), https://doi.org/10.1080/07075332.2019.1694052; Margot Tudor, "Gatekeepers to Decolonisation: Recentring the UN Peacekeepers on the Frontline of West Papua's Re-Colonisation, 1962-1963," *Journal of Contemporary History*, 2021, 1–24, https://doi.org/10.1177/0022009421997894. Greg Poulgrain suggests that Kennedy's and Hammarskjöld's plans for a more expansive role of the UN in West New Guinea played a role in their assassination: see Poulgrain, *The Incubus of Intervention: Conflicting*

*Indonesia Strategies of John F. Kennedy and Allen Dulles* (Petaling Jaya [Malaysia]: Strategic Information and Research Development Centre, 2015), chapter 2; republished in the U.S. as *JFK vs. Allen Dulles: Battleground Indonesia* (New York: W. W. Norton & Co., 2019).
5. President of the Security Council, "Note by the President of the Security Council," UN SCOR, 47th Sess., UN Doc S/23500, 31 January 1992, p. 3, cited in Anne Orford, *International Authority and the Responsibility to Protect* (Cambridge: Cambridge University Press, 2011), 91.
6. Orford, *International Authority*, 91–92. Today, the UN deploys over 100,000 peacekeepers. See "United Nations Peacekeeping," https://peacekeeping.un.org/en (last accessed 25 June 2019).
7. For a discussion of the UN Transitional Authority in Cambodia (UNTAC), the UN Transitional Administration for Eastern Slavonia (UNTAES), the UN Interim Administration in Kosovo (UNMIK), and the UN Transitional Administration in East Timor, see chapter 8 of Carsten Stahn, *The Law and Practice of International Territorial Administration: From Versailles to Iraq* (Cambridge: Cambridge University Press, 2008). Stahn suggests that the millennium brought a return to an "assistance-oriented approach" that in some cases, however, was merely a matter of labels, "which masked the actual degree of international interference." (See chapter 9.)
8. Stahn, *Law and Practice*, 268; Orford, *International Authority* (209) goes further in describing these administrations as "revolutionary regimes, designed to eliminate any existing laws, property relations and political cultures deemed illegitimate."
9. Stahn, *Law and Practice*, 286.
10. Anne Orford, "Book Review Article: 'International Territorial Administration and the Management of Decolonization,'" *International and Comparative Law Quarterly* 59 (2010): 246.
11. Orford, *International Authority*, 199.
12. Orford, "International Territorial Administration," 243, 249.
13. For an early discussion of the problems of the term, see Henry Richardson, "'Failed States,' Self-Determination, and Preventive Diplomacy: Colonialist Nostalgia and Democratic Expectations," *Temple International and Comparative Law Journal* 10, no. 1 (1996): 1–78; also see Jonathan Hill, "Beyond the Other? A Postcolonial Critique of the Failed State Thesis," *African Identities* 3, no. 2 (2005): 139–54.

# BIBLIOGRAPHY

## PRIMARY SOURCES

### ARCHIVAL MATERIAL

*Bodleian Library, Oxford University*

United Nations Career Records Project (UNCRP).

*Charles E. Young Library, University of California Los Angeles (UCLA)*

Ralph Bunche papers (RB).

*George Meany Memorial Archives, University of Maryland Libraries, College Park*

Jay Lovestone papers.

*Hoover Institution Archives, Stanford University (HIA)*

Victor Hoo papers (VH).

*International Labour Organization Archives, Geneva, Switzerland*

Miscellaneous papers relating to David Blelloch.

*Library and Archives Canada, Ottawa, Canada (LAC)*

John King Gordon fonds.
Hugh Keenleyside fonds.

*National Archives at College Park (NAII)*

Record Group 59: General Records of the Department of State.
Record Group 84: Records of the Foreign Service Posts of the Department of State.

## Rare Book and Manuscript Library, Columbia University, New York City (RBML)

Andrew Cordier papers (AC).
Carter Goodrich papers (CG).
David Owen papers (DO).
Finkelstein, Lawrence. "Castles in Spain; United States Trusteeship Plans in World War II." Doctoral dissertation, Columbia University, 1970.
———. "The Trusteeship System: An Analysis. A Study and Interpretation of the Steps Leading to the Conclusion of the First Nine Trusteeship." Masters essay, Columbia University, Public Law and Government, 1948.

## Seeley G. Mudd Manuscript Library, Princeton University

Henry Labouisse papers.

## United Nations Archives and Records Management Section, New York City (UNARMS)

AG-001, Fonds Secretary-General Dag Hammarskjold (1953–1961).
  S-0847 Meeting Minutes Administrative Records.
AG-005, Fonds Secretary-General U Thant (1961–1971).
  S-0845 United Nations Operation in the Congo (ONUC)—Files and Correspondence.
AG-008, Fonds United Nations Operation in the Congo (ONUC) (1960–1964).
  S-0736 Office of the Special Representative of the Secretary-General—Cables.
  S-0849 United Nations Operation in the Congo (ONUC)—Advisory Committee Verbatim Minutes.
AG-011, Fonds United Nations Executive Office of the Secretary-General (EOSG) (1946-present).
  S-0369 Martin W. Hill—numbered subject files.
AG-021, Fonds United Nations Department of Political Affairs (1992-present); AG-021–003, Sub-fonds Department of Trusteeship and Information from Non-Self-Governing Territories (1946–1954).
  S-0504 Subject Files—Office of the Assistant Secretary-General—Dr. Victor Hoo.
  S-0723 Subject Files—United Nations Advisory Council in Somaliland (UNACS).
  S-1555 Subject Files—Office of the Assistant Secretary-General—Office of the Principal/Director—Dr. Ralph J. Bunche.
  S-1559 Subject Files—Office of the Director—H.A. Wieschoff—United Nations Advisory Council for Somaliland (UNACS).
  S-1563 General Problems Section (formerly) and Visits Section—Reports—Visiting Missions to Trust Territories.
AG-025–003 Registry Section.
  S-0175 Technical Assistance.
AG-051 United Nations Commissioner in Libya (1949–1952).
  S-0655 Subject Files—Council and Commissioner in Libya.
  S-0660 Subject Files—Council and Commissioner in Libya.

## United Nations Archives at Geneva, Switzerland (UNOG)

Record Group: GX (Economics) 26 (Economic Development—United Nations Development Program—1948–87) 14, Records of the UN Technical Assistance Board.

## OTHER PRIMARY SOURCES

Atlantic Charter. http://avalon.law.yale.edu/wwii/atlantic.asp. Last accessed 2 April 2016.
League of Nations Covenant. https://avalon.law.yale.edu/20th_century/leagcov.asp. Last accessed 30 August 2019.
Harry Truman Inaugural Address, 20 January 1949 ("Point IV Speech"). https://www.bartleby.com/124/pres53.html. Last accessed 30 August 2019.
UN Charter. https://www.un.org/en/sections/un-charter/chapter-xi/index.html. Last accessed 24 June 2019.

## PUBLISHED UN DOCUMENTS

### *UN Official Records: Economic and Social Council*

Summary Records:
E/SR.942–945, July–August, 1956, 22nd Session.
E/SR.980–983, July 1957, 24th Session.
Documents submitted to the Economic and Social Council:
  E/3017, 10 June 1957, "An International Administrative Service: Memorandum by the Secretary-General."
  E/3121, 19 May 1958, "Proposal for the Establishment of an International Administrative Service: Report by the Secretary-General."
Resolutions:
  E/RES/51(IV), 26 March 1947, "Expert Assistance to Member Governments."
Summary Records of ECOSOC's Technical Assistance Committee:
  E/TAC/SR.146–147, July 1957
  E/TAC/SR.161–164, July 1958
  E/TAC/SR.190–196, July 1959
  E/TAC/SR.221–225, July 1960

### *UN Official Records: General Assembly*

Documents submitted to the General Assembly:
  A/4212, 14 September 1959, "Technical Assistance in Public Administration: Provision of Operational, Executive and Administrative Personnel." Report by Secretary-General.
Documents submitted to the Second Committee:
  A/C.2/L.376, 30 October 1958, "Programmes of Technical Assistance: Establishment of an International Administrative Service." Statement by the Secretary-General at the 539th meeting.
Resolutions:
  A/Res/58 (I), 14 December 1946, "Transfer to the UN of the Advisory Social Welfare Functions of UNRRA."
  A/Res/198 (III), 4 December 1948, "Economic Development of Underdeveloped Countries."
  A/Res/200 (III), 4 December 1948, "Technical Assistance in Economic Development."
  A/Res/246 (III), 4 December 1948, "International Facilities for the Promotion of Training in Public Administration."
  A/Res/289 (IV) A, 21 November 1949, "Question of the Disposal of the Former Italian Colonies."
  A/Res/855 (IX), 14 December 1954, "Financing of the Economic Development Plans of the Trust Territory of Somaliland under Italian Administration."

A/Res/1530 (XV), 15 December 1960, "United Nations Assistance in Public Administration: Provision of Operational, Executive and Administrative Personnel."
Second Committee, Summary Records:
A/C.2/SR.530–536, 544–548, 13th Session, 1958.
Verbatim Records (proces-verbaux):
A/PV.906, 17 October 1960, 15th Session

## UN Official Records: Security Council

Documents submitted to the Security Council:
S/4389/Add.5, 29 July 1960 "First Report by the Secretary-General on the Implementation of Security Council Resolution S/4387 of 14 July 1960."
S/4417/Add.5, 11 August 1960, "Memorandum by the Secretary-General on the Organization of ONUC."
S/4446, 20 August 1960, "Letter Dated 20 August 1960 from First Deputy Minister for Foreign Affairs of the Union of Soviet Socialist Republics Addressed to the Secretary-General."
Resolutions:
S/RES/143(1960), 14 July 1960, The Congo Question.
Verbatim Records (proces-verbaux):
S/PV.888–9, 21 August 1960.

## UN Official Records: Trusteeship Council

Official Records
TCOR: 14th Sess. (June/July 1954), 528th and 530th meeting.
TCOR: 20th Sess. (May/July 1957), Annexes, Agenda item 11 (IBRD, *The Economy of the Trust Territory of Somalia*, Report of January 1957).
Resolutions:
T/Res/1001(XIV), 7 July 1954, 550th meeting, "Financing the Economic Development Plans of the Trust Territory of Somaliland under Italian Administration."

## UN Official Records: United Nations Development Program

DP/TA/L.15, 1 December 1967, "Policy Matters: Operational Assistance under the Technical Assistance Component," Report by the Administrator to the UNDP Governing Council, 5th Session, 9–24 January 1968.

## UN Press Releases

SG/482, 29 May 1956: "Address by Secretary-General Dag Hammarskjold to International Law Association, at McGill University, Montréal, Wednesday, 30 May 1956."
SG/908, 14 April 1960: "Statement by Secretary-General Dag Hammarskjold before the Economic and Social Council on International Cooperation on Behalf of Former Trust Territories Which Have Become Independent."

## UN Sales Publications

Charnow, John, and UNICEF. *Maurice Pate: UNICEF Executive Director, 1947–1965*. New York: United Nations Children's Fund, 1989.
Connelly, Matthew. *The Contributions of the United Nations to the Improvement of Public Administration: A 60 Year History*. New York: United Nations, 2009.

Higgins, Benjamin. *The Economic and Social Development of Libya*. New York: United Nations Technical Assistance Administration, 1953.
Lindberg, John. *A General Economic Appraisal of Libya*. New York: United Nations Technical Assistance Administration, 1952.
*Report of the United Nations Mission of Technical Assistance to Bolivia*. New York: United Nations Technical Assistance Administration, 1951.
*The Trust Territory of Somaliland under Italian Administration: Report*. New York: United Nations Technical Assistance Administration, 1952.
*UN Mission of Technical Assistance to Haiti: Report*. Lake Success: United Nations, 1949.
*Yearbook of the United Nations 1946–1947*. New York: United Nations, 1947.
*Yearbook of the United Nations 1948–1949*. New York: United Nations, 1950.
*Yearbook of the United Nations 1950*. New York: United Nations, 1951.
*Yearbook of the United Nations 1959*. New York: United Nations, 1960.
*Yearbook of the United Nations 1960*. New York: United Nations, 1961.
*Yearbook of the United Nations 1961*. New York: United Nations, 1962.

## PUBLISHED ORAL HISTORIES

Apter, David Ernest. Interview by J. Sutterlin, 27 February 1991. UN Oral History Project. http://www.unmultimedia.org/oralhistory/2013/01/apter-david-ernest-2/. Last accessed 8 August 2016.
Goode, Richard B. Interview by H. Stephen Gardner, 6 March 1998. Baylor University Institute for Oral History & Department of Economics. https://digitalcollections-baylor.quartexcollections.com/Documents/Detail/oral-memoirs-of-richard-b.-goode-audio/975860. Last accessed 10 August 2021.
Linnér, Sture. Interview by Jean Krasno, 8 November 1990. UN Oral History Project. http://www.unmultimedia.org/oralhistory/2011/10/linner-sture/. Last accessed 29 April 2016.
Liu, F.T. Interview by J. Sutterlin, 23 March 1990. UN Oral History Project. http://www.unmultimedia.org/oralhistory/2011/10/liu-f-t/. Last accessed 5 May 2016.
Schachter, Oscar. Interview by William Powell, 14 March 1986. UN Oral History Project. http://www.unmultimedia.org/oralhistory/2011/06/schachter-oscar/. Last accessed 7 June 2016.

## PUBLISHED SPEECHES, ARTICLES, BOOKS, AND BIOGRAPHIES BY UN PERSONNEL AND OTHER PROTAGONISTS

Bloch, Henry Simon, and Bert F. Hoselitz. *Economics of Military Occupation: Selected Problems*. Chicago: University of Chicago Press, 1944.
Bunche, Ralph. "French Administration in Togoland and Dahomey." Doctoral dissertation, Harvard University, 1934.
———. "The United Nations Operation in the Congo." Speech given at Columbia University, 16 March 1964. In *The Quest for Peace: The Dag Hammarskjöld Memorial Lectures*, edited by Andrew Cordier and Wilder Foote, 119ff. New York: Columbia University Press, 1965.
———. *A World View of Race*. Washington, D.C.: Association in Negro Folk Education, 1936.
Cordier, Andrew, and Wilder Foote, eds. *Public Papers of the Secretaries-General of the United Nations*. Vol. 5: *Dag Hammarskjöld, 1960–1961*. New York: Columbia University Press, 1975.
Dayal, Rajeshwar. *Le Gouverneur Général Félix Eboué, 1884–1944*. Paris: Hachette, 1957.
———. *A Life of Our Times*. London: Sangam, 1998.
———. *Mission for Hammarskjöld: The Congo Crisis*. Princeton: Princeton University Press, 1976.
Devlin, Larry. *Chief of Station, Congo: A Memoir of 1960–67*. New York: Public Affairs, 2007.

Eder, George. *Inflation and Development in Latin America: A Case History of Inflation and Stabilization in Bolivia.* Ann Arbor: University of Michigan, 1968.
Finkelstein, Lawrence. "Bunche and the Colonial World: From Trusteeship to Decolonization." In Rivlin, *Ralph Bunche: The Man and His Times*, 109–31.
———. *Somaliland under Italian Administration: A Case Study in United Nations Trusteeship.* New York: Woodrow Wilson Foundation, 1955.
Goodrich, Carter. "Bolivia in Time of Revolution." In Richard S. Thorn and James M. Malloy, eds., *Beyond the Revolution: Bolivia since 1952.* Pittsburgh, University of Pittsburgh Press; 1971: 3–24.
———. "Bolivia: Test of Technical Assistance." *Foreign Affairs* April 1954: 473–81.
Gottmann, Jean, and Jean de la Roche. *La Fédération Française: Contacts et Civilisation d'Outre Mer.* Montréal: Editions de L'Arbre, 1945.
Gullerton, Garry. *UNESCO in the Congo.* Paris: UNESCO, 1964.
Hoffman, Paul. *World without Want.* New York: Harper & Row, 1962.
Hoo, Mona Yung-Ning. *Painting the Shadows: The Extraordinary Life of Victor Hoo.* London: Eldridge & Co., 1998.
Horn, Carl von. *Soldiering for Peace.* New York: D. McKay, 1967.
Kanza, Thomas R. *Conflict in the Congo: The Rise and Fall of Lumumba.* Harmondsworth: Penguin, 1972.
Karasz, Arthur. "Experiment in Development: Bolivia since 1952." In *Freedom and Reform in Latin America*, edited by Fredrick B. Pike, 256–80. University of Notre Dame Press 1959.
———. *International Aid: A Summary with Special Reference to the Programmes of the United Nations.* New York: James H. Heineman, 1966.
Keenleyside, Hugh. *Memoirs of Hugh L. Keenleyside.* 2 vols. Toronto: McClelland and Stewart, 1981.
Lepawsky, Albert. *The Bolivian Operation: New Trends in Technical Assistance.* International Conciliation no. 479. New York: Carnegie Endowment for International Peace, 1952.
Myrdal, Gunnar. *Rich Lands and Poor: The Road to World Prosperity.* New York: Harper, 1957.
O'Brien, Conor Cruise. *To Katanga and Back: A UN Case History.* New York: Simon and Schuster, 1963.
Pelt, Adrian. *Libyan Independence and the United Nations: A Case of Planned Decolonization.* New Haven, CT: Yale University Press, 1970.
Rikhye, Indar Jit. *Military Adviser to the Secretary-General: UN Peacekeeping and the Congo Crisis.* New York: St. Martin's Press, 1993.
Rivlin, Benjamin. "The Legacy of Ralph Bunche." In idem, ed., *Ralph Bunche: The Man and His Times*, 3–27.
———. *Ralph Bunche: The Man and His Times.* New York: Holmes & Meier, 1990.
———. *The United Nations and the Italian Colonies.* New York: Carnegie Endowment for International Peace, 1950.
Singer, Hans. "Obstacles to Economic Development." *Social Research* 20, no. 1 (1953): 19–31.
Urquhart, Brian. ———. *Hammarskjold.* New York: Knopf, 1972.
———. *A Life in Peace and War.* New York: Harper & Row, 1987.
———. *Ralph Bunche: An American Life.* New York: W.W. Norton, 1993.

## SECONDARY SOURCES

Abi-Saab, Georges. *The United Nations Operation in the Congo, 1960–1964.* Oxford: Oxford University Press, 1978.

Adebiyi, Adebisis Oluwatoyin. "The Role of the United Nations Visiting Missions in the Decolonisation of East Africa, 1948–1960." MLit thesis, University of Oxford, 1985.
Aksu, Esref. *The United Nations, Intra-State Peacekeeping and Normative Change.* Manchester: Manchester University Press, 2018.
Alacevich, Michele. *The Political Economy of the World Bank : The Early Years.* Stanford: Stanford University Press, 2009.
———. "Postwar Development in the Italian Mezzogiorno: Analyses and Policies." *Journal of Modern Italian Studies* 18 (2013): 90–112.
Alexander, Yonah. *International Technical Assistance Experts: A Case Study of the UN Experience.* New York: Praeger, 1966.
Amrith, Sunil, and Glenda Sluga. "New Histories of the United Nations." *Journal of World History* 19, no. 3 (2008): 251–74.
Anderson, Carol. *Eyes off the Prize: The United Nations and the African American Struggle for Human Rights, 1944–1955.* Cambridge: Cambridge University Press, 2009.
Anghie, Antony. *Colonialism, Sovereignty, and the Making of International Law.* New York: Cambridge University Press, 2004.
Ani, Awni al-. "Libyen, Tochter der UNO." In *Libyen,* edited by Fritz Edlinger, 102–23. Vienna: Promedia, 2011.
Autesserre, Séverine. *The Trouble with the Congo: Local Violence and the Failure of International Peacebuilding.* Cambridge: Cambridge University Press, 2010.
Bandeira Jerónimo, Miguel. "Competing Developments: Intercolonial Organisations and Colonial Education (1940s-1970s)." In *Education and Development in Colonial and Postcolonial Africa: Policies, Paradigms, and Entanglements, 1890s–1980s,* edited by Damiano Matasci, idem, and Hugo Gonçalves Dores, 237–62. London: Palgrave, 2020.
Bandeira Jerónimo, Miguel, and José Pedro Monteiro. "The Inventors of Human Rights in Africa: Portugal, Late Colonialism, and the UN Human Rights Regime." In *Decolonization, Self-Determination, and the Rise of Global Human Rights,* edited by Dirk Moses, Marco Duranti, and Roland Burke, 285–315. New York: Cambridge University Press, 2020.
———, eds. *The Pasts of the Present: Internationalism, Imperialism and the Formation of the Contemporary World.* London: Palgrave Macmillan, 2017.
Belhabib, Cherifa. "The United Nations Trusteeship System, 1945–1961." PhD thesis, University of Cincinnati, 1991.
Berthelot, Yves, ed. *Unity and Diversity in Development Ideas: Perspectives from the UN Regional Commissions.* Bloomington: Indiana University Press, 2004.
Bhagavan, Manu. *India and the Quest for One World: The Peacemakers.* New York: Palgrave Macmillan, 2013.
Bhouraskar, Digambar. *United Nations Development Aid: A Study in History and Politics.* New Delhi: Academic Foundation, 2007.
Bills, Scott. *The Libyan Arena: The United States, Britain, and the Council of Foreign Ministers, 1945–1948.* Kent, OH: Kent State University Press, 1995.
Borgwardt, Elizabeth. *A New Deal for the World : America's Vision for Human Rights.* Cambridge, MA: Belknap Press of Harvard University Press, 2005.
Brewer, W.M. "William Henry Dean." *The Journal of Negro History* 38, no. 1 (1953): 134–36.
Browne, Stephen. *The United Nations Development Programme and System.* New York: Routledge, 2012.
Burke, Catherine. "The Great Debate: The Decolonization Issue at the United Nations, 1945–1980." DPhil thesis, University of Oxford, 1986.
Burns, Alan. *In Defense of Colonies: British Colonial Territories in International Affairs.* London: Allen & Unwin, 1957.

Byrne, Jeffrey J. "Africa's Cold War." In *The Cold War in the Third World*, edited by Robert J. McMahon, 101–23. New York: Oxford University Press, 2013.

———. "Beyond Continents, Colours, and the Cold War: Yugoslavia, Algeria and the Struggle for Non-Alignment." *The International History Review* 37, no. 5 (2015): 912–32.

Calder, Ritchie. *Agony of the Congo*. London: Gollancz, 1961.

Castagno, Alphonso. Review of *The Economics of Trusteeship in Somalia* by Mark Karp. *Middle East Journal* 15, no. 4 (1961): 469–70.

———. *Somalia*. New York: Carnegie Endowment for International Peace, 1959.

Challenor, Herschelle S. "The Contribution of Ralph Bunche to Trusteeship and Decolonization." In Rivlin, *Ralph Bunche: The Man and His Times*, 132–45.

Chand, Ganeshwar. "The United States and the Origins of the Trusteeship System." *Review (Fernand Braudel Center)* 14, no. 2 (1991): 171–230.

Chowdhuri, Ramendra N. *International Mandates and Trusteeship Systems: A Comparative Study*. Dordrecht: Springer, 1955.

Claude, Inis. *Swords into Plowshares: The Problems and Progress of International Organization*. New York: Random House, 1956.

Clavin, Patricia. *Securing the World Economy: The Reinvention of the League of Nations, 1920–1946*. Oxford: Oxford University Press, 2013.

Collins, Carole. "The Cold War Comes to Africa: Cordier and the 1960 Congo Crisis." *Journal of International Affairs* 47, no. 1 (1993): 243–69.

Collins, Michael. "Decolonisation and the 'Federal Moment.'" *Diplomacy & Statecraft* 24, no. 1 (2013): 21–40.

Connelly, Matthew. *A Diplomatic Revolution : Algeria's Fight for Independence and the Origins of the Post-Cold War Era*. New York: Oxford University Press, 2002.

———. "Taking Off the Cold War Lens: Visions of North-South Conflict during the Algerian War for Independence." *The American Historical Review* 105, no. 3 (2000): 739–69.

Cooper, Frederick. *Africa since 1940: The Past of the Present*. Cambridge: Cambridge University Press, 2002.

———. *Citizenship between Empire and Nation: Remaking France and French Africa, 1945–1960*. Princeton: Princeton University Press, 2014.

———. "Writing the History of Development." *Journal of Modern European History* 8, no. 1 (2010): 5–23.

Crawford, Neta. "Decolonization through Trusteeship: The Legacy of Ralph Bunche." In *Trustee for the Human Community: Ralph J. Bunche, the United Nations, and the Decolonization of Africa*, edited by Robert A. Hill and Edmond J. Keller, 93–157. Athens: Ohio University Press, 2010.

Cullather, Nick. "Miracles of Modernization: The Green Revolution and the Apotheosis of Technology." *DIPH Diplomatic History* 28, no. 2 (2004): 227–54.

Dallin, Alexander. *The Soviet Union at the United Nations: An Inquiry into Soviet Motives and Objectives*. New York: Praeger, 1962.

Darwin, John. "Decolonization and the End of Empire." In *The Oxford History of the British Empire*, vol. 5: *Historiography*, edited by Robin Winks, 541–58. Oxford: Oxford University Press, 2001.

Desgrandchamps, Marie-Luce. "Dealing with 'Genocide': Humanitarian and International Organizations during the Nigeria-Biafra War (1967–1970)." *Journal of Genocide Research* 16, no. 2-3 (2014): 281–97.

———. "Du Congo au Biafra. Guerres Civiles et Actions Humanitaires dans les Relations Internationales Postcoloniales." *Relations Internationales* 176, no. 4 (2018): 55–67.

———. *L'humanitaire en Guerre Civile: La Crise du Biafra (1967–1970)*. Rennes: PUR, 2018.

Dimier, Véronique. *The Invention of a European Development Aid Bureaucracy: Recycling Empire*. London: Palgrave Macmillan UK, 2014.
Dorn, Glenn. "Pushing Tin: U.S.-Bolivian Relations and the Coming of the National Revolution." *Diplomatic History* 35, no. 2 (2011): 203–28.
———. *The Truman Administration and Bolivia: Making the World Safe for Liberal Constitutional Oligarchy*. University Park: Pennsylvania State University Press, 2011.
Drake, Paul. *The Money Doctor in the Andes: The Kemmerer Missions, 1923–1933*. Durham, NC: Duke University Press, 1989.
Duara, Prasenjit. "The Cold War and the Imperialism of Nation-States." In *The Oxford Handbook of the Cold War*, edited by Richard Immerman and Petra Goedde. Oxford: Oxford University Press, 2013: 1–22.
Easterly, William. *The Tyranny of Experts: Economists, Dictators, and the Forgotten Rights of the Poor*. New York: Basic Books, 2013.
Eder, George. *Inflation and Development in Latin America: A Case History of Inflation and Stabilization in Bolivia*. Ann Arbor: University of Michigan, 1968.
Eggers, Nicole, Jessica L. Pearson, and Aurora Almada e Santos, eds. *The United Nations and Decolonization*. London: Routledge, 2020.
Ekbladh, David. *The Great American Mission : Modernization and the Construction of an American World Order*. Princeton: Princeton University Press, 2010.
El-Ayouty, Yassin. *The United Nations and Decolonization: The Role of Afro-Asia*. The Hague: Martinus Nijhoff, 1971.
Engerman, David. "The Second World's Third World." *Kritika: Explorations in Russian and Eurasian History* 12, no. 1 (2011): 183–211.
Engerman, David, and Corinna Unger. "Introduction: Towards a Global History of Modernization." *Diplomatic History* 33, no. 3 (2009): 375–85.
Ewing, Cindy. "'With a Minimum of Bitterness': Decolonization, the Arab-Asian Group and Postcolonial Internationalism at the United Nations." *Journal of Global History* (forthcoming).
Feichtinger, Moritz, and Stephan Malinowski. "Konstruktive Kriege? Rezeption und Adaption der Dekolonisationskriege in Westlichen Demokratien." *Geschichte und Gesellschaft* 37, no. 2 (2011): 275–305.
———. "Transformative Invasions: Western Post-9/11 Counterinsurgency and the Lessons of Colonialism." *Humanity* 3, no. 1 (Spring 2012): 35–63.
Feldman, Ilana. "Ad Hoc Humanity: UN Peacekeeping and the Limits of International Community in Gaza." *American Anthropologist* 112, no. 3 (2010): 416–29.
Ferguson, James. *The Anti-Politics Machine: "Development," Depoliticization, and Bureaucratic Power in Lesotho*. New York: Cambridge University Press, 1990.
Ferrari-Bravo, Giuliano. "The Development of International Trusteeship at the United Nations with Particular Reference to British Reactions: 1944–1960." PhD thesis, University of Cambridge, 1976.
Ferraz de Oliveira, António. "Territory and Theory in Political Geography, c.1970s–90s: Jean Gottmann's *The Significance of Territory*." *Territory, Politics, Governance* online (2020): 1–18. DOI: 10.1080/21622671.2020.1733061.
Field, Thomas. *From Development to Dictatorship: Bolivia and the Alliance for Progress in the Kennedy Era*. Ithaca: Cornell University Press, 2014.
Finnemore, Martha. *National Interests in International Society*. Ithaca, NY: Cornell University Press, 1996.
Firestone, Bernard. *The United Nations under U Thant, 1961–1971*. Metuchen, NJ: Scarecrow, 2001.

French, John. "The Robert J. Alexander Interview Collection." *Hispanic American Historical Review* 82, no. 2 (2004): 315–26.

Friedman, Jeremy. "Soviet Policy in the Developing World and the Chinese Challenge in the 1960s." *Cold War History* 10, no. 2 (2010): 247–72.

Fröhlich, Manuel. *Dag Hammarskjöld und die Vereinten Nationen : Die politische Ethik des UNO-Generalsekretärs*. Paderborn: Schöningh, 2007.

——. *Political Ethics and the United Nations: Dag Hammarskjöld as Secretary-General*. London: Routledge, 2008.

——. "The 'Suez Story': Dag Hammarskjöld, the United Nations and the Creation of UN Peacekeeping." In *Peace Diplomacy, Global Justice and International Agency: Rethinking Human Security and Ethics in the Spirit of Dag Hammarskjöld*, edited by Carsten Stahn and Henning Melber, 305–40. Cambridge: Cambridge University Press, 2014.

Gaiduk, Ilya. *Divided Together: The United States and the Soviet Union in the United Nations, 1945–1965*. Stanford, CA: Stanford University Press, 2012.

Gerard, Emmanuel, and Bruce Kuklick. *Death in the Congo: Murdering Patrice Lumumba*. Cambridge, MA: Harvard University Press, 2015.

Getachew, Adom. *Worldmaking after Empire: The Rise and Fall of Self-Determination*. Princeton: Princeton University Press, 2019.

Gibbs, David. *The Political Economy of Third World Intervention: Mines, Money, and U.S. Policy in the Congo Crisis*. Chicago: University of Chicago Press, 1991.

——. "The United Nations, International Peacekeeping and the Question of 'Impartiality': Revisiting the Congo Operation of 1960." *The Journal of Modern African Studies* 38, no. 3 (2000): 359–82.

Gilman, Nils. *Mandarins of the Future: Modernization Theory in Cold War America*. Baltimore: Johns Hopkins University Press, 2003.

——. "The New International Economic Order: A Re-Introduction." *Humanity: An International Journal for Human Rights, Humanitarianism and Development* 6, no. 1 (2015): 1–16.

Glick, Philip. *The Administration of Technical Assistance*. Chicago: University of Chicago Press, 1957.

Gold, Jennifer. "The Reconfiguration of Scientific Career Networks in the Late Colonial Period: The Case of the Food and Agriculture Organization and the British Forestry Service." In *Science and Empire: Knowledge and Networks of Science across the British Empire, 1800–1970*, edited by Brett Bennett and Joseph Hodge, 297–320. Basingstoke: Palgrave Macmillan, 2011.

Gram-Skjoldager, Karen, and Haakon A. Ikonomou. "The Making of the International Civil Servant c. 1920–60: Establishing a Profession." In eadem, idem, and Kahlert, *Organizing the 20th-Century World*, 215–30.

Gram-Skjoldager, Karen, Haakon A. Ikonomou, and Torsten Kahlert. "Introduction." In idem, *Organizing the 20th-Century World*, 1–12.

——, eds. *Organizing the 20th-Century World: International Organizations and the Emergence of International Public Administration, 1920–1960s*. London: Bloomsbury Academic, 2020.

Haakonsen, Jan M. "In Memory of I.M. Lewis." *Nomadic Peoples* 18, no. 2 (2014): 1–9.

Hayter, Teresa. *French Aid*. London: Overseas Development Institute, 1966.

Heerten, Lasse. *The Biafran War and Postcolonial Humanitarianism: Spectacles of Suffering*. Cambridge: Cambridge University Press, 2017.

Heise, Julius. "Right to Petition vs. Rules of Procedure." In *The United Nations Trusteeship System: Legacies, Continuities, and Change*, edited by Julius Heise, Maria Ketzmerick, and Jan Lüdert. Global Institutions. London: Routledge, forthcoming.

Heise, Julius, Maria Ketzmerick, and Jan Lüdert, eds. *The United Nations Trusteeship System: Legacies, Continuities, and Change*. Global Institutions. London: Routledge, forthcoming.
Helleiner, Eric. *Forgotten Foundations of Bretton Woods: International Development and the Making of the Postwar Order*. Ithaca, NY: Cornell University Press, 2016.
Heller, Peter. *The United Nations under Dag Hammarskjöld, 1953–1961*. Lanham, MD: Scarecrow, 2001.
Henry, Charles P. *Ralph Bunche: Model Negro or American Other?* New York: New York University Press, 1999.
Heppling, Sixten. *UNDP: From Agency Shares to Country Programmes, 1949–1975*. Stockholm: Ministry of Foreign Affairs, 1995.
Hill, Jonathan. "Beyond the Other? A Postcolonial Critique of the Failed State Thesis." *African Identities* 3, no. 2 (2005): 139–54.
Hill, Robert, and Edmond Keller, eds. *Trustee for the Human Community: Ralph J. Bunche, the United Nations, and the Decolonization of Africa*. Athens: Ohio University Press, 2010.
Hilsman, Roger. *To Move a Nation: The Politics of Foreign Policy in the Administration of John F. Kennedy*. Garden City, NY: Doubleday, 1967.
Hodge, Joseph. "British Colonial Expertise, Post-Colonial Careering and the Early History of International Development." *Journal of Modern European History* 8, no. 1 (2010): 24–46.
———. *Triumph of the Expert: Agrarian Doctrines of Development and the Legacies of British Colonialism*. Athens: Ohio University Press, 2007.
Hoskyns, Catherine. *The Congo since Independence: January 1960-December, 1961*. London: Oxford University Press, 1965.
———. *The Organization of African Unity and the Congo Crisis, 1964–65: Documents*. Dar-es-Salaam: Published for the Institute of Public Administration, University College Dar-es-Salaam, by Oxford University Press, 1969.
House, Arthur. *The UN in the Congo: The Political and Civilian Efforts*. Washington, DC: University Press of America, 1978.
Huggins, Nathan. "Ralph Bunche the Africanist." In Rivlin, *Ralph Bunche: The Man and His Times*, 69–82.
Iandolo, Alessandro. "Beyond the Shoe: Rethinking Khrushchev at the Fifteenth Session of the United Nations General Assembly." *Diplomatic History* 41, no. 1 (2017): 128–54.
Immerwahr, Daniel. "The Greater United States: Territory and Empire in U.S. History." *Diplomatic History* 40 (2016): 373–91.
———. *How to Hide an Empire: A History of the Greater United States*. New York: Farrar, Strauss and Giroux, 2019.
———. *Thinking Small: The United States and the Lure of Community Development*. Cambridge, MA: Harvard University Press, 2015.
Irwin, Ryan. *Gordian Knot: Apartheid and the Unmaking of the Liberal World Order*. New York: Oxford University Press, 2012.
———. "Imagining Nation, State, and Order in the Mid-Twentieth Century." Rethinking Cold War History in Southern Africa. *Kronos* 37 (2011): 12–22.
———. "A Wind of Change? White Redoubt and the Postcolonial Moment, 1960–1963." *Diplomatic History* 33, no. 5 (2009): 897–925.
Iverson, Kenneth. "The 'Servicio' in Theory and Practice." *Public Administration Review* 11, no. 4 (1951): 223–28.
Jackson, Donna. "The Carter Administration and Somalia." *Diplomatic History* 31, no. 4 (2007): 703–21.
———. *Jimmy Carter and the Horn of Africa: Cold War Policy in Ethiopia and Somalia*. Jefferson, NC: McFarland, 2006.

Jackson, Regine. "The Failure of Categories: Haitians in the United Nations Organization in the Congo, 1960–64." *Journal of Haitian Studies* 20, no. 1 (2014): 34–64.

Jackson, Simon. "Transformative Relief: Imperial Humanitarianism and Mandatory Development in Syria-Lebanon, 1915–1925." *Humanity* 8, no. 2 (2017): 247–68.

Jackson, Simon, and Dirk Moses. "Introduction: Transformative Occupations in the Modern Middle East." *Humanity* 8, no. 2 (2017): 231–46.

Jackson, Simon, and Alanna O'Malley, eds. *The Institution of International Order: From the League of Nations to the United Nations*. London: Routledge, 2018.

Jacobson, Harold Karan. "ONUC's Civilian Operations: State-Preserving and State-Building." *World Politics* 17, no. 1 (1964): 75–107.

———. *The USSR and the UN's Economic and Social Activities*. Notre Dame, IN: University of Notre Dame Press, 1963.

Jain, Devaki. *Women, Development, and the UN: A Sixty-Year Quest for Equality and Justice*. Bloomington: Indiana University Press, 2005.

James, Alan. *Britain and the Congo Crisis, 1960–1963*. New York: St. Martin's Press, 1996.

Jansen, Jan, and Jürgen Osterhammel. *Dekolonisation: Das Ende der Imperien*. Munich: C.H. Beck, 2013.

Jolly, Richard. *UN Contributions to Development Thinking and Practice*. Bloomington: Indiana University Press, 2004.

Kalb, Madeleine. *The Congo Cables: The Cold War in Africa from Eisenhower to Kennedy*. New York: Macmillan, 1982.

Kalinovsky, Artemy. *Laboratory of Socialist Development: Cold War Politics and Decolonization in Soviet Tajikistan*. Ithaca, NY: Cornell University Press, 2018.

Kanet, Roger. *The Soviet Union, Eastern Europe and the Third World*. Cambridge: Cambridge University Press, 1987.

Karp, Mark. *The Economics of Trusteeship in Somalia*. Boston: Boston University Press, 1960.

Kelly, Saul. *Cold War in the Desert: Britain, the United States, and the Italian Colonies, 1945–52*. New York: St. Martin's Press, 2000.

Kendall, Sara. "'Constitutional Technicity': Displacing Politics through Expert Knowledge." *Law, Culture and the Humanities* 11, no. 3 (2015): 363–77.

Kennedy, Dane. *Decolonization: A Very Short Introduction*. New York: Oxford University Press, 2016.

Kennedy, Michael, and Art Magennis. *Ireland, the United Nations and the Congo: A Military and Diplomatic History, 1960–1*. Dublin: Four Courts Press, 2014.

Kennedy, Paul. *The Parliament of Man: The Past, Present, and Future of the United Nations*. New York: Random House, 2006.

Kent, John. *America, the UN and Decolonisation: Cold War Conflict in the Congo*. London: Routledge, 2010.

Kiang, Lu-Yu. "The Development and Operation of the Method of Supervision in the United Nations Trusteeship System." PhD thesis, New York University, 1955.

Kilson, Martin. "Ralph Bunche's Analytical Perspective on African Development." In Rivlin, *Ralph Bunche: The Man and His Times*, 83–95.

Kirk-Greene, Anthony. *Britain's Imperial Administrators, 1858–1966*. New York: St. Martin's Press, 2000.

———. "Decolonization: The Ultimate Diaspora." *Journal of Contemporary History* 36, no. 1 (2001): 133–51.

Kluge, Emma. "Decolonisation in the Pacific: West Papua, the United Nations and the Non-Aligned Movement." Paper presented at the conference *Challenging the Liberal World*

Order: *The History of the Global South, Decolonization and the United Nations, 1955–2000*, Leiden University, 8–9 May 2018.

———. "West Papua and the International History of Decolonization, 1961–69." *The International History Review* 42, no. 6 (2019): 1155–72. https://doi.org/10.1080/07075332.2019.1694052.

Kona Nayudu, Swapna. "'In the very eye of the storm': India, the UN, and the Lebanon Crisis of 1958." *Cold War History* 18, no. 2 (2018): 221–37.

———. "'A Man of Supreme Patience': Rajeshwar Dayal, Hammarskjöld's Envoy." Wilson Center blog, April 23, 2018. https://www.wilsoncenter.org/blog-post/man-supreme-patience-rajeshwar-dayal-hammarskjolds-envoy.

Korn, Hallen. "Law or Order: The Politics of Development and Humanitarian Intervention in the Congo Crisis, 1960–61." Undergraduate thesis in history, Columbia University, 2014.

Kott, Sandrine. "Fighting the War or Preparing for Peace? The ILO during the Second World War." *Journal of Modern European History* 12, no. 3 (2014): 359–76.

———. "The Social Engineering Project: Exportation of Capitalist Management Culture to Eastern Europe (1950–1980)." In *Planning in Cold War Europe: Competition, Cooperation, Circulations (1950s–1970s)*, edited by Michel Christian, Sandrine Kott, and Ondrej Matejka, 123–42. Berlin: De Gruyter, 2018.

Kott, Sandrine, and Joëlle Droux, eds. *Globalizing Social Rights: The International Labour Organization and Beyond*. New York: Palgrave Macmillan, 2013.

Lal, Priya. "Decolonization and the Gendered Politics of Developmental Labor in Southeastern Africa." In Macekura and Manela, *The Development Century*, 173–96.

Latham, Michael. *The Right Kind of Revolution : Modernization, Development, and U.S. Foreign Policy from the Cold War to the Present*. Ithaca, NY: Cornell University Press, 2011.

LeBlanc, Zoe. "'They Are All Lumumbas': Anti-Colonial Solidarities and Media Representations in the United Arab Republic during the Congo Crisis 1960–61." Paper presented at the International Seminar on Decolonization Reunion Conference, Washington, DC, 2016.

Leclerc, Elisa. "Nuclear Testing on the Strategic Trust Territory of the Pacific Islands—How the U.S. Became an Imperial Power in the Region of Micronesia." In *The United Nations Trusteeship System: Legacies, Continuities, and Change*, edited by Julius Heise, Maria Ketzmerick, and Jan Lüdert. Global Institutions. London: Routledge, forthcoming.

Lefever, Ernest. *Crisis in the Congo: A UN Force in Action*. Washington, DC: Brookings Institution Press, 1965.

———. *Uncertain Mandate: Politics of the UN Congo Operation*. Baltimore: Johns Hopkins University Press, 1967.

Lehman, Kenneth. "Article Review: Glen J. Dorn. 'Pushing Tin: U.S.-Bolivian Relations and the Coming of the National Revolution.' *Diplomatic History* 35:2 (April 2011): 233–258." H-Diplo, H-Diplo Article Reviews, no. 303 (May 5, 2011). https://issforum.org/reviews/PDF/AR303.pdf.

———. *Bolivia and the United States: A Limited Partnership*. Athens: University of Georgia Press, 1999.

Lewis, Ioan. *A Modern History of Somalia: Nation and State in the Horn of Africa*. Boulder, CO: Westview Press, 1988.

———. "Review of *The Economics of Trusteeship* by Mark Karp." *Journal of the International African Institute* 31, no. 2 (1961): 190–91.

Limoncelli, Amy. "Great Britain and International Administration: Finding a New Role at the United Nations, 1941–1975." Doctoral dissertation, Boston College, 2016.

Lipsey, Roger. *Hammarskjöld: A Life*. Ann Arbor: University of Michigan Press, 2013.

Lohrmann, Ullrich. *Voices from Tanganyika: Great Britain, the United Nations and the Decolonization of a Trust Territory, 1946–1961*. Berlin: Lit, 2007.

Lorenzini, Sara. *Global Development: A Cold War History*. Princeton: Princeton University Press, 2019.

———. "The Socialist Camp and the Challenge of Economic Modernization in the Third World." In *The Cambridge History of Communism*, edited by Norman Naimark, Silvio Pons, and Sophie Quinn-Judge, 341–63. Cambridge: Cambridge University Press, 2017.

Louis, Wm. Roger. *Imperialism at Bay: The United States and the Decolonization of the British Empire, 1941–1945*. New York: Oxford University Press, 1978.

———. "Libya: The Creation of a Client State." In *Decolonization and African Independence: The Transfers of Power 1960–1980*, edited by Prosser Gifford and idem, 503–28. London: Yale University Press, 1988.

———. *National Security and International Trusteeship in the Pacific*. Annapolis: Md Naval Institute Press, 1972.

Louis, Wm. Roger, and Ronald Robinson. "The Imperialism of Decolonization." *Journal of Imperial and Commonwealth History* 22, no. 3 (1994): 462–511.

Luard, Evan. *A History of the United Nations*. Vol. 2: *The Age of Decolonization, 1955–1965*. New York: St. Martin's Press, 1989.

———. *A History of the United Nations*. Vol. 1: *The Years of Western Domination, 1945–1955*. New York: St. Martin's Press, 1982.

Lüdert, Jan. "Conditions Apply: Non-State Actors Challenging State Sovereignty through Intergovernmental Organizations: An Analysis of National Liberation Movements and Indigenous Peoples at the United Nations." Doctoral Dissertation, University of British Columbia, 2016.

Macekura, Stephen, and Erez Manela, eds. *The Development Century: A Global History*. New York: Cambridge University Press, 2018.

MacFayden, David, Michael D.W. Davies, Marilyn Carr, and John Burley. *Eric Drummond and His Legacies: The League of Nations and the Beginnings of Global Governance*. Cham: Palgrave Macmillan, 2019.

MacKenzie, David. *A World beyond Borders: An Introduction to the History of International Organizations*. Toronto: University of Toronto Press, 2010.

Mahoney, Richard. *JFK: Ordeal in Africa*. New York: Oxford University Press, 1983.

Maki, John. "U.S. Strategic Area or UN Trusteeship." *Far Eastern Survey* 16, no. 15 (August 13, 1947): 175–78.

Manela, Erez. *The Wilsonian Moment: Self-Determination and the International Origins of Anticolonial Nationalism*. New York: Oxford University Press, 2007.

Mann, Gregory. *From Empires to NGOs in the West African Sahel: The Road to Nongovernmentality*. African Studies Series 129. New York: Cambridge University Press, 2015.

Mann, Peggy. *Ralph Bunche, UN Peacemaker*. New York: Coward, McCann & Geoghegan, 1975.

Mansbach, Richard. "The Soviet Union, the United Nations, and the Developing States." In *The Soviet Union and the Developing Nations*. Baltimore: Johns Hopkins University Press, 1974.

Marcus, Nathan. *Austrian Reconstruction and the Collapse of Global Finance, 1921–1931*. Cambridge, MA: Harvard University Press, 2018.

Mark, James, Artemy Kalinovsky, and Steffi Marung, eds. *Alternative Globalizations: Eastern Europe and the Postcolonial World*. Bloomington: Indiana University Press, 2020.

Martelli, George. *Experiment in World Government: An Account of the United Nations Operation in the Congo, 1960–1964*. London: Johnson Publications, 1966.

Massad, Joseph. "Against Self-Determination." *Humanity: An International Journal of Human Rights, Humanitarianism, and Development* 9, no. 2 (2018). http://humanityjournal.org/issue9-2/against-self-determination/

Matena, Karuna. "Popular Sovereignty and Anti-Colonialism." In *Popular Sovereignty in Historical Perspective*, edited by Richard Bourke and Quentin Skinner, 297–319. New York: Cambridge University Press, 2016.
Maul, Daniel. *Human Rights, Development and Decolonization: The International Labour Organization, 1940–70*. New York: Palgrave Macmillan, 2012.
———. *The International Labour Organization: 100 Years of Global Social Policy*. Berlin: DeGruyter, 2019.
Mazov, Sergei V. *A Distant Front in the Cold War: The USSR in West Africa and the Congo, 1956–1964*. Stanford, CA: Stanford University Press, 2010.
Mazower, Mark. *Governing the World: The History of an Idea*. New York: Penguin Press, 2012.
———. *No Enchanted Palace: The End of Empire and the Ideological Origins of the United Nations*. Princeton: Princeton University Press, 2009.
———. "The Strange Triumph of Human Rights, 1933–1950." *The Historical Journal* 47, no. 2 (June 1, 2004): 379–98.
McCullers, Molly. "'The Time of the United Nations in South West Africa Is Near': Local Drama and Global Politics in Apartheid-Era Hereroland." *Journal of Southern African Studies* 39, no. 2 (2018): 371–89.
McNeely, Connie. *Constructing the Nation-State: International Organization and Prescriptive Action*. Westport, CT: Greenwood, 1995.
Meaney, Thomas M. "The American Hour: U.S. Thinkers and the Problem of Decolonization, 1948–1983." Doctoral dissertation, Columbia University, 2017.
Melber, Henning. *Dag Hammarskjöld, the United Nations and the Decolonisation of Africa*. London: Hurst & Company, 2019.
———. "Liberating Namibia: The Long Diplomatic Struggle between the United Nations and South Africa." *Journal of Modern African Studies* 50, no. 4 (2012): 733–34.
Mitchell, Timothy. *Rule of Expert: Egypt, Techno-Politics, Modernity*. Berkeley: University of California Press, 2002.
Mockaitis, Thomas. *Peace Operations and Intrastate Conflict: The Sword or the Olive Branch?* Westport, CT: Praeger, 1999.
Mohan, Jitendra. "Ghana, the Congo, and the United Nations." *Journal of Modern African Studies* 7, no. 3 (1969): 369–406.
Morone, Antonio. "How Italy Returned to Africa: From the Loss of the Colonies to African Independence." In *Colonialism and National Identity*, edited by Bartella Farnetti and C. Dau Novelli, 126–44. Newcastle upon-Tyne: Cambridge Scholars Publishing, 2015.
———. "Somali Independence and Its Political Connections with Nasser's Egypt." In *The Horn of Africa since the 1960s Local and International Politics Intertwined*, edited by Ylonen Aleksi and Jan Zahorik, 109–22. Basingstoke: Routledge, 2017.
Morrell, Gordon. "A Higher Stage of Imperialism? The Big Three, the UN Trusteeship Council, and the Early Cold War." In *Imperialism on Trial*, edited by R.M. Douglas, Michael D. Callahan, and Elizabeth Bishop, 111–37. Lanham, MD: Lexington Books, 2006.
Mountz, William. "Americanizing Africanization: The Congo Crisis, 1960–1967." Doctoral dissertation, University of Missouri, 2014.
Moyn, Samuel. *Not Enough: Human Rights in an Unequal World*. Cambridge, MA: Harvard University Press, 2018.
Muhammad, Faqir. "United Nations Technical Assistance in Public Administration with Special Reference to the Provision of Operational and Executive Personnel." Doctoral dissertation, Syracuse University, 1960.
Murphy, Craig. *The United Nations Development Programme: A Better Way?* Cambridge: Cambridge University Press, 2006.

Muschik, Eva-Maria. "Article Review 'Beyond the Shoe: Rethinking Khrushchev at the Fifteenth Session of the United Nations General Assembly.'" *H-Diplo* 718 (6 October 2017). http://tiny.cc/AR718.

———. "The Art of Chameleon Politics: From Colonial Servant to International Development Expert." *Humanity: An International Journal for Human Rights, Humanitarianism and Development* 9, no. 2 (2018): 219–44.

———. "Managing the World: The United Nations, Decolonization, and the Strange Triumph of State Sovereignty in the 1950s and 1960s." *Journal of Global History* 13, no. 1 (2018): 121–44.

———. "Special Issue Introduction: Towards a Global History of International Organizations and Decolonization." *Journal of Global History*, forthcoming.

———. "The Trusteeship System, Decolonization and (the Limits of) UN Agency." In *The United Nations Trusteeship System: Legacies, Continuities, and Change*, edited by Julius Heise, Maria Ketzmerick, and Jan Lüdert. Global Institutions. London: Routledge, forthcoming.

Myrdal, Gunnar. *Rich Lands and Poor: The Road to World Prosperity*. New York: Harper, 1957.

Namikas, Lise. *Battleground Africa: Cold War in the Congo, 1960–1965*. Stanford, CA: Stanford University Press, 2013.

Nassif, Ramses. *U Thant in New York, 1961–1971: A Portrait of the Third UN Secretary-General*. New York: St. Martin's Press, 1988.

Normand, Roger, and Sarah Zaidi. *Human Rights at the UN: The Political History of Universal Justice*. Bloomington: Indiana University Press, 2008.

Nunan, Timothy. *Humanitarian Invasion: Global Development in Cold War Afghanistan*. New York: Cambridge University Press, 2016.

Ofuatey-Kodjoe, W. "Ralph Bunche: An African Perspective." In Rivlin, *Ralph Bunche: The Man and His Times*, 96–108.

O'Malley, Alanna. *Diplomacy of Decolonisation: America, Britain and the United Nations during the Congo Crisis 1960–64*. Manchester: Manchester University Press, 2018.

———. "Ghana, India, and the Transnational Dynamics of the Congo Crisis at the United Nations, 1960–1." *International History Review* 37, no. 5 (2015): 970–90.

Orford, Anne. "Book Review Article: 'International Territorial Administration and the Management of Decolonization.'" *International and Comparative Law Quarterly* 59 (2010): 227–50.

———. "Hammarskjöld, Economic Thinking and the United Nations." In *Peace Diplomacy, Global Justice and International Agency: Rethinking Human Security and Ethics in the Spirit of Dag Hammarskjöld*, edited by Carsten Stahn and Henning Melber, 156–89. Cambridge: Cambridge University Press, 2014.

———. *International Authority and the Responsibility to Protect*. Cambridge: Cambridge University Press, 2011.

O'Sullivan, Christopher. *The United Nations: A Concise History*. Malabar: Kriegler, 2005.

Pearson, Jessica L. *The Colonial Politics of Global Health: France and the United Nations in Postwar Africa*. Cambridge, MA: Harvard University Press, 2018.

———. "Defending Empire at the United Nations: The Politics of International Colonial Oversight in the Era of Decolonisation." *The Journal of Imperial and Commonwealth History* 45, no. 3 (May 31, 2017): 525–49.

———. "The French Empire Goes to San Francisco: The Founding of the United Nations and the Limits of Colonial Reform." *French Politics, Culture and Society* 38, no. 2 (2020): 35–55.

Peck, Connie. "Special Representatives of the Secretary-General." In *The UN Security Council: From the Cold War to the 21st Century*, edited by David Malone, 325–39. Boulder, CO: Lynne Rienner, 2004.
Pedersen, Susan. "Back to the League of Nations." *The American Historical Review* 112, no. 4 (October 2007): 1090–1117.
———. "Foreword: From the League of Nations to the United Nations." In *The Institution of International Order: From the League of Nations to the United Nations*, edited by Simon Jackson and Alanna O'Malley, ix–xvi. London: Routledge, 2018.
———. "Getting Out of Iraq—In 1932: The League of Nations and the Road to Normative Statehood." *The American Historical Review* 115, no. 4 (2010): 975.
———. *The Guardians: The League of Nations and the Crisis of Empire*. Oxford: Oxford University Press, 2015.
———. "An International Regime in an Age of Empire." *American Historical Review* 124, no. 5 (2019): 1676-80.
Pepin, Jacques. *The Origins of AIDS*. Cambridge: Cambridge University Press, 2011.
Pinto, Michelle. "Employment, Education, and the Reconfiguration of Empire: Africanization in Postwar French Africa." PhD dissertation, New York University, 2013.
Pomeroy, Earl. *Pacific Outpost American Strategy in Guam and Micronesia*. Stanford, CA: Stanford University Press, 1951.
Porter, Louis H. "Cold War Internationalisms: The USSR in UNESCO, 1945–1967." Dissertation, University of North Carolina, 2018.
Poulgrain, Greg. *The Incubus of Intervention: Conflicting Indonesia Strategies of John F. Kennedy and Allen Dulles*. Petaling Jaya (Malaysia): Strategic Information and Reseach Development Centre, 2015.
———. *JFK vs. Allen Dulles: Battleground Indonesia*. New York: W. W. Norton & Co., 2019.
Prashad, Vijay. *The Darker Nations: A People's History of the Third World*. New York: The New Press, 2008.
Pruden, Caroline. *Conditional Partners: Eisenhower, the United Nations, and the Search for a Permanent Peace*. Baton Rouge: Louisiana State University Press, 1998.
Quammen, David. *Spillover: Animal Infections and the Next Human Pandemic*. New York: W.W. Norton & Co., 2012.
Rachbauer, Tamara. *Egon Ranshofen-Wertheimer—Chronologie eines bewegten Lebens*. Munich: Grinn, 2008.
Reinisch, Jessica. "Internationalism in Relief: The Birth (and Death) of UNRRA." *Past & Present* 210, Supplement 6 (2011): 258–89.
Rempe, Martin. *Entwicklung im Konflikt: Die EWG und der Senegal, 1957–1975*. Cologne: Böhlau, 2012.
Rens, Jef. *Le Programme Andin. Contribution de l'OIT a Un Projet-Pilote de Coopération Technique Multilatéral*. Brussels: E. Bruylant, 1987.
Reyner, Anthony. "Somalia: The Problems of Independence." *The Middle East Journal* 14, no. 3 (1960): 247–55.
Richardson, Henry. "'Failed States,' Self-Determination, and Preventive Diplomacy: Colonialist Nostalgia and Democratic Expectations." *Temple International and Comparative Law Journal* 10, no. 1 (1996): 1–78.
Rietkerk, Aaron. "In Pursuit of Development: The United Nations, Decolonization and Development Aid, 1949–1961." PhD thesis, London School of Economics, 2015. http://etheses.lse.ac.uk/3158/.
Rist, Gilbert. *The History of Development: From Western Origins to Global Faith*. 3rd ed. New York: Zed Books, 2008.

Rodríguez, Magaly, Liat Kozma, and Davide Rodogno, eds. *The League of Nations' Work on Social Issues: Visions, Endeavours and Experiments*. New York: United Nations Press, 2016.

Roes, Aldwin. "World Bank Survey Missions and the Politics of Decolonization in British East Africa, 1957–1963." *International Journal of African Historical Studies* 42, no. 1 (2009): 1–28.

Röhrlich, Elisabeth. "State of the Field Essay on the History of the United Nations and Its Organizations." *H-Diplo*, 20 April 2018. http://tiny.cc/E153.

Rosenberg, Emily. *Financial Missionaries to the World: The Politics and Culture of Dollar Diplomacy, 1900–1930*. Durham, NC: Duke University Press, 2007.

Rowe, Edward. "The Effects of the United Nations' Trusteeship System." PhD thesis, University of California, 1966.

Rubinstein, Alvin. *The Soviets in International Organizations: Changing Policy toward Developing Countries, 1953–1963*. Princeton: Princeton University Press, 1964.

Russell, Ruth. *A History of the United Nations Charter: The Role of the United States, 1940–1945*. Washington, DC: Brookings Institution, 1958.

Saltford, John. *The United Nations and the Indonesian Takeover of West Papua, 1962–1969: The Anatomy of a Betrayal*. London: Routledge, 2003.

———. "United Nations Involvement with the Act of Self-Determination in West Irian (Indonesian West New Guinea) 1968 to 1969." *Indonesia* 69 (2000): 71–92.

Salvatici, Silvia. "Between National and International Mandates: Displaced Persons and Refugees in Postwar Italy." *Journal of Contemporary History* 49, no. 3 (2014): 514–36.

Saunders, Chris. "The Role of the United Nations in the Independence of Namibia." *History Compass* 5, no. 3 (May 2007): 737–44.

Sayward, Amy. *The Birth of Development: How the World Bank, Food and Agriculture Organization, and World Health Organization Changed the World, 1945–1965*. Kent, OH: Kent State University Press, 2006.

———. *The United Nations in International History*. London: Bloomsbury, 2017.

Schlesinger, Arthur. *A Thousand Days: John F. Kennedy in the White House*. Boston: Houghton Mifflin, 1965.

Schlesinger, Stephen. *Act of Creation: The Founding of the United Nations: A Story of Superpowers, Secret Agents, Wartime Allies and Enemies, and Their Quest for a Peaceful World*. Boulder, CO: Westview Press, 2003.

Scott, Rebecca. "Economic Aid and Imperialism in Bolivia." *Monthly Review* 24, no. 1 (1972): 48–60.

Seibert, Julia. *In die globale Wirtschaft gezwungen. Arbeit und kolonialer Kapitalismus im Kongo (1885—1960)*. Frankfurt am Main: Campus, 2016.

Selzer, Will Joseph. "The Trusteeship Council of the United Nations and Self-Government, with Particular Reference to British East Africa, 1947–1951." PhD thesis, University of Pennsylvania, 1959.

Sharma, Patrick. *Robert McNamara's Other War: The World Bank and International Development*. Philadelphia: University of Pennsylvania Press, 2017.

Sharp, Walter. *International Technical Assistance: Programs and Organization*. Chicago: Public Administration Service, 1952.

Sherwood, Marika. "'There Is No New Deal for the Blackman in San Francisco': African Attempts to Influence the Founding Conference of the United Nations, April–July, 1945." *The International Journal of African Historical Studies* 29, no. 1 (1996): 71–94.

Shipway, Martin. *Decolonization and Its Impact: A Comparative Approach to the End of the Colonial Empires*. Malden, MA: Blackwell, 2008.

Siekmeier, James. *The Bolivian Revolution and the United States, 1952 to the Present*. University Park: Pennsylvania State University Press, 2011.

Simons, Geoffrey. *Libya and the West: From Independence to Lockerbie.* Oxford: Centre for Libyan Studies, 2003.
Simpson, Bradley. "The Atlantic Charter and the Imagined Future of Self-Determination and Decolonization, 1941-1945." Paper presented at the conference *Challenging the Liberal World Order: The History of the Global South, Decolonization and the United Nations, 1955-2000,* Leiden University, 8-9 May 2018.
———. *The First Right: Self-Determination and the Transformation of Post-1941 International Relations.* New York: Oxford University Press, forthcoming.
Sinclair, Guy Fiti. "Self-Determination, Human Rights, and the End of Empire in the 1970s." *Humanity: An International Journal of Human Rights, Humanitarianism, and Development* 4, no. 2 (2013): 239-60.
———. *To Reform the World: International Organizations and the Making of Modern States.* Oxford: Oxford University Press, 2017.
———. "The United Nations, Public Administration and the Making of Postcolonial States." Paper presented at the Technologies of Stateness: International Organizations and the Making of States workshop, European University Institute, Florence, 15-16 September 2016.
Sluga, Glenda. "The Human Story of Development: Alva Myrdal at the UN, 1949-1955." In *International Organizations and Development, 1945-1990,* edited by Corinna Unger, Marc Frey, and Sonke Kunkel, 46-74. London: Palgrave Macmillan, 2014.
Speich Chassé, Daniel. "Der Blick von Lake Success: Das Entwicklungsdenken der frühen UNO als 'lokales Wissen.'" In *Entwicklungswelten—Globalgeschichte der Entwicklungszusammenarbeit,* edited by Hubertus Büschel and idem, 143-74. Frankfurt am Main: Campus, 2009.
———. "Decolonization and Global Governance: Approaches to the History of the UN-System." Paper presented to the History of International Organizations Network, Geneva, 2013. https://www.academia.edu/21763722. Last accessed 27 August 2021.
———. *Die Erfindung des Bruttosozialprodukts: globale Ungleichheit in der Wissensgeschichte der Ökonomie.* Göttingen: Vandenhock & Ruprecht, 2013.
Spooner, Kevin. *Canada, the Congo Crisis, and UN Peacekeeping, 1960-64.* Vancouver: University of British Columbia Press, 2009.
Stahn, Carsten. *The Law and Practice of International Territorial Administration: From Versailles to Iraq.* Cambridge: Cambridge University Press, 2008.
St. John, Ronald Bruce. *Libya: From Colony to Revolution.* London: Oneworld, 2017.
Stockwell, Sarah. "Exporting Britishness: Decolonization in Africa, the British State and Its Clients." In *The Ends of European Colonial Empires: Cases and Comparisons,* edited by Miguel Bandeira Jerónimo and António Costa Pinto, 148-77. London: Palgrave Macmillan UK, 2015.
Stokke, Olav. *The UN and Development: From Aid to Cooperation.* Bloomington: Indiana University Press, 2009.
Tamborini, Francesco. "The United Nations, the Italian Decolonization and the 1949 Bevin-Sforza Plan: A Victory for Neo-Colonialism?" In Eggers, Pearson, and Almada e Santos, *The United Nations and Decolonization,* 61-80.
Terretta, Meredith. "'We had been fooled into thinking that the UN watches over the entire world': Human Rights, UN Trust Territories, and Africa's Decolonization." *Human Rights Quarterly* 34, no. 2 (2012): 329-60.
Thomas, Martin, and Andrew Thompson, eds. *The Oxford Handbook of the Ends of Empire.* Oxford: Oxford University Press, 2018.
Thornton, Christy. "'Mexico Has the Theories': Latin America and the Interwar Origins of Development." In Macekura and Manela, *The Development Century,* 263-82.

Tortolli, Alessia. "The Trust Territory of Somaliland, 1950–1960: Trusteeship or Colony?" In Eggers, Pearson, and Almada e Santos, *The United Nations and Decolonization*, 151–70.

Toussaint, Charmian Edwards. *The Trusteeship System of the United Nations*. New York: Praeger, 1956.

Toye, John, and Richard Toye. *The UN and Global Political Economy: Trade, Finance, and Development*. United Nations Intellectual History Project Series. Bloomington: Indiana University Press, 2004.

Tripodi, Paolo. "Back to the Horn: Italian Administration and Somalia's Troubled Independence." *Journal of Modern African Studies* 32, no. 2/3 (1999): 359–80.

——. *The Colonial Legacy in Somalia: Rome and Mogadishu: From Colonial Administration to Operation Restore Hope*. Basingstoke: Macmillan, 1999.

Tudor, Margot. "Gatekeepers to Decolonisation: Recentring the UN Peacekeepers on the Frontline of West Papua's Re-Colonisation, 1962-1963." *Journal of Contemporary History*, 2021, 1–24, https://doi.org/10.1177/0022009421997894.

——. "'Now the UN has its first colony': Technical Assistance and Informal Trusteeship during the UN Peacekeeping Mission in Congo, 1960." Julius Heise, Maria Ketzmerick, and Jan Lüdert, eds., The United Nations Trusteeship System: Legacies, Continuities, and Change, Global Institutions (London: Routledge, forthcoming).

Turner, Oliver. "'Finishing the Job': The UN Special Committee on Decolonization and the Politics of Self-Governance." *Third World Quarterly* 34, no. 7 (2013): 1193–1208.

Twitchett, Kenneth J. "The Colonial Powers and the United Nations." *Journal of Contemporary History* 4, no. 1 (1969): 167–85.

Unger, Corinna. *International Development: A Postwar History*. London: Bloomsbury Academic, 2018.

Urbano, Annalisa. "A 'Grandiose Future for Italian Somalia': Colonial Developmentalist Discourse, Agricultural Planning, and Forced Labor (1900–1940)." *International Labor and Working-Class History* 92 (2017): 69–88.

——. "Imagining the Nation, Crafting the State: The Politics of Nationalism and Decolonisation in Somalia (1940–60)." Doctoral dissertation, University of Edinburgh, 2012.

Van Beusekom, Monica. *Negotiating Development : African Farmers and Colonial Experts at the Office du Niger, 1920–1960*. Portsmouth: Heinemann, 2002.

Van Bilsen, Jef. *L'indépendance du Congo*. Tournai: Casterman, 1962.

Vandewalle, Dirk. *A History of Modern Libya*. Cambridge: Cambridge University Press, 2017.

Van Reybrouck, David. *Congo: The Epic History of a People*. London: Fourth Estate, 2014.

Vanthemsche, Guy. *Belgium and the Congo, 1885–1980*. Cambridge: Cambridge University Press, 2012.

Verna, Chantalle F. "Haiti, the United Nations, and Decolonization in the Congo." In Eggers, Pearson, and Almada e Santos, *The United Nations and Decolonization*, 127–48.

Vitalis, Robert. "The Midnight Ride of Kwame Nkrumah and Other Fables of Bandung (Ban-Doong)." *Humanity: An International Journal of Human Rights, Humanitarianism, and Development* 4, no. 2 (2013): 261–88.

——. *White World Order, Black Power Politics: The Birth of American International Relations*. Ithaca, NY: Cornell University Press, 2017.

Waal, Alex de. "The Wrong Lessons." *Boston Review* 1 December 2003. http://bostonreview.net/world/alex-de-waal-wrong-lessons.

Walker, Lydia. "Decolonization in the 1960s: On Legitimate and Illegitimate Nationalist Claims-Making." *Past & Present* 242, no. 1 (2019): 227–64.

Ware, Gilbert. "Somalia: From Trust Territory to Nation, 1950–1960." *Phylon* 26, no. 2 (1965): 173–85.

Webster, David. "Development Advisors in a Time of Cold War and Decolonization: The United Nations Technical Assistance Administration, 1950–59." *Journal of Global History* 6, no. 2 (2011): 249–72.

———. *Fire and the Full Moon: Canada and Indonesia in a Decolonizing World.* Vancouver, BC: UBC Press, 2009.

Weiss, Thomas. *UN Voices: The Struggle for Development and Social Justice.* Bloomington: Indiana University Press, 2005.

Weissman, Stephen. *American Foreign Policy in the Congo, 1960–1964.* Ithaca, NY: Cornell University Press, 1974.

Wempe, Sean Andrew. "A League to Preserve Empires: Understanding the Mandates System and Avenues for Further Scholarly Inquiry." *American Historical Review* 124, no. 5 (2019): 1723–31.

Wertheim, Stephen. "Instrumental Internationalism: The American Origins of the United Nations, 1940–3." *Journal of Contemporary History* 54, no. 2 (2019): 265–83.

———. *Tomorrow, the World: The Birth of U.S. Global Supremacy.* Cambridge, MA: Harvard University Press, 2020.

———. "Tomorrow, the World: The Birth of U.S. Global Supremacy in World War II." Doctoral dissertation, Columbia University, 2015.

Wilder, Gary. *Freedom Time: Negritude, Decolonization, and the Future of the World.* Durham, NC: Duke University Press, 2015.

Williams, A. Susan. *Who Killed Hammarskjöld?: The UN, the Cold War, and White Supremacy in Africa.* New York: Columbia University Press, 2011.

Witte, Ludo de. *The Assassination of Lumumba.* London: Verso, 2001.

Young, Alden. "A Currency for Sudan: The Sudanese National Economy and Postcolonial Development." In Macekura and Manela, *The Development Century*, 130–49.

———. *Transforming Sudan: Decolonization, Economic Development and State Formation.* Cambridge: Cambridge University Press, 2018.

Young, Kevin. "Purging the Forces of Darkness: The United States, Monetary Stabilization, and the Containment of the Bolivian Revolution." *Diplomatic History* 37, no. 3 (2013): 509–37.

Zanasi, Margherita. "Exporting Development: The League of Nations and Republican China." *Comparative Studies in Society and History: An International Quarterly* 49, no. 1 (2007): 143–69.

Ziemke, Earl. *The U.S. Army in the Occupation of Germany, 1944–1946.* Washington, DC: U.S. Government Printing Office, 1975.

# INDEX

Page numbers in *italics* refer to figures.

Abbas, Mekki, 244, 328–29n121, 336n219
Acheson, Dean, 148
Addis Ababa, 190
Ade, Roger, *233*
Aden, 33
Administrative Committee on
  Coordination (ACC), 183, 314n85
Adoula, Cyrille, 206–7, 236, 244–46, 334n191
Afghanistan, 192
Africa, 2, 10, 27, 50, 95, 122–23, 176–78, 181,
  192, 195, 199–200, 202, 209–10, 214, 220,
  227, 238, 248, 278n124, 322–23n35
Ahmed, Syed H., 284n43
Akabo party, 208
Alaska, 34
Albania, 312n51
Alexander, Robert, 160
Algeria, 8, 10, 94, 317n151
*Alliance de Bakongo* (Abako), 320n18
Alvarado, Julio, 136
American Federation of Labor (AFL), 135
*Amministrazione Fiduciaria Italiana della
  Somalia* (AFIS), 98–99, 101–19

Anglo-American Caribbean Commission,
  34–35
Angola, 202, 246
Angus, J. Houston, 300n48
anticolonialism, 7, 9–10, 28, 32–33, 37–39, 43,
  53–54, 65, 82, 118, 120, 177
Apter, David, 212
Arab League, 75, 284–85n56
Arab States, 318–19n4
Aramayo, Carlos Víctor, 140, 144
Arce, José, 282n19, 301n75
Argentina, 141, 157, 187
Arkadiev, G. P., 220
*Armée Nationale Congolaise* (ANC), 199, 213,
  234, 236, 239, 245–46, 321n26, 331–32n160
Asia, 2, 10, 31, 135, 176, 178, 195, 204
Assad al-Jerbi, Ali, 72
Atlantic Charter, 7, 36; British Colonial Charter
  supplement, call for, 33; signing of, 32, 33
Australia, 28, 43–44, 52, 271–72n7, 279n137
Australian New Guinea, 271–72n7. *See also*
  Papua New Guinea
Austria, 70, 144, 172, 184, 301n71

Ballivián, Hugo, 154
Bandung conference, 176–77
Bank of England, 84
Baradi, Mauro, 108
Barre, Siad, 101
Baudouin, King, 213
Bayalinov, Kassymaly, 45
Bel, Albert J. P. L., 284n43
Belgian Congo, 49–50, 202, 209–10, 235. See also Congo
Belgian Ruanda-Urundi, 271–72n7. See also Burundi, Rwanda
Belgium, 43–44, 49, 53, 193, 198–99, 202–5, 207–9, 212, 218, 228–29, 236, 243, 279n137, 317n151, 320n16, 323n40, 334n192
Benghazi, 75, 282n22
Benson, Wilfried, 51
Berbers, 67, 73
Bernadette, Count Folke, 54
Bevin-Sforza compromise, 65, 69
Bey, Fadel, 101, 104
Bey Mizran, Mustafa, 61
Bey, Selim, 82
Biafra, 230
Blelloch, David, 135, 141–42, 300n48, 301n66, 301n67
Bloch, Henry S., 211, 220–22, 325n58, 327n99
Blowers, G. A., 84–86, 287n102, 287n103, 287n107
Bohan, Merwin, 135
Böhm von Bawerk, Eugen, 119
Bolivia, 6, 12, 23, 25, 81, 93, 124, 172, 175–76, 183, 185–86, 200, 252, 299n33, 301n66, 306n136; Altiplano regions, 133, 153; American loans, dependent on, 134; anti-U.S. sentiment in, 158; currency, devaluation of, 161–62; dire economic conditions in, 161; elite in, 133–34; indigenous peoples, 133, 153; inequity in, 133–34, 141; inflation, 161–62, 164; instability and "underdevelopment" in, 157; junta in, 154; Keenleyside mission to, 138–50, 157, 165; Lend-Lease program, 135; miner's strike, 126; monetary stabilization program, 161–65; old order in, 134; public administration, importance of, 143; "rule of experts," 163; tin industry, 130–37, 141, 145–47, 151–53, 164; UN assistance to, 125–30, 136–38, 155–57, 159–64, 166; UN Indigenous Population Project, 301n66; UN mandate in, 132; UN program, as attack on Bolivian sovereignty, 158; US investment in, 134–36, 162, 164, 308n169
Bond, W., 294n74
Brazil, 56, 89, 157, 184; training and research center or international administration, call for, 173–74, 188–89
Britain, 5, 7–8, 12, 31–32, 36, 38–39, 43–45, 53, 63–66, 69, 72–89, 94–95, 98, 101–2, 104, 121, 124, 134–35, 140, 185, 186–88, 193, 202, 204, 264n23, 277n91, 279n137, 297n125, 315n119, 317n151, 322–23n35, 334n192; international regional commissions, proposal of, 34–35; and Palestine, 54; technical assistance from, 195
British Cameroons, 271–72n7
British Colonial Office, 181–82
British Empire, 32–33, 45, 181
British Guiana, 162
British Military Administration (Somaliland), 100–101
British Somaliland, 100, 291n10. See also Somali Republic
British Tanganyika, 271–72n7. See also Tanzania
British Togoland, 271–72n7. See also Ghana
Broadly, Herbert, 80; "New Rome," dream of, 81
Bulgaria, 172, 312n51
Bunche, Ralph, 12, 20, 27–29, 49, 111, 113, 276n83, 278n124, 281n7, 290n2, 294n79, 294n79, 294–95n85, 321n26, 322n33, 326n78, 328–29n121, 327n96, 328n106, 336n229; colonialism, critique of, 50–51; communist, accusations of, 212, 325–26n68; Congo, mission to, 209–18,

220–21, 223–24, 246; and decolonization, 51–52; Middle East, peacekeeping in, 54; Nobel Peace Prize, awarding of, 54–55
Burma, 57, 189, 323n36
Burney, Christopher, 284n43
Burns, Alan, 45
Burundi, 271–72n7. *See also* Belgian Ruanda-Urundi

Caffari, V., 294n74
Cairo, 75, 104–5, 284–85n56
Calder, Ritchie, 336n215
Cambodia, 190, 253, 312n51
Cameroon, 271–72n7. *See also* French Cameroons
Canada, 138–40, 173, 182, 184, 204, 264n23, 315m119
Carman, John, 160
Carnegie Endowment for International Peace, 69, 122
Carpio, Victorio, 103–4
Castagno, Alphonso, 122, 297n131
Castello, Edmondo de Holte, 104–5, 292n29
Cebe-Habersky, J. J., 121
Central African Republic, 202
Central Bank, 161
Central Intelligence Agency (CIA), 205, 207–8, 321n26, 322–23n35
Cevallos, Jaime Palenque, 305n132
Ceylon, 189, 226, 312n51
Chad, 40
Chile, 14, 57
China, 14, 26–28, 32, 36, 52, 56, 172–73, 207–8, 264n23, 312n51
Churchill, Winston, 32
Cold War, 4–5, 7, 11, 13, 25, 27, 168, 176–77, 179, 188, 198–203, 211–12, 218, 248–49, 251, 253–54, 268n72
Collins, Carole, 211–12
Colombia, 15, 56, 66, 98–99, 103–4
colonialism, 1, 10–11, 42, 50–51, 54, 200, 213; colonial world, 36, 41; internationalization of, 78

*Compagnie du Chemin de Fer du Bas-Congo au Katanga* (BCK), 319n11
*Confédération des Associations Tribales du Katanga* (CONAKAT), 320n19
*Conferenza per la Somalia*, 100–101
Congo, 6, 25, 92–93, 124, 201, 209–10, 252–53, 322n33, 327n101, 332–33n171, 336n215, 337n235; agriculture, 235; as American colony, 337n234; Baluba ethnic group, 229, 243, 331–32n160; Belgian soldiers in, 213, 218; colonial bureaucracy of, 202–3; Congo Fund, 246; constitutional crisis of, 205, 234–35, 241, 321n26; Council of Commissioners, 205; debt of, 203; decolonization, 245; emergency food relief program, 218–19; experts in, 334n192; famine conditions, 229–30, 243; *Force Publique*, 208, 213; and genocide, 204–5; houseboys, 331n157; joining forces against UN, 244; judicial system, 236–37; on-the-job training, 233; Kasai Province, 230, 238, 240–41; Katanga, 199, 202–8, 217–18, 224, 236, 240, 244–45, 319n11, 321n24, 322–23n35, 330–31n144, 331–32n160; Kitona, 208; Kivu, 323n38; "Luluabourg Constitution," UN drafting of, 237; medical teams, 227; mining, 235–36, 331–32n160; mutiny in, 203; new civilian government, election of, 244–45; Orientale, 323n38; public debt, 320n16; public works, 228; OPEX services, 222–23; resident representative, 210–11; resource extraction, 202; and secession, 204–7, 217–18, 224, 229, 236, 243, 245–46, 327n96, 331–32n160; education, 232–34; and self-government, 212; South Kasai, 204, 229, 236, 243–44, 321n24, 331–32n160; sovereignty of, 225, 244; Soviet takeover, threat of, 211–12; state-building, 237–38, 248; Ten-Year Development Plan, 320n16; unemployed, as threat to, 228–29; UN civilian effort in, 218–20, 223–24, 226, 229–31, 233, 241–42, 246; UN "Congo Club," 212, 220, 221,

Congo (*continued*)
  328n106; UN consultants, 222–23, 225–26, 245; UN intervention, repercussions of, 249; UN military assistance, request for, 217–18; UN neutrality, problem of, 241–42; UN peacekeeping force in, 248–50; UN relief programs, 239; UN restoration of law and order, 236–37, 245, 247–48; UN technical assistance, 213–16, 218, 224–25, 234, 241–42, 244, 246–48; UN troops in, 199, 204–7, 224, 238–39, 246, 248
Congo Crisis, 13, 193–94, 198–99, 201–2, 217, 232, 248–49, 254
Congo Group, 220, 328n106
*conquistadores*, 133
Cordier, Andrew, 78, 205–6, 211–12, 220, 234–35, 283n37, 321n25, 322n33, 328–29n121, 329n125
Corea, Claude, 226
Costa Rica, 174
Council of Foreign Ministers, 64–65
Coursin, Leon H. E., 300n48
Cremona, Paul, 284n43
Crespo Gutiérrez, Alberto, 305n132
Crespo Rodas, Alfonso, 154
Cripps, Stafford, 177
Croatia, 253
Cuba, 207–8
Cyprus, 338n3
Czechoslovakia, 184

Dahomey, 49, 51, 209–10
Danzig, 172
David, Jean, 329n125
Dayal, Rajeshwar, 206, 212, 220, 240, 243–44, 321n26, 322n33, 328n106, 328–29n121, 329n125, 330n143, 332n167, 336n219
Dean, William H., 78–79, 81, 111, 113, 294n74, 294n79, 294n80, 294–95n85; racism toward, 112
decolonization, 2, 4–5, 8, 10, 13, 17, 27, 29, 51–52, 59, 62, 67, 96, 122–24, 129, 166–68, 176, 179, 188, 191–93, 196, 199, 204, 245, 249, 252–53; nation-state, as logical outcome of, 251; "natural" course of, 197; state sovereignty, 197
Deeb, Goro, 107
de Gaulle, Charles, 68, 291n10
de la Roche, Jean, 1–2, 12, 21–22, 39–43, 103–4, 106, 108, 116–17, 276n78, 293n54, 296n111
Denmark, 279n137
"developing countries," 2, 17–18, 20, 62, 165, 168, 170–75, 179–80, 185–89, 195–96, 252, 261n5, 309n8, 309–10n19, 313n63, 317n151
Di Stefano, Mario, 294n79
Djibouti, 291n10. *See also* French Somaliland
Djojohadikusumo, Sumitro, 311n41
Dominican Republic, 98
Dorn, Glen, 133–34, 145, 151, 160, 303n95, 303n100, 308n169
Dorsinville, Max H., 328–29n121
Drummond, Eric, 71
Du Bois, W. E. B., 38
Dulles, Allen, 315n110
Dutch East Indies, 70, 174

East Africa, 49, 98, 194–95, 286n98
East Asia, 7
East Timor, 25, 249, 253
Éboué, Félix, 40
Eden, Anthony, 283n28
Eder, George Jackson, 164–65
Egypt, 26–27, 54–55, 57, 65–68, 70, 73–75, 77, 83, 85, 89, 94, 98–99, 104–6, 174, 186–87, 227, 284–85n56, 297n125, 312n51, 317n151, 318–19n4
Einstein, Albert, 302n90
Eisenhower, Dwight D., 161–62, 325–26n68
Eisenhower, Milton, 162
Eritrea, 63–65, 290n2; as autonomous territory, 66; Ethiopia, merge with, 282n21
Estonia, 172
Ethiopia, 65–66, 84, 98, 100–102, 106, 172, 190, 192, 214, 217; Eritrea, merge with, 282n21

"Eurafrica," 177
Europe, 2, 7, 11–13, 16, 25–26, 31, 33, 50, 53, 55, 57, 92, 146, 174, 182, 190, 202, 240, 317n151; Eastern Europe, 168, 177, 192, 227, 314n87
Export-Import Bank, 132–33, 135, 153, 190

"failed states," 20, 27–28, 249, 254
Fasasi-Ayeni, 229
federalism, 41–42
Federated States of Micronesia, 271–72n7
Feldman, Ilana, 318–19n4
Feral, G., 294n74
Ferguson, James, 18
Fielding-Clarke, A., 294n74
Finkelstein, Lawrence, 52, 290n2
Finnemore, Martha, 264n24
Florman, Irving, 146–49, 302n90, 303n95
Ford Foundation, 16, 96, 195, 231
Fornari, Giovanni, 101, 113–14
France, 5, 7, 32, 36–37, 43–44, 53, 63–66, 69, 72–75, 77–80, 82–83, 85, 87–89, 94–95, 98, 124, 185, 187, 202, 204, 207, 237, 277n91, 315n119, 317n151, 334n192
Free French, 7, 40, 68
French Cameroons, 271–72n7. See also Cameroon
French Colonial Information Service, 40
French Empire, 40
French Equatorial Africa, 67
French Somaliland, 291n10. See also Djibouti
French Togoland, 271–72n7. See also Togo
French West Africa, 67
French Union, 53
Fritzle, Carl, 300n48
Frobenius, Leo, 220

Gaiduk, Ilya, 314n87
Gardiner, Robert, 230–31, 244, 328n106, 328–29n121, 336n219
Gaza Strip, 318–19n4
Gbenye, Christophe, 323n38
Geneva (Switzerland), 6

German empire, 7
Germany, 7; ordoliberal school, 169
Getachew, Adom, 10
Ghana, 209, 214, 230, 244, 271–72n7, 325n58
Gillifan, Donald W., 300n48
Gilpin, Antony, 238–241, 334n196, 334n197, 335n201, 336n219
Gizenga, Antoine, 225, 244
global governance, 5–6, 40, 254
Global North, 184
Global South, 10–11, 14, 184, 226
González-Fernández, Alberto, 284n43
Goode, Richard, 144, 300n48
"good governance," 163, 252
Goodrich, Carter, 78–83, 111, 132–33, 136–38, 143–44, 153, 155, 157–60, 162–64, 281n7, 285n65, 298n20, 299n36, 305n132, 306n136, 307n157
Grand, Albert, 284n43
Great Britain, 31–32, 64, 69, 104, 121, 188, 279n137
Great Depression, 7
Greece, 64, 89, 172, 334n192
Grossen, J., 236
Guam, 34, 37, 271n3
Guatemala, 162
Guevara Arze, Wálter, 160
Guinea, 209, 214

Hague, The, 263n19
Hahmoud, Saleh, 284n43
Haiti, 56, 84, 111, 129, 130, 137, 139, 173–74, 237, 299n38, 334n192
Hamdy, Mahmoud Moharran, 108
Hammerskjöld, Dag, 14, 24–25, 93, 124–25, 167, 170–71, 173, 178, 192, 194, 196, 198–200, 204, 209–12, 214–20, 222–24, 230, 232, 234–35, 242, 244, 248–49, 309n7, 315n110, 321n25, 324n44, 327n89, 327n99, 327n101, 328n106, 329n125, 330–31n144, 331–32n160; death of, 207, 245, 322–23n35, 326n78, 336n219, 338–39n4; International Administrative Service (IAS), proposal of,

Hammerskjöld, Dag (*continued*)
    165–66, 168, 172, 175–77, 179–91, 252;
    neocolonialism, charges of, 225–26;
    ordoliberal school, aligned with, 169;
    "underdeveloped countries," emphasis on,
    310n21; as "world's troubleshooter," 169
Harrington, Mario, 164
Hawaii, 34, 271n3
Helleiner, Eric, 268n72
Hertzog, Enrique, 126, 130, 133
Higgins, Benjamin, 89–92, 94, 220, 252,
    287n107, 288n128, 311n41
Higgins Report, 90, 93
Hitler, Adolf, 325–26n68
Hoffman, Paul G., 96, 179, 289n153,
    311–12n47, 313n63
Hoo, Victor, 28, 48–49, 54, 278n109
Hoskyns, Catherine, 329n125
Hull, Cordell, 135
humanitarianism, 253, 325n68;
    humanitarian disasters, 200, 243;
    humanitarian intervention, 230, 250;
    humanitarian rescue operations, 207–8
Hungary, 144, 172, 312n51
Hussein, Hagi Mohamed, 292n35

Idris, Sayyid, 72, 75
imperialism, 40, 50, 121, 189–90; age of, 33;
    *Yanqui* imperialism, 157
India, 14, 26–27, 70, 98, 173, 186–87, 227,
    264n23, 273n22, 312n51, 322n33
Indonesia, 8, 89, 174, 188–89, 253, 311n41,
    315n110, 338n252
inequality, 165, 169
Institute of Pacific Relations, 274n29
International Administrative Service (IAS),
    165–66, 168, 172, 175–83, 189, 252; aid
    recipients, 190; and decolonization, 188;
    donor nations, 190; feedback toward, as
    positive, 190–91; further study, suggestion
    of, 188; opposition to, 184–85, 187–88;
    reservations toward, 186–87; support for,
    191; as UN overreach, 186

International Atomic Energy Agency
    (IAEA), 269n78
International Bank for Reconstruction and
    Development (IBRD), 15, 79, 119, 155, 158.
    *See also* World Bank
International Civil Aviation Organization
    (ICAO), 227, 269n78, 331n149
International Commission of Jurists, 333n188
International Cooperation Agency (ICA),
    117, 296n109. *See also* U.S. Agency for
    International Development (USAID)
International Court of Justice, 263n19
International Labor Organization (ILO), 40,
    56, 78, 83, 132, 135, 146, 183, 222, 228–29,
    269n78, 331n158; Non-Metropolitan
    Territories Division, 142;
    Recommendation on Minimum
    Standards of Social Policy in Dependent
    Areas ("Charter for the Colonies"), 51–52
International Monetary Fund (IMF), 12–13,
    15, 79, 84–86, 129, 155, 158, 164–65, 208,
    234, 269n78, 270n86, 286n97, 320n16
internationalism, 197
internationalization of social policy, 51
International Red Cross, 327n101
international relations: Westphalian notion
    of, 2
International Telecommunications Union
    (ITU), 222, 227, 269n78
International Trade Organization (ITO),
    334n196
Iran, 190, 227, 312n51
Iraq, 8, 98, 249, 271–72n7, 312n51
Ireland, 184, 204
Iron Curtain, 184
Israel, 28, 54–55, 210, 236, 282n22, 317n151,
    318–19n4
Issa, Abudullahi, 108
Italian Somaliland, 291n10. *See also* Somali
    Republic
Italy, 11, 43–44, 66, 69, 72–73, 79, 85, 90–91,
    98–100, 110, 117, 121–22, 236, 276–77n90,
    334n192; African territories of, 63;

colonies of, 59, 61, 64–65, 68; settler colonialism, 68

Jamaica, 192
Japan, 7, 135, 138, 221, 227, 317n151
Jebb, Gladwyn, 177, 264n21
Johnston, D., 294n74
Jordan, 54–55, 312n51

Kabila, Laurent, 323n38
Kalonji, Albert, 229, 321n24, 331–32n160
Kanza, Thomas, 214, 225, 337n234
Kaplan, Robert, 337n247
Karasz, Arthur, 129, 161–65, 307n165
Karp, Mark, 118–19, 122, 296n109
Kasavubu, Joseph, 203, 205–8, 213–14, 217–18, 223, 234–35, 241, 320n18, 329n125, 334n191
Katmandu, 192
Keenleyside, Hugh, 23, 138, 140–51, 153–55, 157, 183, 186, 252, 269n79, 301n75
Keenleyside Report, 150, 154–55, 157, 163, 165. *See also* Report of the United Nations Mission of Technical Assistance to Bolivia, The
Kennedy, John F., 315n110, 328n106, 338–39n4
Kenya, 8, 49–50, 100, 210
Kenyatta, Jomo, 210
Kernan, Henry S., 300n48
Keynes, John Maynard, 169, 304n115
Khan, Muhammad Zafrullah, 282n19
Khiari, Mahmoud, 244, 336n219
Khrushchev, Nikita, 212, 226
Kirghizia (Kyrgyzstan), 45
Kismayo incident, 108
Koo, Wellington, 52–53
Kooy, W. A., 78–79
Korea, 102
Korean War, 309n12
Kosovo, 25, 249, 253

Labouisse, Henry, 328n106
Lakhdari, Abdelamek, 108
Lagos, 181

Laos, 192, 312n51
La Paz (Bolivia), 23, 93, 126, 128–34, 137, 140, 144–45, 150, 153–58, 162–63
Latin America, 9, 15, 40, 43, 65, 71–72, 132, 134, 138–39, 141, 148, 153, 155, 171, 173, 188
Laugier, Henri, 149–50
League of Nations, 4–5, 9, 31, 37, 48, 71, 102, 144, 301n71; Committee on Technical Cooperation, 14; Covenant, 271n3; International Labor Organization (ILO), 14–15; mandates system, 8, 27, 29–30, 32, 34–35, 43, 46, 49, 51, 54, 209–10, 261n3, 271–72n7, 273n24; reconstruction efforts, 172–73; resident "commissioners," 172; Secretariat Information Section, 70
Lebanon, 15, 54–56, 89, 210, 271–72n7, 312n51
Lechín, Juan, 160
Lehman, Kenneth, 299n27, 303n95, 308n169
Leopoldville, 205–7, 209, 211, 213, 216, 220, 223–24, 226, 231, 233–34, 238, 240, 244, 323n38, 331n157
Lepawsky, Albert, 300n48
Lewis, I. M., 122
Liberia, 84, 144, 172, 214
Libya, 6, 9, 11–12, 21, 59–60, 63–64, 66, 71, 81, 99–100, 105, 111, 113, 117, 124–25, 172, 177–78, 192–93, 200, 214, 220–22, 252, 254, 281n7, 283n30, 284–85n56, 285n65, 286n83, 286n97, 289n153, 290n2, 311n41, 312n51; Bevin-Sforza plan, 69; civil service, 93–95; currency of, concern over, 84–88; Cyrenaica, 67–69, 72, 75, 283n25, 283n28, 283n29, 284–85n56; development institutions, 94; economic development, 88, 90, 92–93; and education, 91; ethnicities in, 67; experience of, as sobering, 96; Fezzan, 65, 67–69, 72, 75, 94; financial assistance, 83; financial dependence, on other governments, 95; food production, 88; government, forming of, 74–76; foreign personnel in, 94; hostile natural environment of, 67; independence of, 65, 69–70, 74–75, 77, 95;

Libya (continued)
  infrastructure, 91–92; oil in, 94; Palestinian refugees, 288n123; Sanusi Order, 72; social welfare, 91; state-building, 79, 334n191; state creation, 61; technical assistance to, 77–80, 82–85, 88–89, 93–94; territories of, 67; transformation of, as UN model, 96; Tripolitania, 61, 65, 67–70, 72–76, 85, 87, 283n25, 284–85n56; trusteeship, 69; UN goal for, in agriculture, 90–91; women's work, on volunteer basis, 91
Libyan-American Technical Assistance Service, 92
Libyan Finance Corporation (LFC), 94
Libyan Public Development and Stabilization Agency (LPDSA), 94
Lie, Trygve, 43, 54, 56, 65, 70, 76, 84, 95, 102–3, 130, 146, 150, 177, 264n21, 283n37, 309n12, 31m25
Lindberg, John, 12, 83–84, 86–88, 90, 147, 286n97, 287n107, 300n48, 302n90
Linnér, Sture, 210–11, 216, 220, 222–23, 240, 244, 328–29n121, 329n125, 334n195, 336n219
Lippmann, Walter, 33
Liu, F. T., 211
Lohrmann, Ulrich, 48, 273n16
Lorentzen, Helge, 300n48
Loufti, Omar, 71
Louis, Wm. Roger, 27, 32, 69, 273n16
Lovanium Medical School, 233–34
Luard, Evan, 46, 48, 59, 282n21, 312n51
Lucas, A. J., 103–4, 292n23
Lumumba, Patrice, 203–5, 213–14, 217–18, 223–24, 234–35, 241, 320n18, 321n24, 321n2, 323n38, 329n125, 331–32n160; and genocide, 243–44; murder of, 206, 244, 330–31n144

MacFarquhar, Sir Alexander, 328n106
MacPherson, Sir John, 47
Magruder, Calvert, 135–36, 142, 299n33
Malagodi, Giovanni, 117–18, 296n109

Malik, Charles, 56
Malinowski, Bronislaw, 210
Malraux, André, 181
Manchuria, 70
Mann, Gregory, 309n9, 338n1
Mann, Peggy, 278n124
Marchino, Giacomo, 72–73
Marcus, Nathan, 301n71
Marshall Islands, 271–72n7
Marshall Plan, 96, 110
Martelli, George, 332n168
Martínez Cabañas, Gustavo, 130
Martino, Enrico, 108
Marx, Karl, 288–89n140
Matadi (Congo), 218
Matienzo, Eduardo Anze, 130
Maul, Daniel, 51–52
Mauritius, 33
Mazower, Mark, 31–32, 168; "strange triumph," 261n3, 309n9
McCarthy, Joseph, 12, 212, 325–26n68
McGill University, 177–79, 181
McLeod, A. N., 84–86, 287n102, 287n107
Meeting of Experts, 86–87, 284–85n56
Mensing, Johann P., 284n43
metropoles, 2, 7–8, 12–13, 196, 213
metropolitan policymakers, 7–8, 40, 181
Mexico, 138, 139, 187, 264n23
Middle East, 10, 28, 54, 82, 215
Miller, Edward, 148–49
Ministry of Overseas Departments and Territories, 181
*Mission de l'Organisation des Nations Unies pour la Stabilisation en Republique Democratique du Congo* (MONUSCO), 249–50
Mitchell, Timothy, 270n86
Mizran, Mustafa Bey, 72
Mobutu, Joseph, 201, 205–6, 208, 235–36, 242–44, 333n182, 333n185, 336n215; coups of, 241, 247, 321n26, 337n234, 337n235
modernization theory, 212, 304n115
modernity, 91

INDEX 371

Mogadishu, 61–63, 65–66, 97–99, 101, 103–6, 108, 114–17, 121, 290n5; "the Lido," UN headquarters of, 107
Mohamud, Abdullah Issa, 106
Montenegro, Walter, 305n132
Monture, G. C., 300n48
Morocco, 214, 312n51
*Mouvement National Congolais* (MNC), 320n18
*Movimiento Nacionalista Revolucionario* (MNR), 128–29, 134, 154, 156–58, 160–64, 302n78, 307n165; land reform, 159; mining business, nationalization of, 159
Mulele, Pierre, 323n38
Myrdal, Alva, 81, 131, 151, 298n15
Myrdal, Gunnar, 298n15, 304n115

Namibia, 10, 43, 338n252. *See also* South West Africa
Namikas, Lise, 211, 321n26, 322n33, 330n143, 334n191
Narasimhan, Chakravarthi V., 328n106
National Association for the Advancement of Colored People (NAACP), 38
National Bank, 94
National Congress Party, 72
nationalism, 1, 31, 41–42, 48, 68, 212
National School of Law and Administration, 231
National Stabilization Council: "Fifty-Step-Plan," in Bolivia, 164–65
nation-states, 4, 19, 25, 42, 122, 124, 251; multilateral cooperation, 2
Nauru, 271–72n7
neocolonialism, 184, 186, 225
Netherlands, 70, 174, 185, 253, 279n137, 315n110
New Deal, 78
New International Economic Order (NIEO), 14, 15, 56, 309–10n19
New York, 6, 19, 28, 98–99, 168, 189, 197, 199, 223, 227, 238, 263n19, 263–4n20
New Zealand, 43–44, 48, 271–72n7, 279n137
Nigeria, 181–82, 230, 244, 271–72n7

noninterference, 11, 59, 173, 200, 223, 225, 247–49, 251–52
North Africa, 64, 68, 223
North America, 16, 174, 190, 223
Northern Mariana Islands, 271–72n7
Nwokedi, Francis, 244, 328n106
Nyasaland, 202

O'Brien, Conor Cruise, 326n78
Office of Inter-American Affairs (OIAA), 132, 135
Ofuatey-Kodjoe, W., 278n124
O'Malley, Alanna, 263n16
*Opération des Nations Unies au Congo* (ONUC), 25, 198–199, 201, 205–7, 212, 220–21, 224, 226–27, 230, 231, 232, 233, 234–35, 250, 253, 321n26, 322n33, 329n125, 330n143, 332n167, 332n168, 333n185, 335n212, 336n215; civilian operations, 228, 237–39, 244–45, 252; domestic security, 236; end of, 246; noninterference, 200, 223, 247, 249; peacekeeping, 249; relief work, 243; social welfare work, 229; as turning point, 252; UN consultative group, 241
Operation Dragon Rouge, 208
Operation Rum Punch, 206–7
Operations in the Congo. See *Opération des Nations Unies au Congo* (ONUC)
Orford, Anne, 169, 254, 264–65n26, 309n7, 309n11, 339n8
Organization for Economic Co-operation and Development (OECD), 194
Ortiz Benítez, Lucas, 300n48
Osorio-Tafall, Bibiano F., 328–29n121
Ottoman Empire, 68, 283n29
Owen, David, 78, 177–78, 209, 264n21, 311–12n47, 334n196

Pakistan, 65–66, 70, 73–75, 77, 85, 94, 173, 184, 227, 284–85n56
Palau, 271–72n7
Palestine, 14, 28, 43, 54, 210, 271–72n7, 276n83

Panama, 192
Pan-Arabism, 105
Pandit, Vijaya L., 29, 273n22
Papua New Guinea, 47. *See also* Australian New Guinea
Paris Peace Conference, 48
Paris Peace Treaty, 63
Pastrana, Vicente, 103
Pate, Maurice, 219, 327n101
Paz Estenssoro, Víctor, 128, 154, 159, 161, 163–64
Pearson, Jessica L., 10, 54
Pechanec, J., 294n74
Pedersen, Susan, 8, 168, 261n3, 273n24
Pelt, Adrian, 12, 21–22, 65–66, 69–73, 75–88, 90, 92–96, 209, 281n7, 282n19, 283n37, 283n38, 284n43, 284–85n56, 286n83, 287n112, 324n44; advisory nature, 74; Council for Libya, relationship with, 74
Pérez-Guerrero, Manuel, 131
Peru, 57, 140
Philippines, 52, 66, 89, 98–99, 103, 105–6
Pintos, Jerome, 284n43
Poland, 173–74, 264n23, 314n87
Porter, Louis H., 267n56
Portugal, 279n137
postcolonial world, 2, 8, 10–11, 19, 24, 62, 103, 123, 169, 176, 180, 183–84, 198, 203, 249, 252, 270n86
Poulgrain, Greg, 315n110, 338–39n4
Power, Thomas, 71, 84, 98, 284n41, 284n43, 285n65, 290n2
Poynton, Hilton, 45
Prashad, Vijay, 309n6
Prebisch, Raúl, 14, 325n58
Price, Byron, 149–50
Pruden, Caroline, 188
public administration, 16–18, 25, 62, 77, 80, 89, 95, 99, 142–44, 156, 173, 178, 182, 184, 188–89, 191, 196, 222; development, link with, 172; as universal technical skill, 17, 174–75

Qadara, Mansur Bey, 87

racism, 111–12, 213
Ranshofen-Wertheimer, Egon, 102–3
Reconstruction Finance Corporation, 145
Red Cross, 227
Report of the United Nations Mission of Technical Assistance to Bolivia, The, 150, 152, 153; "Bolivian Paradox," 151. *See also* Keenleyside Report
Republic of China (Taiwan), 173, 204
Republic of Congo (Congo-Brazzaville), 202, 214
Restrepo, Carlos Lleras, 56
Reynalds, Jean, 232
Rhodesia, 202, 246, 322–23n35
Rico, Remberto Capriles, 305n132
Rietkerk, 334n195
Rikhye, Jit, 220, 333n185
Rivlin, Benjamin, 282n10, 282n11
Rockefeller Foundation, 16
Rockefeller, Nelson, 132
Rojas, Casto, 305n132
Romania, 312n51
Rome, 68, 110–11, 113–14
Romulo, Carlos P., 38, 52
Roosevelt, Franklin D., 32, 36, 135; international trusteeship, conception of, 33–34
Rosenborg, Ansgar, 324n44
Rosenstein-Rodan, Paul, 311n41
Rostow, Walt Whitman, 122, 288–89n140, 304n115, 311n41
Ruanda-Urundi, 202
Russia, 297n125. *See also* Soviet Union
Rwanda, 49, 271–72n7. *See also* Belgian Ruanda-Urundi

Saar Territory, 172
Salah, Kamal al din-, 292n35
Samoa, 37, 271–72n7. *See also* Western Samoa
Sanusi-al, Sayyid Idris, 283n29

Sanusi Order, 68–69, 283n29
Schachter, Oscar, 220–21, 328n106
Schlesinger, Arthur, 246
Schreiber, Marc, 284n43
Schumpeter, Joseph, 304n115
Seldenrath, Theodore R., 300n48
self-determination, 7, 10, 166, 197, 251; government bureaucracies, impediment of, 95; state sovereignty, 252; as term, vagueness of, 276n78
self-government, 9, 20, 29–30, 32–34, 37–39, 48, 58–59, 65, 69, 78, 97–98, 108–10, 122, 181–82, 212, 224, 262n10, 276n178
Sen, B. R., 186–87, 235
*servicios*, 132
settler colonialism, 68
Sharia law, 71
*shir*, 109
Shore, Taylor, 55, 103–4, 107, 112, 292n23, 292n29, 293n49, 294n80, 294–95n85
Siles Zuazo, Hernán, 156, 158, 160
Sinclair, Guy Fiti, 2, 264–65n26
Singapore, 33
Singer, Hans, 14, 151, 304n115
Slim, Mongi, 226
Smith, George Ivan, 26, 328n106
Société Internationale Forestière et Minière du Congo (Fominière), 319n11
Somalia, 21–22, 64–65, 101, 106, 119, 122, 292n35, 293n49; clan system, 123; clientelist relationship, with sponsor countries, 99; decolonization, 123; ethnic warfare, 123; international development assistance, dependence on, 123; state-building, 99–100; state collapse, 123. See also Somaliland
Somali Constitutional Independent Party (HDMS), 106
Somali Republic, 62, 122–23. See also British Somaliland, Italian Somaliland
Somaliland, 6, 9, 11, 21, 27, 59–60, 63–64, 78–79, 104, 112, 125, 172, 178, 209, 221–22, 254, 271–72n7, 276–77n90, 281n7, 282n12, 290n2, 290n5, 294n79; anti-American Egyptian influence in, 121; Arabic, widespread use of, 105; as "backward," 97; children, mortality rate of, 115; diseases, campaign to fight, 115; District and Municipal Councils, 109–10; economic development, 116–17, 120–21; education in, 114–15; famine, combating of, 115; foreign capital assistance, 119; granting of sovereignty, as mistake, 120; independence, 97, 103, 122–23; international agencies, support from, 117; international ground assistance, 115–16; "Italian" plan, criticism of, 118–19; Legislative Assembly, 109; nomad population, 103, 110; patronizing attitude by UN officials, 107; post-independence financial support, 121; psychological malaise in, 117; recommendations for, 113; self-government, transfer to, 109; state creation, 61; state-building, 99, 102–3, 105–6, 108; technical assistance, 110–11, 115–16, 124; Territorial Council, 109, 117; tribalism, 110; troops in, 101; as UN trust territory, 66–67, 98–99, 100–102, 107, 123; UN visiting mission, 118; U.S. assistance to, 116. See also Somalia, Somali Republic
Somali Youth League (SYL), 100–102, 106, 109, 117, 292n35, 293n57
Soumialot, Gaston, 323n38
South Africa, 10, 43, 49–50, 139, 210, 271–72n7, 279n137, 322–23n35, 338n252
South America, 131
South West Africa, 10, 43, 271–72n7. See also Namibia
sovereignty, 1–2, 8, 18, 20, 23, 31–32, 35, 42, 59, 62, 76, 80, 98–99, 120, 122–24, 173, 177, 179. See also state sovereignty
Soviet Union, 7, 9–10, 16, 32, 36, 39, 44–45, 64, 66–67, 143, 189–90, 201, 204–5, 207–8, 210, 218, 224–26, 248, 264n23, 309n12, 317n151, 325–26n68, 330n143, 331–32n160; national liberation, 26. See also Russia

Spain, 279n137, 334n192
*Special Comité du Katanga*, 319n11
Speich-Chassé, Daniel, 19
Spinelli, Pier Pasquale, 101, 209
Stahn, Carsten, 339n7
Stalin, Joseph, 16, 149
state-building, 6–7, 13, 18–19, 21, 31, 60–63, 67, 70, 79, 95, 97, 99, 102, 237–38, 248, 251, 334n191; de-politicizing of, 105; as technical challenge, 96, 123–24
state creation: deadline method, 61
state sovereignty, 2, 4, 18, 251; administrative capacity, tied to, 168; and decolonization, 166–67, 197; and self-determination, 183–84, 197, 252; "strange triumph," 261n3
Stimson, Henry, 36
Stockholm School, 169
Storie, R. Earl, 300n48
strategic trust territories, 36, 275n54, 276–77n90, 283n30. *See also* Trust Territory of the Pacific Islands
Sudan, 168, 184, 192, 202, 214, 217, 312n51
Suez Crisis, 200, 210, 318–19n4, 326n78
Suharto: New Order regime, 311n41
Sweden, 54, 204; Swedish socialism, 12, 83
Switzerland, 237, 334n192
Syria, 54–55, 271–72n7, 312n51

Tanganyika, 48, 202
Tanzania, 271–72n7. *See also* British Tanganyika
technical assistance 4, 16, 17, 31, 55–59, 129, 149, 172, 174, 176, 186–87, 193–97, 199, 251, 317n151; to Bolivia, 125, 131, 142–43, 154, 157–63; to Congo, technical assistance, 213–16, 218, 224–25, 234, 241–42, 244, 246–48; to Latin America, 132; to Libya, 77–80, 82–85, 88–89, 93–94; to Somaliland, 110–11, 115–16, 124
Thant, U, 207, 245–46, 323n36, 336n219
Third World, 4, 11, 14, 24, 168, 188, 211, 226, 267n56, 309n6

Togo, 271–72n7. *See also* French Togoland
Togoland, 49, 51, 209–10
Touré, Ahmed Sékou, 324n44
Toye, John, 171, 310n21
Toye, Richard, 171, 310n21
Transjordan, 271–72n7
Treaty of Friendship, 323n40
Tripoli, 61–63, 65–66, 70–71, 73–76, 79, 82–84, 90, 93–95, 282n22, 285n65
Truman, Harry S., 147, 325–26n68; Point IV speech, 13–16, 57, 139, 171–72
trusteeship, 20, 69; colonial, 9, 29, 32, 59, 262n10; international, 4, 11, 27, 33–34, 36, 39–40, 49, 123, 252, 274n38; trusteeship system, 8–9, 20, 27–28, 58, 60, 64, 97, 210
Trust Territory of the Pacific Islands, 271–72n7. *See also* Strategic Trust Territories
Tshombe, Moïse, 203, 206–7, 217–18, 224, 229, 246, 320n19, 327n96, 327n97, 334n191
Tunisia, 67–68, 73, 89, 95, 214, 226, 244, 312n51, 334n192
Turkey, 94, 174

Uganda, 49–50, 202, 210, 212
*Union Minière de Haut-Katanga* (UMHK), 319n11, 320n19
United Arab Republic, 214, 334n192
United Libya Kingdom, 62
United Nations (UN), 13, 17, 26, 31, 33–47, 49, 52–53, 71, 101, 107, 116–17, 122, 136–39, 141, 147–48, 151, 153, 154, 170, 203, 208; "administering authorities," 58–59, 61–62, 77–78, 81–83, 88, 90–92, 98; administrative assistance, 145–46, 166–68; administrative assistance, as unbiased, 167; African member states, admittance to, 192; assistance programs, 190, 312n50, 315n119; behavioral guidelines, 90; "Bolivian Dilemma," 156; capital assistance, 14; claim to neutrality, hollowness of, 190; and colonies, 58–59; colonialism, ending of, 4, 30; colonial trusteeship, 9, 29, 32, 59,

262n10; competence, questioning of, 173–74; Congo Crisis, response to, 193–94, 198–201; as coordinating agency, 173; Declaration by the United Nations on National Independence, 35; decision-making process, as cumbersome, 183, 188; decolonization, 10, 29, 59, 62, 67, 96, 124, 129, 168, 177, 191, 196–97, 199, 204, 249, 251–53; "dependent peoples," 33–35, 41–42; "dependent territories," 9–10, 37–38, 42; "developing countries," 62, 174–75, 180, 252, 309–10n19; development assistance, 18–25, 62; European Office of, 70; experts, 19, 22, 62, 79–80, 88, 90–91, 93–94, 124, 130–31, 140, 144, 150, 152, 160–61, 163, 184, 187, 189, 222–23, 234, 236, 243, 245, 311n41, 332n170, 334n192; experts, as "birds of passage," 89; failed states, 254; founding of, 2, 4, 8, 36; founding member states, 32, 36, 43–44; functional units of, 5; imperial powers and former territories, bridge between, 181; as important actor, in global history, 6; industrialized world, focus on, 56; international bureaucracy of, 5; international development assistance, shift of attitudes toward, 196–97; Libya, experience in, as precedent, 96; membership of, 2; member states, 58, 61, 94, 98, 123, 129, 143, 173, 176–77, 183, 189, 191–93, 201, 205, 209, 226, 246, 250, 252–54, 282n21; member states, inequalities among, 56; nation-states, 2; noninterference, mandate of, 11, 59, 200, 225, 248, 251–52; overreach, worries over, 18, 186; peacekeeping missions, 19, 210, 248–49, 253; post colonial world, central role in, 2; public administration, 173–75, 182; rehabilitation and reconstruction, work of, 55; resident representatives, 16; scientific rationality, 19; security, concept of, 253; self-determination, 4, 95, 251–52; self-government, 59; significance of, 59; and sovereignty, 173, 177, 179; state-building, 61–63, 67, 95–97, 99–100, 102–3, 105–6, 248, 251; state-building, as technical challenge for, 96, 123–24; state sovereignty, 197, 252; as stopgap organization, 167; system of, as vast, 5; Tanganyika, visiting mission to, 48;, 55–59, 78–79, 82–85, 88; technical assistance 55–59, 78–79, 82–85, 88–89, 93–94, 110, 111, 124–25, 129, 131, 143, 149, 172, 174, 176, 186–87, 193–94, 196–97, 199, 234, 251, 317n151; too little power of, 248; trusteeship system, 8–9, 20, 27–28, 58, 60, 64, 97, 210; trust territories, 8–9, 58, 271–72n7; underdeveloped countries, assistance to, 56–57, 172; United States, as synonymous, 12, 155–58; U.S. government, working relationship with, 129; world order, shape of, 1; visiting missions, 118. *See also* specific UN agencies

UN Advisory Committee on the Congo (UNACC), 226, 335n212

UN Advisory Council for Somaliland, 66–67, 98–99, 101–4, 107, 110, 115–16; dysfunction of, 106; watch-dog function of, 105, 108

UN Charter, 15, 28, 40, 46, 52–53, 150, 175, 225, 262n10, 264–65n26; and colonies, 37; Declaration Regarding Non-Self-Governing Territories, 9, 20, 27, 29, 32, 37, 271n3; security, and global welfare, 170; self-determination, 4; self-government, 29–30

UN Children's Emergency Fund (UNICEF), 115, 218–19, 233, 327n101

UN Conciliation Commission, 330n143

UN Conference on Trade and Development (UNCTAD), 14, 309–10n19

UN Conference on International Organization: in San Francisco, 29, 32, 284n41

UN Council for Libya, 70–73, 76, 79, 85, 284–85n56; advisory nature of, 74; developmental appraisal, 82–83; and state-building, 96

UN Department of Economic and Social Affairs, 87, 129–32, 177
UN Department of Trusteeship and Information from Non-Self-Governing Territories, 27, 30–31, 40, 48, 51–52, 54–55, 57–58, 115, 182, 210, 220; Trusteeship Division and Palestine, 54
UN Economic Commission for Asia and the Far East (ECAFE), 334n196
UN Economic Commission for Latin America (ECLA), 173, 268n64
UN Economic and Social Council (ECOSOC), 5, 58, 165, 183–84, 225, 304n108; "Expert Assistance to Member Governments" resolution, 56; UN Technical Assistance Committee, 150
UN Educational, Scientific and Cultural Organization (UNESCO), 15, 77, 79–80, 94, 183, 194, 222, 231–32, 233, 245, 269n78, 331n158; Five Year Program for Educational Development, 114
UN Emergency Force (UNEF), 318–19n4
UN Expanded Program for Technical Assistance (EPTA), 93, 193–94, 269n78, 280n155. See also UNDP, UN Special Fund for Development
UN Food and Agriculture Organization (FAO), 15, 40, 56, 79–80, 132–33, 183, 222, 235, 269n78, 304n108
UN General Assembly, 4, 11, 14–15, 21, 28, 39, 43, 56, 75–78, 87, 92, 94, 97, 105–6, 109, 119, 121–22, 130, 173, 183, 189, 193, 205, 216, 225–26, 246, 282n21, 304n108; Bevin-Sforza plan, defeat of, 69; Committee of 24, 59; colonialism, 54; Committee on Information from Non-Self-Governing Territories, 9–10, 30, 38, 52–54, 59, 209; Congo Fund, 246; Council for Libya, 65–66, 70–74; Declaration on Granting Independence to Colonial Peoples, 10; "Disposal of the former Italian colonies," 65; Fourth Committee on Trust and Non-Self-Governing Territories, 48, 59;

Fourth Committee for Non-Self-Governing and Trust Territories, 116; self-determination, 10; Special Committee on Palestine, 54; state-building, 61; "Technical Assistance for Economic Development," 57
UN Indigenous Population Project: in Bolivia, 301n66
UN International Administrative Service (IAS), 165–66, 169, 197; as consequential, 168; state sovereignty, administrative capacity, tied to, 168
UN Monetary and Financial Conference, 15
UN New International Economic Order (NIEO), 14, 15, 56, 309–10n19
UN Palestine Commission, 54
UN Program for the Provision of Operational and Executive Personnel (OPEX), 24–25, 168–69, 191–93, 196, 215, 311–12n47, 315n110. See also UN International Administrative Service (IAS)
UN Relief and Rehabilitation Administration (UNRRA), 55–56, 130–32
UN Relief and Works Agency for Palestine Refugees (UNRWA), 288n123, 328n106
UN Secretariat, 2, 9–10, 13, 29, 39, 43–44, 46–47, 49, 53, 56, 61, 63, 66, 67, 94, 98, 99, 102, 106, 112, 116, 124, 130–31, 138, 150, 155, 158, 177, 179, 188–90, 199, 208–11, 223, 225–27, 242, 252–53, 263–4n20, 269n78, 277n91, 310–11n33; Africa Unit, 111; agenda, pursuit of, 6; as apolitical, presented as, 5; "Congo account," 222; decolonization, facilitating of, 4, 6, 8, 11, 30; Department of Conference and General Services, 70; Department of Economic Affairs, 78, 111, 238; dependent territories, 11, 30; development thinking, contributions to, 6; diversify, push to, 12; empire building, 185; Expanded Program

for Technical Assistance (EPTA), 16–17, 57; OPEX, 191–97, 200; Public Administration Division, 174; public administration guidelines, 174–75; Social Activities Division, 78–79; state-building, shaping of, 6–7, 70, 237–38; technical assistance, 4, 16–17, 31; Technical Assistance Administration (TAA), 16, 183, 186; trust territories, 59. *See also* UN Department of Trusteeship and Information from Non-Self-Governing Territories

UN Security Council, 4, 36, 43–44, 54, 169, 201, 213, 237, 276–77n90, 304n108, 309n12; Congo Crisis, 199–200, 204, 206, 215–16, 218–19, 221, 224, 226, 244; UN Military Observer Group in India and Pakistan (UNMOGIP), 318–19n4

UN Special Fund for Development, 96, 313n63

UN system, 5, 15–16, 32, 186, 194–95, 197, 200

UN Technical Assistance Board (TAB), 209, 281n7, 304n108

UN Technical Assistance Committee (TAC), 183, 304n108

UN Temporary Executive Authority (UNTEA): in West New Guinea, 253, 338n252

UN Transition Assistance Group, 338n252

UN Truce Supervision Organization (UNTSO): in South West Africa/Nambia, 318–19n4

UN Trusteeship Council, 5, 9, 36, 39, 43–46, 48, 52, 54, 58–59, 98, 103–5, 107–8, 116–17, 119; trust territories, 53

UN Trusteeship Division. *See* UN Department of Trusteeship and Information from Non-Self-Governing Territories

United States, 5–9, 11, 13, 16, 26, 38–39, 43–44, 52, 64–66, 85, 87, 91–92, 94–95, 98–99, 104, 115–16, 121, 128, 134–36, 138–39, 145–48, 151, 153–54, 162–63, 165, 182, 188, 201–3, 208, 210, 217–18, 225, 236, 245, 264n23, 276–77n90, 277n91, 290n2, 315n119, 317n151, 320n16; anticolonial self-image, 271n3; Congo, investment in, 246–47; empire, internationalization of, 34; foreign aid, 120; Latin America, technical assistance to, 132; Pacific, postwar control of bases in, 35–36territorial expansion of military power, 36; trusteeship, 27; UN, setting up of, 31–32; UN, as synonymous, 12, 155–58

United States Agency for International Development (USAID), 246–47

Universal Postal Union (UPU), 269n78

Únzaga, Óscar, 301n75

Urbano, Annalisa, 282n12

Urquhart, Brian, 54, 211, 213, 215, 221, 226, 324n44, 325–26n68, 326n78, 327n96

Urriolagoitia, Mamerto, 133, 136, 145–48, 154, 161, 302n86

U.S. Agency for International Development (USAID), 117, 270n86. *See also* International Cooperation Agency (ICA)

Vandewalle, Dirk, 283n26
van Mook, Hubertus, 174
Van Reybrouck, David, 327n97
Vanthemsche, Guy, 320n16
Veillet-Lavallée, Francis, 238, 240–41
Venezuela, 174
Vietnam, 190
Villaroel, Gualberto, 134, 299n27
Virgin Islands, 111
von Horn, Carl, 223

Wachtmeister, Wilhelm, 328n106
Wake Island, 37
Walton, Edith, 118, 296n111
Watt, Robert J., 135–36
Webster, David, 311n41
Weintraub, David, 131–32

Welles, Sumner, 33
Wertheim, Stephen, 32
West Africa, 49
West Germany, 204
Western Samoa, 48, 271–72n7. *See also* Samoa
West New Guinea, 253, 315n110, 338n252, 338–39n4
Wieschoff, Heinz, 220–21
Williams, Susan, 322–23n35
Winslow, Anne, 122
World Bank, 13, 178, 190, 208, 234, 268n72, 269n78, 270n86. *See also* International Bank for Reconstruction and Development (IBRD)
World Health Organization (WHO), 56, 77, 79–80, 115, 146, 183, 194, 227, 229, 232–34, 239, 269n78, 285n65, 304n108
World Meteorological Organization (WMO), 227, 269n78
World War I, 1–2, 7–8, 27, 34, 43, 283n25, 283n29
World War II, 2, 7, 15, 31, 34–35, 50, 55, 61, 68, 83, 130, 134, 145, 150, 195, 210, 220

Yalta, 39
Yemen, 338n3
Yenga, Pierre, 233
Young, Kevin, 162
Yugoslavia, 189, 264n23
Yumbu, Joseph, 208–9

Zanzibar, 271–72n7

# COLUMBIA STUDIES IN INTERNATIONAL AND GLOBAL HISTORY

Cemil Aydin, Timothy Nunan, and Dominic Sachsenmaier, Series Editors

Cemil Aydin, *The Politics of Anti-Westernism in Asia: Visions of World Order in Pan-Islamic and Pan-Asian Thought*

Adam M. McKeown, *Melancholy Order: Asian Migration and the Globalization of Borders*

Patrick Manning, *The African Diaspora: A History Through Culture*

James Rodger Fleming, *Fixing the Sky: The Checkered History of Weather and Climate Control*

Steven Bryan, *The Gold Standard at the Turn of the Twentieth Century: Rising Powers, Global Money, and the Age of Empire*

Heonik Kwon, *The Other Cold War*

Samuel Moyn and Andrew Sartori, eds., *Global Intellectual History*

Alison Bashford, *Global Population: History, Geopolitics, and Life on Earth*

Adam Clulow, *The Company and the Shogun: The Dutch Encounter with Tokugawa Japan*

Richard W. Bulliet, *The Wheel: Inventions and Reinventions*

Simone M. Müller, *Wiring the World: The Social and Cultural Creation of Global Telegraph Networks*

Will Hanley, *Identifying with Nationality: Europeans, Ottomans, and Egyptians in Alexandria*

Perin E. Gürel, *The Limits of Westernization: A Cultural History of America in Turkey*

Dominic Sachsenmaier, *Global Entanglements of a Man Who Never Traveled: A Seventeenth-Century Chinese Christian and His Conflicted Worlds*

Perrin Selcer, *The UN and the Postwar Origins of the Global Environment: From World Community to Spaceship Earth*

Ulbe Bosma, *The Making of a Periphery: How Island Southeast Asia Became a Mass Exporter of Labor*

Raja Adal, *Beauty in the Age of Empire: Japan, Egypt, and the Global History of Aesthetic Education*

Mona L. Siegel, *Peace on Our Terms: The Global Battle for Women's Rights After the First World War*

Nicole CuUnjieng Aboitiz, *Asian Place, Filipino Nation: A Global Intellectual History of the Philippine Revolution, 1887–1912*

Michael Christopher Low, *Imperial Mecca: Ottoman Arabia and the Indian Ocean Hajj*

Jessica Namakkal, *Unsettling Utopia: The Making and Unmaking of French India*

GPSR Authorized Representative: Easy Access System Europe, Mustamäe tee 50, 10621 Tallinn, Estonia, gpsr.requests@easproject.com

www.ingramcontent.com/pod-product-compliance
Lightning Source LLC
Chambersburg PA
CBHW031230290426
44109CB00012B/226